DAVID LEWIS was trained as a research biochemist, with degrees from the University of Bristol. He worked for his entire career for a large pharmaceutical company in Nottingham. On retirement, he and his wife emigrated to Cyprus, where they lived for more than six years, Now seventy, and back in Britain, they enjoy life near their children and grandchildren.

David has been associated with the United Reformed Church (formerly the Congregational Church) all his life, but it was only after retirement that he really started to think deeply about the character and message of Jesus. This book is the result of that study.

THE REAL JESUS?

THE REAL JESUS?

David Lewis

ATHENA PRESS
LONDON

THE REAL JESUS?
Copyright © David Lewis 2006

All Rights Reserved

No part of this book may be reproduced in any form,
by photocopying or by any electronic or mechanical means,
including information storage or retrieval systems,
without permission in writing from both the copyright owner
and the publisher of this book.

ISBN 1 84401 810 5

First Published 2006 by
ATHENA PRESS
Queen's House, 2 Holly Road
Twickenham TW1 4EG
United Kingdom

Printed for Athena Press

*To my wife, Eleanor,
for without her encouragement,
this book would not have been written or published.*

Contents

Foreword	11
Baptism	21
The wilderness	35
The first of the few	49
Jesus starts work	64
More new friends	79
Pentecost at Jerusalem	96
Jesus finalises the twelve	107
Magdala	126
Cana and Nazareth	139
More teaching – and more trouble	149
The end of the first mission	162
Winter in Jerusalem	176
The second mission begins	187
Retreat to the North	197
The mission to Judaea	211
The end of the second mission	226
Judas, John and Jericho	240
Jerusalem at last	256
The last week	271
The tension mounts	283
The arrest	298
Trials and tribulation	316
Crucified, dead and buried	335
Victory	350

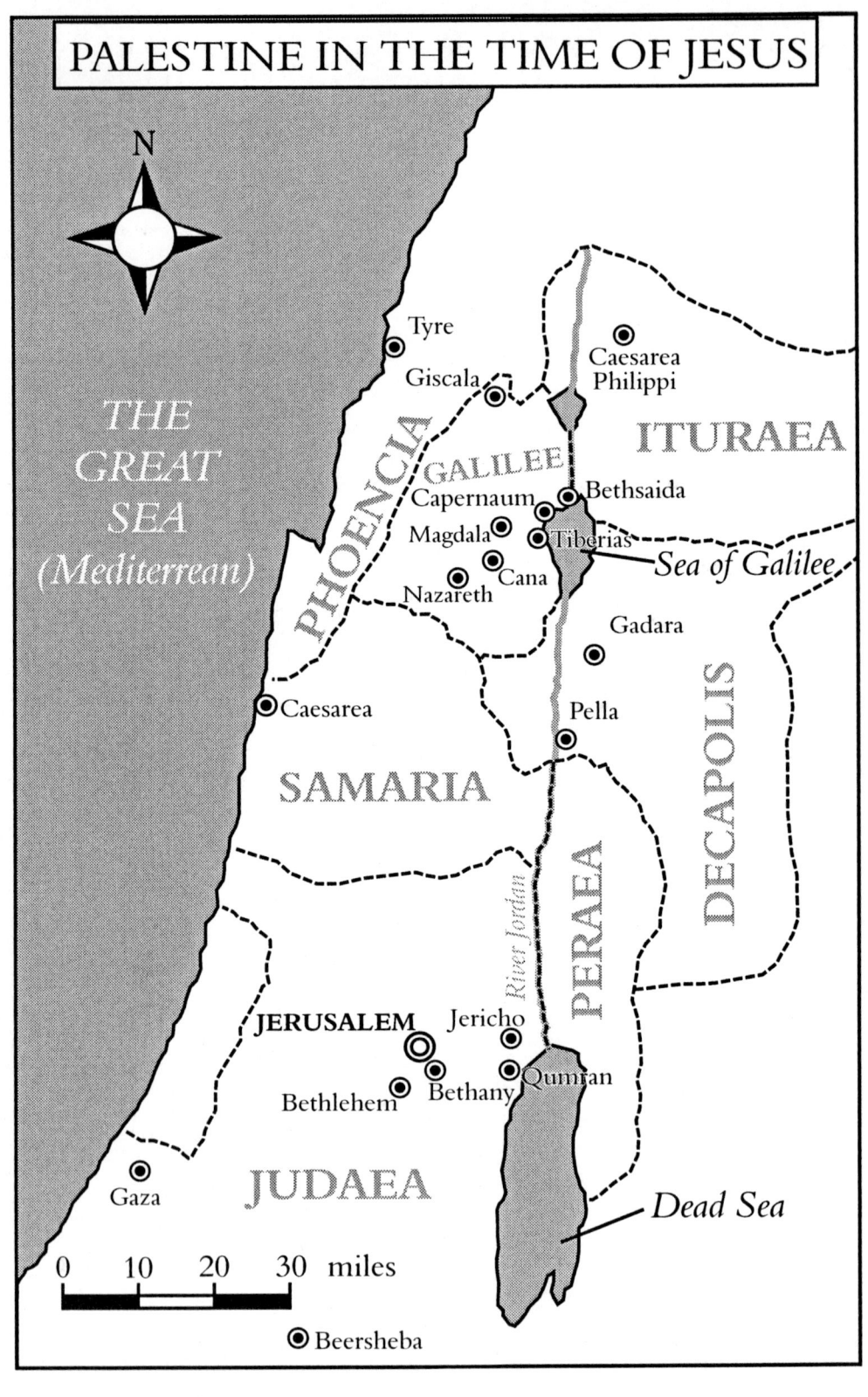

Foreword

Those who have the temerity to attempt to write the story of the life of Jesus are bound to upset some, and probably many, of their readers. This is quite inevitable, for everyone interested in Jesus will have his or her own ideas about him, and these notions are bound to vary very considerably. Nowadays, we frequently see representations of Jesus in films and TV plays, and all too often he is portrayed with a pale face, blond hair and blue eyes, his head surrounded by a mystical light. His words are intoned to the accompaniment of beautiful music, played by well-modulated strings. But this Westernised, romantic representation cannot possibly reflect the actuality in Palestine two thousand years ago, for Jesus was a first-century Jew and must have had a typical Middle Eastern appearance – black or dark brown hair, brown eyes set in a bronzed face – and he was certainly much more down-to-earth. The Jesus I imagine when I read the gospels was often tired, dirty and dishevelled – there was no halo. It seems pretty certain that, for many months of his ministry, he lived essentially the life of a gypsy – there was certainly no orchestra in the background! However, there will be many that will disagree with my version. The truth is that there may be as many views about the person of Jesus as there are persons willing to consider the matter.

Although the gospels give us quite a lot of information about Jesus and sometimes some tantalising isolated details, there are many gaps in the story and much of the background is missing. No doubt we all fill in the missing material, consciously or, more likely, unconsciously, every time we read the Bible, and, when we compare our ideas with those of others, the differences emerge. But the problem is not just about the gaps left in the gospel records. Many Christians today, and surely all non-believers, do not accept that the gospels are literally true in every particular. There are many variations and contradictions in the biblical accounts, and scholars have spent years studying them and discussing why they occur. There are several reasons for them.

Firstly, it is clear that the gospels made no serious attempt to give an exact chronology. They do not attempt to provide a precise day-by-day account of the life of Jesus, but often group together his teachings, his parables and the healing incidents. Some biblical scholars think that the gospel writers used previously written material, now lost, in putting together their 'good news'. They think that earlier writers had recorded these little collections of teachings, or parables, or healings, for the benefit of their local churches and that it is these smaller works, sometimes referred to as pericopes, which were later incorporated, perhaps more or less unchanged, into our gospels. The person who seeks to tell the story today has, therefore, to consider for himself (or herself) what might be the most likely order of events and rearrange the gospel sequence accordingly.

Secondly, the gospel writers unashamedly tell us that they are writing their accounts solely in order to 'convert' the reader to the Christian way. Matthew probably wrote for Jewish readers, very likely those far away from Judaea in the diaspora: the others wrote for Gentiles in different parts of the Roman empire. The gospels, therefore, are 'slanted' – told very much from the Christian point of view – and their stories, inevitably, set Jesus and his followers in the most favourable light.

Thirdly, it seems clear that some of the earliest records of incidents, which showed characters who became important in the early church at a disadvantage, were modified later to minimise embarrassment.

Lastly, as we all know, with time memories tend to fade and incidents may be remembered incorrectly or embellished. In all these ways, differences and contradictions occur between the scriptural accounts, and it seems fair to assume that, for the most part, the later the account was written, the greater is the chance of the story becoming misreported, adjusted, exaggerated or overlaid with new ideas.

Everyone accepts that the gospels were not written down at the time of Jesus. The gospel writers were certainly not like modern day reporters, whose writings are published only hours after the events they record. There must have been quite a considerable gap between the events in the ministry of Jesus and the first written accounts of them, but fierce arguments continue among scholars as to exactly how big that time gap was and who exactly eventually wrote them. However, there is general agreement that our gospel of 'Mark' was the first to be written and some biblical scholars date its composition as the mid-Sixties of the first century, i.e. approximately thirty-five years after the crucifixion. However, a few have suggested a date as early as AD 50, while others think that the gospel dates from shortly after the fall of Jerusalem in AD 70. In any event, it is quite clear that there is a lengthy period between the *events* of the gospel and the *first written record* of them and, for most experts, it seems most unlikely that the author would have been an eyewitness of the events he describes.

The gospels of Matthew and Luke have been variously dated anywhere between AD 70 and 90, according to which 'expert' you happen to consult, while the gospel of John almost certainly came last and has been dated anywhere between AD 90 and 110, though a few people favour an earlier date. Again, it is very unlikely that any of these authors were themselves eyewitnesses of the events they described.

Many people have written at length commenting on the differences of detail between the four gospels. Even though it seems very likely that Matthew and Luke had Mark's text available to them as they wrote, for there are many similar passages, there are still many interesting and suggestive differences between the three accounts. But the greatest differences occur between John and the others, the so-called Synoptic gospels.

I will not attempt here to comment on the minutiae, which have been discussed in depth by many experts (e.g. G Vermes in *The Changing Faces of Jesus* is very helpful in this regard). Instead, as someone with a lifelong interest and some experience in the theatre (albeit only as an amateur), I would draw the reader's attention to the differences in the *character* of Jesus as portrayed by the four gospel writers. There is no way that an actor could possibly portray the historical Jesus on stage and be true to the all the characteristics described by all four evangelists. The actor and his director would have to make some difficult choices.

Jesus as portrayed by Mark is almost invariably a somewhat diffident man, reluctant to 'push' himself, modest, even almost shy. He seeks the lowest places in life, and encourages his followers to do the same. He wants his healing miracles kept quiet. He never promotes *himself* – he always points his listeners to God. He waits for others to acknowledge him as the Messiah. The first time he claims to be the Messiah in public is in the last week of his life, on Palm Sunday, and then only in an oblique way, recognised by people actively looking for him. He is finally forced to admit to his claim to be the Messiah under duress at his trial, and does so only reluctantly. Throughout the gospel, he is interested primarily in the message, rather than pushing his own claims.

In the main, Matthew and Luke concur with Mark's delineation of Jesus, but occasionally they record Jesus as saying things that simply do not fit this pattern. In some places, they portray Jesus as promoting himself, in addition to the message. Matthew and Luke certainly report that several others recognised and proclaimed Jesus as Christ even at his birth. However, in *John*, Jesus himself tells many people throughout the ministry that he is the Messiah. Throughout this gospel, Jesus makes stupendous statements about himself, claiming to be 'the resurrection and the life', 'the way, the truth and the life', 'the bread of life', and so on. He says that nobody can come to God except through him. These claims are truly staggering in their import, and light years away from the reticence of *Mark*. The writer of *John* is in no doubt – Jesus *himself* is the message and actively promotes himself as such.

It is clear that these divergent characters cannot be reconciled – they cannot all be factually correct. Some explanation for these differences must be offered. Most people approach the problem by saying that, with time, the followers of Jesus became more and more convinced about what they perceived to be the significance of who he had been and what he had accomplished. Matthew and Luke, to some extent, and even more so John, put words into the mouth of Jesus which they felt represented what he was and who he was, rather than what he had actually said at the time. Thus, the relatively straightforward story told by Mark, of a man in Galilee, who had a message and who went round helping, befriending and challenging people, gradually became overlaid with new insights.

I ask my reader to try to leave on one side, for the moment, the question of whether these later insights were correct or not. The point I wish to make is that the later writers were claiming things on Jesus's behalf that Jesus did not actually claim for himself during his lifetime. Having considered what actually happened, it is, of course, open to each of us to decide for ourselves how far the later interpretations are correct.

Of course, there was one New Testament author writing even earlier than Mark. Most biblical scholars agree that the letters to Rome, Corinth (two), Galatia, Philippi, Thessalonica (certainly one, maybe two) and Philemon were written over the period AD 50-62, and are from the hand of Paul of Tarsus. There is still disagreement over the letters to the Colossians and Ephesians, but the earliest date for them seems to be early 60s. Most scholars agree that the pastoral letters to Timothy and Titus are written by another hand, later on, while the letter to the Hebrews is definitely not Pauline and probably dates from the late 60s. So, if we are looking for the earliest records in our New Testament, it is to the seven, eight or nine genuine Pauline letters that perhaps we should look. However, in the event, this course of action is of very limited assistance in yielding material about the historical Jesus; for, while Paul agrees closely with the teachings of Jesus concerning the practicalities of the Christian life, he records almost nothing of the facts of his earthly ministry, mentioning only the Last Supper, the crucifixion and the Resurrection.

Important though these events undoubtedly are, they are not the whole story by any means. We need to know about the whole of Jesus's life, and on these details Paul is mysteriously silent. Of course, we know that he never knew Jesus during his earthly ministry, but he must have been in close contact with many who had known him, and it does seem strange that he has so little to say about his story.

Instead of building on his master's life and teaching, Paul builds virtually his entire theology around the final two days of Jesus's life and the days that followed, drawing not only on the Old Testament, but also on Greek and other local cultures, for his raw material. His ideas are, of course, extremely important as an interpretation of the work of Jesus, but as a source of factual material, they are almost useless. Nevertheless, we read that he not only accepts Jesus as the Christ, but also (like John) as a figure existing with God from all time. In the early 50s, Paul writes to Corinth, saying that God effected creation through Christ,[1] but at that time he clearly holds that Christ is subservient to God.[2] Later on, however, writing to Philippi in the late 50s or early 60s, he apparently comes to regard Christ as equal to God.[3] If the letter to the Colossians is also Pauline, and written about AD 62, there is support therein for the same idea.[4]

Contrast this with Mark, probably writing in the mid-60s or later, who portrays Jesus as the Christ, but has nothing whatever to do with the rest of these beliefs. Neither do the other two synoptic gospels, written in the 70s or 80s. It seems that different Christian traditions were developing in different regions at this time. Communications were obviously limited and there was no overarching authority insisting on uniformity then. The early Church continued to interpret Christ's character over more than four centuries, with first one idea, and then another, making the running. In places, Jesus the Jew came to be accepted not only as the Messiah, but also as the Son of God (and that term became enriched with new meanings as time went by), coexistent with the Father from all time, God's agent in creation and finally revered as the second person of the Trinity, equal with God the Father.

Once Christianity became the official religion of the Empire, uniformity was required and eventually the creed was finalised at Nicea in AD 325 and confirmed later at Chalcedon in AD 451. The conferences laid down the belief that Christ was God. Details of this progression of thought are well described by Jonathan Hill in his book *The History of Christian Thought*, and discussed in great detail by Paula Fredriksen, in her book entitled *From Jesus to Christ* (2nd edition, 2000).

It is interesting to note that nowhere in Old Testament prophecy is the Messiah thought of as divine; ideas on the subject were extremely varied, but he was always some kind of very special human. I feel certain that the Jesus of history, a Jew, whose first and great commandment began 'The Lord thy God is One', would have shuddered at the very idea that he could be regarded as equal with God, his Father. Mark's Jesus always pointed away from himself to God. He did not seek to promote himself, but God. It is reasonably clear – though some have questioned even this – that Jesus became sure that he was God's chosen Messiah, but that is very different from saying that he was and is equal with God and should be worshipped as such.

So, in seeking to represent the Jesus of history and tell his story in the same way as any other, I have relied primarily on Mark, the earliest gospel writer, while realising that even he was writing with pressures on him to produce a certain outcome to the reading of his story. I have, however, included some stories found only in Matthew and Luke, when they are consistent with the Markan character. In addition, in spite of the misgivings I have expressed above, I have included some material derived solely from John's gospel, for there is a body of scholarship that thinks that *John* has two distinct strands within it. One involves the long interpretive discourses which embody the claims he made and describe his relationship with God, while the other contributes some interesting factual details of the story, particularly concerning Jesus's ministry in Judaea and Jerusalem, and especially describing events in the last week of Jesus's life. This second strand is thought to be of much earlier origin, which was later incorporated into the longer work which we now know today as 'the gospel of John'. It seemed to me important not to lose these elements.

In making these choices, of necessity I have had to exercise judgment based on what I feel I know of Jesus through my own experience of him today. It surely is the case that, if the Resurrection is really true, then Jesus is alive today and can make himself known to anyone who looks for him in the present time. Of course, the dangers in doing so are very real, for my experience of Jesus could well be flawed, but I can only offer what I think I know.

As we have seen, there are many episodes in the life of Jesus on which the gospel records are completely silent. I have tried to fill in these gaps and provide a possible background, in an attempt to make sense of the events which are recorded in the gospels. Some of this background comes from 'tradition' – material that has been passed down to us in the non-canonical scriptures and the writings of ancient churchmen. Some material repeats what others who have tried to fill in the gaps have proposed more recently, but much has come solely from my own imagination, which is obviously no better than the readers'. It goes without saying that nobody should place any firm reliance on anything other than the scriptural record. Where information in this story is based on scripture, I have indicated this by endnotes at the conclusion of each chapter.

I could not have written this book without the benefit of reading many books written by others much more learned than myself. It is impossible to remember, much less quote, all of them, but I am particularly indebted to the following:

>Paul Johnson, *A History of Christianity* (Weidenfeld & Nicolson, 1976)
>Geza Vermes, *Jesus the Jew* (SCM, 1983)
>Ian Wilson, *Jesus, The Evidence* (Weidenfeld & Nicolson, 1984)
>John Shelby Spong, *This Hebrew Lord* (Harper Collins, 1988)
>——, *Rescuing the Bible from Fundamentalism* (Harper Collins, 1992)
>E P Sanders, *The Historical Figure of Jesus* (Penguin, 1993)
>Geza Vermes, *The Changing Faces of Jesus* (Penguin, 2000)
>Jonathan Hill, *The History of Christian Thought* (Lion, 2003)
>The Bible references are mainly taken from the *New English Bible* (Oxford University Press, 1961 and Cambridge University Press, 1970).

Writing this story has been very difficult. For years, I have been able to set certain incidents in the gospel story on one side, to be 'considered later', or to be left as open questions, but when one sets out to tell the full story, one has to be more definitive. No longer can things be left hazy – 'maybe this, maybe that'. Facts are black and white. There can be no more sitting on the fence. But this is by no means to say that I would go to the stake for every detail! What I have written is just my best guess, in so many instances; and in time to come I may well wish I had chosen differently!

The miracles of Jesus obviously present a difficulty to the modern writer and reader. What really happened in Palestine all those years ago? What seems possible, when judged against the background of today's scientific knowledge? What might have been exaggerated or misrepresented with time? Which information is consistent with the character that emerges from the gospel of

Mark, the earliest account of Jesus's life? My own approach has been to regard as unlikely all the miracles which do not have as a motive Jesus's care for others. So, for example, I have dismissed the stories of Jesus walking on water, or changing water into wine. It seems to me that these 'incidents' are in the same category as the notion of casting oneself from the top of the temple – something done simply to attract favourable attention. We know that, very early on, Jesus discarded this idea as unworthy.[5]

However, the stories of Jesus healing people and his care for those who were handicapped are too deeply embedded in the gospel story to be dismissed entirely. I have to accept that there must be some truth in at least some of these records, unlikely though they may seem at first sight to modern man. All the gospels record that Jesus healed a wide variety of diseases and conditions. Some cures seem quite plausible, being in response to conditions probably caused by mental and spiritual deficiencies; but others, like blindness and deafness, would not seem to be capable of cure by word of mouth – certainly not instantly, as recorded in the scripture.

After much consideration, I decided to omit such miracles as being unlikely and unbelievable to people in our day, though it is worth noting that history records that other men living at about the same period as Jesus were known to be healers in the same tradition as him, so perhaps we should not discard the possibility too quickly. Maybe, as we progress in our study of disease, we too will recover more of this power of healing. It is already abundantly clear that it is not possible to separate physical, mental and spiritual illnesses – the whole individual must be considered – and the physicians of today could perhaps learn something from those who heal by other means.

The final and greatest miracle in the gospel story is, of course, Jesus's Resurrection. Many people today feel that this event certainly has to be regarded as quite impossible. There have been many attempts to explain the story away. Among these, *The Passover Plot*, by Hugh J Schonfield, is as good as any. The trouble with all these accounts is that they imply either Jesus and/or the early church knowingly proceeded on the basis of a lie, which I really cannot accept. Jesus is certainly not a liar, and real people, like the disciples, don't put their lives on the line for something they know perfectly well to be untrue. Whatever the explanation, it cannot be that these people deliberately sought to mislead others.

I am impressed by three certain facts in the situation. Although there are many anomalies and uncertainties in the scriptural accounts of the resurrection, one essential fact upon which they all agree is that the body of Jesus disappeared and was never recovered. This has to be explained. The book by Frank Morrison *Who moved the stone?*, written many years ago, deals in great detail with this question and can still be highly recommended.

The second incontrovertible fact is the changed lives of the disciples. On Good Friday, they were demoralised and craven, scared and scattered. By the evening of Easter Day, however, their spirits had apparently revived. Within a short time, they were appearing in public, loudly proclaiming their faith and their belief that Jesus was alive. They went out into the whole of the known world, sometimes in the face of severe persecution, to tell Jesus's story. Something enormously significant must have happened for this tremendous change to come about in their lives.

Lastly, there is the undeniable fact of the many thousands of Christians down through the years who have claimed to know Jesus and feel his influence in their lives – not in the general way in which one may be influenced by others – say, Isaac Newton, William Shakespeare or Ludvig van Beethoven – but on a day-to-day, personal level. People today can and do know Jesus as a friend – and more. It seems to me that the only plausible explanation for these three facts is that something dramatic happened to convince the disciples that the Resurrection (in some form) actually occurred. The followers of Jesus became convinced that he had acquired a new and powerful life after death – impossible though that may seem on first consideration.

So, despite all the difficulties, on the main thrust of the story I feel relatively content. I submit that Jesus was a first-century Jew, operating against the background that we know from the history books, as well as from the gospels. God poured himself into Jesus in a way that made the man from Nazareth totally unique. He knew God as nobody else has or can. He identified with God's purposes completely, better than anyone else has, before or since. He provided a transparent window into the heart and mind of God. If we say that Jesus was only a man, however wonderful, we have not said enough – he was much more; but if we go as far as to say that he was and is God, we have said too much. He was, and is, not God. He was, and is, quite simply, in a class of his own – unique – not fitting into either category, 'God' or 'man'. He was, and is, God's Messiah, or, in Greek, the Christ. To his followers, he was, and is, the best friend they could ever find. He made such an impact on the life of his times that his story has been told and retold for nearly two thousand years, all over the world. That the story has become embellished and misinterpreted over the years is almost inevitable.

In the face of all this, many scholars have asserted that it is impossible to arrive with any certainty at the truth of Jesus's earthly life. No doubt they are right, but the attempt, not only for me, but for everyone who is interested, is well worth the effort. For Judaism and Christianity are movements which are locked into history – God has actually interacted with his people on earth down through the ages. Christianity starts with facts, not just theories and ideas. Therefore, it must be the case that we need to know as much as we can about the life of Jesus in order to have any real chance of interpreting him properly and coming to know the Christ of faith, who still walks and talks with his followers today, if we will let him. At any rate, I hope that this will be the experience of the reader.

David Lewis, March 2006

NOTES

[1] I Cor. 8:6.
[2] I Cor. 11:2–33 and I Cor. 15:24–25.
[3] Phil. 2:5–11.
[4] Col. 1:15–20.
[5] Matt. 4:5-7 and Luke 4:9-12.

Baptism

It was likely to be pretty hot later on, considering it was only mid-April. The sun shone out of a hard blue sky, dotted with a few clumpy white clouds. The two men had to think in terms of walking up to twenty miles that day, with the sun on their backs, so they could look forward to getting quite warm. It would be necessary to keep the neck and head well protected, but at least, heading north, the glare in the eyes would not be a factor. They walked steadily forward, picking their way carefully along the rough track which followed the valley of the Jordan for about sixty miles, from near the north end of the Dead Sea to the southern tip of the Sea of Galilee. They had hardly started so far. They had forded the river about five miles east of Jericho and turned north towards Galilee, but that was only about half an hour ago. The feet of thousands of Galilean pilgrims had trodden this path over the years, coming to Jerusalem for the festivals, only to return a week or so later. The main throng came and went at this time of the year for Passover, as the law required, but the route was, of course, used all year round, both for the other festivals and by traders.

'Someone should improve this track,' muttered James. At twenty-eight he was the younger but taller of the two, well built and muscular. 'Heaven help us, we pay enough taxes!'

'I doubt whether anyone in authority cares much about the state of the tracks,' replied his companion, Andrew. 'They are all too preoccupied by building their palaces and maintaining a good lifestyle – and finding their taxes for Rome, of course. Herod Antipas, who rules here in Peraea, has to be prompt with his payments or he's in trouble, and the Roman Prefect, who rules in Judaea – what's his name? – Pilate, or something similar, will be in the same boat.'

This was quite a long speech for Andrew, who was not given to holding forth. He was usually to be found in the background, listening. At home, his elder brother, Simon, did most of the talking. Big, brash, bullying Simon, some called him, yet he had a good heart underneath it all. In a way, Andrew felt more at ease with James. True, James could 'let forth' himself, when he had a mind, but, on the whole, he was more restrained than Simon. Nevertheless, it would be good to be back in Capernaum and see the big fellow again. They had only been away for a couple of weeks, yet it felt like half a lifetime.

'What did you think of Jerusalem this year?' he asked.

'I like Passover,' replied James. 'It's a part of life that doesn't change. It's always crowded and the ritual never alters. We go to the Temple as Jews have done over the centuries, buy our sacrifices, say our prayers and enjoy our meals together in the evenings...'

'Jews haven't been going to this Temple for that long', corrected Andrew, who was inclined to be precise on occasions. 'Old Herod, Antipas' father, the one they called "The Great", built this Temple – what, only fifty or sixty years ago.'

'Not quite true, if you want to be completely accurate,' replied James, 'Herod only extended the second Temple, the one built after the return from Babylon. Of course, the original Temple – the one that was destroyed by the Babylonians – was built nearly a thousand years ago by King Solomon.'

'The feast itself, of course, goes way back before that, though – right back to Moses's time and the escape from Egypt,' observed Andrew. He paused before continuing thoughtfully, 'Moses was supposed to have been able to do wonderful things – mainly with his staff, if I remember rightly. Didn't it turn into a snake one time – and didn't he make water flow out of a rock in the desert?'

James looked incredulous. He pursed his mouth and kicked at a pebble in his path, sending it skipping off into the nettles growing thickly either side of the track.

'I'm not sure I believe some of those old stories,' he muttered.

'God was with Moses,' said Andrew, much in the manner of old Hezekiah, their local rabbi.

James laughed. 'You'd better look out, or you'll get to look like Hezekiah too, if you're not careful,' he said, 'and serve you right!'

Andrew sniffed. 'You can never be serious for long, James. I like observing the festivals and I think it's important to remember our history. We Jews go back a long way, and ...'

'We're different, I know.' James's voice was still slightly mocking. 'We don't associate with others – not with Samaritans, nor Greeks, nor Egyptians – and particularly not with Romans, of course...'

'Well, I think there is value in keeping ourselves to ourselves as a nation.' Andrew was getting more into his theme now. 'We are the only nation that knows who God really is. Over the centuries, we have worshipped him and he has cared for us. We very soon pay for it, if we don't. The other nations have a great miscellany of Gods – idols, statues – but these Gods aren't real. Even the so-called worshippers don't really worship them half the time, but just go through the motions. They can't really believe that blocks of wood or stone can make any difference in their lives, can they?'

James decided it was time to take Andrew more seriously, since he had to share his company for a few more days.

'I think that perhaps that some of them believe that there really are Gods called Jupiter, Mercury or Mars, or whoever, but the statues are just reminders – perhaps not very different from us having altars. We reverence our altars, don't we, without believing that the actual table, or tablet of stone, is a god?'

Andrew said nothing for a while. Then he admitted, 'Good point. Perhaps you're right.'

They walked on in silence for several hundred yards before Andrew spoke again.

'Anyway, I'm glad I went this year for Passover. I feel better for going. We don't get there very often, what with having to get cover for the business and the travelling and all that... It is as well that the law allows us to miss going to Jerusalem if we live a long way from it.'

'But then someone has to decide what constitutes a "long way",' said his companion. 'I suppose that's another task for the scribes to decide on... Of course, they like to get their fingers into every pie!'

James paused, before continuing. 'Anyway, we needn't worry about the businesses. Simon will look after yours, and my dad keeps ours going – what with Nathan, Japheth, and the rest of the hired men. Then there's always my young brother, John. Not that he's a lot of use. Half the time – he's got his head in the clouds, thinking strange thoughts! Perhaps he's in love!'

'Really?' said Andrew, surprised.

'No, not him!' said the other, grinning. 'I was just kidding!'

'At twenty, he's the right age.'

'Not him,' repeated his brother, knowingly.

'Well, we can't talk, I suppose. Neither of us is married and we're fast getting past it!' Andrew looked slightly crestfallen.

'I'll marry when I'm ready,' said James somewhat gruffly. 'Anyway, marriage isn't always a bed of roses. Look at your brother! His Ruth is a lovely girl – nothing against her at all – but fancy having to live with your mother-in-law!'

'Oh, Abigail's all right,' said Andrew, but he didn't look too sure. 'Anyway, mothers aren't always so easy to live with either! I live with mine – you live with yours and your dad. Possibly marriage would be a better alternative!'

Andrew looked slightly wistful. 'It might be nice to have someone to look after us in our old age!'

'Damn it all, I'm not thirty,' retorted James, 'I'm not worrying about old age yet. You're only thirty-two, and far too young to concern yourself with age!'

Andrew grimaced. 'Well, old age seems to start around fifty, it seems to me. You see people starting to get more aches and pains then – and they're more likely to get sores and swellings. We're all right now, fit as fleas, but—'

'It's all that fishing,' James cut in. He prodded his companion in the arm. 'Look at those biceps!'

It was true. Both men were brown as berries, tough and sinewy, muscular in the arms and shoulders through dragging nets regularly – nets that were frequently full of fish, much to their satisfaction. Theirs was a good life, even if it was a hard one. In reality, the families were well knit together and supported each other, and the fishing community generally rallied round to support all its members. It had been quite easy to arrange to be away for a fortnight. Next year, they'd do the same for someone else, though it seemed unlikely that the rather irreligious Simon would want to bother. John? Well, who could tell with the enigmatic John.

The path, previously winding between the little fields in the Jordan Valley, now ran immediately alongside the river itself. The water flowed quite freely at this time of year and looked quite inviting. James suggested stopping and bathing their feet, but his more earnest companion was for pressing on, at least till lunch time. They had a little bread and some fruit packed in a bag and he felt that it would be better to press on before it got too hot. They could enjoy the water just before the food. Perhaps they might even take a short nap after lunch. The prospect was distinctly appealing.

'You're probably right,' said James. 'I just thought that this looked like a good place. Mostly, the banks are too overgrown at this time of year.'

'We'll find somewhere,' soothed Andrew. 'Never fret.'

So they pressed doggedly on. Conversation lapsed, except for the occasional remark – when the swallows dipped into the water to bathe themselves, or when they saw some pretty wild lilies growing in a vast swathe across a patch of land. They stopped to look for a moment at the beauty of the purple carpet of blooms. Mostly, however, the land was cultivated, with barley ready for harvest soon and wheat not far behind. Above their heads, there was the occasional apricot tree with swelling fruit, making the mouth water. The fig trees were sprouting new foliage. It was a lovely time of year.

As noon approached, they came to a place where the path ran alongside the river and there was a tiny beach with a stretch of sand running away from the water for a small distance. A small crowd, perhaps a couple of dozen people, had gathered and was listening to someone making quite a speech. He was a rather striking fellow of about their own age, unkempt, his black hair and beard long and tousled, his clothes, what there were of them, ragged and dirty, made from what looked like camel hair. He was standing on a rock and holding forth in no uncertain terms. His voice was authoritative, strident, compelling. Andrew and James stopped in spite of themselves and found themselves listening to the spellbinding voice.

'You need to save yourselves,' it was saying. 'Save yourselves from the judgement to come. It'll be no use later on – you'll be too late.'

The crowd were muttering. Some looked sheepish. Others poked out their chins defiantly.

The voice continued. 'I'm telling you – warning you – now. The one who is to come will soon be among us.'

'Who do you mean?' came a voice from the crowd.

'I'm talking about the one the prophets foretold. For hundreds of years, they've been telling us that we can expect a prophet – no, more than a prophet – God's anointed one. He will come to release us from bondage. He will set us free.'

'Free from the bondage of Rome, d'you mean?' came the voice again, clearly incredulous.

'Free to be God's people again!' was the reply from the rock. 'But first, you must welcome him in your hearts by turning away from your sins and cleansing your lives.'

'Who says?'

'*I* say. I am warning you that the time is running out. The one we look for, the Messiah, is coming and we must be ready for him. Wash yourselves. Get clean, so that he will find us suitable for his salvation and allot you a place in his new Kingdom.'

'And who are you? Are you this Messiah?' The voices from the crowd were still scornful.

'No. No, I am not the Messiah. My name is John. I am just his messenger, sent to announce his coming.[1] It is exactly as the prophet Isaiah foretold:

"Comfort, comfort my people; it is the voice of your God.

Prepare a road for the Lord. Clear a highway across the desert for our God."[2]

'I am the one who has come to lay that highway, but the one who follows is much greater than I am, or ever can be. Why, I am not worthy so much as to lace up his sandals.'

'When did you say he was coming?' asked someone else, a little less aggressively.

'At any time now,' replied the scarecrow. 'So you must prepare. Confess that your lives are not all they should be and wash yourselves clean while you can. He mustn't find you wallowing in your sins.'

'What makes you think I'm all that bad, anyway?' cried another voice. 'I keep the law as best I can.'

'Look,' said John. 'There isn't a person living who can claim to have kept the law in all its particulars. None of us remembers to reverence God in our whole lives. We frequently forget about him. We forget to pray, we don't give enough time to searching the holy scriptures, and we fail to love him with all our hearts, minds and strength, as we have been commanded to do. That's why our High Priest goes into the Holy of Holies in the Temple, once a year, on the Day of Atonement, to seek God's cleansing for us all. But that's not the end of the matter, by any means. We all know, if we are honest with ourselves, that we could live better lives – lives free from cheating at business, lives free of lies and little deceits, lives that are more cheerful and joyful and helpful. Can any of you claim to be living lives like that – all the time? Of course, we can all be pleasant on occasion, when it suits us, when life treats us well, but what about the rest of the time? I'm saying you must turn away from the dark side of life. Look for a life which is free of selfishness and hypocrisy, and genuinely seek to treat others as you want them to treat you. That's written in the law too.'

The crowd were quieter now.

John's voice became a little less strident, more coaxing.

'My friends, take this opportunity. Here is water. Here is the holy River Jordan, used by our fathers and all the prophets through the centuries for washing and sometimes for healing. Remember the story of Naaman the leper? He was healed by bathing in the Jordan.[3] Come and be baptised and become clean.'

John stepped down from the rock and, putting his arm round the nearest man's shoulder, led him gently down the little beach, which gradually sloped into the water.

'Come along, my friend.'

Almost against his will, it seemed, the man allowed himself to be taken forward till his feet were touching the water. There, he removed his tattered sandals, threw off his outer garment and waded with John into the stream. When he was nearly up to his waist, John stopped him, and asked, 'What is your name?'

The man muttered a reply. Then, cupping his hands together, the preacher took up water and lifted it high over the man's bowed head. He raised his voice for all to hear.

'Ruben – I baptise you this day, so that you may be clean of all your sins. Go and lead a better life from now on.'

The water splashed down over Ruben's head and shoulders. Again and again John lifted water to anoint him, until he was completely soaked.

Then the prophet spoke quietly. 'Go in peace, with God's blessing.'

Without a word or glance for anyone, the drenched figure splashed his way to the shore and up the beach, snatching up his clothes as he went. The others cleared a path for him, watching in amazement. Then another fellow, quite an old man, with white hair and stooping shoulders, started forward into the water, calling:

'I'm coming, John. Baptise me too, please.'

'Come along then, father,' said John, smiling, holding out his arms out to help him.

'Me too,' said another.

Pretty soon there was quite a queue, waiting for John to carry out his little ceremony. The beach ran with water, streaming from the newly baptised as they made their way up to the path, where they gathered under a fig tree to towel themselves off as best they could and sit to contemplate what they had done. One or two knelt in prayer.

Andrew turned to look at his friend.

'What do you make of all this?' he asked.

James took him by the arm and started to lead him away, out of earshot, further down the path.

'I'll tell you what I think,' he said. 'I think that by next week, or certainly by the end of next month, these people will be back to their old ways and none the better for their experience. It's all very well saying that they want to get rid of the past and turn over a new leaf, but will they actually do it? Human nature being what it is, they won't be able to keep it up. That's why the High Priest has to go into the Holy of Holies and seek the nation's forgiveness every year on the Day of Atonement.'

Andrew paused before replying.

'Yes… you're quite right,' he said eventually, with some reluctance. 'They won't keep it up. But' – and here he looked up keenly into James's face – 'isn't it better for them to have tried… to have made the effort?'

James grimaced and shrugged his shoulders.

'If you say so, but I wouldn't go through that washing hocus-pocus myself, not for anything. I'd just be sorry and get on with it. Come on, let's go on. I'm looking forward to my lunch – and bathing my feet.'

Andrew hesitated.

'You go on, if you want to,' he said. 'I want to hear this man, John, speak again, and talk to him one to one, if I can. I'll follow you later. I may catch you up tonight, but if I get delayed, I'll see you back in Capernaum.'

It was James's turn to hesitate.

'I don't like to leave you, old chap,' he said.

'Oh, I'll be all right here and you'll come to no harm on this track. The way is quite clear and there are no robbers on this stretch. It's not like that bit between Jerusalem and Jericho, where I wouldn't travel alone for anything.'

Andrew took James's hand. 'Off you go, now, and I'll see you soon. Give my best to Simon and tell him I'll be home soon and tell him all about it.'

James grinned. 'Your brother has little time for religion,' he reminded him. 'He'll have no time for washing away sins and looking for new prophets! I'll not try to explain it to him, but I'd like to be there when you try! Good luck! Take care. I'll see you soon – I hope!'

Reluctantly, the two parted and Andrew watched while his friend set off, with increasing pace, north along the path. He turned at the bend and waved; then he was out of sight. As soon as he was gone, Andrew started to wonder if he had done the right thing. It wasn't really like him to decide, on the spur of the moment, to change all his carefully laid plans and go off on a wild goose chase. Well, it was done now, he thought. He retraced his steps but found the little beach deserted. He looked under the fig tree where those who had been baptised had assembled, but they too had disappeared. Andrew groaned. He had done the wrong thing. If he hurried, he thought that perhaps he would be able to catch up with James. As he hesitated, trying to decide what to do, the bushes parted near him and he found himself confronted by the unkempt prophet himself.

'Ah, I wondered who it was,' John said. 'Can I help you?'

Andrew, never very articulate, was momentarily lost for words. Eventually he stammered out, 'Yes. Yes, I was hoping to see you – speak to you. I heard part of your – address – this morning. I felt sorry for you, with the crowd being so – well, rude – scornful – at times…'

'Yes, but in the end, several did listen to what I was saying,' said John, with a smile. 'And they wanted to be baptised and made clean. Even if only one person takes that step, I am content. Come along with me and share our lunch – it isn't much, but it'll suffice.'

It was only then that Andrew realised that he had let James go off with the bag in which the lunch was packed.

'Thank you,' he murmured. 'I don't like to intrude…'

'Nonsense,' said the other. 'There's just a few of us – we can talk over lunch, before our siesta. I always try to take a nap after lunch when the sun is at its hottest. I get up early and I shall be preaching again towards the end of the afternoon, so I need to refresh myself. Hopefully I'll baptise a hundred later! Come along.'

He led the way through the bushes to a little clearing where three men were sitting round, preparing a few items for lunch – bread, fish and fruit.

'Come on, sit down, and let's hear about you,' said John. 'You haven't even told me your name yet.'

Still shy, Andrew introduced himself and shook hands in turn with John's three followers. He particularly took to a big fellow called Matthias, who sported a large bushy beard and reminded him a little of Simon, but the resemblance stopped short at that point, for Matt was reluctant to speak much. John was soon the centre of the conversation. He again told Andrew that he believed strongly that he had been called by God to foretell the coming of the long-expected Messiah. He didn't claim to know exactly where and when the Messiah would come, but he felt sure it would be soon, and he felt certain that he would recognise him when he saw him. Andrew, summoning up all his courage, asked him where he, John, had come from, and what his longer-term plans were. John explained that he had been given by his parents, at birth, to the religious life. He was a Nazarite. Andrew recalled hearing about Nazarites – they were usually dedicated at birth and given totally to God's service. They didn't drink alcohol; they didn't cut their hair – they were really quite weird, Andrew thought. That would account for John's rather disreputable appearance!

John was still talking. He just wanted to be present when the coming Kingdom was established, he was saying. He himself wouldn't be anything special in that Kingdom – everything would be taken over by 'the one who was to come'. His job would be finished once the great one had arrived.

'But what kind of kingdom is it to be?' asked Andrew. 'Is this new King – the Messiah – going to sweep the Romans into the sea and liberate us from political slavery? This would mean war on a tremendous scale. Who will attempt to fight – who *can* fight – the might of Rome? When – if – one of their armies is defeated, they simply send another, bigger than the one before. We'd all finish up butchered.'

John was evasive. 'When the Messiah comes,' he said, nodding his head sagely, 'all will be revealed. I don't have the secrets, but I have the certainty.'

'Well,' said Jonathan, one of the other followers, 'Rome will take some shifting. Perhaps the Messiah will bring an army of angels with him and ride through them on a chariot of fire.'

'In that case,' said Matt, 'it'll be the end of this world as we know it. It will be a completely different place, with God in command of everything. It could be wonderful.'

'Maybe,' said the other disciple; Andrew struggled to remember his name, but thought it was David. 'But, alternatively, maybe God will expect the nation to mobilise and create its own army – as they did a hundred and fifty years ago under the Maccabees. It was the Seleucids who oppressed us then, not the Romans, and we got rid of them. It's the only time we've been really independent, as a nation, since before the exile to Babylon – oh, more than five hundred years ago.'

John intervened. 'All this is very interesting,' he said. 'History is all very well, but I prefer to look forward rather than dwelling on the past. I have only one mission – to prepare for HIM.'

And he spoke the word in such a way that it could only be written in capital letters. Turning to Andrew, and looking at him full in the face, he said, 'Are you with me, Andrew? Will you throw your lot in with us? We shall need fellows like you to swell the army of God, no matter what kind of kingdom is on offer.'

Andrew squirmed. What should he say? It was all so sudden. This morning he had been a fisherman, returning home from a holiday – a religious holiday to be sure, but a holiday all the same – and here he was, being confronted by a religious, well, 'freak' was the word which came to mind, and offered a completely different proposition.

'I really haven't had time…' he faltered.

There was a pause which seemed to Andrew to last for ten minutes. Eventually, John said quietly, 'Well, sleep on it. I'm turning in for a nap myself; we can talk again another time.'

Andrew breathed a sigh of relief. At least for the present he had been spared from making up his mind. He would think it all over, but almost certainly he'd find the opportunity to slip away a little later and dodge the question permanently. Looking up, he noticed that the sky was beginning to cloud over a little. There were still great patches of blue sky, but certainly there were more clouds than before. He would need to find somewhere to sleep under cover tonight, for there might be rain, and rain at that time of the year might well be heavy. But he wouldn't embarrass his host or himself by walking out immediately. He took the cue from the others, found a comfortable spot and lay down to sleep.

But sleep didn't come. Too much had happened to keep his mind from resting. What was this kingdom that John promised? Who was the expected one? Would the world really end? In his mind's eye, he could see a cohort of angels brandishing flaming swords, carving through the Roman legions, destroying them all to a man. Then he saw a man arrayed in white robes from head to foot, wearing a golden crown, coming on the clouds in a chariot of fire, with John standing beside him, leading a victory parade and stopping beside a flight of marble steps, that led up, up, it seemed for ever, to a great throne. On the throne… it must be God. Oh, no, he couldn't look at the throne, because nobody could look at God and live. Yet he had to know. So he tried to turn to see the throne – and started from sleep, in a cold sweat, with his mind all aflutter.

As the worst of the heat of the afternoon passed, the little band stirred back to life. They all washed and drank water, then made their way back to the little beach. John climbed on to the rock and started to address the passing pilgrims, causing another small crowd to gather. The main thrust of his message was the same and the questions not very different.

However, after about half an hour, the little throng was joined by a group of well-dressed men, Pharisees and Sadducees, who, it seemed, had come specially from Jerusalem to find out for themselves exactly what this man, John, was up to. Not that John was at all abashed. He saw the group approaching and immediately turned his withering fire on them.

'You brood of vipers!' he shouted. 'Who warned you to come here to escape the wrath to come?'[4]

'Don't take that tone with us,' said the man who appeared to be their leader. 'Don't you know who we are?'

'It's precisely because I know who and what you are that I said what I did,' retorted the baptiser. 'I know full well that you are "high-ups" from Jerusalem – the supposed holy men of the Temple staff.'

'Then you should show some respect,' snarled the chief Sadducee.

'I'll gladly show respect for you when your actions match your words,' countered John. 'You think because you are sons of Abraham and religious and Temple-goers that you will be safe from the coming conflagration, but I'm here to tell you that you, like everyone else, will be judged and found wanting. Repent! Change your ways, for already it is high time. The axe is already being plied to the root of your tree, and you are about to be hewn down.'

'And who are you to tell us what to do? Whoever do you think you are?'

Once again John spelt out his message of the coming Messiah and his own role as the messenger of the great King that was coming. The men from the Temple were unimpressed. The arguments raged on for many minutes, with the ordinary pilgrims becoming more and more confused at the turmoil, not knowing which side to believe. Eventually, the leader of the official group called to his companions and declared that he had had enough of this banter.

'It is pointless wasting time on such a man as this,' he sneered.

So saying, he turned on his heel and strode away, followed promptly by the others of his party.

'Go on your way, you vipers!' yelled John after them. 'Nothing can save you from the wrath to come.'

The little procession departed with much wagging of heads and pulling at beards.

'But what about us?' said one of the pilgrims. 'What must we do?'[5]

'Turn your lives around. Be prepared to live for others as well as yourselves. Share what you have with those less fortunate. Live at peace with all around you,' was the reply.

'What about me?' said someone from the back, a man who had previously kept very much on the edge of the crowd. 'I'm a tax collector, and nobody will deal willingly with me, because they think I have sold out to the authorities. I am shunned and despised by my local community.'

'What do you expect?' said another, turning belligerently. 'You're even worse than the Romans – you're a Jew who works for the occupying forces, which is worse in my book.'

'I have to earn a living, like everyone else,' whimpered the luckless fellow. 'I was trained as an accountant, and so—'

'Make sure, then, that you only collect what is due,' cut in John. 'We all know that most tax collectors take more than the tax required and feather their own nests. Just because many folk can't read or write or figure numbers is no reason to cheat them.'

'I'll do that, Rabbi,' said the unfortunate accountant. 'Thank you.'

'Come and confess your past and change in the future,' said the prophet. 'Come along, all of you, and wash away the past and make sure the future is different.'

Once again John descended to the beach and encouraged those in the crowd who were wavering. He led the taxman by the elbow into the water and started to baptise him. The others followed, one or two breaking into the singing of a psalm. Andrew watched, amazed, at the mood of the people, as they came smiling out of the water.

It was getting towards the end of the afternoon by this time and the sun was sinking towards the west, causing a glittering stream of gold to form on the waters of Jordan, nearly half a mile wide at this point. From Andrew's viewpoint, John, well out in the stream, was bathed in the twinkling pathway and seemed to take on an angelic glow in the radiance.

As the queue waiting for baptism began to shorten, Andrew noticed a newcomer walk purposefully off the path and down to the water's edge.[6] This man didn't hesitate for a second, but, as soon as he had removed his sandals and his outer garment, he waded out to the waiting group. When it came to his turn to be baptised, Andrew noticed John hesitate before he started to reach down for the water of baptism. The two men exchanged a few words and then, as if reluctantly, John turned the newcomer so that they stood together in the brilliant, glittering, golden stream across the water. As he lifted up the water, a clump of thick cloud suddenly pushed across the sun, momentarily blocking out the glorious light, but the cloud rapidly passed and, as the man rose from baptism, the sun returned in all its brilliance, seemingly even more glorious than before. The man then waded ashore, picked up his belongings and walked off in the direction of Jericho without a word to anyone.

With nobody else waiting, John, too, waded ashore. He seemed unusually quiet, and yet buoyed up, as if he was suppressing some news of great importance. That evening, after supper, John called them together round the fire. As soon as they were all assembled, he blurted out, 'It's happened! He's here. I've seen the one we are all waiting for. I've seen the Lamb of God.'[7]

'What do you mean?' Jonathan asked. 'When did you see him?'

'This afternoon, out there in the river. The last man who came for baptism. I feel sure that that was the person we are looking for. His name is Jesus. He's from Nazareth, in Galilee.'

'What makes you think he's our man?' queried Jonathan. 'I didn't notice anything special about the last man.'

'As I baptised him,' replied the prophet, 'the light suddenly dipped and then blazed up behind him. It seemed in that moment to turn him into an angel – the sun lit his hair and into my mind thundered the words of the psalm: "You are now my son; this day I became your father."[8]

'And somehow I knew that God was speaking to this man, Jesus. His head was ringed in the setting sun and it was as if a presence came into him, surrounding him with something, or someone. Just as if a golden bird had alighted on his head. Don't ask me to explain it – it is just how I felt.'

'But, surely, if he were really the Messiah, you should have sought baptism from him, not he from you.' David still sounded sceptical.

'That's exactly what I told him myself,' replied John. 'I asked him to baptise me, but he wouldn't. He insisted that he wanted to share in the ceremony here with us.'

'Why ever didn't you tell us?' cried Matt. 'Why didn't you let us talk to him? Why didn't you invite him here to supper with us, so that we could meet him?' There was genuine disappointment in his voice, and the others seemed to share in his feeling, even Andrew, who found himself drawn into the excited, yet disappointed, mood of John's followers.

'I'm sorry,' said John, 'really sorry. I too wanted to have a long conversation with him, because there is so much we have to discuss, but he said he had to go. He has an urgent meeting with a mutual friend of ours.'

'Ah, you know him, then,' David said.

'Oh, yes. I knew him quite well at one time, not long ago. We were both at Qumran, just a few miles south of here, on the shores of the Dead Sea, studying with the Essene community there. I had been there for some months before he arrived, but our study periods overlapped for several weeks. We didn't see a lot of each other, but I saw enough to realise that this was a rather special man, with some really good ideas. He thought deeply and, once he had made up his mind about something, he seemed to glow with authority on the topic. He didn't agree with the Essenes on several aspects, so he left the community and I lost touch with him. I haven't seen him for about six months now – not since the autumn. But today I saw him in a new light – quite literally.'

'I'm afraid I don't know a lot about the Essenes,' said Andrew timidly. 'What are their main beliefs? Why are they different from the rest of us? Are you still—'

'No, I'm not an Essene, Andrew,' John cut in. 'Like Jesus, I couldn't agree with many of their ideas and practices. I learnt a lot from them that I value, but I couldn't take it all. So I too left the community. But I do agree with them that the Temple authorities are completely on the wrong track. The Sadducees actively cooperate with the Romans, which can't be right.'

'We all hate the Romans and everything they stand for,' said Andrew, 'but I had always supposed that the High Priest and the Sanhedrin cooperated with them rather than initiate open warfare, which would do nobody any good. That way, Rome leaves us Jews to run our own affairs – to a large extent.'

'Are you sure that that is their reason?' queried John. 'Don't you think that also they rather enjoy their high status and don't want to lose it? I feel sure that they very much like being the ones who do the organising on behalf of Rome.'

'Well, no doubt that helps,' admitted Andrew.

'But it's not only that,' said John. 'They have turned the Temple into a market, which is abhorrent. They buy and sell animals and birds in the outer precinct as if they were tradesmen or butchers. Why they still rely on sacrifices at all beats me. The prophets, Amos, Hosea, Micah and others, six hundred years ago, realised that God prefers a godly life to a burnt ox.'[9]

'Did you not want to continue with the community life, though?' asked David.

'In the end, life has to be lived in the world,' replied John, 'at least as far as I am concerned. The world is where the need is, and that is, therefore, where I have to be. The Essenes like their exclusive little sect, believing that they are different, the only ones who know the truth. I thought I knew better than that and so I left the community, to set up here with you, my friends, to wait for the Messiah, who will answer all our questions.'

'But now,' said Andrew, 'now you think that you may have found the man you are looking for? What will you do? What should we do?'

'I will wait for the Messiah to tell me. You must decide for yourselves what you must do,' replied the prophet. 'I have told you that I think Jesus is the man you need to follow in the future. If he proves to be as I hope, then my work is done. I shall fade away as his work blossoms.'

'Did he tell you where he was going?' asked Matt.

'He said he was going to Jericho,' replied John. 'We have a mutual friend there, also called John. He too was at Qumran, learning and studying with us. He also disagreed with the Qumranis, but for different reasons: he came to different conclusions. He is a priest, actually on the Temple staff, working for the High Priest, but he is still a friend of mine, even though I disagree with him. At least he's not a hypocrite, like so many of them. He is genuinely trying to live by his concepts. If you go to Jericho and ask for John barHelez, I'm sure you'll find him; he's quite influential. And I feel sure that there's a good chance you'll find Jesus with him.'

'Then I'm going to look for him,' declared Matt. 'I'll set out first thing in the morning.'

'Could I join you?' said Andrew, immediately surprised at his own impulsiveness. As soon as he thought about it, he realised that, on this occasion, he had acted more like his brother. It was much more like Simon to offer to do such a thing on the spur of the moment.

'Of course,' said Matt, sounding genuinely pleased. 'Glad to have your company.' Then, turning to the others, he continued, 'I'll report back to the rest of you here as soon as I can, and by then Andrew can make up his mind what he intends to do.'

'Well, I'm going to move north tomorrow,' said John. 'The Galilean pilgrims to Passover have almost all set off from Jerusalem by now and passed this place. Besides, after our experiences today, we could do without the close attentions of the Temple hierarchy! I think it would be best to work our way gradually northward towards Galilee. You'll pick us up somewhere along the river bank, Matt. You won't be able to miss us!'

And so it was agreed. The rain never materialised and Andrew slept out in the open near the fire, in the company of his new friends. This time, he slept soundly, in spite of the challenging events of the day and the cool of the night.

NOTES

[1] John 1:20.
[2] Isaiah 40:1,3.
[3] II Kings 5:14.
[4] Matt. 3:7.
[5] Luke 3:10.
[6] Mark 1:9.
[7] John 1:29.
[8] Psalm 2:7.
[9] Amos 5:22; Hosea 6:6; Micah 6:6–8.

The wilderness

Andrew and Matt started out for Jericho soon after first light, pausing only for a quick rinse and a meagre breakfast. They soon reached the ford, recrossed the river and walked on to Jericho without incident. John barHelez seemed to be well known, for they were able to find his house after only two enquiries. With some trepidation, Matt knocked at the door of a large and well-appointed dwelling, set in a spacious garden, all in marked contrast with their own modest homes. A well-dressed servant answered and asked them in, while he enquired if the master would see them. After a few minutes, a tall, graceful man in a long white robe came walking on to the terrace, where they were waiting. Unusually, he had bright blue eyes, which contrasted oddly with his swarthy appearance.

'Good morning, friends,' he began. 'I am John barHelez. What can I do for you?'

'We are looking for Jesus, from Nazareth in Galilee,' answered Matt. 'We believe that he may be staying with you – or perhaps you know where he is?'

'Indeed I do,' said the householder, smiling. 'He is at present on my roof, praying; but, when he is finished, I will tell him you are here and I feel sure he will want to meet you. Please sit down and I will have some refreshment brought. Do you prefer fruit juice, beer or wine?'

'Thank you. Fruit juice for me,' Matt answered.

Andrew nodded. 'Me too, please.'

John inclined his head and went away and, before long, the servant returned with their drinks and asked if they were comfortable. The two friends were, in fact, more comfortable, sitting on the cushioned chairs on the shady terrace, than they had been for some time. Ten minutes passed very easily and then they saw John returning down the stairs from the roof with another man. The newcomer looked keenly across at them on the terrace, smiled and started in their direction. He was of average height, with dark brown, kind eyes, brown hair down to his shoulders and a well-groomed beard of the same colour. His face was tanned to a mid-brown colour and housed a wide smile. He was perhaps a year or two younger than Andrew and simply dressed in a homespun robe. The fisherman tried to recall the man in the water with John the previous evening, but he couldn't. He hadn't taken sufficient notice. He wouldn't make that mistake again!

'I am Jesus, from Nazareth,' said the newcomer. 'How can I help you?'

His voice was soft and gentle, yet had depth and the quality of velvet. Suddenly, the two visitors realised that they really had no clear idea of their reasons for coming. Neither could articulate the thoughts that were coursing through their minds. Jesus waited patiently, a gentle smile on his face. Eventually, Andrew managed, 'We are… followers of John, who is baptising down at the river. He said that he baptised you yesterday and that you – well, that we should seek you out – and talk to you.'

'… That you had many things to tell us – about the coming Kingdom,' Matt chimed in, anxious to help his faltering friend.

'John told you that, did he?' said Jesus, half to himself. 'That is very interesting. I'd be very happy to talk to you both, but, actually, I have to be on my way shortly. I'm going back to the river. Which way are you two going?'

'We've got to go back that way,' said Matt. 'Could we all walk along together?'

'That's a good idea,' replied Jesus. 'I must just take my leave of John barHelez and thank him for his hospitality and then we can be on our way.'

Fifteen minutes later, the three travellers were on the track back to the river. As he journeyed, Jesus told the other two a little of what he proposed. They found him easy to relate to; they felt as if he took them into his confidence very readily, opening his personality to them and making them feel comfortable when asking any questions. His voice was reassuring, mostly soft, but with a depth that suggested that it could be raised to a considerable volume if roused. His eyes, brown and twinkling, were kind and welcoming, yet they seemed to see right into any object of their interest, searching for explanations. Andrew felt the strength of Jesus's character and personality; here was one who could command attention and, he felt, devotion too.

'I have been increasingly feeling that God has some special work he wants me do for him,' Jesus explained. 'This feeling started years ago, when I was quite young – in fact, so long ago I can't really remember not feeling that way. The process has taken years to mature – and even now, there are many uncertainties left.'

Jesus paused, as if expecting a question, but none came, so he continued.

'I feel called to announce a new world – God's world. It is time. High time. God is going to act, and act decisively, in some way. It is as John indicated – God is going to inaugurate a new Kingdom, in which things are going to be so much better. Prisoners are to be liberated, those who are broken-hearted will be comforted and those who are sick will be healed – just as the prophets foretold.'[1]

'How will these things happen?' said Andrew. 'Will God sweep away the Roman empire? Are the Jews to rule the earth? Or will this new Kingdom be confined to Jewry?'

'You must not think that I have all the answers. God is the only one who knows everything. But he is telling me more and more, and soon I believe I shall be ready to speak for him to the people.'

'When will that be?' asked Matt.

'Very soon, my friends,' said Jesus softly. 'I must leave you at the river. You are going north, are you not? I must carry on eastwards.'

'But that'll take you into some pretty rough country, won't it? It's practically desert up there.' Andrew was already concerned for Jesus.

But Jesus only smiled. 'Don't worry, Andrew. I'll be all right. I need the solitude. I need to have many days on my own with God to decide more precisely how to go about the task that he is setting me and, exactly, the part he wants me to play. I shall talk it through with him in great detail and than I shall come to Galilee to tell you all about it. John baptised me yesterday. That was the symbol, the outward sign, that I have started this great work – and it is interesting, and encouraging too, that he knew something special happened then. What did he say about it?'

It was Matt who tried to find the answer.

'Well, John said that he thought – you are the person who could – bring about – initiate the Kingdom that he is looking for. He is asking everyone to prepare for the Kingdom by cleansing themselves. He hopes that you are the one that the prophets predicted would come and bring God's plans to fruition—'

'But he doesn't know just what is implied by that,' Andrew broke in. 'He's at a loss to know what kind of kingdom it will be…'

'We must be patient and wait for God to reveal his plan,' said Jesus, smiling. 'I hope and believe that, while I am in the wilderness of Jordan, God will tell me the answers to some of these questions – at least enough to make a start. When he does, as I said, I will come to Galilee and tell you – and anyone else who will listen.'

There didn't seem to be much more to say after that. The three men walked on until they came to river, where they parted with warm handshakes. Jesus smiled at the other two, warming them in a way they hadn't felt since they were children at their mothers' knees. They felt reassured. This man, Jesus, seemed to know what should be done, even if he did not have all the answers 'off pat'. He would tell them, as soon as God had told him.

★

Andrew didn't dawdle on his way northwards to Capernaum in Galilee. He had much to think about, but he kept striding forward meantime, completing the eighty miles or so in under five days. He saw little of the Jordan Valley in all its spring splendour. The lush meadows, the array of wild flowers – marigolds, crown daisies, fennel and the rest – the blossoms on the trees, all went unnoticed as he strode along, intent on getting home, yet simultaneously churning over in his mind all that had happened. Time and again, he relived the previous few days, especially the time spent with John and then Jesus. He arrived home mid-afternoon on the fifth day, just as Simon was preparing to leave home for work.

'Oh, there you are at last,' said the big fellow, clapping him on the back and making him recoil. 'James said that you had been delayed... or should I say waylaid?'

'I'd like to tell you all about it, Simon,' returned his brother, more solemnly. 'Have you got to be off just now? Stop a few moments and share a mug of wine with me.'

'Well, I ought to get off and get the boat ready for the night's fishing,' grumbled Simon, 'but I rarely say "no" to a drop of wine. I suppose I can spare you a few moments.'

Then, before Andrew could get his mind into working order, with the excitement of a little boy, Simon burst out, 'Listen, we had a hell of a catch last night – seldom better! It should make a tidy sum at the market. I wonder what the news will be when I get down to the waterside?'

'Never mind fish for a moment,' said Andrew. 'I've much to tell you. It won't take long.'

So the two brothers sat facing one another across the rough kitchen table, clutching their wine. However, they had hardly seated themselves when the door opened and Ruth, Simon's pretty, young wife, and her mother, Abigail, appeared.

'Welcome home, Andrew,' said Ruth, kissing him lightly on both cheeks, much to Andrew's secret delight.

'Good to see you again,' said the older woman. 'Did you have a good visit to Jerusalem?'

'Yes – very good,' replied Andrew. 'I was just going to tell Simon all about it.'

'Well, we'll get in the kitchen, then, and start preparing the evening meal. You'll stop with us, won't you, Andrew?'

Andrew nodded gratefully.

'We'll leave you to your talk,' said Ruth, knowing that Simon liked to discuss business with his brother without being overheard by mere women. 'Come on, Mother,' she said, and the women departed, chatting about the price of flour.

'Now,' said Simon, slightly impatiently, 'out with it! What have you been up to?'

'Well...' When put to it, Andrew hardly knew where to begin. Slowly he got into his stride. 'The festival passed off quite well, much as usual. We made our sacrifices, said our prayers and enjoyed the company... saw many old friends. I like Passover and all that it stands for...'

'Yes, yes,' broke in Simon, 'but that isn't all, is it? You've been to Passover several times, but never dallied on the return journey before. What happened then? James was pretty secretive about it all.'

'I expect he told you that we met a – well, I suppose you could call him a prophet.'

'Oh, come on,' jeered his brother. 'Which prophet? Elijah? Jeremiah? Leave it out!' And he went off into gales of forced laughter.

'Jeer all you like, Simon,' said the younger man, hurt. 'He spoke like a prophet, anyway. Several people who were there were convinced by what he said and accepted baptism at his hands.'

'And what's baptism, when it's at home?' demanded the big man.

'It's a sort of – bath, a wash. John – that's the prophet – told us to wash ourselves clean from the past and prepare for "the one who was to come" – you know, the Messiah – the one that the Rabbi has often told us must come sometime to redeem the nation.'

Andrew couldn't look at his brother, for fear that he would continue his mockery. Instead, Simon paused, grimaced, pushed his chair back and strode over to the side table where the wineskin promised a refill of his mug. He sensed that Andrew was serious and realised that he shouldn't damn him too quickly.

'And what did you think about that?' he queried, quite quietly.

'I don't know, Simon,' returned Andrew, relieved at the change of tone. He rose too and caught his brother's arm. 'I really don't know,' he repeated. 'It's been going round and round in my mind ever since. What if the Messiah is really coming?'

'There have been plenty of false alarms,' grunted the other. 'Anyway, did you go in for a bathe in the River Jordan with the prophet?'

'No, I didn't,' said Andrew slowly, 'but I spent several hours with John and his friends, to try to find out more about this coming King – or whoever he is – and the Kingdom he will inaugurate. There are many different ideas on what this Kingdom will be like and how it will come…'

He paused before venturing his most incredible news. Then, falteringly, he spoke again.

'But that's not all, Simon. John told us that he had actually seen and baptised the man he believed to be Messiah that very day!'

'What?' Simon's interest was now fully aroused. 'Did you meet him?'

'Not at that time, but I went with one of John's followers, Matt, to find the man next day. We had quite a long talk with him as we journeyed together.'

'Where was he going?'

'He was off to the desert of Jordan, east of the river – to think and to pray, he said. Then he promised to come to Galilee to tell me – us – everyone – what he intends. He is a Galilean himself – from Nazareth.'

'Huh! Nothing very spectacular ever comes from that God-forsaken little village,' retorted Simon. 'You know what they say about Nazareth! Every other person there isn't worth a half-denarius!'

'We'll see,' returned his brother.

The two brothers eyed one another challengingly, before Simon spoke again.

'So that's it, is it?'

'For the present.'

'Well, when this chap comes… what's his name, by the way?'

'Jesus. When you see him, you'll see just an ordinary man in many ways, but he's – well you just have to meet him. His eyes hold you – his voice the same. He's so friendly and he seems to understand you, even before you speak to him. But the situation he represents is all confusing; I really can't make up my mind what I think about it all.'

'Let's just wait and see,' said Simon. 'In a few days, you might forget all about this fellow. Meantime, I'm going fishing!'

*

It was already halfway through May. The weather was simply wonderful, warm and sunny, yet not so warm as to be uncomfortable – that is, unless you had housework to do. Even in the mid-afternoon, Martha was still busy; she was always busy. She had been busy for the past thirteen years, ever since the death of her parents, which left Lazarus, her elder brother, and herself to fend for, and bring up, the rest of the family. There were three more daughters and one more son. Lazarus had been nineteen at the time, Martha just sixteen. She had been busy!

Nobody could accuse Martha of excessive beauty. She was a 'plain Jane' if ever there was one. She had kindly eyes, but her chin was weak, her skin poor and blotchy and her general appearance reflected her obsession with housework.

She felt more than slightly aggrieved at being lumbered with a family when only sixteen years old. It meant long hours of work, six days a week, all year round. Nothing much could be done on the Sabbath, of course; well, thank God for the Sabbath! The responsibility for the family had also meant that her chance of marrying had gone – she was too busy looking after her parents' children to consider having any of her own. There was Adina, who was fifteen when Mum died, but quite useless about the house and with her head always full of boys, and Ammiel, two years younger, who was not much better. Then there was the younger brother, Jacob, just ten when orphaned, and little Mary, only three.

Lazarus had done his best to bring in the money, but Martha had had to run the home. There was the washing of all the clothes, the cooking of all the food, the fetching of all the water to cook it in and the finding of the firewood to cook it on. Then there was the interminable cleaning; how on earth could one keep a house full of children clean, when it had a mud floor and a roof that leaked. In summer there was dust everywhere; in winter, patches of oozing mud, where the roof had leaked. Mother had never worried too much about the housework, being of an easy-going disposition, but Martha couldn't abide muddles and dirt, disorganisation or filth! Oh, yes! It had been a struggle.

It should have been easier as time went by. The two older girls, Adina and Ammiel, had both married three or four years ago and had their own homes and families just down the street. But Mary had taken after her mother. Even now, at sixteen, she wasn't much use in the home. She would do as she was bidden, but could never think for herself or offer to help out. What she was thinking about all day, Martha couldn't imagine. Perhaps she too was thinking of marriage; she was pretty enough, but no likely lad had yet emerged to take her off Martha's hands.

Jacob, now twenty-three, had recently married and moved into a little house about a half-mile away on the outskirts of Bethany with his new bride. Lazarus had handed the business over to Jacob three years ago and had more or less left home. To be fair, Lazarus had certainly tried to fill his father's shoes for some long time. Left to head the family at nineteen, he had tried to continue father's market garden business, working long hours in the fields below the house. He had done his best but his heart wasn't really in it. He lacked the experience and the 'green fingers'. His crops of vegetables, tomatoes and cucurbits were not as plentiful, nor of the same quality, as those his father had produced. Nor did he have his father's business skill to get the best prices when he took the crop to market in Jerusalem. Martha could remember her father taking loaded cartfuls of produce to market, with poor old Job, the donkey, straining to cope, even though the route was mainly downhill; but, for Lazarus, the crops dwindled and the profits dropped each year. He had struggled on for ten years, with Jacob gradually taking more and more responsibility. Fortunately, Jacob seemed to have inherited his father's gift, and latterly things had looked up a little. But now Jacob had his own wife to keep and soon there would be children. How long would he support his sisters? Martha wondered.

Lazarus just couldn't seem to knuckle down to work nowadays. He had always felt the call to the religious life. That was all very well, thought Martha; religion is fine, in its place. But shouldn't keeping the home going come first? Lazarus had begun by spending a good deal of time talking with old Simeon, the local rabbi. He thought about becoming a rabbi himself, but had never quite decided. Then he had started to go more and more often to Jerusalem, to sit at the feet of the scribes and doctors of the law who taught every day in the Temple Precinct, but still he couldn't decide exactly what he ought to do with his life. He couldn't agree with either the Pharisees or the Sadducees, and seemed to be lost in a religious fog.

At last, he had packed his bag and taken himself off to the shores of the Dead Sea, where, surrounded by desert, the monastic community of the Essenes sect was located. Qumran: the very name seemed, somehow, mysterious and a little menacing. Lazarus had spoken very little about his life at Qumran, but Martha had gathered that the routine was very strict. The brethren (there were no women in the community – at least, that was the official rule) rose at five every morning, summer and winter. Much time was given to prayer and cleansing. Ritual bathing was practised before each meal and every act of worship, and it seemed that there were many more of the latter than the former! Much time was given to reading, copying and interpreting the ancient scriptures, as well as cleaning the communal house and tending the fields. It was, of course, useless to try to till the ground near the community, but several fields were rented out to the brethren down in the Jordan Valley. Apparently, Lazarus had been sent there several times to work for the community.

But, after a while, Lazarus had decided that community life was not for him either. He had completed the first year as a novice, but had decided that, after all, he should not proceed with his candidature. He had failed again – or the community had failed him. God didn't seem to be sure what he wanted for Lazarus. Now he flitted about, doing a little work here and there, arriving home in Bethany from time to time, staying a few days or a week or two, then drifting off again in search of… Lazarus wasn't sure what.

All their problems had started that awful day when Mother and Father had been killed. What a day that was. Martha remembered it as if it were only yesterday. Mother had been coming down the village street and had stopped to talk to their neighbour outside her house, just across the road from their own garden gate. Suddenly, she had heard the sound of galloping horses and, looking round, she had seen a Roman chariot, pulled by two enormous stallions, thundering towards her down the narrow street. Mother had sprung towards the garden gate, but slipped and fell, right in the path of the oncoming chariot. To make matters worse, Father, in the garden, hearing her cry, but not seeing the immanent danger, had rushed to help her, and both had been trampled under the flying hooves.

Father had been killed outright, but Mother, partially protected by his body, had lingered on for several dreadful days and nights, till she finally succumbed to infection in her many wounds. Martha had tried to nurse her. She pleaded with her to live, but it was of no avail. Mother, her kindly if slightly scatter-brained mother, had gone to be with Father. They had been an affectionate couple and would have wanted to be together, even though they were scarcely forty when the accident happened. Martha and her sisters had wept, of course, but the practical side of Martha could not mourn for long. She had quickly assumed the role of housewife and mother. Lazarus would have to be 'father'. They would have to bring the others up in a right and proper manner.

Some of the villagers had not been as quick to move on. There was fierce resentment towards the charioteer, for Father and Mother were popular and the family had lived in the village for as long as anyone could remember. However, it was later established that some of the village dogs had startled the horses, causing them to bolt. The driver really couldn't be blamed; indeed, he was lucky to escape injury himself as the chariot careered madly along the narrow streets, crushing everything in its path, only coming to rest about two miles away, as the horses finally tired and the driver regained control. But some of the villagers still muttered in their beards about the hated Romans and their attitude to the subservient Jews.

'My goodness, I must get moving!' Martha muttered to herself. 'I've been reminiscing too much and there's so much to do! I must put all that washing away…'

But, just at that moment, a knock came at the door. Puzzled, Martha approached the door rather warily. If it had been Lazarus or Jacob at the door, or one of the girls, or even a neighbour, they would have just walked in – that was the way in the village. So who on earth would knock?

Martha opened the door and her face immediately changed. Her dark brown eyes lit up and her face broke into a smile as she recognised Jesus and, behind him, John barHelez.

'Jesus, fancy seeing you!' she cried. 'Come in – and welcome.'

'Thank you, Martha,' replied Jesus. He stumbled a little through the narrow doorway and Martha reached out to support him.

'Whatever's happened?' she said. 'You look really poorly – and weak…'

'He'll be fine,' said John, coming in after Jesus. 'He's been out in the wilderness for many days, looking for answers to difficult questions, and he hasn't bothered to look after himself. He just needs food and sleep – and a bit of kindly care.'

'I'll be fine,' said Jesus, slumping down into a chair.

'Let me get you some fruit juice,' said Martha. 'Orange or lemon?'

'Whatever's handy.'

Martha flew away to the kitchen area at the back of the house to find the necessary.

'Where's Lazarus?' asked Jesus, once he had sipped the refreshing juice.

'I'm expecting him at supper time,' replied his sister. 'He went into Jerusalem early this morning, but he will be home shortly. He's still got a good appetite! What about you?'

'I shall enjoy your supper, Martha,' smiled Jesus.

'You'll stop too, John?'

'If I may, Martha. That would be very kind,' came the prompt response.

'Whatever has happened, Jesus, that you've been out in that awful wilderness?' Martha was always curious to know what was going on.

'I'll tell you the story tonight, Martha, if you don't mind. When we are all together. Then I shall only have to do so once!'

'Of course, Jesus. It'll keep till then. John, come and sit down here.' Martha was a good hostess and enjoyed fussing over them both, but she had scarcely drawn up a chair for herself when the door opened again and in came Mary, carrying a pot full of water. As soon as she saw Jesus, she put the pot down, spilling a fair amount in her haste, and ran to greet him, kissing him warmly on both cheeks. It was difficult to believe that Martha and Mary were sisters. Martha, at twenty-nine, looked almost an old woman, whereas Mary, at sixteen, was a ravishing beauty, with long flowing black hair, dark brown eyes and perfect skin. Martha always looked a bit like a scarecrow, but Mary carried her fine figure with dignity wherever she went.

Jesus heaved himself up in the chair and tried to stand.

'Sit down, Jesus,' both sisters cried out almost together.

'You look all in,' said Mary. 'Whatever has happened to you?'

'Later, Mary,' replied the visitor. 'I'll tell you all about it later, when Lazarus is here, and we've had supper.'

So it was that the family and their guests sat around the table that evening in the courtyard at the back of the house, where they could talk quite privately. The area was enclosed, and beautiful trailing flowering bushes grew all over the walls. Overhead, the stars shone bravely, the Milky Way standing out in a great stream of haze across the sky. In the trees nearby, cicadas were scratching busily, trying to attract mates for themselves. Jesus was talking in that soft, persuasive voice of his. Every eye, with the possible exception of Martha's, who thought she had heard a mouse in her kitchen, was on the soft-spoken Galilean.

'I believe that God has called me,' he was saying. 'I've always felt it – I know you have too. Lazarus, John and I have all been drawn away from our homes to study; we all finished up at the Qumran community, in response to that call. In the end, for different reasons, we all rejected their teaching and went our various ways. Lately, God's call to me has become more insistent – more intense. I am now sure that God wants me to go out and tell people that he is going to act – soon – decisively – to establish a new era.'

'Do you mean that you believe the promised kingdom is coming?' asked Lazarus, his voice intense with expectation.

'What do you mean by that phrase, my friend?' asked Jesus.

'Well, we've always been told, haven't we, that one day God would send a Messiah – or two Messiahs, a King and a Priest – to set up a heavenly Kingdom, where God would rule unchallenged. Then things would be done on earth, as they already are in Heaven. In this new Kingdom, everyone would be—'

'Everyone?' John broke in. 'Surely you don't think that the Gentiles will be included in God's Kingdom?'

Lazarus turned to his friend. 'You know well that there have been arguments about that matter for years – centuries. Of course, we Jews will always be God's chosen race, but some people think that one day even the Gentiles will be included in God's favour.'

'Even Romans?' John looked pained.

'Perhaps even the Romans,' said Jesus. 'You two seem to think that the Kingdom will necessarily be a political reality, where, as has always happened in the past, one nation will be set up over against another. Such a Kingdom would have to be protected by armies, and this involves coercion – force of arms – with all that this implies by way of pain and suffering. Do you think that this is consistent with God's love? Perhaps God has a completely different kind of Kingdom in mind.'

There was a moment's silence while they all digested this last remark. Then Jesus continued.

'While I was in the desert, I was led to believe that that Kingdom might involve an entirely different situation. It wouldn't depend on arms – it will not rival either Greece or Rome – it will be more an attitude of mind, a way of living, that each individual embraces for himself and that like-minded individuals join together to propagate and foster.'

'What sort of Kingdom would that be?' John sounded very dubious.

'It will be a Kingdom of the heart and mind,' replied Jesus. 'An inner Kingdom, where, in the centre of every individual's life, there will be peace, serenity, and, above all, love. Love for God; love for one another.'

'Love for God and love for your neighbour is certainly what the law commands', said John.[2]

'But can love be commanded?' asked Jesus, softly. 'Surely, love can only be given voluntarily, willingly, in response to someone loving you.'

'Someone has to love first,' put in Lazarus.

'God loved us first, and loves us all, all the time,' replied Jesus. 'Because God loves us, we can all respond. As we realise that his love and his life are springing up in our lives, we can reflect a little of that love to other people, then they, too, can reflect that love to others, and so on. The process is a bit like yeast leavening a lump of dough. The yeast works away in the lump gradually leavening the whole loaf, making the bread light and pleasant to eat, not dull and stodgy.'[3]

'So are we not to expect a visible Kingdom?' Lazarus sounded disappointed.

'One day, everything will be God's. God will bring everything under his own control in time. Earthly Kingdoms cannot last for ever. But when that final state of affairs will come, only God knows.[4] Meantime, I'm sure that the Kingdom I have described can begin in our lives today – it is already flooding my life and can be yours too.'

'So what will you do to ensure that this Kingdom comes?' asked John.

'Starting in Galilee, I will tell the people what I have told you. I will explain that their period of slavery and uncertainty is over, just as foretold by the prophets.'

'They will misunderstand you, just as we did,' said Lazarus, shaking his head. 'They will think of freedom from Rome – and an earthly Kingdom.'

'I shall try to tell them the truth as I see it,' replied his friend. 'I shall tell them about a Kingdom of "right relationships" that is there for everyone who seeks it.'

'Will they listen to you?' asked Lazarus. 'I mean – no offence, old friend, but why should they listen to someone who is not a priest or even a village rabbi? Some know you as a simple carpenter! Why should they listen to a mere joiner?'

'They will listen,' replied Jesus, with quiet confidence. 'After all, none of the prophets of old were highly qualified men. None were trained rabbis or priests – people like Jeremiah, Amos, Hosea … God spoke to them and they just stood up and spoke to the people. Sometimes they spoke to kings and they listened. In the same way, the people will listen to me. They listened to John, when he preached down by the Jordan and offered them baptism there.'

'John has the idea that the Messiah will come in his lifetime – any time now,' said Lazarus. 'Are you claiming to be the Messiah – the "one who should come" – "the anointed one"?'

There was a lengthy pause. Nobody in the group could take their eyes from the Galilean. Eventually Jesus spoke again.

'I know that I am called by God to do this work. It would be a great privilege to be the Messiah, but also a great burden. In the end, we all have to try to do God's will.'

'Why should being the Messiah be a burden?' John was incredulous.

Jesus turned to him and smiled.

'My friend, you know as well as I do that there are many references to the work of the Messiah in the scriptures. Some speak of the Messiah as a great king, or priest, or leader, with the world at his feet. Many speak of his privileges. But some – especially Isaiah – emphasise his service to others and his suffering for others. He is to be led "like a sheep to the slaughter".[5] I'm sure you remember the text. What does that mean?'

Only the cicadas replied, so Jesus continued.

'This paradox occupied a great deal of my thinking while I was away in the wilderness. What is really the work of the Messiah? He is sometimes called the "Son of God". Of course, we are all sons of God, in one sense – he is our father, we are all his sons and daughters...'

At this, Jesus turned and smiled at the two women, who were keeping very quiet in the presence of the three men.

'Yes, we are all Israelites and part of the chosen race, but the Messiah will be the first of all, perhaps the "Son of God" in a different sense. What will that mean? What powers will the Messiah have?'

Jesus paused to see if any of his friends would respond, but they seemed to be reluctant to try to answer the question. So the carpenter went on, slowly.

'When I was in the desert and feeling very hungry, a thought kept haunting me: If you are really the Messiah, you should be able to turn these stones into bread.[6] And – I thought – not just for my own needs, but also to feed all the hungry folk who are around us every day. Wouldn't that be a splendid thing to do for the poor, I wondered... Feed them and let them see that God cares.'

Once again there was a pause, while they all pondered. Then Jesus continued.

'But in the end, I came to the conclusion that, whether I could turn stones into bread or not, this was not God's way. God would not want me to bribe people by giving them bread, or gold, or anything else, for this would not involve their hearts and wills – their inner selves. They would be glad of the bread, temporarily, but be hungry again. No, the Kingdom is a matter of the heart and will, first of all. It can't be bought with bribes.'

'So you won't feed them?' said Martha, greatly daring.

'God has provided corn in the fields and strength in their arms,' replied Jesus. 'Everyone can be fed if only people will share what is already potentially available. What is needed is not free handouts, but the will to work together willingly for the benefit of all.'

'Then what is the Messiah's work?' persisted John.

'That was the question that haunted me, when I was in the desert.' Jesus seemed to be a long way away, reliving the experience. 'I heard a voice in my heart saying, "If you are really the Messiah, you ought to be able to cast yourself down from the topmost pinnacle of the Temple and no harm will come to you".[7] People would see this miracle, recognise that you are someone special and be drawn to believe in all that you say.'

'Would you really do that?' Lazarus's eyes were alight.

Jesus shook his head solemnly. 'No. After some thought, I realised that that wouldn't do either, Lazarus. The Messiah is not some kind of magician or wizard. Men's hearts are not to be won by tricks. Even if they were impressed by the miracle, the effect would not last, because, as in the case of the bread, there is no change in the heart – nothing has happened in the inner man. We have all seen magicians working at fair-grounds. We are impressed for the moment by what they do, but half an hour later, we have forgotten the whole thing. No. Even a miracle like that would not reach the souls of the people.'

'Then?'

'I concluded that no amount of dabbling in worldly matters would do.[8] Even if I were to become master of the whole world, I would be no better off than Tiberius Caesar – and we all know how much he is revered in the hearts of ordinary folk! Does he satisfy the heart? Does he provide the real blessings of life – love, truth, beauty, goodness…? Of course not. These things spring from God, who works like the yeast in the lump of dough. When we feel his love aglow within us, then, and only then, will we be drawn to treat other people properly, lovingly, and they, in their turn, will love others also.'

'It would be a lovely world,' said Mary, with a sigh. 'If only everyone could think like that. But I can't see the Romans thinking that way – not Pontius Pilate, for example. Nor even our beloved Tetrarch, Herod Antipas.'

'All in God's good time,' said her guest. 'I believe that I know enough to begin my ministry in Galilee. I propose to rest up for just a few more days, then go to Galilee and start work.'

'Well,' said John slowly. 'I shall think about all you have said, my friend, but I have yet to be convinced. I shall continue to pray for guidance – and for you. But, for my part, I shall continue at my place on the Temple staff.'

Lazarus spoke up. 'We all studied together at Qumran,' he said. 'You'll remember that there we were taught to despise the High Priest and the Temple worship. The Essenes believe that the priests have got it entirely wrong. They believe that all their sacrifices are worthless, because the priests have sold out to the foreigners. They are nothing better than collaborators.'

'I understand their reservations,' replied John, 'but Caiaphas believes that it is better to cooperate with Rome rather than risk a full-scale riot, or rebellion, and have even the small amount of freedom we have taken away from us. At present, we are left to run our own affairs to some extent – we do not have to join in Emperor worship, as do all the other vassal states of Rome. We don't have to recognise their many gods. That's surely worth something.'

'True,' said Jesus, 'but it also means that the High Priest and his entourage live in great luxury, while the common people go short.'

'That's inevitable,' retorted John. 'There will always be the rich and the poor. Would you have our High Priest look like a ragamuffin? So long as the rich have a care for the poor…'

'But do they? Do the priests care for the poor, today?' Jesus sounded doubtful. 'From what I can see, neither the priests, nor the scribes, nor the Pharisees, really care for the poor. If they do good, it is usually for show.' He shook his head sadly. 'But you must do as you think right, John, I know that. It is good to know that there are some good souls among the priests on the Temple staff, who will listen for God's voice among the clamour of all that goes on there.'

'I just wish I was as sure as you two are,' said Lazarus. 'Both of you think that you are following the right path, yet they turn out to be quite different! I don't know which is worse – to be sure, but possibly wrong, or unsure and lost, like me!'

The others had to smile. Poor Lazarus meant well, but he could never make up his mind.

NOTES

[1] Isaiah 61:1.
[2] Deut. 6:5; Lev. 19:18.
[3] Matt. 13:33.
[4] Acts 1:6–7.
[5] Isaiah 53:7.
[6] Matt. 4:3.
[7] Matt. 4:5.
[8] Matt. 4:8.

The first of the few

Jairus was a pillar of society in Capernaum. In his mid-forties, he was fit and in the prime of life. His was a prosperous business; he maintained and operated several mills and processed a good proportion of all the wheat grown in the district. He had a reputation for being fair with all customers, both large and small, and dealing equally with both communities in the town, both Jew and Greek. Perhaps it was for this reason that he was normally known by the Greek form of his name, rather than the Jewish form, Jair. But Jairus was also a pillar of the Synagogue, the most influential layman in the local congregation. He was involved with old Hezekiah, the rabbi, in all the major decisions effecting the religious life of the community. So it was that, near the end of May, Jesus sought out Jairus's house and asked if he might address the congregation on the following Sabbath.

Jairus was initially caught in two minds. On the one hand, he had never met Jesus himself, nor did the aspiring preacher offer any references from local rabbis. He said he came from Nazareth, which was about twenty miles away and had a bit of a reputation for producing weird customers. On the other hand, he did look the part and was highly articulate. Yes, he had certainly presented himself well. His voice, in particular, had impressed Jairus with its soft melodic character, and his choice of words was very apt. His eyes certainly held the listener and there was no doubting his sincerity. It was not unusual for suitable laymen to address the meeting. Traditionally, Judaism had always been open to God's word from whatever quarter it might flow. Over the centuries, numerous individuals had arisen from obscurity to bring the nation back to God. Perhaps this Nazarene might have a word from God in the prophetic tradition.

Although the authentic prophetic voice had been silent for many years, there was always hope; the man John, who was baptising down on the Jordan River, had shown that things might be stirring again. After consideration, Jairus decided that Jesus should be allowed to speak on the Sabbath. And so it was, that, towards the end of the morning worship, Jesus stood up in the Synagogue to address the congregation. His theme was 'the successful life'.

'Everyone is entitled to want to lead a successful life,' he began. 'Nobody is likely to seek anything else – how foolish it would be if anyone sought failure! But how many of us know where to look for success, or, indeed, what to count as success?'

Jesus paused and looked round the room. Then he continued.

'For some, success involves the getting of plenty of money. For some, success means the acquisition of positions of power. For others, success is equated with happiness, and they believe that is to be found in eating, drinking and making merry.'

Jesus's voice now became quieter. He leaned forward and continued.

'But none of these things, my friends, brings real success or lasting happiness. Of course, everyone needs some money in order to live, and there is nothing wrong with a certain amount of power and influence, if properly used. Nor is there anything wrong with having a happy time together, so long as it isn't at the expense of someone else. But none of these things brings lasting joy, real happiness or abiding success. In fact, real happiness does not come by acquisition, but by distribution, not by getting but by giving.'

Jesus's hands and arms were being used to good effect as he spoke. The congregation could see him 'getting' and 'giving' – his facial expressions, too, told the story. He went on.

'Real joy comes not by taking from others but by sacrificing for others; not by having power over others, but by sharing influence with others. Having a good time is only really fun if everyone is involved – it must be inclusive, not exclusive. In short, life can only be successful if it is lived in accordance with ancient saying of scripture: "Always treat others as you would like them to treat you".'[1]

There was long silence following Jesus's address. The content of the theme was not controversial, for it echoed one of the greatest commandments, which devout Jews repeated every day. But the style of the address was quite different from usual. Normally, preachers began with scripture, and expounded from the text, carefully taking every point from the written word, thus deriving authority for what they were saying. Jesus, on the other hand, had simply spoken from the heart, expressing the truth in new ways, and only finally demonstrating that what he had said was consistent with the scripture. In fact, what he said seemed to go beyond the word of scripture to the very essence of the matter.

There was a buzz of comment from the congregation as they left the Synagogue. Everyone wondered where this new preacher had come from and whether he would speak again soon. Andrew, listening from the back of the Synagogue, had certainly felt again the tug of Jesus's personality as he listened. Those appealing eyes, those expressive gestures, that velvet voice… Certainly Jesus could hold an audience, and Andrew felt the pull of his charisma. What he said would be right, as far as Andrew was concerned. What a pity that Simon, as happened far too often, had overslept and missed going to the Synagogue! Of course, they had been very busy that week. Somehow, night work always took it out of you more than the same number of hours worked by day, but Simon was used to it – he was just lazy!

Andrew made his way swiftly to Simon's house, bursting in on Ruth, who was preparing a meal.

'Where's the big fellow?' he asked.

'On the roof, with a mug of beer – where else?' came the cheerful reply.

Andrew skipped up the steps to confront his brother, whom he found lounging in characteristic attitude, his enormous frame draped casually over a sagging basket chair, his beard damp with beer slurped from the mug which he held aloft in his gigantic hand when he saw him.

'Welcome, little brother!' he roared, grinning widely.

'Simon, you old layabout! You should have come to Synagogue with me this morning,' exclaimed the other.

'Why? What was so special about today?' His brother leered at him over the rim of the mug.

'Jesus, the man I told you about, has arrived in Galilee – he was there in the Synagogue and spoke to us.'

'And what did he have to say for himself?' Simon sounded sceptical. Andrew hesitated.

'Well, what did he say?' Simon persisted.

Slowly Andrew got himself together.

'It wasn't so much what he said, as the way he said it,' he explained. 'His eyes, his voice, his gestures – he's just so … I can't explain, Simon. You'll just have to come and hear him for yourself.'

'What did he say?' Simon was nearly shouting now.

'Well – he talked about living a successful life. He said that actually giving was better than getting. Happiness couldn't be acquired, he said – it came through sharing with others. In the finish, he related it to the law we all know – "love your neighbour as yourself" – but he taught from the heart, not from scripture. His message comes from within him, not on an old scroll.'

'So you were impressed?' Simon didn't sound very impressed himself.

'You would have been too, Simon, if you had been there. You should have come.'

'Is he going to speak again next Sabbath?'

'I don't know – perhaps he will.'

But, in fact, the brothers didn't have to wait that long, for the very next evening, as they were walking towards the shore to prepare for the night's fishing, they saw Jesus coming up the road towards them.

'Hello, Andrew,' said Jesus.

'Fancy you remembering my name,' replied Andrew, taking the proffered hand.

'I never forget a face,' said the Nazarene, 'and I try never to forget a name either.'

Andrew turned to his brother. 'This is Simon, my elder brother,' he said.

Jesus immediately thrust out his hand and took Simon's huge fist, clasping it firmly. His brown eyes flashed.

'I'm very pleased to meet you,' he said.

Simon was caught somewhat off balance. On the one hand, he didn't usually have much time for preachers but, on the other, this man, with his friendly disposition, his warm handshake and those blazing eyes, certainly struck a chord with him and invited a positive response. He took Jesus's hand and pumped it vigorously.

'I was hoping to see you,' continued Jesus. 'I need a favour.'

And somehow, before they knew it, the brothers were agreeing to meet the preacher at the seashore late next afternoon on the following day. Jesus explained that he had been preaching on the beach that day and drawn quite a crowd. He planned to do the same the next day.

'However, the trouble is that the crowd all push and shove to get a better view, and I have nowhere from which to address them properly. It would be better if I could stand in the prow of your boat, just a few feet out from the waterline, and then we could get everyone else to sit comfortably on the sand to listen.[2] As it is, those at the front get pushed forward and forced right into me. It was chaotic this afternoon. I'm worried someone might get hurt.'

'No problem,' said Simon, organisation being one of his strong points. 'We'll soon sort it for you.'

And they did. For an hour or more, the brothers provided their boat as a floating pulpit and persuaded the crowd to sit on the beach to listen. Nobody was inconvenienced; everyone saw and heard the preacher. Simon was very pleased with himself; Jesus was pleased too.

That evening, after Jesus had gone into town for supper and a rest, the fishermen were gearing up for their nightly toil, mending the nets and checking the boat, when their friends, James and John, came down to the beach on similar business. After the usual fishermen's gossip, James ventured, 'I hear you've been helping this preacher, Jesus, from Nazareth.'

'We just lent him the boat for an hour or so,' replied Andrew.

'What did you think of him?'

'You know that I've always been impressed by him. I met him first in Jericho, after we'd both heard John the baptiser by the river. He talked a lot of sense then, and again on the two occasions I've heard him since.'

'And you, Simon?' asked James.

Simon chewed his lip for a moment before replying. Finally he replied, 'I've always been a bit wary of preachers, as you know. But I have to admit that this chap has something. It's not just what he says; it's what he is – his manner.'

'He holds you – well, he holds me,' burst in Andrew, normally reluctant to interrupt Simon. 'You just have to listen, and respond to him.'

'Perhaps we should come to the beach tomorrow' said James. 'He's coming again, is he?'

Andrew nodded. 'Yes, we'll all be here.'

'I'll make the effort,' said James. 'What about you, little brother?' They all looked at John.

The young man, who thus far had seemed far away in his own thoughts, suddenly returned to consciousness.

'Oh, yes, if you wish,' he said. His attitude was indifferent.

However, once they had heard Jesus speak, and even more after they had been introduced to him, both the barZebedee brothers became keen to spend more time with the Nazarene. John, in particular seemed to warm to Jesus. It was as if his previously wandering mind had now found a focus. His eyes, which, in the past, had seemed glazed over, now shone with a new interest and vitality that was evident to all who knew him.

So the two pairs of brothers took it in turns to provide the 'pulpit' for Jesus, and helped to keep the crowds who came to hear him in some semblance of order. As the days went by, the crowds grew bigger and, soon, not only the people of the town of Capernaum, but also folk from the surrounding villages were talking of the 'new prophet', who seemed to know the way that life should be lived. He talked to them of a new relationship between people, of a world where everyone would have a place, a society of equal opportunities, a community for God. He did not criticise the law – rather he developed it and transcended it. He went beyond the words to the heart of the matter.

But after a week's preaching in Capernaum, Jesus suggested to the fishermen that it was time to move east, to the next town, Bethsaida. The ministry needed to move on and move out.

★

Bethsaida was Philip's town now,[3] but he had been born and brought up in Pella, a town in the Decapolis, about thirty miles to the south, just a little to the east of the River Jordan. His origins, his name, his culture and first language were all Greek.

Pella was a bustling little town, set in a delightful valley served by a refreshing stream that gushed water all through the winter and spring, but subsided to a mere trickle during the long hot summers. Little houses, some made of stone, some of mud bricks, were dotted about all over the valley floor, but in the centre stood an imposing temple, a gymnasium and a theatre. The latter was used not only for performances, but for all public meetings; the elders of the town were often to be seen there discussing local politics. Set on the surrounding hills overlooking the valley were three more temples, dedicated to various gods and goddesses. Their graceful columns and beautifully carved statues were frequently admired by passing strangers. Pella was a town that was proud of itself.

Philip's father had been well known and respected in Pella; he had had a thriving business as a potter. The family had been raised there, amid the Greek-speaking, theatre-going community, accepting the ancient gods and keeping the local customs. Philip had been quite a good athlete at one time, competing fiercely in the races and starting to show some considerable promise as a discus thrower.

But Philip's father often had to take his wares to be sold either in Galilee or Peraea, and so, inevitably, he had come into contact with Jews and Jewish ideas. Thus it had come about that he had met, in Bethsaida, a man called

Nathaniel, a Jew of about his own age, and after many months of careful debate within himself, he had decided to renounce his old faith and culture and become a Jew. He, and all the males in the family, Philip among them, had been circumcised according to the law. He had sold up in Pella and moved home to Bethsaida, where they had immersed themselves in their adopted race and religion. All this had happened a dozen years ago, when Philip was only eleven. Now he was fully grown, tall, strong and, many said, handsome and a good potter himself, following in his father's footsteps. He and his elder brother, Demitri, were likely to take on more and more responsibility for the business as Father got older – already, at fifty-two, Father was failing; his eyes were not as good as they had been and his joints were often painful. His fingers were by no means as sure on the clay as they had been in his prime. Somehow he couldn't be bothered any more.

Philip was sitting one afternoon early in June in his workshop, situated on the edge of town, turning another pot, running his fingers gently over the clay, trying to work it into an item of both beauty and utility. But he wasn't having a good afternoon – things weren't going well at all. Normally, he was a gifted craftsman, but today the first two pots he had cast after his siesta had not turned out well and had had to be destroyed. He had failed to produce that smoothness of finish that he usually achieved and had decided not to compromise his standards. The clay had been crushed and remoulded twice – and Philip was decidedly irritated with himself at his lack of progress, which was unusual. Once more, however, his fingers failed to persuade the clay into its correct shape and Philip muttered a stifled curse. He was just about to sweep the clay aside and start yet again when a quiet voice behind him interrupted him.

'Excuse me. Could you give me a mug of water, please?'

Philip looked up, startled for a moment. He had been concentrating so hard on his wheel that he hadn't noticed a stranger coming up the street towards his workshop. He now saw a man of about his own height, dressed in a simple homespun robe, with dark brown eyes and hair. Those eyes were darker than any Philip had ever seen before, like deep pools in a forest.

'A drink?' he queried. 'Yes, of course.' Hospitality to a traveller was part of the Jewish tradition – indeed, it is common to all the nations of that region. He got up and walked into the back of the workshop and spooned water from a jar into a mug for the stranger.

'You're not from round here, are you? I don't think we've met before,' he ventured.

'That's right. My name is Jesus. I'm from Nazareth. I haven't been to Bethsaida for some years now; I came a few times as a boy, but that's longer ago than I care to think about!'

'Well, sit down a moment and tell me what brings you here,' said Philip and he drew up a chair so that the two of them could sit in the shade.

Jesus told Philip that he was a preacher and that he intended to speak at the lake side that afternoon, when he had met up with Simon and Andrew, who were sailing the boat along the coast. He himself had walked, being in need of the solitude to prepare his mind for his sermon. Philip found himself telling this friendly person about himself and his family, and how they had changed their faith and become Jewish. Jesus seemed very interested, inquiring gently how Philip felt about his father's decision, and whether he had ever questioned for himself the need for the change. Philip reflected on this for a moment before replying.

'I suppose, at that age, I just followed my father's wishes,' he said. 'After all, at eleven, you don't really know your own mind too well, do you? But I don't think I ever regretted leaving my Greek friends and coming to Bethsaida. Of course I enjoyed the sport and the theatre in Pella, but I can do without them, and we have made many friends here. I owe most of all to a man called Nathaniel, who helped us all to find our way, especially when we first arrived here. He was appointed by the rabbi to help us integrate into Jewish society. He's much older than me – nearer Dad's age than mine – and he's become a sort of father in God to me. He helped me learn the scriptures and understand just why the Jews are so special. He taught me the essentials of the faith – about Abraham and the Covenant, Moses and the Law, about David the great king, and Elijah the great prophet. He told me how the ten tribes were lost and about the exile in Babylon – and about the return to Jerusalem. He also told me about the uprising under the Maccabees, the Hasmonean Kingdom and how Herod the Great built the present Temple. All I know about the faith I got from Nathaniel.'

'He seems to have done a good job,' observed the man from Nazareth, smiling. 'You must introduce me to him sometime.'

'I'd like to,' said Philip.

'But I have to go now and meet my friends who have come by boat. Time is getting on. Perhaps you would like to come and hear me speak sometime?'

'I'll come now,' said Philip. 'I wasn't having a good afternoon anyway – as you probably noticed. Nothing seemed to be going right. I'll give it up for the afternoon and come to the lake with you.'

So the two men left the workshop together and made their way to the lake side, where they found Simon and Andrew waiting with the boat. Jesus introduced the young man to his fishermen friends. They were at first surprised to find that Jesus had found a new friend in Bethsaida so quickly; but, talking about it later, they decided that Jesus's personality was such that he was likely to find new friends quickly everywhere!

'Actually, we too were from Bethsaida, originally,' said Simon. 'We moved to Capernaum about fifteen years ago – my father thought that there were better fishing and mooring facilities there.'

'That's why we've never met, then,' replied Philip. 'We arrived here about twelve years ago.'

They chatted on until, a few minutes later, Jesus started to speak to the people. Only a few people stopped to listen that afternoon, but Jesus did not seem bothered.

'Word will get around,' he said. 'We'll come again tomorrow and, in all probability, things will go better.'

He had spoken again that afternoon about the Kingdom of God – or, as he called it sometimes, the Kingdom of heaven. While not ruling out the possibility of a total reorganisation of the existing order, in which God would act decisively to control the whole world, Jesus had again stressed his idea of an inner 'Kingdom', a revolution of the heart and mind, in which people embraced a new way of living and thinking. Philip had, evidently, been greatly impressed by the preacher's ideas.

'You really must come and meet my mentor, Nathaniel,' he insisted.[4] 'He would be most interested to share his thoughts with you. He has so much background in the faith.'

So the little party had made their way through the town to a small house, surrounded by fruit trees, situated about a half a mile away from the lake. There they found the older man, approaching fifty, with hair already beginning to go grey at the temples, eyes rather deep-set and a tanned face lined with years of smiling and questioning.

'Come and sit down, all of you,' said Nathaniel. 'Let me get you a drink.'

'You're most kind,' returned Jesus. 'I wouldn't mind a seat – I've been standing too long!'

When they were all seated, served with cool lemon juice and shaded by the large fig tree from the afternoon sun, Philip started to tell Nathaniel all about their afternoon.

'Jesus really gave me a new slant on the meaning of life,' he enthused. 'He told us about the coming of the Kingdom – the fulfilment of the Law and the Prophets.'

'Did you say that you hailed from Nazareth?' asked Nathaniel, with a wide smile. 'Don't they say that Nazareth is incapable of producing anything worthwhile?'

'I believe it has been said,' replied Jesus, also smiling. 'You'll have to make your own mind up on that score – I'm afraid I can't help my background! I was born in a poor house and grew up to be a village carpenter – but now I believe that God has called me to be more than a carpenter, just as he called you to be a true Israelite and father in God to this young man, Philip.'

'How did you know that?' said Nathaniel.

'Philip has been telling me all about you and just what a help you have been to his family since they moved to Bethsaida.'

'I was glad to give the family a hand. They came here rather ignorant of Jewish affairs, but they wanted to learn, and it was pleasure to teach them.' Nathaniel looked with pride and affection at his young pupil.

'You certainly helped me,' said Philip, 'and I'm very grateful.'

Then turning to the others, he said, 'By the way, I should have mentioned that this fellow has two names, Nathaniel and Bartholemew.[5] Some use one name, others use the other. It can be confusing!'

'I answer to either,' chuckled the older man. 'Nathaniel is my given name, but at the Synagogue they call me Bart because there's another Nathaniel. There's no real mystery.'

The conversation rattled on easily enough until Nathaniel's wife, Lydia, came to see about supper.

'I hope you'll all stay,' said Nathaniel. 'I'm sure we can stretch what we have in the kitchen.' This with a quick glance at Lydia, who confirmed the position with a quick nod and a smile.

'Do stay,' she said.

'Well, if you're sure we are not overwhelming you,' said Jesus.

It was a happy evening. Conversation flowed freely. Lydia proved to be an excellent cook and Nathaniel a warm host, quickly putting everyone at ease. Jesus obviously loved dinner parties and had them laughing when he told amusing stories and asked them riddles. But he also encouraged the others to speak of their own experiences of life, and, one by one, they shared their memories, both amusing and, in some cases, heart-rending. The light faded, but still the group chattered on under the gleaming stars.

Eventually there was a slight lull in the proceedings and Simon, greatly daring, caught Jesus's eye and asked, 'What about you, Jesus? We've all spoken of our own lives. Will you not tell us about your own background? Why did you decide to be a preacher?'

Jesus hesitated, then smiled – just a little smile at the corner of his mouth.

'Why does a river decide to flow?' he replied. 'It just happens. And so it was with me. I just knew that that was what I had to do. God spoke and I had to listen – and then speak myself.'

'Did you go to rabbinical school?' asked Philip.

'I have studied a great deal, in many different centres of learning,' replied the preacher, 'but, before I could do that, I had to earn a living for myself and the family. I grew up in Nazareth, with four brothers and two sisters.[6] I was the eldest. Our village lies only a few miles from the important regional town of Sepphoris, but we rarely went there – it has a high percentage of Gentiles, and Antipas and the ruling class were often there, until he moved his headquarters to Tiberias. Dad used to get work there sometimes, however, which helped our household budget. He was a carpenter, as you know, and we lads were introduced to the trade as quite little boys. It was just as well, too, because, unfortunately, my father died when I was only fourteen. He was only forty-five. It started as just an ordinary cold, but soon it turned to a fever, his breathing was badly affected and within a few days, it failed altogether and he died. I wonder whether working in an atmosphere of sawdust all his life was partly responsible for his early demise. We shall never know.

'Mother was inconsolable – they were very much in love – and to become a widow by the age of only thirty-one was very hard on her, especially since she had such a large family to fend for. There was nothing else for it – we all had to knuckle down to it and make a living somehow. Luckily, as I say, Father had taught us the rudiments of the trade, and we just got on with it as best we could. James, my next brother, was only twelve, Joseph was eleven, Simon was nine and Jude was only five! Jude was excused work for some long time, of course! Gradually our standard of workmanship improved. The villagers were very understanding – they knew the circumstances.

'When I was nineteen, the situation changed. I fell in love. I had known Sarah for several years – she lived just down the street from us – but suddenly, for no apparent reason, we became much more aware of one another. I don't know whether the same thing has happened to the others of you who are married, but that's how it was for us. Suddenly, she wasn't just the girl down the road, she was the one for me. I realised just how beautiful she was, both in body and in spirit, and how much I wanted her.'

The other married men in the circle smiled and nodded, thinking of their own experiences. Nathaniel looked across at Lydia, who blushed and smiled back. Philip grinned. Jesus continued, very quietly.

'We were married quite soon and I moved to a little house round the corner from my home. We were very happy.'

Here, his eyes began to moisten.

'But it was not to last. Only eight months later, Sarah became ill. Her lovely face was covered with a rash – large blotches – and she ran a high fever. Nothing I could do would reduce that fever, which raged night and day for nearly a week. Then, she was gone and I was heartbroken. In addition to losing her, I had lost a child, for Sarah was six months pregnant at the time. I lost my wife and child at single stroke.'

Jesus paused, his face working with emotion. Nobody in the group could speak – the silence was tangible. At last, the carpenter continued.

'I wondered what on earth I had done to deserve such treatment at the hand of God. Why did Sarah have to die? I felt lost – far from God, and far from happiness. People around me, especially my mother and the family, did their best to support me, but it took many weeks before the despair I felt lifted even slightly. Eventually, I told myself that there had been many others left in similar, or even worse, circumstances. I thought of Job in the scriptures: he was not at fault, yet he had to endure terrible suffering. Perhaps it was not my fault that Sarah had died. Perhaps even that terrible experience would teach me something that God wanted me to know. Was it even possible that good could come out of that excruciating pain?

'I started to think about illness and healing, and to study what was known about it. I knew I didn't want to be a conventional doctor, but I'd heard that there had been healers in time gone by. In most generations in our history, there have been men who have had a special gift of healing. I tried to find out about them and how their gift was acquired. I started to learn more about the power of prayer, which brought me back to God, and, indeed, nearer to him than I had ever been before. I spent many hours with our local rabbi, pestering him with questions and discussing all the matters on my heart. Bless his heart. He was so patient with me. He introduced me to a couple of the local scribes and a group of Pharisees, and they gave me much to think about.

'As soon as the younger members of the family could manage the home and business, I left home and went to Jerusalem, to learn from the rabbis there.

'I learnt about the different groups within Judaism: Pharisees, Sadducees and, more remote, Essenes, all with their own beliefs. All these groups have contributed to our religion and culture; all have some elements of the truth, but I found that I couldn't agree with any of them completely, learned though they were. But the discussions I had with them sharpened my thinking and honed my faith. I became more and more sure that their emphasis was in the wrong place. It was then, as things became clearer to me, that I started to feel the urge to preach and to share what I had discovered with others.'

Jesus's face became even more serious. He leaned forward across the table, his hands working to emphasise his comments as he went on.

'One thing I became absolutely convinced about was that some of the practices going on in the Temple were totally unacceptable. The system there has become just a money-grabbing business, far from the worship of God. The businessmen in the outer courtyard of the temple are there to change everyday currencies into Temple coinage, so that the worship will not be offered with heathen coins with the image of Caesar or some other local king on them. That's understandable enough, but the rates of exchange charged by these traders are nothing short of extortion, and the rates are set, I believe, by the High Priest himself! That's not all! The prices of sacrificial animals are set at extremely high rates, which can hardly be afforded by the ordinary pilgrims, many of whom have already had to give up so much to make the journey to Jerusalem in the first place. The whole thing is a racket! The fact is that the priests have become more concerned with wealth and influence than with godliness; they seem to care neither for their own relationship with God nor the people's. They are just businessmen, not priests. That's a terrible thing to have to say, but I'm afraid it's true. While the ritual of the Temple is impressive and the notion of a perfect sacrifice being offered for sin is helpful, nothing covers up the dirty side of the Temple business. Nor is there any excuse for the way in which the High Priest cooperates so actively with the Roman Governor.'

'But doesn't the High Priest have to cooperate with Rome?' asked Andrew. 'If he didn't, he'd be stripped even of the small amount of influence he's got today and we'd be governed by the Romans themselves. We'd be forced into Emperor worship and the Temple would be defiled. That would be awful – wouldn't it?'

'Yes, of course, Andrew,' said Jesus, 'but in my opinion the High Priest is too cosy by half with Pilate. He has more influence than you think, and he could use it for the benefit of the people, instead of using it to line his own pocket. He could stand out against Pilate on points of principle if he wanted to, but he doesn't do so nearly often enough. He's afraid he might lose his position. Of course, I recognise that he has to move carefully, but I'm sure he could do more for the people if he really wanted to.'

'That's certainly what John the baptiser thought,' said Andrew. 'He was pretty strong on that point.'

'I know. As you know, we were students at Qumran together. There were two other fellow-students who were seeking help at this time: John barHelez, whom you have met, Andrew, and a fellow called Lazarus, both of whom were from the Jerusalem area. John had actually already been ordained into the priesthood and was serving on the Temple staff. As you probably know, a priest is not required to be present in the Temple all the time – they work in rotas. They serve in the Temple for, say, a month, then have several months to do other things. John, who is quite wealthy, was able to use this time off for study and to try to work our many things that were bothering him about the faith. So it came about that we four met at Qumran, where each of us hoped to learn from the Essenes there. But it was only later that I found out that the idea of going to Qumran had been fed to John by the Temple authorities themselves; they felt that they needed to find out more about the Qumranis' beliefs and practices. In short, he was a kind of spy for the High Priest.

'Anyway, we all enrolled there. The brethren take in students initially for a period of three months, so that they can assess each person and enable each student to find out if they wish to proceed to full membership of the community, which entails living in full-time and giving up all contact with the world outside. I was always doubtful whether I would stay there indefinitely, but I wanted the opportunity to reflect and learn for the three-month period.

'John, the one who later started the mission on the river baptising people, was already part-way through his probation period when the rest of us arrived, but we included him in our little group and he contributed much to our thinking. It was a happy, if disturbing, time.'

'I understand that the regime in Qumran was pretty formidable,' said Nathaniel. 'There wouldn't be many pleasant meals under the stars in the community, like we have had tonight!'

'Indeed,' replied Jesus, 'the brethren are very austere. It was strict discipline all the way. But the teaching was worth considering. The Qumranis reject completely the Temple worship as soiled and polluted. They are even more critical of the High Priest than I am. They feel that the Temple has become bankrupt, spiritually, which is why they have cut themselves off completely from the rest of society and are living isolated in the desert. They think that the priesthood has sold out totally to Rome and it is only a matter of time before the nation will rise to oppose them and all they stand for. They believe that the priests will one day be thrown out with their Roman masters.'

'Are the Qumranis planning open rebellion, then?' asked Simon, astonished.

'Not as such, in the sense of collecting arms and money – not as far as I know,' replied Jesus, 'but their writings are full of military ideas and prophesies. They are certainly open to the possibility, I believe, when the right moment comes.'

'When the right leader comes, presumably?' Nathaniel asked astutely.

'If the Messiah shows himself, I wouldn't be surprised to see the Essenes in the vanguard of any revolt against Rome,' said the Nazarene. 'Meantime, they purify themselves by prayer and washing many times a day, together with endless study and discussion of the scriptures.'

'How do they manage to get all the water needed for washing so often?' asked Simon. 'They live in the desert, surely.'

'Yes they do,' replied Jesus, 'but they have excellent engineers in their midst, who have devised clever ways of collecting and storing the winter rains that come gushing through the ravines in winter. They've cut out special channels, which divert the water into underground reservoirs cut into the rock below the community buildings so there is always enough to see them through to the next winter.'

'So at what points did you differ from the Essenes?' asked Nathaniel.

'Well, firstly, I couldn't believe that it was right for me to cut myself off from the world. I felt I had a message for the world and a ministry to perform in the world. It is the world that is in need – I have to try to meet that need.'

'That was exactly what John said – the man by the river,' recalled Andrew.

'We agreed about that,' said Jesus, 'as we did about many things. But John and I differed on some matters. He was very strident. He felt that God would come and strike down so many who were on the wrong track. I felt – and still feel – differently. God loves us all, even the worst of us, and seeks to win us back to himself. He doesn't want to strike down anyone but rather to build them up into people worthy to be called sons of God. But John is a great man, doing a great job, in many ways. He is a wake-up call to the nation.'

'Will you be seeing him again and working with him?' asked Andrew.

'I'd like to see him again, of course,' replied Jesus, 'but I heard the other day some disturbing news, which I hope is wrong. I heard that John had been taken prisoner by Herod Antipas and thrown into jail.'[7]

'Why would Herod do that?' asked Nathaniel. 'John wasn't hurting anyone.'

'That's what most people would think,' returned Jesus, 'but it's not, apparently, what the Tetrarch thinks. It may be that he's afraid that John's talk of a coming Kingdom is too revolutionary. Perhaps he's afraid that the people will take it upon themselves to seize arms and proclaim the new era. He'd hate an uprising, because that would bring Rome down on him and he'd lose his job, if not his life. You know how it is – there might well be hotheads who would use the excuse of John's teaching to start a riot. So Herod does perhaps have a point.'

'But you, too, talk about a Kingdom, Jesus. Are you also in danger?' Simon sounded worried.

'I have to be careful,' replied Jesus. 'Anything I say – or anyone says – has the possibility of being misunderstood, either accidentally or deliberately.'

'What about John's followers?' Andrew was thinking of Matt.

Jesus shook his head. 'I don't know. As I said, I only heard about John the other day and I can't really rely on that report. We shall have to keep our ears to the ground. Of course, there is another reason why Herod may have been after John's blood. Apparently, he has been very vocal in his criticism of Herod's latest marriage.'[8]

'Who's he married this time?' asked Nathaniel.

'I understand that he has married Herodias, who was previously his brother Philip's wife. Philip divorced her, and Antipas got rid of his wife to marry Herodias. Of course, these Herodians do tend to marry and divorce regularly, but this is really pretty scandalous – and John has been saying so, in no uncertain terms, by all accounts.'

'But why should Herod care a fig what a ragged man in the desert says? It can mean nothing to him.' Simon sounded incredulous.

Jesus threw up his arms in perplexity. 'I agree,' he said, 'but who can say what goes through the Tetrarch's mind – if he's got one.'

Nathaniel grimaced, but Jesus continued, 'Anyway, poor John is languishing in prison, it seems, and it might be a long time before he gets to see the sun again. It's the end of his ministry for now.'

'You must be careful, Jesus,' said Philip. 'We don't want anything like that to happen to you.'

'I must be about my father's business,' replied the preacher. 'He has called me to preach and tell people what he has in mind for us all. A better way of life. A loving relationship with each other, arising out of a better understanding and love of God.'

There was a pause before Philip spoke again.

'What happened to Lazarus?' he asked.

'He too left Qumran after the three-month period. Poor Lazarus is still searching for the truth – he has yet to find somewhere he feels comfortable to lie. John barHelez, on the other hand, has continued on the Temple staff, in spite of his reservations. In fact, he has become quite senior – a sort of secretary to the High Priest himself. He still thinks that the Temple is the key to the nation's survival and salvation, even though he agrees that there is much that needs to be changed there. I still see him from time to time and we discuss the matter endlessly.'

'Let me say we wish you well, Jesus,' said Nathaniel softly. 'I feel sure that you have a great future in front of you, my young friend. Keep in touch with me, won't you?'

'Of course I will. I might do more than that!'

NOTES

[1] Matt. 7:12.
[2] Mark 4:1.
[3] John 1:44.
[4] John 1:46.
[5] Mark 3:18.
[6] Matt. 13:55–56.
[7] Mark 1:14.
[8] Mark 6:17.

Jesus starts work

The next Sabbath, Jesus was invited to address the congregation in the Synagogue in Capernaum. Simon made sure that he was up in time on this occasion, as did James and John. In addition, Philip had walked over from Bethsaida, but Nathaniel had excused himself, being on duty in his own Synagogue.

Jesus began his address by recalling his visit to Philip's pottery. He did not mention him by name, of course, but, with cleverly chosen words, he painted a word picture of the potter hard at work in his little workshop, gently working the clay with his strong fingers. He reminded the congregation of how, from time to time, the potter needs to throw water on the clay until it has just the right consistency and then he turns the lump, moulding it gradually into the vessel of his choice. But Jesus spoke of how, on this occasion, the potter had failed to make the pot just as he would have wanted. The vessel became misshapen, unsymmetrical, an ugly thing. He then referred to the story of Jeremiah, who had also observed a potter failing at his work, centuries earlier. Jesus unrolled the scroll containing the writings of Jeremiah and read the text:

'"A vessel he was making of the clay would be spoilt in his hands, and then he would start again and mould it into another vessel".[1]

'My friends,' said Jesus, 'the potter's experience is a parable of our own lives. Often we fail, just as the potter fails in his task. God knows when things go wrong with our lives. He knows that sometimes we fail to relate lovingly with one another. He sees that often we fail to help one another. He grieves that we fail to sustain and support one another, as we should, but he wants us to put failures behind us and try afresh to make life what it should be. He will support us, doing for us what we find impossible on our own, but we have to be prepared to destroy the spoilt pot and start afresh; that is, we must put aside our old way of life and begin completely again. The old, spoilt vessel must go back to being just an amorphous lump of clay and be worked again from the beginning. We can't go on working on the marred pot – we need to start afresh with God's help and make a completely new vessel. We need to believe that God is able and willing to sustain us in this endeavour.'

Jesus paused and looked round at his listeners. He saw that his picture had impressed itself on their minds. He leaned forward as he sought to make the idea tell, his voice intense, as usual, his eyes holding first one, then another, in their embrace. He continued talking.

'We should note, however, that the potter does not throw the clay away. The clay can be used again; it is the artistry that has to start from scratch. This too is a picture of our lives. God does not throw us away as useless material. He knows that, with his help, we can still make something good of our lives.'

Just then there was a commotion at the rear of the Synagogue. Someone was clearly ill. A young man was foaming at the mouth and shaking all over in a kind of fit. He staggered forward, his eyes rolling and his arms flailing.[2]

'What are you saying?' he yelled. 'Why have you come here, Jesus? You should have stayed in Nazareth – they need holy men like you over there!'

Jesus stopped speaking and fixed his eyes on the suffering youth. When he did speak, his voice was not loud, but low and very authoritative.

'Be silent,' he said. 'Be calm.'

He walked swiftly down the room to the man and took him by the shoulder. 'Be at peace. There is nothing to fear,' he urged.

The young man slumped forward into Jesus's arms, all his violence gone. Jesus was struggling to hold him and others had to assist him to seat the man on a chair, hurriedly brought from the wall. Jesus put his arm round the lad's shoulder and spoke softly to him.

'Believe me, you have nothing to fear. Your illness has gone and will not return. You are free of the problem you have been labouring under. Put it behind you and begin your life afresh.'

After a moment more, Jesus stood up and signalled to the rabbi that his contribution to the worship was ended. Not surprisingly, the crowd leaving the Synagogue were all aflutter with amazement. The young man who had been ill had been taken home by his family, apparently entirely normal and free of his malady. It transpired that he had been subject to these violent outbursts from time to time for several years; nobody was sure why or when the problem would occur. Most thought that it was a devil in him. Whatever it was, Jesus seemed to have dealt with it.

Simon had invited the others back to his house for lunch after worship. It was growing quite hot as the sun reached its zenith, and the friends in the little party were more than ready for refreshing drinks and seats in the shade. However, when they arrived at the house, Ruth met Simon at the door, saying that Abigail was far from well.[3] When she had tried to get up that morning, she found that she had a high fever and a raging headache. There was no way that she was fit to help serve the lunch.

'I'm sorry, folks,' said Ruth, 'you'll have to make do with my cooking today.'

They all trooped into the house and Andrew immediately offered to help in the kitchen. But Jesus pulled Simon's sleeve and whispered, 'Let me have a word with Abigail.'

'Of course,' said Simon, but he was puzzled. 'Come with me.'

He led the way to the back of the house where his mother-in-law was lying on her bed behind a screen, while the others moved through into the back garden. Jesus sat on the bed and gently took Abigail's limp hand, at which the older woman opened her eyes. Jesus smiled at her and placed his other hand on her fevered brow. He closed his eyes briefly, and then said, 'Don't worry about anything – just relax. We are all friends here.'

He paused again, then, with great authority in his voice, he continued.

'Come along, Abigail. You feel better now, don't you?'

A strange look came into the patient's face. She gripped Jesus's hands tightly and struggled to rise.

'What have you done?' she murmured. 'I do feel so much better.'

She sat up and held her forehead, then shook her head.

'That's amazing,' she cried. 'My headache has virtually gone, yet only five minutes ago it was thumping like a demented man trying to break the door down. And I feel so much better…'

'Just stay calm, Abigail,' said the preacher, smiling, 'and then you'll stay better.'

'I'll get up,' said the woman. 'I feel well enough to give Ruth a hand with the lunch.'

And she was as good as her word. She waved them out of her little room and before long she had washed and dressed, and was heard humming in the kitchen.

The men gathered on the terrace under the shade of a trailing vine. Jesus seemed quite unperturbed, but the others were bursting to ask him how he had acquired this amazing gift of healing – first, the demented man in the Synagogue and then Simon's fevered mother-in-law. Jesus seemed to read their thoughts.

'A great many problems affecting the body are basically a malady of the mind and/or spirit,' he said. 'Take, for example, the case of that poor young man at the Synagogue. I suspect that he had had a terrible experience sometime earlier in his life – someone terrified him, or perhaps he did something for which he felt extremely guilty and ashamed, and this resulted in bouts of hysterical crying and uncontrollable shaking, such as we saw this morning. What he needed was someone who would befriend him and assure him that everything was going to be all right – that the experience was over and there was no need to be afraid. The person befriending the boy needed to have a real care – a deep care – for the tortured mind and to make that concern available to God, who can use it to bring about a cure. It is as if God uses our care like a ray of sunshine, to beam into the troubled mind and burn away the damaged area. He then replaces it with new, living tissue.'

'And will he be all right always now?' asked James.

'Oh, yes, provided that he is supported by a loving family. It's the love and concern that counts. Of course, if he feels threatened again, or falls into despair, he could relapse – but I doubt it.'

'But Abigail wasn't mentally ill,' said Simon. 'How did you cure her fever and headache? What caused that?'

Jesus replied, 'She wasn't as ill as the man in the Synagogue, of course, but I think, nevertheless, that she may have been worrying about dealing with the meal for all of us today. We're strangers, some of us, and it's a big responsibility for anyone to cater for so many of us. She's probably been fretting over it for a couple of days now – ever since your kind invitation, Simon. If you ask Ruth, I expect she's also been a bit stressed, but she's younger and able to cope – and her disposition is also different, isn't it?'

'Nothing much worries Ruth,' agreed Simon.

Just then, his wife appeared and invited them all to sit down for lunch. Both women waited at table and lunch was seldom a more enjoyable occasion.

*

When Ruth awoke next morning, just as the sun was rising, she remembered that Jesus had accepted their offer to stay the night with them; they had put him up on a couch on the roof, where it was nice and cool. Simon had been away all night fishing, of course. She hurried to dress and prepare some food for breakfast. She then filled a cup full of orange juice for her guest and gently mounted the outside stairway to the roof of the house. However, to her surprise, Jesus was nowhere to be found. There was the bed, which had obviously been slept in, but no guest. Ruth hurried to consult Abigail. Whatever could have happened? Simon would be home soon for breakfast and disappointed not to find Jesus, for the big fellow was certainly warming to the Nazarene. Before long, both Simon and Andrew came in, tired after their long night's fishing on the lake.

'Jesus has gone,' said Ruth.

'Already?' queried Simon, frowning. 'I had hoped to see him again and talk some more.'

'I went upstairs with a drink for him, just after daybreak, and he was already up and away.'

They were all disappointed. They had all looked forward to more conversation with the mysterious preacher, who had these marvellous healing powers. The men hoped that they could be of some use to him during the week. Simon was also slightly miffed that he had failed to wait to bid him goodbye and thank him for their hospitality. They ate their breakfast, mostly in a somewhat gloomy silence, their minds wandering over the events of yesterday. But just as the men were preparing to head for their beds, the door opened and the missing guest stood in the doorway.

'Good morning, everyone. It's a lovely day!'

The others moved quickly to greet him and find him a place at the table.

'Where have you been? We've been wondering what had happened to you,' cried Ruth.

'I'm sorry if you were concerned,' replied Jesus. 'Please forgive me. I thought you would realise.'

Ruth hurried to get him some breakfast – bread, cheese, and fish, followed by fruit. The others gathered round the table as Jesus continued.

'I always use the first part of the day for prayer and planning.[4] I have a full week in front of me, and I have to know what I should do with it, so I have a long talk with my father.'

'Your father?' burst out Simon. 'But you said...'

'My heavenly father, I mean,' said Jesus. 'God is a father to all of us – he is certainly mine. He looks after me better than any earthly father, or mother, could. You should always think of God as your parent, you know. The scriptures always use the word "father", because, in our culture, we regard the man as the head of the household. But God has all the best qualities of both a father and a mother; he encompasses every virtue and good quality. You know how some humans, both male or female, can show qualities which are most often shown by the opposite sex. Thus, males are often regarded as outstanding leaders, but there are women who can certainly lead exceptionally well. In the same way, some men can be very gentle and patient, and exhibit qualities that we associate, perhaps, more with women. Now God has the whole range of wonderful qualities and so can be both father and mother to us, as necessary.'

Just as Jesus finished speaking, there came a sharp rap at the door. Simon answered it and found two men there, dressed in the unmistakable robes of Pharisees, with tassels hanging from their sleeves. He courteously enquired of them their business.

'We're looking for Jesus, the preacher from Nazareth,' said the first, rather sternly.

'He's here. Please come in and meet him.'

He showed the two men into the little room, while Ruth rapidly cleared away a few household belongings that were cluttering the place. Jesus rose and faced his visitors.

'Simon, perhaps it would be better if we went outside on to the terrace, where we can talk quietly without being in Ruth's way,' he suggested. 'It's nice and shady out there.'

He led the way outside, followed by the two Pharisees. The fishermen hesitated.

'Come along, Simon, and you too Andrew,' said Jesus; then, to the Pharisees, 'Now, gentlemen, please be seated.'

'No need for that,' said the first Pharisee, gruffly. 'We shan't need to be here very long. Were you the man preaching at the Synagogue yesterday?'

'That's right,' returned the preacher. 'Hezekiah and Jairus kindly invited me to speak to the congregation.'

'But they didn't ask you to perform magic – and to work on the Sabbath,' said the other Pharisee.

'What do you mean?' Jesus' voice was soft, but steel-like.

'I mean that you healed a young man who was devil-possessed yesterday, on the Sabbath – and in the Synagogue! Working on the Sabbath is contrary to our Law, as you must know.' The second Pharisee was getting quite worked up and red in the face as he spoke.

Jesus sighed, a deep sigh. He looked at the two Pharisees for a long moment before replying.

'Do you mean to tell me that you would prefer a young man to suffer, rather than be made better, just to keep the Sabbath regulations? If your cow falls into a ditch, you pull her out, don't you – even on the Sabbath?'

'The Law is the Law,' snarled the red-faced man.

'We can't allow any breach of the Law to go unchallenged,' said the other, a little more reasonably, 'or where will it end? The Sabbath has to be protected.'

'Look, I too approve of keeping the Sabbath,' said the Nazarene. 'It is very sensible to keep one day in the week as a time for worship, for rest and refreshment, different from the working week. I certainly don't quarrel with the principle, but, surely, when someone has an urgent need…'

'Just keep the Law,' broke in the florid Pharisee, wagging his forefinger. 'Keep to the straight and narrow, and don't try to get clever with us!'

So saying he turned on his heel and stalked pompously out of the house, closely followed by his companion. Jesus watched them go without another word, then he sat down, shaking his head. He was evidently very disappointed.

'Surely,' he said, scratching his head in bewilderment, 'it is better to do good on the Sabbath than not… I simply don't understand their thinking. The Sabbath was made for the sake of man, not man for the Sabbath!'[5]

Less than a quarter of an hour later, there came another knock on the door. Three men were there, asking for Jesus. This time, Simon was more wary and asked Jesus to come to them. It transpired that the newcomers had not been able to get to the Synagogue on the previous day and were hoping that Jesus would speak again, so that they could hear him. They had to work all day, so they wanted to know if Jesus would talk to them in the early evening. Jesus consulted with Simon, and it was agreed that they could come to the house; Jesus would speak to them then.

Jesus went later on in the morning to speak to the people down by the seashore. All the fishermen had been up all night at their work, so he had to manage as best he could without the boat. The result was quite chaotic; the crowd was very excited by reports of the healing at the Synagogue the previous day. The result was that Jesus was close to being mobbed, and he arrived back at the house quite tired just before lunch.

During the morning, Jesus heard confirmatory reports of the imprisonment of John the Baptist by Herod Antipas. Several people expressed their regret, for John had been a popular figure, but, however much they wrung their hands, there seemed to be little that they could do about it. Such was the power of the King.

Evidently, word that Jesus was going to speak at the house early in the evening spread during the day for, by the appointed hour, quite a crowd turned up at Simon's door. There must have been thirty or more, including Hezekiah, the rabbi, and a couple of local scribes. Simon decided that it was better if the people went out into the little enclosed courtyard at the rear of the house, so that Jesus could address them from the terrace, which was at a slightly higher level.

Jesus began by talking about salt.

'We all need salt,' he said. 'You all know that. Without salt, we become ill and eventually die. Salt is so important that Roman soldiers are sometimes paid part of their wages in salt rather than in coinage. But what if the salt is polluted?'

Jesus paused and looked round at the little group.

'Let us imagine that a trader, seeking to make a quick profit, tries mixing salt with flour, or chalk – or even sand. The adulterated salt is quickly found to be valueless, isn't it? It is still salt, but it has lost its value and is fit for nothing but to be thrown away.'

Here Jesus looked at the people before him more intently, his brown eyes aflame as he continued.

'You must ensure that you have the unadulterated salt of God's message – not something that is contaminated. Hold fast to the truth and share the true message among yourselves.'[6]

Just then, there was a disturbance on the roof. Four men appeared in view, carrying what looked like a bulging hammock. They started pulling back the vines and other climbing plants covering the terrace, which provided the shade, and lowering their burden on ropes, till it arrived at Jesus' feet.[7] The preacher looked bemused.

'Whatever are you doing?' he demanded.

One of the men above, seeing that he now had Jesus's attention, shouted down to him.

'We are bringing my father to you. We heard that you are able to heal the sick, and Dad is in great need. We couldn't get through the house or into the garden, so we've used the outside stairs and the roof. Please help him. Please…'

Jesus stepped forward to look into the hammock. Inside, he saw a thin, frightened man approaching fifty years of age. He stretched out his hand and took the claw-like hand offered to him. Clearly, the man had suffered and was suffering still. He had the palsy, a creeping paralysis which was slowly taking over his entire body. Jesus knelt by the rough bed, continuing to hold his hand.

'Don't be fearful,' he said, smiling at him. 'Your mistakes are behind you, dealt with, forgotten and forgiven. God knows that you have done wrong, but that's all a thing of the past.'

One of the scribes in the group pushed forward and pulled at Jesus's sleeve.

'Just a moment,' he said sternly, 'You can't go round saying that sins are forgiven, just like that! That's God's prerogative, not yours. Who do you think you are? Are you setting yourself up as God? That's blasphemy!'

'Why do you say that?' asked Jesus, rising. 'I know that this man's sins are forgiven because I know that God is always ready to forgive anyone, whoever they are. It is not that God disregards sins as if they are of no importance – I don't think that for a moment. Sin always grieves God, but just as you can forgive your children, no matter what they have done, so God too does the same, however much he has to bear the hurt in the process. And so that you will know that I am right about this...' and here he turned to the palsied man and knelt by him again... 'I say to you, it is time to get up and walk.'

So saying, he took the man's hands, and gently pulled him into a sitting position. Soon, to everyone's amazement, the man struggled to his feet and staggered into Jesus' waiting arms.

'Go along, my friend, back to your home and your loving family, who have had the faith to bring you to me, so that God could cure you. Take your mat and go.'

The man, gaining confidence with every step, staggered the few steps into the house. Up on the roof, his relatives, who had been smiling and crying by turns, turned and made for the stairs to meet him. They met at the front door, amid great scenes of emotion. The crowd pressed forward through the house to witness the reunion, overturning chairs and other household items. Everyone was in confusion except for Jesus, who stood still on the terrace with a tiny smile playing on his lips, but with tired eyes. After a few minutes, he slumped into a chair and held his head in his hands.

Eventually, peace was restored to the little house and the crowd dispersed. Simon and Andrew joined Jesus in the garden. Ruth came out with some wine for each of the men.

Simon looked at the tired face of the preacher, and burst out, 'You did it again! You cured that man of that terrible disease.' He was overcome with excitement, but puzzled at Jesus's look.

'Of course I am happy for the whole family,' said his guest. 'It is always good to see people well after an illness, well and able to face life again, freed from any sense of guilt or despair. It was good to see the trust of the family who brought him here rewarded. But look at the downside. I had hoped to help the whole group, by talking to them and showing them the way to a better life – and I hardly got started. They won't remember anything of what I said; they're too taken up with the palsied man's good fortune. I'm not here to be a kind of magician, or even a doctor, just to cure people's bodies. I want to minister to the whole man – indeed, to the whole nation.'

The friends of Jesus could hardly believe their ears.

'Surely,' said Andrew, 'this wonderful healing will convince everyone that you are indeed a prophet, a really holy man whom God has sent and they will listen even more carefully to what you have to say now.'

'Perhaps,' said Jesus, 'but, more likely, I'm afraid they'll just bring more and more unfortunates for me to heal and totally ignore their own need of healing of mind and spirit. Of course, I'm happy to help all those who are ill, but...' He broke off, shaking his head.

'I had hoped to help so many more whose lives are just as seriously flawed, and they simply don't know it.'

'What did you... when did you begin to... how did you learn to heal like you do?' Andrew hesitated as he struggled with the question.

Jesus looked at him, then down at his hands. There was long pause before he spoke again.

'After my wife, Sarah, died, I was devastated. I suppose every loving husband feels the same way. How on earth can one carry on? And yet, there is no choice but to carry on. I never forgot the feeling of bereavement, but neither did I forget my own feeling of inadequacy. Why hadn't I been able to help her – to cure her? Others have been great healers in the past. Could I find their secret? God has almighty power. How could I reach through to that power? What is the secret? Indeed, should we seek to cure? There are no easy answers to these questions. Obviously, we all have to die someday – nobody can live for ever, that's quite clearly not part of God's plan for us. But should people die in their teens or twenties, when they have so much promise in front of them?'

Jesus looked round slowly at the little group and then continued.

'I felt that God would give me the power to heal, so long as I used it sensibly. But, above all, I knew that I must not use the gift for my own ends – for example, as a way of attracting attention to myself. In the desert, before I started preaching, this was borne in on me very forcibly. I came to realise that even if I could cast myself down from the pinnacle of the Temple and fly gently to earth unharmed, such a miracle would merely convince people for a few moments that I was a magician, but it would have no lasting effect on the way they lived their lives, or their relationship either with God or each other. And it is this improvement in relationships that I am really called to promote.

'But I did discover the practice of healing and, when I can heal without attracting the wrong kind of response, I have done so – with increasing confidence – from shortly after Sarah's death until now. The thing that worries me about this issue is that most people associate sickness or handicap with moral weakness. "If someone is sick, they must deserve it," they say. "God is punishing them for their wickedness." Now, that simply isn't so. People who are ill need our sympathy and understanding, not our condemnation. They may have a burden of guilt or terror in their lives that contributes to their sickness, but that is different from saying that God is punishing them. So I studied, I prayed and then I practised. You too could do it, if you do as I did. Perhaps you will do, someday.'

'Not I,' said Simon. 'I could never...'

'Never say never,' said Jesus, smiling. 'Who knows what you will do, one day?'

There was silence for a few seconds, as each of the listeners digested this remark. Then Jesus spoke again.

'I think I had better leave Capernaum for a while,' he said. 'No doubt the local scribes will be scandalised at what has happened here and make a protest – perhaps worse. I'll move out temporarily, till the excitement has died down.'

'Why don't you go across the lake to the Decapolis for a visit?' suggested Simon. 'We could take you there by boat. That way, nobody can even speak to you en route, let alone do anything worse.'

'We could be away at first light,' said Andrew. 'We could go right down to Gadara, at the far end of the lake, right away from all the problems.'

'I'm not sure about Gadara itself,' replied Jesus. 'I'm not too keen on towns – especially Greek ones. Besides, the town must be six or seven miles from the lake – that's a long way, there and back, in addition to the boat trip. But it would be useful to get away into the area surrounding the town and have some time together – the three of us – if you really are prepared to spare the time.'

'Sure. I'm game.' Simon was keen. 'We can spare a day without any difficulty.'

Andrew nodded. He always followed his brother's lead – this time enthusiastically. They set off, next day, early in the morning. The day was pleasant enough at first. The sun shone from time to time, peeping out from behind fleecy clouds, warming their hearts and giving them hope of even better things to come. Jesus settled down in the stern of the boat, initially thinking about his future ministry, but later relaxing to such an extent that he actually dozed off, lulled to sleep by the warmth of the sun and the gentle lapping of the water against the sides of the boat. The brothers let him sleep. He had had a trying time and there was nothing that needed doing. In any case, they were the practised sailors, not Jesus, whom they regarded as an honoured passenger.

But after they had been afloat for just over an hour and were about half way across the lake, the clouds quite suddenly began to thicken and a dirty squall blew up from the west, causing the lake's surface to become really very choppy.[8] The little boat grew quite lively, to the extent that both Simon and Andrew, hardened sailors though they were, became anxious for their safety. They had seen similar situations before, of course, for the lake was notorious for these sudden squally conditions, but this particular one was unusually severe. They got the sail in quickly and headed into the wind, but several times the boat nearly capsized as the water broke over the bows, leaving the boat inches deep in water. Andrew began to bale furiously, while Simon continued to battle at the helm. To their surprise, Jesus slept on peacefully, as if in his own bed in Nazareth! Eventually, there came a slight lull in the storm and Andrew was able to cease baling long enough to see how their passenger was faring. He shook the preacher gently on the shoulder, wakening him.

'Are you all right?' he yelled above the wind. 'I'm surprised this squall hasn't woken you and scared you. It's had me worried, I can tell you!'

Jesus jerked awake and started into a sitting position. Simon called from the tiller, 'This is a bad storm, Jesus. We've only just managed to keep afloat! Don't you care?'

His guest pulled himself to his feet and moved unsteadily to join Simon.

'I haven't been aware of anything untoward,' he said quietly. 'In any case, we are in God's hands. The storm will soon pass. Don't fluster yourselves. We'll be quite safe.'

The two fishermen were astounded at his calm and his faith. They felt that they should have been the ones who ought to have been reassuring him, as a mere landlubber; but instead it was Jesus who was able to calm their minds. Andrew returned to his baling feeling much more certain that they would get through all right, while Simon, at the tiller, was sure that the storm had lifted noticeably since the preacher had woken. In fact, it wasn't too much longer before the squall died away completely, just as quickly as it had blown up, and pretty soon they were able to hoist the sail again and resume their course south to the shores of the Gadarenes. They pulled the boat up on to the shore with some difficulty and sat talking until it was time to eat. The two fishermen wanted to discuss the matter of the storm again and ask Jesus about his calm assurance, but somehow the words wouldn't come. They made a meal out of the provisions they had brought with them, though some of the bread had become uneatable, being soaked. However, they enjoyed the salad and fruit and, luckily, the beer had survived uncontaminated!

After their lunch and a short rest, Jesus suggested that they went for a stroll along the waterside. They had walked about a half a mile, when they saw that they were approaching a small village by the lake. On the outskirts of the village, as usual, was the village cemetery, with its collection of little gravestones and monuments, commemorating the lives and burial places of bygone village folk. The three men stopped to look at the place, thinking how peaceful it looked. The swallows streaking across the sky and swooping occasionally were the only moving creatures in sight. The cicadas kept up a constant rattle of sound in the background, but, apart from that, all seemed still and at peace. It was a lovely moment. However, the tranquillity of the scene was suddenly abruptly broken. A large, unkempt man jumped out from behind one of the gravestones, roaring his protest at their presence.[9]

'What do you want here? What have you to do with me?' he demanded. 'Get away from me – clear out, d'you hear!'

He started forward, bearing down on the three friends. He was nearly naked, with many large wounds on his body, which appeared to be have been self-inflicted with sharp stones. His arms were covered in patches of congealed blood and scars from earlier misfortunes. His bulging, bloodshot eyes stared insanely into the eyes of the three visitors.

'Get away from me, I say! I want nothing to do with you!' he shrieked, and he flung himself at Jesus.

The fishermen drew back in alarm, but Jesus stood stock-still.

'He's totally mad,' whispered Simon, clutching at Jesus's sleeve. 'Watch out, or he'll do you some mischief!'

'He's just ill, my friend,' said the preacher, gently releasing himself from Simon's grasp. 'He needs help. He'll be all right soon.'

To the surprise of the fishermen, Jesus bent forward to touch the madman, who was by now grovelling at his feet, and caught him by the hands. The man drew back, uncertain what to do, for nobody had approached him kindly for years. He had been left severely alone by the locals, who had brought him a little food from time to time, but otherwise steered well clear of him.

'Be calm, my friend,' said Jesus, in a quiet, soothing voice. 'You can be freed from whatever it is that is troubling you.'

'I am – I'm – something is – I have a devil inside me,' the man stammered out. 'He won't let me alone, to be myself.'

'That's no devil,' said Jesus. 'You are ill, but you have suffered enough.'

Then, in a more commanding voice, he said, 'Let go of it.'

The man emitted a tremendous scream and shook violently. The two fishermen thought for a moment that he was about to turn on his helper, but, having thrashed about with his arms uncontrollably for a few seconds, he suddenly slumped down on the floor in a faint. But the scream and commotion had disturbed a large group of pigs who were grubbing about in the field next to the graveyard. They became extremely agitated, biting at one another, honking noisily, each one disturbing and confusing its neighbour. The result was a full-scale stampede away from the scene; the entire herd crashed through the rough fence work around their enclosure and careered out of all control right into the lake.

The fishermen were by now thoroughly alarmed. The farmer was not going to be pleased, to say the least! What had started as a quiet country walk was rapidly deteriorating into a nightmare, but Jesus was not taking any notice of the pigs. Instead, he was holding the shoulder of the slumped figure at his feet. Soon, the man opened his eyes, and, for the first time, looked with normal eyes into the face of his healer. Gone was the insane look, the loud screaming, the violence and the heartache. Instead, the man exhibited all the appearance of a sane, but puzzled, child. He gazed about him as if he scarcely recognised his whereabouts. He looked with horror at his appearance – the bleeding arms, the scars and the dirt.

'How did I get like this?' he asked.

'It looks to me as if you've cut yourself,' replied his new-found friend. 'At other times, it looks as if you've been chained up, but clearly the fetters were ineffective – you've broken out of them. The villagers couldn't control you, so they left you here, out of the way, to fend for yourself. You mustn't blame them; they were afraid. You are very strong.'

Then, smiling at him, Jesus asked, 'What is your name?'

'I don't know – I can't remember. They used to call me "Legion" – I think. I suppose that was because they thought I had a legion of devils in me, and it seemed to me that they were right. But I'm – I feel – better now.'

At that moment, a couple of men appeared on the scene. They had evidently been brought there in response to the noise – first of the madman, then the herd of stampeding pigs.

'What on earth is going on?' exclaimed the first. Then, seeing the pigs loose and the damage to the fencing, he swore. 'Hell! What the hell…?' He was lost for words in his confusion.

The second newcomer was also swearing profusely under his breath, but soon his attention was taken by the man now sitting quietly at Jesus's feet.

'Is that Legion?' he asked incredulously. 'My God! He's as quiet as my grandmother!'

'He's quite well now,' said Jesus calmly. 'He'll do you no harm.'

'But how...? When...?' The two men struggled in their surprise to ask the right questions.

'Take him back to the village with you,' said Jesus, in a voice of quiet authority. 'He needs clothing, food and care. Has he relations there?'

The men muttered their assent, then, as their brains and their tongues gradually regained their normal usage, they implored Jesus and his friends to leave their village.

'We aren't used to this kind of thing here,' they said. 'Go away – leave us in peace.'

Jesus turned to comply but the man who had been insane grabbed at him, then struggled to his feet, intent on following him.

'Let me come with you,' he implored. 'I want to be near you. I feel safe with you.'

But Jesus prevented him, gently pushing the man away from him.

'You'll be safe now – and much better with your own family, among your own people,' he said. 'Just give thanks to God for your healing, and try to live a useful life in future.'

The Galileans eventually made their way back to the boat. Not much was said, but the minds of the two fishermen were in turmoil. What kind of man was this, that could do such things? They remained quiet throughout their return to Capernaum, too stunned to venture any more questions.

The following day, Jesus again announced his intention to leave town.

'I must get away from here for while at least. I think I shall go again to Bethsaida. Perhaps they will listen to me there. Maybe I shall see Philip and Nathaniel again.'

'I'll come too,' Simon burst out. 'I'll bring the boat as the pulpit. Andrew can look after the business for a day or two – he can hire a boat from Zebedee.'

Andrew nodded, but it was clear from his face that he would have preferred to be going with Jesus and Simon.

★

That evening, the fishermen prepared for work by the lake side. In spite of the incredible happenings of the past few days, work had to go on and Simon was there to help prepare the hired boat, examine and mend the nets and stow all the equipment with Andrew. His brother was bitterly disappointed at the prospect of being left behind while Simon went with Jesus, but someone had to do the work, and he had had several days off in Jerusalem recently. He would work alongside James and John in their boat and do his best to keep things going. Fortunately, they made a reasonably comfortable living, enough for their fairly simple requirements, so one or two thin nights wouldn't be disastrous to the family's livelihood.

But the talk wasn't of work. The fishermen could make their routine preparations without much thought, their nimble fingers and strong arms moving mechanically, while their minds and thoughts churned over the astonishing events of the past few days. Simon and Andrew couldn't wait to tell the others of the happenings at the other end of the lake. It was Simon, of course, who had to speak first.

'Jesus just spoke the word and this man, who was even bigger than me, and as strong as an ox with an insane strength, fell quiet. All his insanity was expelled – in a moment. And Jesus never lifted his voice…'

'He was magnificent,' agreed Andrew. 'I must admit, I was a bit scared. If that man had attacked us, the three of us together would have had a hard time controlling him, but Jesus just stood there – and held the fellow's hand!'

'It's hard to believe,' replied James, 'but we saw what he did in the Synagogue last Sabbath – and, anyway, you fellows wouldn't lie to us.'

'And it was strange on the lake, too,' said Andrew. 'This storm suddenly blew up – you know how it can happen occasionally. It was really quite nasty for a while, but Jesus just slept thought it – as if it was nothing. Then, when I did wake him, he just exuded calmness. He hadn't a trace of fear… I thought, as a landlubber, he would be terrified, but not a bit…'

Simon took up the story.

'It was almost as if he stilled the storm – his calmness transferred itself to us, and suddenly we too lost our nervousness. Pretty soon, the storm blew itself out anyway and all was peace and tranquillity again. It was truly amazing.'

'He's certainly one in a million,' said John. 'I think I'm a little afraid of him. No, not afraid – in awe of him, I think.'

The fishermen worked in silence for a few moments. Then, John, thinking back to a couple of nights earlier, said, 'Fancy Jesus being a widower, at such a young age. No wonder it had such a profound effect on his thinking.'

'And he lost a child at the same time,' said Andrew.

'I didn't know that,' replied John. 'How awful.'

'That sort of thing happens all too often,' Simon said. 'So many folk have sickness and then death in their families and are cut off in the prime of life. It's terrible. I don't know how I'd cope if it were Ruth.' He shook his head sadly.

'If you have to, you get by.' James could be rather unfeeling on occasion.

'It's certainly made Jesus more sympathetic than you are,' said his brother. 'He always seems to care for those who are in trouble. It also encouraged him to study healing techniques. So some good did come out of tragedy.'

There was another lull in the conversation. Eventually, James rather startled the others when he said, 'What do you lot really make of this man? I mean, who is he? Why does he have this healing power? What about his ideas? And what's this "Kingdom" he speaks about?'

Rather surprisingly, it was Andrew who found his tongue first.

'I've never met anyone like him,' he volunteered. 'Nobody could fail to be impressed by the healings, of course, but his personality is also quite amazing. He's always fun to be with, yet he's serious too, profound…'

'What about his message?' persisted James.

'I'm for him, anyway,' said John. 'I'll stick with him even if I don't always understand all he's saying.'

'What about you, big brother?' Andrew turned to Simon.

Simon shrugged his massive shoulders.

'You know me. I'm not really much for preaching as a rule, but this fellow certainly has more about him than anybody I've ever heard. Didn't I say I would go with him tomorrow?'

'You did,' said Andrew, rather ruefully. 'Perhaps he'll make a follower of you yet.'

'We'll see.'

NOTES

[1] Jeremiah 18:4.
[2] Mark 1:23.
[3] Mark 1:30.
[4] Mark 1:35.
[5] Mark 2:27.
[6] Mark 9:50.
[7] Mark 2:3–4.
[8] Mark 4:37.
[9] Mark 5:2.

More new friends

The next day, Jesus and Simon set out to sail the three miles to Bethsaida. It was a glorious day, with a clear, hard blue sky, framing a sun which would be roasting by early afternoon. But it was pleasant enough mid-morning on the water, with a little breeze that both cooled the travellers and swept the little boat towards their destination. Galilee was at her best at this time of the year – warm enough, without being overpowering, yet still green on shore, for the rainy season had not been over long enough for the ground to be scorched and brown. The two men were able to relax and reflect as they sailed comfortably along. There was no need to talk much. Each had plenty to think about.

They moored up at a little bay where the local fishermen were already working on their boats and tackle. Simon knew them all, of course, and he was able to make the introductions. Jesus seemed to be at home with the men right away, asking them questions and listening with interest to their unlikely stories of big catches from the lake and life-threatening storms, as well as more homespun yarns about their wives and sweethearts.

Before long, while Simon stayed with the fishermen, Jesus moved further up the beach to a place where half a dozen little stalls had been set up, with fish, fruit, vegetables, bread and other household necessities on sale. Some women were doing their shopping there and using the opportunity for a lengthy chat about anything and everything. Jesus quickly made himself known and seemed to have the knack of being accepted by them too. Before long, he told them that he would be preaching at the beach shortly and he hoped they would stay to listen, or return soon, perhaps with a friend.

Just a few yards from the stalls was a tax booth,[1] where the local tax gatherer was sitting, surly-faced, looking out for any boats coming into the anchorage from across the border in the Decapolis or Ituraea. The two burly soldiers on guard at the booth would then quickly escort the visiting sailors to the taxman to pay their dues. Any foreigner had to pay a tax and a further amount on any goods imported into Antipas' territory of Galilee.

To Simon's surprise, he saw that Jesus did not stop when he reached the end of the row of stalls but continued towards the tax booth to talk to the official and his guards. Simon couldn't believe what he was seeing. People generally avoided all contact with tax gatherers for, so often, they cheated simple people, extracting excess revenues. Many people could not read, write or calculate, so they became easy prey to unscrupulous officials who could easily line their pockets at the expense of the unwary or uneducated. The Tetrarch did not concern himself with how the money was collected, so long as he got his due. He did not pay the tax gatherers a regular wage; he expected that they would charge a commission to cover their living, but the 'commissions' were always exorbitant, and consequently tax gatherers were always very wealthy, and always intensely disliked.

But that was not all. The Galileans knew that a good proportion of their taxes went from the Tetrarch to Tiberius Caesar in Rome, the hated Emperor of the world. Thus, the tax gatherer was seen as an agent of the occupying powers, people who had no business in their country at all, let alone exercising power there.

All this tumbled through Simon's mind as he watched his friend talking to the taxman, who was, at first, unresponsive and monosyllabic, but gradually relaxed a little as Jesus got through with his astonishing charisma. After a few minutes at the tax booth, Jesus rejoined the fishermen at the water's edge and they began preparing the boat as their makeshift 'pulpit', as they had done in Capernaum the week before. Simon threw out an anchor at the stern and ran a line to a stake on the beach from the bow. Jesus stood up in the prow and called to the people to approach and seat themselves. At first a little unwillingly, the people gathered round but they were later joined with increasing enthusiasm by others as the preacher started to speak. The stallholders craned their necks and cupped their ears to hear. Even the taxman cocked an ear in Jesus's direction.

'Let me tell you a story,' began Jesus.[2] 'It's a simple tale of a shepherd, who had a decent sized flock of good-looking sheep – in fact, he had about a hundred animals, of which he was very proud. He used to take them off into the hill country near his home so that they could graze. Of course, he watched them very closely in case any were in danger, for the country was quite wild and rugged, and they might very well be attacked by wolves or foxes, or wander off on their own and get lost. Every night, he would ensure that they were provided with water and then safely penned against a cliff. All night long, he himself would lie across the entrance to the pen, so that no sheep could get out and no predator could get in to attack the sheep.

'But, in spite of all his care and precautions, one day he noticed that one of his sheep was missing. Yes, that little black she-lamb, not very old, the one with a slightly misshapen left front leg, was not in the flock. What should he do? If he left the rest of the sheep alone, they would be exposed to danger, but, if he didn't look for the missing lamb, she would have no chance at all on her own in the wild hills. What should he do?'

Jesus looked around at the crowd, now very quiet, as if he expected an opinion, but nobody ventured a comment.

'The shepherd didn't hesitate,' said Jesus. 'He made the flock as safe as possible in the pen, leaving food and water, and set out to find the lamb that was lost. He retraced his steps, moving as quickly as he could over the ground he had covered that day, searching each side of the route to see if he could see the animal that was in danger. When night fell, he still had had no success. He slept fitfully during the hours of darkness but was up and off at the first streak of light, continuing the search. At last, he heard a plaintive bleating from up on the cliff and then, to his delight, he found the little lamb, trapped on a narrow ledge, crying for help, frightened and very hungry.

The shepherd was, of course, jubilant. He took the little creature on to his shoulders and carried it back to the pen, where he found the rest of the flock none the worse for his absence. The pastor was able to tend to every animal and did so with a feeling of great relief and joy.'

Jesus paused and looked round at the little group sitting on the beach in front of him. He smiled and continued.

'I want to tell you that God is rather like that good shepherd. We are his sheep, whatever our defects. He loves us all and looks after us, giving us all that we need. He has no intention of losing any of us. If any of us should go off on our own and get lost, God searches for us. He goes to tremendous lengths to ensure that we are rescued and brought back to the flock. Some people may feel that they have strayed too far away ever to be rescued. They have, for whatever reason, decided to leave the rest of the community and go off on their own. They have opted to leave the decent, happy, honest life for the sake of monetary gain, or increased power or some other soiled existence. After living that way for a while, they may feel that they are lost for ever to decent living, and it's too late for them ever to be taken back.'

Here Jesus paused as he looked around, before speaking with great emphasis.

'I am here,' he said, 'to tell you, if you feel like that, that it simply isn't so. It's never too late. Nobody is beyond recall. God can and will find a way to rescue all his lost sheep, however far they have strayed from the rest of the flock. God will search until he finds the lost one, no matter what the cost and the time involved. When he finds it, he has great joy in his heart. Believe me.'

There was a hush in the crowd at the end of Jesus's homily. Some listeners looked indifferent and left shrugging their shoulders and muttering, but many had obviously been affected, their faces betraying their emotion as they considered the implications of what had been said. Simon hurried forward to the prow of the boat and grasped Jesus's hand warmly.

'Thank you for that,' he said huskily. 'I – well – I haven't been too much up on religion in the past. I haven't taken seriously enough God's claim on my life. I feel a bit of a lost sheep myself, and you have been like a good shepherd to me, reaching out...'

'God is the good shepherd, Simon,' replied Jesus. 'He's reaching out to you and everyone else who feels the need of him. He will find you and will welcome you back into the flock.'

Jesus clapped Simon on the shoulder.

'You'll do!' he said. 'But now, I must go and talk to these people who kindly stayed to listen to me.'

So saying, Jesus stepped on to the beach and greeted the women, the fishermen, the stallholders – anyone and everyone who still lingered on the shore. Then he walked slowly up to the top of the beach and looked over to the tax gatherer. This time, it was the official who beckoned to him. Jesus walked slowly over and took the hand hesitantly offered to him. He saw a short, squat man, seemingly huddled within himself. His beard was straggly and beginning to turn grey, as was the hair at his temples, but the eyes were bright and piercing. The tax gatherer spoke in a low voice.

'Do you think that God would consider even a tax gatherer worth rescuing?'

Jesus smiled, a broad, winning smile.

'Even a tax gatherer,' he said. 'You're a person too, aren't you? You are a part of God's family, aren't you? Why not?'

The unhappy accountant grimaced and shook his head.

'You know what people think of us,' he said. 'They say that we cheat them – and often we do, when we think we can get away with it. I've been no better than the rest. It's easy money. People also say we are working for the Romans, that we've betrayed our own nation and sold out to the Gentiles. That isn't true. We pay our taxes to the Tetrarch's office; what happens to them after that isn't our affair. I'm still a Jew and proud of it and I still want to be accepted by my own people and within my own community.'

'Of course you do – and why not?' Jesus's voice was reassuring. 'You can be accepted. I accept you. God accepts you. He has never lost sight of you. You must believe that, and act on that belief. There is no reason why you cannot be part of God's Kingdom – the new Kingdom that he will be setting up – that he is already setting up, in our midst. Come along with me now and we'll get some lunch together.'

'I want to do better than that,' replied the tax gatherer. 'I'd like you and your friend to come to my house tonight and eat dinner with me. I'll invite a few of my friends and colleagues, and we can talk some more.'

'Thank you,' replied Jesus. 'I'm sure Simon and I would be very pleased to come. Will you tell me your name and where we are to come?'

'My name is Levi,' replied the official, now smiling himself. 'But more often I'm known, in professional circles, as Matthew. Either will do. Take your pick!'

He quickly explained where his house was to be found. Jesus called Simon over to meet his host for the evening and, rather hesitantly, Simon joined his friend to take the taxman's hand. Simon was soon to get used to taking the hands of all and sundry, through his friendship with the carpenter from Nazareth!

★

Matthew had obviously spared no expense in preparing the evening meal for Jesus and Simon. He had sent out to several friends, inviting them in for the evening and was delighted that most could come. Matthew's wife, Joanna, was still all aflutter, supervising the arrival and preparation of a veritable mountain of food – several kinds of meat, fish, vegetables and fruit, as well as many good wines. The table sagged under the weight of all the good things. The tablecloth was crisp and white, the pottery tableware was spotless and the cutlery shone brightly from much polishing.

Servants waited on Jesus and Simon as they arrived and courteously washed their feet. Then they were seated at the splendid table with Matthew and Joanna and their four friends and their wives. Simon felt distinctly uncomfortable amid so much splendour; he hadn't ever been in such a grand house, except to sell fish at the tradesmen's entrance, but Jesus seemed to take it all in his stride, seemingly equally at home in a rich, as in a poor, house.

Matthew looked a little sheepish when Jesus gently suggested that he should offer thanks to God for such a meal, but his prayer was so simple and straightforward, and so unusually brief as compared with the long-winded prayers of the Pharisees who were often seen praying in the street,[3] that Matthew quickly relaxed and settled down to a splendid evening. The time went happily by, with conversation flowing back and forth across the table. Matthew proved to be a considerate host, ensuring that everyone was served with the food they really liked and that nobody was left out of the conversation for long. Jesus was in his element, laughing frequently, telling stories and listening intently to all those round him.

When, at last, the company had eaten their fill and the ladies had left them, Matthew tapped on his wine cup and called for silence.

'Tonight,' he said seriously, yet with a smile on his lips, 'marks a turning point in my life. This morning, I heard Jesus here telling me that I still have a place in the community and in the human race – something that, frankly, I had begun to doubt.'

Turning to his colleagues, he said, 'You know how it is, my friends. Those of us working in the tax department of the government are always being accused of greed, hypocrisy and treachery. Some of it is undoubtedly true, some is an exaggeration. The net result is, however, that we are outcasts in our own town, considered in the same category as prostitutes or Gentiles. We are lost to the nation of Israel as far as most of our neighbours are concerned. I hate that. Jesus assured me today that this doesn't have to be the case. I can turn my life around and be accepted again.'

'What do you have in mind to do?' enquired one of his friends, a fellow taxman. He looked rather sceptical. 'Are you going to leave the department? What then? How will you live?'

'I don't know yet in any detail,' replied Matthew soberly. 'Of course, I know there will be difficulties, but I will not be charging exorbitant commissions any more, for a start. I shall probably give up altogether and seek alternative employment as an accountant. I may be able to help small-time traders to avoid paying excessive tax bills in the future, by giving them sound financial advice.'

'Your colleagues won't like that!' snorted another. 'You can't expect the rest of us to allow our profession to be challenged. There's bound to be a reaction.'

'We'll see,' said his host. 'I may give up my profession altogether and seek a completely new life. What do you think I should do, Jesus?'

Jesus had been watching the exchange between the financiers with evident interest. 'Time will tell, Matthew,' he replied. 'You will need to sleep on it and pray about it. Perhaps you will find a completely new occupation soon – maybe I can find you a job.'

The company looked at Jesus in some amazement, but he didn't elaborate on his last statement. Instead, he said, 'Let me tell you all another story, a bit like the one I told by the shore earlier today.[4] It concerns a young woman, not long married. She discovered one day that she had mislaid a coin, part of the wedding gift that her husband had given her on their wedding day. You know the rather pretty headdresses that some husbands give their wives, chains with coins hanging off them? Well, it was a coin from one of those that the woman had lost, and, not surprisingly, she was very upset. It wasn't just that she was a bit nervous about what her husband would say when he found out; she was genuinely very proud of the headdress and loved to wear it. It reminded her of that wonderful day when she had married – a happy, happy day, which she had looked forward to for so long. But the decoration was spoilt now. One coin was missing.

'Straightaway, she put aside all her other household duties and started to look for the missing coin. She took out all the chairs, moved the tables and larger items of furniture and swept the floors, searching carefully. She cleaned in all the corners, turned out all the drawers and dusted along all the shelves. At last, when she thought she would never find it, right in a far corner of the room, she saw a glint from the light from her oil lamp and there, at last, was her missing coin.

'Can you appreciate how she felt? You can surely understand her delight and relief. It wasn't just the monetary value of the coin that mattered to her, but that special, sentimental value, the significance to her marriage and her relationship with her husband. She had found the lost coin! She straightaway went next door to her neighbours and invited them in to her house for a mug of wine. It was that important! "Let's rejoice together," she said, "I thought I'd lost my coin and spoilt my wedding present. But, thank goodness, I've found it."'

Jesus looked at the assembled guests, smiling, yet serious.

'I tell you this. God is similarly pleased when he finds somebody who was lost to him. His heart is similarly delighted. As you know, I told Matthew a similar story today about a shepherd who had lost his lamb, and it's clear that he's seen the point. He has felt God's joy, as well as his own, that he is once more a member of God's family.'

Silence fell on the company and there was an awkward pause, until, just then, a servant came in and whispered something in Matthew's ear. He smiled and then announced:

'And now, my friends, I have some entertainment for you. We have in the town a group of singers, who visit homes to entertain. I've persuaded them to sing for us tonight, so I know you'll make them welcome.'

As he spoke, three beautiful girls entered the room, one holding a small harp. They grouped before the table, and, at a nod from Matthew, started to sing, at first a little nervously, but with increasing confidence. The voices blended beautifully together, the harmony falling gently on their ears. Simon felt that he had never heard such a wonderful sound, nor seen such loveliness. But as he listened, he realised that the words were of unbridled passion and rather indelicate, to say the least. Such a song was all right for rough fishermen, Simon thought, and would be accepted well enough by the tax gatherers, but he wondered how Jesus would react. He stole a glance at his friend's face and was rather surprised to see that Jesus did not seem to be embarrassed. He sat there, smiling, and joined in the applause at the end of the performance.

The evening continued without further incident, the conversation continuing until well into the evening. Simon kept wondering when Jesus would bid his host goodnight, as they had, as yet, made no arrangements for the night; but Jesus seemed content to stay and enjoy the company. Eventually, Matthew pressed them to stay at his house overnight, which they thankfully accepted.

The following morning, Jesus and Simon were given an excellent breakfast outside on the terrace. The morning air was again wonderful – calm and warm as the sun climbed up into the deep blue sky. The whole earth seemed to be at peace as they sat there in the garden. Of course, they knew this to be an illusion, but they enjoyed the moment while it lasted. Matthew joined them as they finished their breakfast, apologising for his absence. He had been talking to Joanna. He was still bubbling with excitement from the events of the previous day and revelling in the idea of making a new start in life. He told Jesus that he had decided to resign his post at the tax department and seek employment as an accountant with some of the small traders who worked nearby. Jesus wished him well but reminded him of the opposition he would inevitably face from his former colleagues, as evidenced by their comments on the previous evening.

'I realise it won't be easy,' said Matthew with a grimace. 'I know that my life is going to change completely and that I shall be far less well off. But I want to give it a try.'

'What does Joanna say about it?' enquired Jesus. 'It will affect her too.'

'I know,' said his host, with a shrug. 'She's pretty fed up with me for giving up my job, but I just feel I have to do it. She'll have to economise.'

'Don't be too hard on her, Matthew,' advised Jesus. 'You have made the right decision, I'm sure, and it's a courageous one, but she may well resent being "pulled down", socially, without being consulted. I just hope that there is no great rift between you.'

'So do I,' said Matthew, 'but this is what I feel I have to do.'

'There is nobody who leaves behind family, or friends, or riches, or anything else, for the sake of God's Kingdom, who will not find that it has been worthwhile in the long run,' said Jesus.[5]

There was a pause at that. Then Jesus announced that he intended to stay in Bethsaida for a few days, preaching each day, either on the shore or in the town centre. Matthew immediately offered his house as a base while they were there, and this was gratefully accepted.

Soon, Jesus and Simon set out for the seashore, but they had hardly gone a few steps when they were approached by three men, dressed unmistakably as Pharisees, who blocked their pathway and demanded to know who they were. Jesus told them in an even voice and they quickly rounded on him, saying, 'So you are the ones who were entertained by Levi, the tax gatherer, and his friends last night?'

'That's so,' replied Jesus. 'Is there a problem?'

'The problem, as you call it, is yours, not ours,' retorted the senior Pharisee. 'You come here, setting yourself up as a preacher, a holy man, and yet you hobnob with Levi and his sort, cheats and Roman-lovers. That's your problem – how do you explain that?'

'Very easily,' replied the Nazarene. 'I was graciously invited to supper and I accepted – as any polite human being would do when kindly invited by another. Not to have gone would have been a real snub and most impolite. The fact that my host felt that his life was all mixed up and in need of a complete overhaul was, surely, all the more reason to go, to support him. He has decided to change his ways and rejoin God's family – isn't that a cause for rejoicing?'

'People like him are beyond redemption,' was the surly reply.

'Nobody is beyond God's love,' replied Jesus. 'Nobody.'

'And what about those unsavoury women who entertained you at dinner last night?' enquired another of the Pharisees. 'They have a reputation in this town. They are thought to be little better than prostitutes!'

'There was nothing unseemly in their conduct last night,' said Jesus. 'Their choice of singing material could be improved, I agree, but apart from that—'

'Exactly!' broke in the Pharisee. 'Weren't you affronted when they sang songs like that?'

'If they are supported and helped, they will see for themselves that there are better songs available,' replied the preacher.

The Pharisees nearly choked with indignation.

'You aren't worthy to preach God's message. You had better leave this town, before you do real damage,' their leader demanded.

'I shall stay for a few days at least,' came the calm reply. 'It is not the healthy people who need a doctor, but those who are sick; I did not come to call virtuous people, rather those who had lost their way.'[6]

★

But Jesus decided to change his plans two days later. The authorities of the Synagogue had turned down his request to use the steps of the building to preach in the town centre, and his sermons on the beach had been interrupted by hecklers – scribes and Pharisees and their friends, out to make mischief and undermine his ministry to the people. So Jesus decided to move on inland and visit some of the smaller villages there.

He and Simon set out early next morning, before the sun became too hot, and walked about five miles to a small village called Urta. There they found, as usual, a well in the centre of the village and sat down to take a drink. A pleasant woman who was nearing forty was drawing water and kindly lent them a cup. They started chatting to her, discovering that her name was Rachel, and that she was the wife of the local basket maker. Jesus asked her if she could direct him to the home of the village rabbi, as he would like to talk to the people from the steps of the Synagogue – if they could be persuaded to listen. Rachel responded pleasantly, directing them to the house and saying that she would tell her husband, Thomas, about the possibility that Jesus would preach. He, in his turn, would, no doubt, put the word around the village that there would be a meeting.

Thus, all was soon arranged and Jesus was confronted by quite a good crowd when, at the end of the working day, he arrived to speak. Thomas was already present as the preacher strolled up the street towards the Synagogue. He introduced himself to Jesus and was, in turn, introduced to Simon.

The basket maker was rather a stern-looking man of about forty, with gaunt features and a hard mouth. His fingers were long and his hands expressive – he used them frequently as he spoke, making expansive gestures in the air, but he seemed to lack geniality. Simon thought that he wouldn't take to this rather cold-looking fish, but Jesus, smiling as usual, greeted him cordially.

'You've gathered quite a big crowd to hear me – I'm very grateful,' he said.

'It's nothing,' growled Thomas. 'Think nothing of it.'

Jesus chose to talk again that evening about the coming Kingdom. As before, he stressed that God's Kingdom was immanent.

'In fact, it is already here, in one sense,' he said.

'Then why are the Romans still occupying of our land?' asked someone in the crowd.

'I have no doubt that the Roman Empire will be swept away one day,' responded the preacher. 'How and when this will happen, I don't know – only God knows. I only know that no earthly kingdom can stand for ever. Our nation has been ruled by many outsiders in the past – Egyptians, Babylonians, Persians, Assyrians, Greeks – all are now swept away. God's Kingdom, on the other hand, will surely survive eternally in the hearts and minds of his people – all those who respond to his call.'

'What do you mean?'… 'How can this be?' Voices were being raised all round the crowd.

Jesus raised his arms to restore quiet. He smiled winningly before continuing again.

'You need to reorder your lives,' he said, 'and look at things from a different point of view – God's point of view. See everyone around you as God's family – we are all brothers and sisters of one heavenly Father. Treat one another accordingly. Let me put it to you this way. Go back to your childhood. Do you remember how you thought about the world when you were a child? You did not worry about the Roman occupation, paying taxes, making a living, or even where the next meal was coming from. You just believed that your parents would take care of you and your needs – and they did! So, in the same way, God will look after you now. I tell you, whoever does not accept the Kingdom of God like a child will never enter it.'[7]

There was a murmur in the crowd and one sceptic from the back of the crowd said jeeringly, 'You think that we can all knock off work, sit back and it will all just happen?'

'Not literally, of course,' replied Jesus, smiling broadly, 'but I do think that people worry themselves quite unnecessarily about all these things, whereas, if they took a more relaxed attitude to life and concentrated their effort on supporting each other, life would be happier all round. If everyone looked after the next man's needs, there would be sufficient for everyone. Children don't fret – you'll often see them playing together, sharing their toys and other little possessions, such as they are. Why can't adults be the same?'

The questions and answers went on for some time. Eventually, the gathering broke up and Jesus started to walk away with Simon, but they had hardly gone more than a hundred paces when Thomas caught up with them and asked if they would take supper at his house that evening. Naturally, they were delighted and accepted at once. Rachel turned out to be an excellent cook and made them very welcome. The little house was simple but well furnished and very neat. Everything was spotlessly clean and nothing seemed to be even an inch out of place. The supper table was beautifully laid, plates and cutlery all set with great precision.

'There's a place for everything and everything in its place,' said Thomas – rather grimly, Simon thought. 'That's how Rachel is!'

Simon thought of his Ruth and the contrast with their own home. Muddles frequently were the order of the day there, and housework certainly not the highest priority!

They ate their meal exchanging pleasantries and local chit-chat. When they had finished and Rachel had retired to the kitchen to wash the plates and pots, leaving the men to sip their beer, Thomas suddenly launched out on a more serious topic which, Simon thought later, he had probably been keeping bottled up all the evening.

'You were talking today about children,' he said, looking hard at Jesus. 'Become like a child and see things through childish eyes, you said.'

'That's right,' said Jesus, quietly. 'I think that's a good way to approach life.'

'But what if you have no children?'

Thomas's voice was low and he looked at the table as he spoke. 'Rachel and

I wanted children; we have been married for nearly twenty years and still we have no children. How can we be like children? We have none. We've forgotten what it is like to be a child – and we have no pattern.'

'What can I say?' replied Jesus, softly, his hand on Thomas's arm. 'It must be – it obviously is – a real burden to you that your marriage has not been blessed with children. I do understand. I too have none. My wife died just a few months after we were married and she was pregnant at the time, so I really do share your pain.'

'I hate it,' muttered Thomas. 'Most Sabbaths, Rachel and I go to visit my twin brother who lives a few doors away from here.[8] He has six children and another on the way. Of course, it's nice to play with his children – I'm their uncle, after all – but all the time I'm thinking, "Why haven't we got children of our own?" I think I shall stop going there – it upsets me so much.'

'And Rachel – what does she think about it?'

'I think she has given up all hope. She shuts herself off from the problem and never mentions it, these days. She gives all her time to cleaning and tidying this place. It isn't a home anymore – it's more like an exhibition! Not a chair, not a cushion, is out of place. I daren't leave my sandals under the table – they have to be put away!'

Thomas sighed deeply.

'Life seems to have lost its real meaning,' he said. 'You talked of a new way of life, God's Kingdom. I certainly wish I could find it!'

'You will,' promised Jesus. 'I will help you to find what you are looking for.'

★

It was getting hot, working outside the blacksmith's shop at Gischala. The sun beat down on the little town, reflecting off all the walls of the houses and scorching the earth, so that clouds of dust were raised with every passing set of feet or hooves, or any little breath of wind. Not that there was much air; the morning was almost still. What with the ever-increasing heat, as June approached, and the heat of the forge fire, Simon was roasting uncomfortably, and his young assistant, James, was suffering similarly.

Simon was in his mid-twenties, tall, bronzed and muscular. His hair and beard were dark and unkempt, and he had an ugly scar down one side of his face, which marred his otherwise craggy good looks. His assistant was still in his late teens, short in stature, but likely to become similarly broad and muscular as he matured. Both were distinctly sweaty at the moment, hard at work making a plough for their neighbour, Joseph.

'What a trade to follow,' grumbled Simon. 'As if it isn't hot enough, we're stuck over a roaring forge fire!'

'I suppose we have to work at something,' replied his assistant sympathetically, well used to the moans of his boss. 'We're nearly done, aren't we?'

Just then the gate clanged and a man slipped into the yard. He seemed rather furtive, as if he was reluctant to be seen, but as soon as Simon noticed him, he motioned to the newcomer to go inside the forge, saying to James, 'Take a break.'

Simon followed the man into the forge and cleared a seat on a rough wooden bench in the corner.

'No time for sitting,' said the newcomer. 'Have you got the goods ready for us?'

'Yes, all done,' replied the blacksmith, 'but would it not be better to come for them after dark?'

'That's what I have in mind,' growled the other. 'I will come with some comrades tonight, about an hour after sundown. How many fellows will I need?'

'It's not the weight – it's the noise that might be a problem. Bring just one other fellow and a handcart. I've made several swords, about a dozen, five daggers and a stack of arrowheads. If you drop that lot, it'll make a devil of a row! I suggest you bring a cart with something in it – vegetables, fruit, manure, anything – and you can hide the weapons in the load.'

'Right,' said the stranger. 'I'll see you tonight!' And with that he slipped out of the forge and down the road as quickly as he had come.

'Who was that?' asked James, as the blacksmith resumed his work.

'Oh, nobody in particular,' replied his boss, with feigned indifference. 'A fellow from one of the small villages further up in the hills.'

'A stranger in these parts. What did he want?' James was always full of questions.

'I've been doing a little job for him, that's all. He came to see if it was ready.' Simon tried to sound nonchalant, but was becoming rather uncomfortable under the inquisition.

James dropped to a low voice. 'Did he come for the swords?'

Simon started, then hesitated. James continued, 'I found the weapons the other day when I was tidying the forge – stacked away at the back, behind that old disused door.' Seeing Simon's look of concern, he added, 'Don't worry, I haven't said anything to anyone about the weapons – and I won't.'

Simon gave his assistant a long hard look, then motioned him inside. Once inside, they sat together on the bench.

'I'd better tell you, since you're already involved, it seems. Yes, I made the weapons for the man. Mum's the word, mind. I'm sure you'll have guessed who he is and what they're for.'

'The Zealots!' breathed James. 'Out in the hills. Are you one of them?'

Simon glanced over his shoulder to the window before he answered.

'Well, obviously I don't live up in the hills, so I'm not involved in the raids they carry out on rich property and camel trains – but I'm involved, to a point, I guess, as a supplier. I certainly don't want it known too widely around the town, just in case of informers.'

'I shan't tell anyone – I've already said. But do you agree with these people, with their aims and methods?' James was running on.

'Look, I certainly want to get rid of Antipas,' growled Simon. 'He's just a Roman puppet and I'd like our country to be free of foreigners totally. I want to be part of a free nation again, like we were under the great King David, a thousand years ago. Whether the Zealots are using the right methods is another matter. I help them, but—'

'At a distance?' interrupted James. 'I agree. I'd like to help, too, but I'm not sure how it's best done. It's risky to be associated with Zealots, of course. Most of the town is sympathetic, I know, but there's always the chance of a government spy.'

'Would you be prepared actually to fight?' It was Simon's turn to ask the questions. 'What would your father have to say about that?'

'I've been thinking about it a lot recently,' replied the younger man, perplexity written all over his face. 'The chances of success are bound to be very small. Rome is so powerful. Is it worth taking the risk? My friend Thaddeus and I have talked about it quite a bit, without coming to any conclusion.'

'What about your father?'

James grimaced and shook his head.

'Oh, Dad manages to face both ways. He wouldn't give anyone away, but he won't get involved himself. He's very religious – goes to Synagogue regularly and so on. He can read, and he reads the scriptures a lot.'

'What would he feel about you becoming active, though?' Simon persisted.

'I don't know. I think he'd pretend he didn't know, so he didn't have to take any action.'

The conversation continued for several more minutes. Eventually, Simon decided that enough time had already been wasted on speculative politics and insisted that they went back to fixing the plough, but they hadn't been at it for more than ten minutes when they were interrupted again, this time by another man, very different in character. There was nothing furtive about this second visitor; he came steadily and purposefully down the street and called out over the wall to them, 'Could you spare a drink of water for a traveller, please?'

As hospitality for the stranger is the invariable rule in the Middle East, Simon replied straightaway, 'Of course, come in and take the weight off your feet a moment.'

He downed tools again and went off to find a cup of water for the newcomer, who drank thirstily.

'It's warm today. I've just walked up from Urta.'

'That's far enough on a day like this,' agreed the smith. 'Are you from there? I don't think we've met before.'

'I'm originally from Nazareth, but based nowadays mainly in Capernaum. I'm doing a tour round this area. My name is Jesus – I was a carpenter, but now turned preacher.'

Simon pursed his lips at the mention of 'preacher'.

'I'm the blacksmith hereabouts, as you can see – Simon's my name. This is my assistant, James.'

'I'm very pleased to meet you both,' said Jesus. 'I was hoping that you could direct me to the local rabbi, so that I might ask if I could speak to you all in the Synagogue tonight, or, maybe, outside the building – it's more pleasant to be outside at this time of year.'

Simon was rather at a loss. The rabbi wasn't in his immediate circle of acquaintance, to say the least of it. He hadn't attended worship for some time, and had little time for religion, other than the almost obligatory recognition of the main feast days. James was little better, even though he came from a religious family.

'I'm afraid I – don't know much about Synagogue affairs,' he said eventually. 'I suggest you ask at the village square. Someone there will know where to find the rabbi.'

'I could take you to our home,' said James. 'Father is always at the Synagogue and would be pleased to help.'

'That would be kind,' said Jesus. 'I am interested, though, in what you said, Simon. You say you don't know much about religion – but you want a successful life, I'm sure…?'

'Well, yes, of course,' said Simon, puzzled.

'How do you expect to be successful, by which I mean happy, contented, fulfilled – you choose the word you like best – how do you expect to be any of these things without thinking about the source of all life?' Jesus was smiling that winning smile of his.

Simon felt a little on the defensive. 'I don't really know,' he replied falteringly.

'I have good friend, also called Simon, a fisherman. He was with me until yesterday, but has had to go back to Capernaum to help his brother with the business. He, like you, is a bit confused about life, its purpose and the best way to approach it. I'd like you two to meet sometime and compare notes. It would be interesting. Strangely enough, I also have another fisherman friend called James…'

Jesus looked over at the younger man. 'My friend James is somewhat older than you and a lot taller. You'd like him. Very straight-forward sort of fellow. Yes, we shall have to try to have a get-together for us all sometime. Meantime, why don't you two come down to the Synagogue tonight and hear what I have to say – assuming I can persuade the local rabbi, of course.'

'I guess I could,' replied the blacksmith, a bit reluctantly. 'What do you think, Jim?'

'I'll be there. I'd never hear the end of it from Father if I missed.' This last with a sly wink at Jesus, who smiled in return.

'Well, thanks for the refreshment,' said the preacher. 'I'll hope to see you later, then,' and he held out his hand to each of them. Then, with a sudden change of topic, he said, 'By the way, I'm told that there is an active band of

Zealots in these hills? Have you seen any evidence of their operations in this village?'

Simon managed to keep his face entirely non-committal as he replied, 'I've seen nothing of them myself. There are always rumours, of course.'

James chimed in, 'The north of Galilee has produced many Zealots in the past, it's true, so now people down south assume we are all troublemakers.'

'And are you?' Jesus was smiling. 'No – you don't need to answer that. You don't know me well enough yet to trust me. I could be a government spy – but I'm not! I'll see you tonight.' And with that, he was gone.

The town of Gischala had quite a sizeable Synagogue and, by the end of the afternoon, several dozen men had gathered outside it to hear what this preacher from the south had to say for himself. It soon got around the town that something new was in the air. Even some of the womenfolk gathered around to hear what was going on. Jesus stood up on the steps in front of the building and began by thanking the rabbi for his kindness in allowing him to speak. He went on to refer to the reports of Zealots in the area – men who had been raiding local farms and houses for food and other supplies, and stealing money and valuables from the camel trains moving south.

'Can it ever be right to steal?' he asked. 'No doubt, the Zealots believe in their cause and perhaps there are those here who might agree that things should be changed, but is this the way to do it? Can anyone break the Law with impunity? I refer, of course, not to Caesar's law, or Antipas' law, but to God's Holy Law: "You shall not steal".'[9]

'Our history shows clearly,' came a voice from the rear, 'that there *is* such a thing as a just war. When right is on your side, then it is quite right to fight – indeed, it is quite wrong to stand aside and do nothing. When Israel left Egypt, centuries ago, led by Moses, and Joshua took them into the Promised Land, the whole nation fought their way into Canaan to possess it…'

'The Maccabees took up the sword against the Seleucids and threw them out,' said another voice.

'Yes, that's right,' agreed Jesus, 'but how long did the peace that they won last? The nation was at war constantly under the judges and the kings, and again under the Hasmoneans. There is no lasting happiness or peace to be had by taking up the sword. Bloodshed gets us nowhere in the end, even if we manage a temporary victory or two.'

There was a pause as the crowd digested this remark.

'I believe we ought to think in quite a different way,' continued Jesus. 'Instead of working for an earthly kingdom, I envisage a different kind of Kingdom altogether – God's Kingdom – where, one day, God will be acknowledged as supreme by everybody, and there will be no Caesar.'

'But when?' The question came from the back of the crowd.

'I don't know when,' replied Jesus, 'but the day will come. It may take many years, maybe centuries, but it will come. But meantime, the new Kingdom can begin in the hearts and lives of each of us. We can each prepare for that Kingdom by living life as we know God wants us to live it – we can begin now. Yes – his Kingdom can come today as far as we are concerned, as individuals and as a group of committed people. We are not politicians; we are ordinary folk living ordinary lives as carpenters, blacksmiths, farmers, potters, basket weavers, housewives and so on, but we can be first in this new movement. Long before the kings of this world have even heard of this new deal, we can be living the life that God intends for us. The people who count least in the present set-up can be first in the new Kingdom – the first shall be last and the last, first'.[10]

'All that sounds all too good to be true,' said one man at the front. 'How is this to come about?'

'Just by caring about one another more, as God cares for us. If we emulate God, who treats us all equally, sending his sunshine and rain on everybody equally,[11] then there can be justice for all and no need for people to fight and squabble. We can do it, my friends.'

Jesus's face was all smiles; he held his arms out to them all in a gesture of embrace.

'I doubt whether Caesar will go along with your plan,' said another sceptic.

'I don't believe it!' Comments were coming at Jesus from all sides.

'I promise you,' said Jesus, 'that in the end, the way I have outlined will break through. In the final analysis, force cannot win. There is no power greater than love.'

After the meeting broke up. Jesus found himself ignored by many people in the crowd; but James, followed by Thaddeus and, more reluctantly, by Simon, made their way over to see the preacher. James introduced his friend and Jesus shook his hand warmly. Thaddeus was another young man, hardly twenty, with a fresh complexion, good bearing and jet black, well-groomed hair and beard.

'You got quite a hostile reception,' said James, sounding sympathetic.

'It's bound to take time,' said Jesus confidently. 'Do you think what I said was poppycock?'

None of the other three rushed to answer that question. Finally, Simon replied, 'We'll have to think it over. No doubt we shall talk it over when you've gone.'

'I shall return,' came the ready response. 'Never doubt it.'

NOTES

[1] Mark 2:14.
[2] Luke 15:3.
[3] Mark 12:40.
[4] Luke 15:8.
[5] Mark 10:29.
[6] Mark 2:17.
[7] Mark 10:15.
[8] John 11:16.
[9] Exodus 20:15.
[10] Mark 10:31.
[11] Matt. 5:45..

Pentecost at Jerusalem

It was just one week into June. Jerusalem was teeming with pilgrims again, this time for the festival of Pentecost. Jews were visiting from all over the known world, from places as far apart as Alexandria, Antioch, Ephesus and even Rome itself. The market places were bustling with trade, the streets stiff with visitors and the Temple courts thronged with pilgrims. The sun beat down out of a cloudless sky of deepest blue. Everywhere was shimmering in the heat. Even if headdresses had not been culturally correct, they would need to be worn simply for protection.

Below the Temple stood many public baths. These were provided for the pilgrims by the Temple authorities, so that the pilgrims could wash and purify themselves ritually before entering the precincts of the Temple itself. However, just below the baths, near the sheep market, was a pool of a quite another kind, called locally Bethesda, and round it was a crowd of quite a different sort. In the colonnaded walkway which ran round the pool, lying on rough mats and mattresses, in cots and on chairs, were gathered the lame, the blind and many more who were handicapped and suffering. Day after day, month after month, they lay there, begging from passers-by, hoping that someone would show pity on them. They stayed there sustained by their belief, that, from time to time, an angel was sent from God to bathe in the waters of Bethesda.[1] He was never seen himself, of course, but it was his presence that stirred the surface of the waters, and it was believed that the first person to enter the water after the angel would be cured of all his suffering. So the company of the infirm were there waiting for the surface to move, in the hope that they would be the first to bathe themselves in the healing waters.

Jesus was visiting the Holy City for the festival, accompanied on this occasion by John, the fisherman. They were staying in Bethany with Lazarus, Martha and Mary, journeying into town every day and returning to the village each evening. John was, by now, becoming utterly devoted to Jesus. He had heard him speak many times, both in public and at various smaller gatherings at the seashore and around the meal table. He was fascinated not so much by the message, as by the charisma of the preacher, who seemed to John to have a mesmeric quality about him, such that he could have charmed the birds from the trees if he had so wished. John felt that Jesus's eyes saw you for what you were, rather than for what you professed to be. To John, Jesus's voice was sheer music, usually quiet and persuasive, but occasionally resonant and compelling. Altogether, John had fallen completely under the Jesus spell. Since it had been James who had visited Jerusalem at Passover, all the family agreed that it was John's turn to go this time, though Zebedee constantly complained that his sons were 'for ever off to the big city' leaving him to do all the work and run the business.

Jesus and John had spent most of their time in the inner courtyard of the Temple, the court of the Israelites, discussing points from the scripture with the scribes and lawyers there. For most of the time, Jesus did the discussing while John contented himself with listening, but both, in their different ways, were appreciating their visit to the capital. Quite often, Jesus would address the group gathered round the scribe. It usually happened that many pilgrims would stop to listen in, for Jesus's style was quite different from the others, being much more direct and authoritative, and less dependent on meticulous references to one text after another. People heard him speak from the heart and responded warmly.[2]

This morning, however, Jesus and John were making their way past the sheep market, overlooking the crowd assembled by Bethesda. John looked enquiringly at his hero.

'There are many here who could benefit from your healing powers, Jesus,' he said quietly. 'Do you not think…?'

'No, John,' interrupted Jesus, gently. 'Of course I feel drawn to help, but, as we have seen in Capernaum, healing is so often seen as mere magic, and misunderstood by the people. I hate to see suffering, but I cannot help them all and the presence of the crowd could lead to all sorts of complications.'

They looked down at the sorry spectacle for several minutes more without a word being spoken. Then Jesus pointed out a man set apart from the rest at the back in a corner. He looked as if he were in his eighties, but that was almost certainly a huge overestimate; the effects of a prolonged illness had aged the man unmercifully, adding perhaps twenty or even thirty years to his real age.

'Perhaps we could go and talk to that poor man,' said the Nazarene.

They descended the stairs to the poolside and threaded their way through the collection of sufferers, lying recumbent. Some were snoring noisily as they lay in the shade under the porches, others moaned in pain. Eventually, Jesus and his friend reached the man that he had pointed out. The preacher approached him with hand outstretched. The man blinked up at him and slowly responded with a claw-like hand of his own.

'How are you today,' asked Jesus.

'The same as usual,' was the weak reply.

Jesus introduced John and they learnt that the man's name was Alpheus. They talked together briefly about the festival and the throng of people visiting the capital, but Alpheus had difficulty in showing any interest in his surroundings, having long since withdrawn from the world into his own suffering and boredom. His life, like his body, seemed to have wasted away and shrunk almost to zero.

'How long have you been here?' asked John.

'I was taken ill about thirty-eight years ago,' replied the skeleton, in a lifeless voice. 'Since the doctors couldn't do anything for me, I was brought here, to see if I could be first into the water when it moved, but my relatives couldn't stay with me for long and so there was nobody to help me when the time came. Others always beat me to it into the pool. As time went by, my relatives gave up all hope and now I have no chance. I've given up hope. They placed me here at the back, out of the way, and here I've stayed. I shall die here.'

The frail body twisted and tried to turn away, as if in despair.

'You must not give up hope,' said Jesus. 'Trust in God. Look at me – I'm here to help you.'

The man's attention was caught by the quiet authority in Jesus's voice. He turned back and gazed doubtfully at the brown eyes of the preacher.

'Do you really want to be better?' asked Jesus, urgently.

Alpheus stammered, 'Well, yes, of course… but…'

'Don't say "but",' said Jesus. 'Only believe. Trust that God loves you and that all your mistakes are forgiven.'

So saying, he took hold of both the man's arms.

'Come on,' he said, 'you can do it. Stand up and walk.'

He assisted the man, who was making feeble attempts to rise.

'Come along,' said the quiet, persuasive voice. 'You can do it.'

The man made a further tremendous effort and came first to a sitting position and then, after another struggle, shakily to his feet. He took a faltering step on his emaciated legs, wobbling weakly, but then, as he managed first one step, then another, with increasing confidence, he stood taller and walked more surely. He turned round to Jesus, with eyes brimming.

'Rabbi,' he said, 'how do I thank you?'

'Say nothing to anyone, Alpheus. Take this matting away with you and go home,' replied his healer. 'Go along, now – and say nothing more.'

The man, hardly daring to believe his good fortune, stooped down and caught up the rough matting that had been his bed for so long and started to stagger away.

'Peace go with you,' said Jesus. 'And we will go too,' he said quietly to John, 'before anyone notices. Then there will be no chance of a stir.'

Fortunately, Alpheus hadn't far to go to reach his relatives' house. If he had, he might have started to doubt his ability to walk that far. His legs ached from lack of use as he climbed the steps, dragging the matting behind him. At the top of the stairway, he stopped to get his breath and his bearings, and to recall the direction to his home. As he did so, a couple of Pharisees, passing by, noticed him and said, scowling, 'What are you doing, fellow, carrying that load? Don't you know it's a Sabbath today? It's against the Law to carry anything today.'

'I'm sorry, sir. I didn't realise that it was the Sabbath,' replied Alpheus.

'You didn't know? Well, you should do,' came the curt reply.

'I've been ill, sir,' pleaded Alpheus. 'When you're ill, and laid aside, you lose all track of time. The man who healed me told me to take the matting home; so, of course, I did as I was bidden.'

'Who was it that told you to break the Sabbath?' enquired the Pharisees.

'I don't know who he was – I really don't. He just… arrived… out of the blue.'

'Well, just leave the matting there – you can collect it tomorrow.'

A couple of mornings later, Alpheus made his way slowly to the Temple. He knew that he should make a thanksgiving sacrifice for his cure. He purchased a sacrificial dove in the outer courtyard and made his way to the priest with the bird. He followed the required procedure, said his thanksgiving prayer and turned to go. Just then, he saw Jesus, sitting with John and two scribes, discussing the scriptures. He caught the carpenter's eye, and Jesus excused himself from the discussion and hurried over to him, shaking him warmly by the hand.

'Alpheus – how are you now?'

'I'm feeling well,' replied the other. 'I'm a new man, thanks to you. My family just can't believe it. Neither can I, after all this time.'

'That's really good,' said Jesus. 'Give thanks to God. More than that, live a thankful life – a life of usefulness.'

'I've just left the priest, having given my thanks,' replied Alpheus, 'but I want to thank you too. You never even gave me your name.'

'My name is Jesus,' replied his healer. 'I'm from Nazareth in Galilee.'

'I am forever in your debt,' said Alpheus. Then they shook hands and parted.

But just a couple of minutes after Alpheus had left Jesus, he saw the two Pharisees who had stopped him just after he had been healed. They crossed the courtyard and accosted him again.

'Who was that we saw you talking to?' they demanded sternly.

'That was the man who healed me,' said Alpheus, nervously.

'And who is he?'

'He told me his name was Jesus. He's from Galilee – Nazareth, I think he said.'

The two Pharisees looked triumphantly at one another briefly, then turned back to the other.

'Oh, yes, we know him,' sneered one, wagging his head. 'It was Jesus who told you to carry the bed on the Sabbath, then?'

'Well, yes… but he healed me…'

'He told you to break the Sabbath. That's against the Law.'

They turned on their heels and stalked away, leaving Alpheus bemused.

A little later, as Jesus and John were crossing the courtyard of the Gentiles, where all the traders were conducting their business, a small, dark-skinned man with long dark hair and a very prominent nose, about thirty years old, came up to Jesus and whispered, 'Can I have a word with you?'

'Of course,' said Jesus, surprised. 'What's the matter?'

The man shook his head slightly, then said, 'Follow me, please.'

Without another word, the little man hurried away, glancing behind him from time to time to be sure that the others were following. He led them out of the crowded courtyard, down the long stairway and over to the side of the main street. He walked along until he came to a gap in the wall, in the shade of a tall palm tree, where they could not be overheard. There, he turned to face Jesus.

'You are Jesus, of Nazareth?' he began, almost accusingly.

'Yes, that's right,' replied Jesus evenly.

'My name is Judas – Judas Iscariot. I come from Gaza, in the far south.'

'I know of it. I'm pleased to meet you, Judas.' Jesus's ready hand reached out to grasp the other's and give it a warm handclasp. 'This is my friend, John, who's from Capernaum in Galilee.'

More handshakes, then Judas spoke again.

'I've been watching and listening to you over the past two or three days,' he said. 'I've seen and heard you talking to the scribes and lawyers – and to the pilgrims who have stopped to listen. You seem to be different from the others. You seem to carry more weight than them – you have real authority. The others seem to rely entirely on what has been said in the past.'

'I believe that God, my Father, has called me to speak. He speaks through me. It is the Father who dwells in me doing his own work,' said Jesus slowly.[3] 'I do nothing by myself, only what he tells me to do. Others rely on the words of scripture for their authority, but I feel mine comes from within me. That is not to say that scripture is not helpful – of course it is. Scripture is sacred and records what God has said and done over the centuries. Of course that history provides us with guidance for today. But God is still speaking today; I feel it, I know it for myself.'

'Exactly,' said Iscariot, 'and I hear God speaking when I hear you speak. I would like to hear so much more from you. I have so much that I want to share with you.'

Jesus paused and looked keenly at the stranger.

'Let's have a meal together,' he said, 'then you can tell us all about yourself and what it is that is concerning you. You seem to be somewhat troubled at present. You can tell us how you come to be here talking to us.'

They met that evening for supper at the little inn at which Judas was staying. John had had to walk to Bethany during the day to warn their host there that they would be in town that night, and as he walked he turned over in his mind the strange encounter with the man from Gaza. He wondered what he was really worried about, what his trouble was. What, exactly, had stimulated him to accost Jesus so suddenly? Jesus seemed to take to him readily, but John wasn't sure.

Judas seemed to be very pleased to see them both that evening and hosted a good meal. Conversation moved easily and light-heartedly while they ate, Jesus saw to that. He was affable, as always, laughing frequently and telling stories from his childhood and early life. After the meal, however, when they were sipping their wine, Jesus invited Judas to tell them what it was that was bothering him.

'I suggest you start, if you will, by telling us a little about your background,' he said, 'then we shall be able to understand more clearly why you are concerned.'

It transpired that Judas had been orphaned at a very early age – he didn't remember either of his parents – and that he had been brought up by an elderly uncle and aunt who had no children of their own. They had certainly looked after him as far as his physical needs were concerned, but had shown him little affection. He had felt unwanted, unloved and desperately lonely, often without playmates and rather bored. He had made one friend, Jacob, a lad of his own age who lived across the street from his uncle; but his friend's parents had not got on with his relations, so they had not been permitted to see each other very often. His uncle had provided him with a good education, though, and Judas had profited from it, becoming a skilled accountant. As soon as he could support himself, Judas had left his relations in Gaza and journeyed to Jerusalem, where he had found employment in the Temple, helping to manage the running of the stalls where money was changed.

'My job,' Judas said, 'is to assist in managing the changing house, but I know that the rates of exchange are scandalously high. The pilgrims are robbed – and the rates are set by the High Priest himself! He must know that he is robbing the people. I feel increasingly uncomfortable to be part of this whole business. Furthermore, it isn't as if the money goes exclusively to support the Temple or to help the poor. A good slice goes into the High Priest's pocket. Have you seen the way he lives?'

Jesus nodded. He and John had seen the High Priest's palace every day on their way to the Temple from Bethany. It was as good a house as any in Jerusalem, better than most. It would compare favourably with the Governor's residence, being a place of great splendour and riches.

'I've been listening to you teaching, Jesus,' Judas went on, 'and it seems to me that you have hit on the essential truth. Religion is not a matter of following rules, regulations and rituals, or observing the proper festivals. It's a matter of the heart and spirit. This lifts life out of the rut of habit and law onto a different level, where everyone accepts everyone else as sons and daughters of the living God.'

'You have been listening,' said Jesus, smiling. 'I believe those are my very words.'

'I remember them well,' muttered Judas. 'I told my boss what I thought of his job today when I gave him my notice – and I quoted you! I told him that I was sure you would have nothing to do with this kind of racket! It wouldn't be part of your new Kingdom – your "Kingdom of right relationships".'

Jesus's face looked serious, and John winced as Judas mentioned his confrontation with one of the Temple hierarchy. John knew that Jesus wanted to avoid any conflict with the authorities during this visit, but he noted that his friend did not refer to the matter.

'Can I come with you, Jesus?' said Judas. 'I want to follow you and help you. Can you use me?'

Jesus hesitated for barely a second.

'Of course I can use you, Judas,' he said, 'but we're due back in Galilee shortly, so you'd better get ready to move north soon.'

★

The next day, Jesus and his two followers were again sitting in the Temple courtyard, discussing a point of scripture with one of the scribes. They were contrasting a text in the Torah which reads, 'Ye shall bring your burnt offering and your sacrifices and your tithes...'[4] with the text in the prophets which reads, 'loyalty is my desire, not sacrifice, not whole offerings but the knowledge of God.'[5]

Jesus was saying that clearly God was honoured by any sacrifice, provided it was offered in the right spirit. It needed to be offered with a thankful heart – a heart that was clean through confession. But, even greater than all this was the need to live life in a kindly spirit, being prepared to forgive anyone who had given offence.

'In fact,' he said, 'the two texts do not conflict. They complement one another. The first is derived from the great Moses, who brought the people out of Egypt, long before there was a king in Israel, while the second is from Hosea, who was a prophet after the kingdom split into two, hundreds of years later. One can see how the faith of the fathers developed with time, bringing new insights.'

Just then, a young Levite of the Temple staff approached Jesus and whispered something to him. The latter nodded, then looked round for John and Judas with a puzzled look on his face as he said, 'That's strange. Apparently I'm wanted in the outer courtyard. We'd better go and see what's happening.'

The three friends followed the Levite across the courtyard and into the Court of the Gentiles, where, as usual, they skirted round the area set aside for trade and made their way to the far corner, by the north cloister. There they found a group of Pharisees and scribes, clustered round what appeared, at first glance, to be a dead body. As they approached, however, they could see that it was not a corpse. It was a young woman, terrified and browbeaten, who lay slumped on the floor at the feet of one of the senior Pharisees.

'You are Jesus, the new teacher from Galilee?' This was said as if the speaker was reading a charge in court.

'Yes,' replied the carpenter.

'You see this – thing?' said the Pharisee, indicating the body with his foot.

'This is a fallen creature – an adulteress. She was caught in the midst of her sin. Now, you know the Law, Jesus. Moses said that the correct punishment for such an offence is stoning. What do you say?'

There was silence. Jesus turned away from the accuser, scratched his chin, then squatted down on the ground, deep in thought. As he turned the matter over in his mind, he doodled idly in the sand of the courtyard with his finger. After a moment or two, the Pharisee spoke again, with an obvious sneer in his voice. He believed that he had presented this upstart preacher from the provinces with a problem he couldn't solve. If Jesus agreed that the woman should be stoned, it would clearly conflict with his preaching about God's love and kindness; but if he didn't, he would equally clearly be disregarding the Law of Moses.

'Come along, Rabbi,' he said, with mock respect, 'what should we do with her? Isn't it obvious, in view of the Law?'

Jesus finally looked up. He glanced kindly at the woman and then turned to her tormenter.

'I suggest that the person here who has never sinned should cast the first stone,' he said,[6] and then he bent his head and continued his doodling.

John looked at the expressions of the Temple staff, grouped round the fragile body of the prisoner. They had clearly not expected such a reply. They looked at one another with annoyance written all over their faces. One by one, shaking their heads, but with malevolent glances at the top of Jesus's head, they turned on their heels and left the scene. Soon, only Jesus and his friends were left with the woman. The carpenter looked up again. Slowly he rose, stretched out his hand and helped the woman rise painfully to her feet.

'It seems that nobody accuses you now,' he said softly. 'Nobody's left to condemn you.'

'No, sir,' said the woman, under her breath.

'Neither do I condemn you.' Jesus caught the woman under the arms, forcing her to look him full in his face. 'So go on home – but don't make the same mistake again,' he said with great emphasis, but with a slight smile still playing at the corner of his mouth.

The woman looked at Jesus for a long minute and then responded simply, 'Thank you, sir'. Then she departed, at first slowly, but soon breaking into a run. A moment later, she was out of sight through the main gate of the Temple.

Jesus turned to John and Judas with a slight grimace.

'And we were talking about forgiveness just now!' he said, shaking his head. 'I know nobody who doesn't need mercy from time to time.'

He shook his head again and pulled at his beard. 'It seems that I've made some enemies here in Jerusalem; these people may not show me mercy if they get the chance – so it is just as well we intended to depart north tomorrow.'

That evening, they had their last supper with the family at Bethany. Lazarus had asked John barHelez, the priest, to join them, which pleased Jesus immensely, for he had always got on well with John, even though they often disagreed.

'I understand you've been causing a stir in the courtyard today,' said barHelez, as he joined the company.

'Good news travels fast.' Jesus was still smiling as he spoke, however.

'You haven't done yourself much good, Jesus,' said John. He wasn't smiling.

'I know. I'll be careful.'

'Let's have some supper; we can talk later.' Lazarus was playing the role of host and peacemaker. 'You don't know Judas?'

John barHelez looked keenly at Jesus's new friend, while offering his hand. 'I seem to think I have seen you somewhere,' he said.

'I've recently left the Temple's employ,' Judas volunteered. 'I've often seen you around in the Temple precinct. I used to work in the changing house.'

'But you've stopped now?' John was incredulous. 'It's an excellent position – a job for life! Why give it up?'

Jesus came to Judas's rescue.

'Judas has much the same feelings as I do about the trading in the outer courtyard,' he explained. 'You know that I think it's a racket – we've talked about it often enough. He agrees with me.'

'I see,' said the priest doubtfully. 'So you've left us?'

'Yes. I'm following Jesus now.'

Even John barHelez didn't have much to say to that, so Lazarus quickly invited everyone to sit down at the table for the meal. They enjoyed this greatly and the slight strain in the relationships was soon put on one side. Jesus, as always, was the centre of the conversation, making them all laugh with his mimicry of the Pharisees and Scribes that John and he had been meeting during the week.

'They're so pompous!' he said. 'They put people off religion. Nobody wants to be like them, with their formality and their pride. They seem to have a special "religious" voice, some of them, that they use for praying and preaching! They give all of us preachers a bad name!'

He went on to mimic of one of the men he had met that morning.

'How do they expect people to listen to them when they not only make the faith so difficult, but do so in such incredibly stupid voices?' he finished.

The others were all giggling, especially John and Mary.

'You see,' said Jesus, with a gesture to the two younger members of the group. 'Young people won't take them seriously. We shan't have any followers of the faith if it's left to the Pharisees and scribes to educate them.'

'I can't allow you to make fun of my colleagues on the Temple staff,' complained barHelez. 'They are good men, trying to do their best. They are simply following tradition – tradition which has stood the test of time, coming down to us over many centuries. It's all right for us, younger men, not being steeped in years of Temple tradition. We may be able to see things differently. They can't.'

Mary changed the subject by remarking how lovely the stars were that night. They were eating their meal sitting out in the back garden of the little house. The night was moonless so the Milky Way cascaded across the sky brilliantly. Occasionally, a shooting star flashed. It was all incredibly lovely. The cicadas were sawing away furiously in the trees all around them, adding to the atmosphere. Now and again, a bat fluttered by, seeking its supper. The conversation drifted away from serious topics until after the women had cleared the table and gone into the house to wash the dishes.

John barHelez then turned to Jesus, looking rather solemn.

'You must be careful, my friend,' he said. 'You've upset some important people during your stay in Jerusalem, this time. There are reports in the office that you were encouraging some fellow to break the Sabbath Law. Then there was the brush with a number of officials over that adulteress, and all this against a background of your teaching in the courtyard which rather upstages the local rabbis. They don't like it, Jesus, and they will only tolerate it for a while before they act against you.'

'As far as I can see, I've done nothing they can act against me for,' countered Jesus. 'The question of the Sabbath Law was surely a trifle – the man was healed and going home just a few yards. I can't believe that they can make a case on that. The adulteress – well, they left of their own accord, condemned by their own consciences. I didn't tell them not to stone her. As for my teaching, I only say what I believe God is saying to me. I am not trying to make the rabbis look small – I ask them questions and listen to their answers. Sometimes, I feel that they haven't fully grasped the truth – sometimes that they are misguided. Our tradition has always allowed discussion and even dispute. If I am wrong, I'm sure they will tell me, but there should be no need for me to fear. I don't want trouble – but I must be free to complete my ministry. I've hardly made a start yet. Mind you, we've had some brushes with the Pharisees in Galilee.'

'What happened then?' asked Judas.

It was the young fisherman who insisted on answering.

'I can tell you that,' he said. 'Jesus healed the sick on the Sabbath, and the Pharisees objected to that. Also, just as here, Jesus teaches like nobody else and people prefer to hear him. He's so much clearer and more helpful than the local scribes and Rabbis, and what he says makes real sense! His message is simply good news – a new start – a new Kingdom. Mind you, some people misunderstand the nature of the Kingdom – they think in terms of an armed uprising against Rome.'

'Now that is something you really must avoid even giving a hint about in Jerusalem, Jesus,' said barHelez. 'There must be no suggestion of a call to revolution, however oblique. The High Priest would certainly react if he thought there was going to be any kind of riot – Rome holds him responsible for peace and tranquillity in Judaea. Let anyone threaten to disturb the peace, and Caiaphas will be down on the one who is responsible like a ton of bricks. It won't just be a ticking off, either – he'll have the hide off whoever it is.'

'I agree,' chimed in Judas. 'Caiaphas' position is at stake and he doesn't want it challenged! I fancy he likes his position, both socially and politically.'

'I'll be careful, don't worry,' replied Jesus, with a grin. 'God's kingdom will come in spite of Caiaphas, whatever he says or does. When and how, I don't know, but it will come. Meantime, what can be wrong with preparing the people's hearts and minds for a better, kinder life?'

'Put like that, nothing at all,' said the priest, 'but you know how people misrepresent situations and turn things to their own advantage. Be careful, Jesus. Any sort of talk of changing the political situation is treason, and there's only one response to that – death!'

NOTES

[1] John 5:3–4.
[2] Mark 1:22.
[3] John 14:10.
[4] Deut. 12:6.
[5] Hosea 6:6.
[6] John 8:7.

Jesus finalises the twelve

A week later, Jesus and his friends were back in Capernaum. The weather was really hot by this time and would be even hotter soon, as June moved into July. The earth was scorched and brown. Gone were all the colourful flowers and the green grasses. Only a few deeper-rooted plants were growing – thistles, capers and a few others. The capers had beautiful flowers, but their sharp thorns made the passer-by wary.

Jesus again approached Hezekiah and Jairus to see if they would allow him to speak in the synagogue on the Sabbath and outside the building in the village square during the week. When he did not receive an immediate answer, he felt rather surprised, but next day Jairus's servant came to say that he would be welcome to speak. The congregation on the Sabbath was full of expectation. Word had obviously got round that Jesus had returned to town and would be preaching and, remembering what had happened when he had spoken on the last occasion, they turned out in force. Jesus made his way to the building in good time, accompanied by Judas and all his local fishermen friends. Ruth and Abigail also came along, listening to the service from the side room reserved for women.

Jesus decided to tell another story, this time concerning a farmer.

'It was early springtime,' he began, 'and a farmer was beginning the new season's work. He carefully ploughed the majority of his field, but there was one area of the field where it was so stony that it was impossible to risk his plough there – it would soon have been broken had he tried. Then there was another patch where the weeds were so thick that he decided he would have to leave it until later, when he could deal particularly with the problem. But, as I say, everything else was carefully prepared, so, one fine day, he decided that the time had come to sow the seed. The farmer walked up and down, scattering the seed liberally so that he could look forward to a good crop, but, of course, the birds took advantage of the opportunity and followed him along the field, eating a fair proportion of the seed before it disappeared out of sight into the tilled earth.

'The farmer was fortunate. Enough rain came to nourish the crop, but none was heavy enough to wash the seed away. The farmer rubbed his hands, expecting a fine yield, and visited the field regularly to see how things were progressing. He saw that, after all, some of the seed he had scattered had fallen on the stony ground; this seed had germinated all right, but, having no depth of soil, the little seedlings soon got parched and withered in the sun. He observed too that some had fallen in the weedy patch. These had also germinated, but very soon the resulting seedlings were crowded out by the stern competition and had failed. However, the bulk of the seed had fallen into the ploughed ground and had germinated, matured and come to harvest. Inevitably, some plants had fared better than others, but the overall yield was highly satisfactory.'[1]

Jesus paused and looked round at the crowded Synagogue. 'What do you think this simple story illustrates?' he asked.

Since nobody made any attempt to answer, he continued.

'Well, in a way, the farmer is like God, and the seed represents the message. God spreads his message throughout the world, just as the farmer scattered the seed over the field in my story...'

At this point, there was disturbance at the back of the Synagogue, for a man was being pushed forward towards the preacher. Jesus paused with a puzzled expression on his face. The man hesitated, looking behind him, as if for guidance. Then he turned round and walked slowly towards Jesus again. He finally reached the front, and Jesus's friends, who were close to the front of the congregation, were able to see his problem. His right arm was hanging limply by his side, useless and unsightly.[2] He looked up at Jesus with imploring eyes but said nothing. The preacher looked kindly at the man, then over the man's shoulder to the back of the room. There he saw old Hezekiah, the rabbi, and a couple of local Pharisees watching him closely to see what transpired. He then realised that he had been tricked. The handicapped man had been brought there deliberately by the authorities to trap him into healing someone else on the Sabbath – giving them something more about which they could criticise him.

Jesus didn't hesitate. He went close to the man with the useless arm and held him by both shoulders.

'You have come for healing?' he whispered.

'Yes, please, Rabbi. I hope that my useless limb can be made to work again. Help me, please.'

Jesus turned the man round to face the congregation. Standing behind him, he spoke in a loud voice over the man's shoulder.

'Is it lawful to do good on the Sabbath day, d'you think, or should I do evil?' he asked.

Not surprisingly, nobody was inclined to offer a response.

'Is it better to enhance this life, or would you prefer me to allow this life to go on being handicapped?'

Again, nobody answered. Jesus stared long and hard at the rabbi and his colleagues at the rear of the room, but the silence was deafening. Jesus sighed deeply and asked, 'Isn't it obvious? I can't believe anyone would think it right to withhold healing from this man just because today is the Sabbath. Anyone who did so must have a heart like a stone.'

Then he said, more quietly the man's ear, 'Stretch out your arm. You can do it.'

The man hesitated and glanced over his shoulder at the preacher. Jesus turned him towards him again and repeated his command.

'Stretch out your arm. I promise you, you can do it.'

The man's face was working with many emotions. Doubt, fear and uncertainty were all present, but there was also hope. Eventually, the element of hope triumphed and, looking down, he found that he was able to open his fingers and turn his palm upwards, and then to raise his arm, first a little, then more. The man's face broke into a smile of joy, mirrored by Jesus, who was standing with his own hand outstretched to grasp his in a firm handshake.

'Give thanks to God, my friend. Go, and use your arm in his service.'

'I will,' said the man. 'Thank you, Rabbi.'

'Go, then, and live a life of thanks.'

The man turned and showed his arm to the congregation, who crowded forward to see what had happened. Then he walked out of the building, hesitating as he approached Hezekiah, not relishing catching that official's eye. The rabbi glowered at him but said nothing. The man stepped swiftly through the door, relieved to be out of the building.

Hezekiah paused, then came forward to close the meeting. The disturbance had once again been too great for Jesus sensibly to continue his sermon, so the rabbi simply said the closing prayers and signalled the end of the worship. The people streamed out of the building, all chattering and discussing what they had seen.

When Jesus and his friends reached Simon's house, the preacher seemed very despondent. He flopped down in a chair on the terrace, shaking his head.

'They set me up!' he said. 'They wanted to accuse me of working on the Sabbath again. I couldn't fail that man, though, could I? But nobody will remember the message, or think about it if they do. They were all chattering like magpies about the healing when they left.'

'But they will give thanks to God for the cure, won't they?' said Judas.

Simon intervened. 'We had this conversation before, Judas, the last time this happened – you weren't here, of course. You see, Jesus is afraid that the people will simply ascribe the healing to magic, and have the same reaction as we all have to the local magician when he makes coins appear out of folks' ears. They quickly forget all about it – it means nothing in terms of their way of living.'

'But the healing was marvellous, Jesus. What a gift! How do you do it?' Judas was clearly awestruck. Jesus spoke softly to him.

'I can't tell you precisely how healing works, any more than I can tell precisely how prayer works. It is all in God's hands – a profound mystery. But it has to do with focusing concern and real care on the sufferer and convincing him, or her, that there is nothing to fear. Disease is not always the result of sin and guilt, but these factors can certainly affect people's health in some cases. It isn't that God wants people to be ill – he doesn't send disease as a punishment for wrongdoing – but if we allow ourselves to be dragged down by guilt, then this can result in illness, which may manifest itself as fits, which some call demon-possession, or headache or a fever. It can also show up as a skin complaint – a rash, or sores, which in some cases can even look like leprosy. Even in the case of the man with the useless arm, or people suffering with palsy, there may still be an element of fear or guilt involved, but there are clearly other features that I cannot explain. I just know that I have to trust in God and concentrate my care, like a beam of light, on the invalid. I have to be very certain and assure the sufferer that healing is possible.'

Jesus paused and looked at the sober faces surrounding him. He smiled briefly, then continued.

'One day, you too will be able to heal, if you stay with me and learn and pray. Perhaps, in years to come, men will be clever enough to understand all these things and be able to heal on a grand scale. It takes a lot out of the healer, you know, and you will find that there are limits to what can be achieved.'

Jesus nodded gratefully as Ruth came out on to the terrace to the men and offered them beer or fruit juice to drink. They sipped thankfully, for it was hot even in the shade of the vine which trailed over the wooden frame over the terrace.

'I've been thinking about the story you told in the Synagogue, Jesus,' said John. 'You didn't have time to explain it. You started to say that the farmer represents God and the seed is the message being spread in the world – the field. But what about the rest? I suppose – would the seed that failed because it fell in the weedy patch perhaps represent the message being crowded out by all the trials and tribulations in the world?'

'That's right!' Jesus smiled in delight. 'That's it exactly. What do you think about the seed eaten by the birds?'

Andrew volunteered. 'Might the birds represent the evil in the world? The good message has to compete with the evil in men's hearts and lives, and, in some cases, no doubt, the evil wins against the good. People aren't strong enough to resist temptation. The message is lost just as the seed was lost to the birds.'

'Good – right again,' said Jesus. 'What about the stony places?'

Judas looked up and said, 'I think they could represent the people who accept the message for a while – just as the seedlings germinated in the story – but, because there is no depth to the soil, or, in real life, no depth to the purpose in the person's heart, the seedlings die back and are lost – that is, the person fails to follow through and keep the faith.'

'Excellent,' said Jesus. 'You have expressed the meaning very well. People fail for all these reasons, and then there is no harvest in their lives.'

He looked round at the little group with approval.

'I shall teach a good deal through little stories like that. It is a good way because people like yarns and remember them. If they have any depth to them, they will also work out and remember what lies behind the story as well and hopefully take note and apply it in their lives. The trouble is, as we have seen today, the healing and the teaching can interfere with one another. The other trouble I have to face is the increasing criticism I am attracting from the Synagogue officials and the Pharisees. I feel sure now that I shall be banned from using the Synagogue here again, and it's likely that, before long, it will be impossible for me to preach anywhere in the local towns – word will spread and our experience here will be repeated. I shall have to preach more and more out in the open. Then I shall need you to go into the villages and towns to persuade folk to come out to hear me and to assist me in keeping things reasonably organised when they do come.'

'I can do that,' said Judas. 'No problem. With your reputation, it should be easy.'

'I intend to go all over Galilee, Judas,' warned Jesus. 'It's a big undertaking.'

'I agree that news will travel fast,' said Judas, 'but although the authorities may react negatively, the ordinary people will want to hear what you have to say after what you've done. It shouldn't be very difficult to get them out to hear you.'

The fishermen had been looking at one another while this exchange was in progress. Simon spoke up. 'Andrew and I will help you too,' he blurted out.

Andrew looked in amazement at his brother, but then had to smile. Impulsive Simon again!

'James and I will help too.' John was not going to be outdone.

James grinned and shrugged his broad shoulders. Jesus beamed at them all.

'I'm very grateful for your support, my friends,' he said. Then, suddenly more serious, he said, 'But, Simon, what about Ruth? How will she react to you going off with me for weeks at a time?'

'I'll talk to her. She'll be all right with Abigail.' Simon grinned. 'You never know – she may even be glad of a rest from me! It isn't as if we shall be away for ever!'

Jesus didn't laugh. 'Just put things right with her, my friend. I need your support, but I want her to understand.'

Simon nodded. 'I'll talk to her.'

Jesus turned to the others. 'What about your businesses?'

'Father can manage very well with the hired men,' said James.

'We can get by for a while,' said Andrew. 'There's a little saved. How do you live, Jesus?'

'Like you, I had a little saved before I began, but I've found that people are very generous. As I minister, especially if am able to help folk, I get offered meals, and/or a bed for the night.[3] Look how often you have provided me with hospitality! At this time of year, of course, it is often more comfortable to sleep out of doors anyway. I find I can exist very cheaply. Yes, God does provide, through many ways and means. We shall have to see how we go, but I don't propose to worry about it. I was preaching the other day about leaving things to God, and that is exactly what I propose to do. Of course, once the winter rains start, we won't be able to live outside. I'll stop preaching for a few months then. Over the winter, we can earn some money to tide us over the next spring, summer and autumn. At least I now know that I have a small team I can rely on and you will all learn and be able, in due course, to pass the message on yourselves.'

'Wait a minute,' burst out Simon, 'I'm not sure that I can preach myself! I didn't volunteer for that.'

The others looked similarly concerned.

'All in good time, Simon,' laughed Jesus. 'Things may take time. Just stay with me and we'll see what God can make of you! I can tell you now that I hope soon to add to the party several more men who have shown an interest in my message. Eventually I'd like to have a group of twelve of you – symbolic of the twelve tribes of Israel, which seems appropriate. I shall spend the next few days – or as long as it takes – contacting them all, and we'll see how things develop from there. Judas can come with me, so I shan't lack company.'

★

Jesus and Judas set out next day, early in the morning, to walk to Urta. It was going to be another hot day. Fortunately, they didn't have to hurry. On the way, Judas pressed Jesus further on the topic of the Kingdom of God.

'You said the other day that God's Kingdom would come, but I'm not at all clear as to how you think it will happen. You didn't specify at all.'

'That's because, in truth, I don't know, Judas.'

Jesus stopped walking and caught the other's arm. 'I am convinced that God will act himself to bring about a change for good – and soon. I am also convinced that men can and should prepare themselves for change; they should begin to soften their hearts and change their attitude to life – by seeing things from God's viewpoint, rather than their own. These two things aren't mutually exclusive; God initiates the change and men need to respond. Both God and man can bring about change in different ways. The two effects can – must – coexist.'

'But doesn't God invariably use men to bring about change? If Rome is to be defeated, isn't it up to us men, in the end, to do God's will and raise an army to achieve that?' Judas stuck out his chin defiantly.

'I agree that we – men – are used by God to achieve his purposes – sometimes. But God can also act independently. Look at the sky at night, Judas. Count the stars, if you can. You can't. God built that wonderful heaven without any help from us. Look at the mountains, or the sea. God didn't need our help in creating either of these, did he? Think of the seasons; they come round without any help from us men. Of course God uses men sometimes, but he doesn't invariably do so.'

'Do you envisage him sending an army of angels with flaming swords, then?' Judas persisted.

'I really don't know, Judas. The Kingdom of heaven will come – that I know – but how or when it will happen are questions for God. Perhaps you will be involved. We must remain faithful.'

Jesus paused, then continued.

'The only thing I feel sure about is that it shouldn't involve us in arming ourselves to fight. The people we are going to, these fellows in the northern part of Galilee, are notorious for starting rebellions against the authorities. There are many Zealots in the area. We can expect them to want to fight, if we give them any encouragement – indeed, they're already fighting in a small way.'

'They only need leadership, Jesus. Don't you think that with your leadership—?'

Jesus interrupted. 'No, I don't think so, Judas. That is not in my mind at all. There must be other ways.'

There was nothing said after that for several minutes. They covered the four miles or so before the sun became too hot and they arrived in the village square more than ready for a drink at the well. One or two women were at the well and lent them cups. One remembered seeing Jesus when he had visited earlier and they soon got into conversation, but Jesus soon excused himself and led Judas down the road to Thomas's house, where the basket maker was hard at work at his trade, sitting in the shade in front of the house.

'Good morning, Thomas,' began Jesus. 'How are you today?'

'As you see,' replied that worthy. 'At least I have a trade that permits me to work sitting down in the shade at home. I'm glad I'm not a farmer or a builder! How they continue throughout the summer beats me.'

'I want you to meet a new friend of mine – Judas Iscariot. He's from way down south, from Gaza. He's an accountant by profession – or was. He's given it up to help me.'

Thomas's eyebrows shot up into his forehead. He grimaced.

'Was he a taxman?' he asked.

'No, not guilty!' replied Judas. 'I worked for the Temple authorities, helping with the exchange of coinage for the pilgrims.'

'Still, a very lucrative job, no doubt. Whatever made you give that up?' Thomas was highly impressed.

Jesus cut in swiftly. 'Judas felt that the exchange system was unfair and immoral,' he said. 'He decided instead to come and help me.' Then, with a broad smile, he added, 'I don't pay very well, but he seems content for the present.'

'What will he do for you?' Thomas looked doubtful.

Jesus summarised the conversation of the previous evening, outlining the difficulties he faced in his ministry. He pointed out that he would need help to bring the people out to him in the countryside, if and when the authorities were hostile or unhelpful. He might need help to control excited crowds, especially if healings were involved. Finally, he hoped that his friends would learn the message and eventually be able to do some preaching themselves. At least they should be able to prepare the way for him to come later on. Thomas still looked doubtful.

'I had hoped that you might like to join us too, Thomas,' said the carpenter, softly. 'What do you think?'

'Really? Why on earth would you choose me?' Thomas looked even more dubious. 'What can I bring to the party?'

'Just bring yourself, Thomas – your honesty, your straight-forwardness, your experience of life. You've not had an easy life. There have been difficulties and disappointments – you told me something about them when we met last. You will, I feel sure, be understanding when people come and want to tell us about their troubles.'

Jesus paused and looked at Thomas fully in the face.

'I want you to come,' he said.

There was another longish pause.

'I'll have to talk to Rachel, of course,' Thomas said, eventually. 'It would mean being away from her for quite a bit of the time, I guess. Fortunately, with no children to feed or clothe, we can afford it; we don't live extravagantly anyway. I'll think it over and let you know… will tomorrow do?'

'Yes, of course,' responded Jesus. 'We're going north to Gischala now; we'll call in on you on our way back. It might take a day or two – we don't quite know.'

'Fair enough,' responded the basket maker. 'Look, you might as well have your lunch here and a rest until the worst of the heat has passed. Then you can walk on the six or so miles to Gischala. You'll make it in good time for supper with your friends there.'

'They don't know we're coming,' smiled Jesus, 'but we'll take a chance on their kindness. Thank you for the offer of lunch. We can talk more over our meal, if you wish.'

A couple of hours after their meal, Judas and his new boss set out for Gischala. The sun was still very hot, but the worst of the blistering heat had passed and, provided the two men stepped out at a reasonable pace without pushing themselves, the walk wasn't too exhausting. The terrain wasn't easy, though. They took a track that followed the course of a small river, tumbling down from quite high hills through a little valley. Near the water, there were plenty of grasses and shrubbery growing. The two men kept a wary eye out for snakes, which tend to inhabit the damp ground near rivers. Open sandals were not much protection, should one be faced with a poisonous snake!

'Do you think Thomas will want to join us?' asked Judas.

Jesus jerked his head up in a gesture of uncertainty.

'I don't know,' he said. 'He's basically a close character, though once he decides to trust somebody, he can open up. It's difficult to tell – we've only met the once, but he did confide in me before we had finished.'

'I get the feeling he won't risk it. He's a bit older and might be set in his ways, don't you think?'

'We shall see,' replied Jesus. 'I get the feeling that, if Thomas did give his mind to something, he'd give it all he's got. He's a tough fellow, that one, if I'm any judge of character.'

'And you are!' Judas was sure of that.

They walked on for several minutes, clambering up a particularly steep gradient. There was no shade, so they were glad of their headdresses. They paused at the top of the little hill and surveyed the scenery.

'It's beautiful, isn't it – in a rugged kind of way,' said Judas. 'More beautiful than the area round Gaza, anyway, which is not much better than desert.'

'As we get higher, there will be more trees and therefore more shade,' replied the carpenter. 'It'll be easier going.'

They walked on in silence. Judas was wondering how to raise the Zealot question again. Eventually, he said, 'Are we in any danger in these parts? You said that there were Zealots here, already engaging in guerrilla warfare.'

'We're all right, I think,' said his companion. 'The Zealots aren't going to antagonise poor Jews – they want our support. No, they only attack richer people and especially traders, the rich camel trains that come down from Damascus and beyond, making for Caesarea and ultimately Jerusalem and other towns in the south. People like that keep to the main roads – they don't use little tracks like these.'

'What did the folk at Gischala think of your message when you visited last time? Did you tell them that fighting wasn't on the agenda?'

'Yes, I did,' said Jesus, 'and they weren't very impressed, I'm afraid. I'm going to have to work hard to convince people round here to give up their traditional antagonism towards the authorities. They would fight whoever it was in power, I think, just to keep up tradition! It wouldn't matter who was in charge – he could be Jew or Gentile – they'd still fight him! Mind you, Rome is a rather obvious and juicy target.'

'And you still don't think you ought to harness that fighting tradition for God?'

Jesus snorted. 'I'll give you full marks for persistence, Judas. No, I don't think so. I am not interested in fighting. It isn't God's way, I'm sure. But it'll be interesting to see if anyone else from round here thinks I should try to lead an armed uprising. We shall see!'

Before long they came to the top of a rise and found that the track joined a good Roman road.

'At least the Romans have made travelling easier!' joked Jesus. 'How good they are to us!'

Judas merely grunted and they walked along in silence the rest of the way to the town, which was a little to the west of the river. Jesus very soon recalled the way to Simon's home and knocked on his door.

'Why, it's Jesus,' exclaimed the blacksmith, pleased. 'You're here again so soon.'

'I told you I would return, didn't I? You said you would think over what I said and I've come to find out what you have concluded. But first, let me introduce a new friend – Judas Iscariot. He's from Gaza, in the far south.'

Simon and Judas shook hands. They sized each other up, each wondering what the other would be like, being from such different backgrounds. Judas could not fail to notice immediately the ugly scar on the side of the blacksmith's face, and it made him wonder what it signified. Simon saw the dark skin and hooked nose of the southerner and pursed his lips. He had never been south and didn't trust strangers readily. But soon Simon remembered his manners.

'I guess you two will be hungry and need hospitality,' he said.

Jesus smiled broadly and nodded. 'If you could oblige us, we'd certainly be delighted,' he replied. 'We've had a longish walk today – not too long, but far enough at this time of year – and your hills don't help!'

'Come along, then, and wash before supper. It isn't very grand, but it'll keep body and soul together!'

After the three men had had their supper, Jesus decided that the time had come to press his question.

'Now, Simon, have you thought any more about what I said? Isn't it time to give up fighting and think about a more kindly, useful life?'

Simon pursed his lips, put his hands together almost as if he was praying and took his time replying.

'James, Thaddeus and I have talked a lot about what you said,' he began. 'You know that we were already wondering about whether and how far we should throw in our lot with the Zealots. You have to realise that this is a town which, for generations, has supported them. Resistance is endemic – it's a part of our tradition round here.'

Simon's voice dropped to a low growl.

'For nearly a hundred years now, the Romans have dominated Israel. They have appointed their puppet rulers – the Herods – but they are the real rulers. How can we feel we are Jews when we are really only pawns in their much larger game?'

Simon paused and fingered the jagged scar on the side of his face nervously. It was a reflex action, which he did any time he was puzzled or on the spot. Jesus gently asked how he got such a dreadful wound.

'It goes back to a day I hate remembering,' replied his host. He paused for several seconds before recalling the story.

'My father must have been in with the Zealots. I became conscious of something unusual going on when was I about eight years old, I think. At that age, it's all a bit vague, of course, but I remember sensing that my father was up to something a bit strange. He would be away for a week or two, quite often. I didn't know where he was, or what he was doing; I just knew that Mother didn't say anything about it to anyone outside the family and seemed frightened until he came back.

'Anyway, one time he returned home all right, but the night afterwards we were raided by a detachment of Antipas' troops. They burst in after dark – I was already in bed – and seized Father. I heard a violent struggle going on. I leapt out of bed to see what the noise was and I saw Mother fling herself at the soldiers escorting my Father away. They turned on her and threw her on the floor and brutalised her. Every time they groped at her, she fought back, and, every time, they beat her. Finally, she was senseless and they had their way with her – I didn't understand what they were doing at the time, but I know now.'

Simon paused, swallowing hard to control his emotions. Slowly he continued.

'I couldn't bear to see her hurt, so I ran over to try to save her. They horsewhipped me for my pains. The whip ripped open my face from just below my eye to the jaw line, as you can see. I was lucky, I suppose, not to lose my sight. I've carried that scar ever since. It reminds me of why I hate the government – as if I need reminding.'

'That must be a terrible memory for you to carry through life, Simon,' said Jesus sympathetically.

There was a pause, and then Jesus asked gently, 'What happened after that?'

Simon looked down at his fingers, which he twisted nervously as he replied in a low voice. He was close to tears.

'My mother died as a result of her injuries. I never saw my father again. I was looked after by an uncle and aunt, who were childless, and I followed his trade and became a blacksmith. They both died a year or so ago and I inherited his business. The townspeople rallied round and were sympathetic throughout, especially when I was young. The neighbours here are always helpful when anyone is bullied by the government.'

'You and Judas here have a great deal in common, then,' said the carpenter. 'You're both orphans, brought up in the extended family.'

'So the sympathy of the whole town is Zealot, is it?' Judas chanced a question.

'Very much so, though to varying degrees. Of course, not everybody in the town is involved in actually taking up arms, but there is sympathy for the guerrillas – they are supplied, supported and protected. Sometimes support is forced, where it is not given willingly. You've probably guessed that, as a blacksmith, I am rather useful to the Zealots as a supplier of weapons, if nothing else. James is young, but he'll be in the same position before long, as my helper here. Thaddeus and his father are bakers. Zealots need their bread supplies. If we don't cooperate willingly, we are pressured into helping. What can we do, in the circumstances? If we refuse to cooperate, there may be more than just social pressure on us – we might end up with our throats cut. What would you do in our place?'

'I've already told you what I think, but it's for you to decide what you must do, Simon,' replied Jesus. 'Only you can do that. I realise the dangers, even more so after hearing of your experiences, and it must be difficult to go against all you have grown up with. But if you do decide to renounce violence, you'd better come south with me, out of the way. Why not throw your lot in with us entirely? What do you think?'

The blacksmith shook his head.

'I don't know. I really don't know.' He looked down at his lap again, his fingers still working nervously.

'What about your two friends? Would they be interested in breaking out from this circle of violence by coming with us?'

Simon shrugged his shoulders wearily.

'You'd better ask them. I think they'll be as unsure as I am – but why not ask?'

The five men met early next morning, before the blacksmiths got to work, and Jesus again set out his invitation to them all. As Simon had predicted, James and Thaddeus were ambivalent. None of them would commit themselves. There were too many factors to take into account.

'Well, I'll tell you what I'm going to do,' said Jesus finally. 'I'm going to go back to Capernaum and I'll continue to hope that some, or all, of you will come to meet me there in a week's time. Ask for the house of Simon the fisherman. We'll be there. You can then meet the rest of the fellows who have thrown in their lot with me.'

Jesus took each of them by the hand and looked them full in the face.

'I want you to come with me and find a new life,' he concluded. 'Don't fail me!'

Jesus and Judas set out immediately to walk back to Urta. It was easier walking downhill, even if it was more tricky on the ankles. However, they made good progress and reached their objective before lunch and went straight to Thomas's house. There he was, as before, sitting in front of the building, weaving his baskets. He looked up as they approached, put aside the half-finished work and rose to greet them.

'Hallo again,' he said. 'Have you made good progress?'

'We saw the fellows I wanted to see,' replied Jesus.

'And did you get the response you wanted?' Thomas was evidently curious.

'They are, like you, thinking things over. They have some special problems of their own, which they have to sort out.'

'Political problems, no doubt.' Thomas grinned. 'Don't tell me – it's better not to know. They're all rebels in that neck of the woods!'

'And you?' asked Jesus. 'Have you decided yet?'

There was lengthy pause before Thomas replied.

'It's difficult. I'd like to come, very much, but…'

'But what?' asked Jesus softly.

'It's Rachel,' said Thomas, sadly.

'Is she so totally opposed to you coming with us?'

'No – it's not that. It's just that I don't like the thought of her being left alone.'

'That does you credit, Thomas,' Jesus answered. 'It's thoughtful of you to think like that. I'll tell you what I'll do. I'll make the same arrangement with you as I have with the others. We're on our way back to Capernaum. If you want to throw your lot in with us, meet us there in a week's time – at the home of Simon the fisherman. Everyone knows Simon; you'll have no trouble in finding the house. We'll hope to see you there, then.'

★

After a brief lunch, Judas and Jesus made their way south to Bethsaida, where Jesus went to Levi's house. Judas was surprised at its opulence – and contrasted it with the humble houses they had just left.

'Oh, yes! We shall get a good meal here!' Jesus smiled. 'Levi – or sometimes he's called Matthew – keeps a good kitchen! He's very hospitable – you'll like him. Don't let the fact that he used to be a tax gatherer worry you. He's given up that dubious trade!'

'What is he doing now, then?' Judas sounded doubtful.

'I don't know – but I'm sure we'll soon find out,' replied Jesus. By now he was knocking at the door.

Joanna came to the door and let them in. Jesus saw at once that she wasn't best pleased to see them. Matthew, on the other hand, seemed delighted.

'Come in, Jesus,' he said, beaming. 'How good to see you again. How's it going?'

'Very well,' replied the preacher. 'I'd like you to meet my newest friend, Judas – Judas Iscariot. He's from Gaza.'

They walked through on to the terrace and sat in the shade. Joanna followed them with drinks and then left, scowling.

'You're a long way from home, then, Judas,' said Matthew. 'What brings you so far north?'

'Jesus,' replied Judas, simply. 'I met Jesus when he was in Jerusalem for Pentecost – that's where I was working. I listened to him speaking in the Temple, and – well – that was it. I decided to give up my rather disreputable trade and enlisted in Jesus's cause.'

Jesus smiled at them both. 'You've got a profession in common – you are both accountants. Judas worked for the Temple in the changing house; Matthew worked for Antipas, collecting taxes at the port.'

'We've got something else in common, too,' Matthew broke in. 'We've both given up rotten jobs because of you, Jesus!'

'What are you doing now?' asked Jesus.

'Not a lot,' replied his host. 'Few want to give me work. My former colleagues shun me. Honest traders still don't trust me and I don't want to work with those who are dishonest, so I'm living on what's left of my ill-gotten gains at present. We're going to have to economise. I was determined to pay back money to all those I could remember I had defrauded. That cost quite a bit, I can tell you! But it did me good. The trouble is that, with nothing much coming in and a lot going out, it's quite clear that I shall have to give up this house and the servants – and Joanna thinks I'm crazy. She's livid with me for her "loss of lifestyle", as she puts it.'

'I can well understand that,' said Jesus, 'but doing the right thing is sometimes very costly. Didn't she realise how unhappy you were, living as you were?'

'She doesn't want to see, but she's going to have reconcile herself to the position, because I've decided, and there's no going back.'

Jesus nodded and leaned forward over the table towards Matthew.

'I'm getting together a group of fellows who will come round Galilee with me, spreading the message,' said Jesus. 'There are the fishermen; you've met Simon and there's his brother, Andrew, and their partners, James and John, all from Capernaum. Then there's Judas here, and I've asked some men I know in Gischala and Urta. Then there are two others here in Bethsaida that I hope to see shortly. But, lastly, there's you – if you'll come.'

'You want me?' Matthew could hardly contain his surprise. 'But I can't preach!'

'I know,' smiled Jesus, 'but you have made an important discovery in life that you can share with others – one to one, to begin with. There will be others who may want to start afresh in life; you can help them do that.'

'Well – I don't know what to say.' Matthew screwed his face up in puzzlement. 'Who would have believed it?'

'Will you come and join the group?' pressed Jesus. 'We shall have to live rough quite a bit of the time. I'm being banned from preaching in some of the towns because I am at odds with the local religious authorities, so I am going to go out into the countryside, and I shall need folk like you to bring the people out to me. There will be some need for what you might call 'crowd control' – which'll need some organisation. Above all, I hope to give the group some special training and teaching in the message, so that, in time, they can go out themselves. Will you come and help?'

Matthew hardly hesitated. 'You know that I'm for you, whatever you want,' he said with conviction. 'Yes. I'll come with you anytime, anywhere. When do we start?'

'That's splendid,' replied Jesus. 'I'd like you to meet me in Capernaum at Simon's house, in a week's time. Then you can meet the rest of the group and we can get going.'

★

After a splendid breakfast next morning, Jesus led Judas across Bethsaida to Philip's pottery. The Greek was busy as usual at his wheel and this time the potter had recovered his touch; the pot appeared from the lump of clay like magic as his clever, nimble fingers gently massaged it. Judas and Jesus stood watching for a few moments until he finished moulding and placed it carefully in the row of pots already made that morning, ready for firing.

'Hello, there, Philip!' Jesus, as usual, held his hand out in greeting as soon as the potter started to rise from his wheel. 'Things are going better this time, I see!'

'Just a bit! Just as well, too, or I'd never sell anything.'

'Let me introduce you to my friend, Judas.'

Greetings over, Philip took the two travellers through the little house and into the rear courtyard. There they sat under the shade of a fig tree, sipping beer. Eventually, pleasantries over, Jesus launched into business. He explained the situation as he had to the others. When he finished, he shot a direct look at the potter and asked simply, 'Would you be interested to join us in this enterprise, Philip?'

The potter responded with a sharp intake of breath. 'You mean you want me to come with you?' he asked, incredulously. 'But I'm a potter – not a preacher!'

'You are someone who has knowledge of Greek and Greek ways and culture. That could be useful to us. You are also someone who has found a new faith in Judaism – you weren't born to it – you went and found it for yourself. That too is something which is quite rare, and is an experience which could be important.' Jesus held Philip's eyes. 'What do you think?'

'It's a bit of a shock,' said the other. 'Actually, it was my father who changed his faith, really, not me. I just followed, hardly knowing at that age what I was doing. I'm not sure that I can fulfil all your hopes for me...'

'I understand about your father,' returned Jesus. 'Certainly, it is true that it was his initiative, but you did follow and continue in the faith when you were older and able to judge for yourself. You've continued to learn from Nathaniel – which is good. By the way, I shall be making the same offer to Nathaniel later. Do you think he will respond favourably?'

Philip opened his eyes wide and lifted his hands, palms upward. 'Who knows? Let's go and ask him.'

They did so. Within a short while, Jesus was at Nathaniel's home, where he was again received very warmly. He put the same challenge to the older man and eventually it was left, as in the case of the others, that if either or both of them were prepared to join the group, they too should come to Capernaum in six days' time.

The invitations had been issued. All that was needed now was to obtain the necessary response!

★

Judas had difficulty in waiting the six days. He was so curious to know which of the seven candidates would accept the challenge to work with Jesus full-time. The six who were already committed – Jesus, Simon, Andrew, James, John and Judas – spent a good deal of time together, discussing the best possible route for a preaching tour within Galilee and all the arrangements that would be necessary for it. It was understood, of course, that Jesus would make the final decisions.

The meeting day arrived and the six were sitting quietly on the terrace, resting in the shade, waiting for Ruth to finish preparing the midday meal. There came a knock at the door and every eye turned to see who would be there. It was Matthew, who had been so keen to join the group. He came in somewhat warily, unused to the rather humble house, but he was soon put at ease in his new surroundings. Jesus greeted him very warmly as usual, introduced him to the circle of friends and explained that he would be saying nothing very important until everyone had assembled. He had every hope that there would be more coming before long. Indeed, they had hardly reseated themselves when there was another knock on the door, this time heralding the arrival of Philip and Nathaniel. More introductions – and a further waiting period. Eventually, they took lunch, as nobody else seemed destined to show up with a midday meal in mind.

The group waited all the afternoon, enjoying the unaccustomed leisure, but frustrated and impatient at the uncertainty. At last, as the sun was moving towards the horizon, there was a further knock on the door, and Thomas was welcomed. Jesus again made the introductions, and Simon made sure that Thomas was offered the opportunity to wash and take refreshment. Jesus managed to get a quiet word with him to find out what arrangements he had made for his wife.

This time, Thomas seemed more content with the situation, saying, 'In the end, she decided to go to live with her sister-in-law and help her through the period of her confinement. It'll be a big squash, with all of them in that little house, but she thought it was better than being on her own. And Rebecca will appreciate the help. No doubt it will work out well in the end.'

Jesus nodded, pleased. 'That's good. I'm so pleased that you found an answer that you can both live comfortably with,' he said.

'I'm sorry I arrived so late,' said Thomas, 'but I wanted to spend most of the day with Rachel.'

'Of course. That's quite right.' Jesus understood.

Nobody else arrived before sundown. Jesus seemed disappointed about that. He had evidently hoped that all his chosen men would respond. They sat down to supper, glad to have as many in the group as they had, but still wishing that they had had the full complement. When supper was over, Jesus called for silence and rather more formally welcomed all of them to the group.

'I have been very interested to see who would respond to God's call,' he began. 'You have all made sacrifices to be here, and you will have to make more. Thank you for that. Each of you, in different ways, has indicated that you didn't think you could be of service – that you weren't worthy. That's good. God doesn't want the kind of person who thinks he knows it all. Such arrogance is not in the character of the person he wants. Nevertheless, I have chosen you because each of you can bring different important gifts to the group.'

Looking around at the fishermen, with a smile, he continued.

'Some of you bring physical strength, which might be necessary in controlling excited and overwrought people. All of you bring strength of purpose and character, of different kinds. Some of you have had great disappointments in your own lives, which will make it easier for you to sympathise with others who will come to you, disappointed and even in despair. Philip brings a Greek dimension; Nathaniel brings great knowledge of the Jewish scriptures and culture; Judas has worked in the Temple precinct and can inform us of some of the detailed happenings there; Matthew and Judas are educated and read fluently and can figure things out – we shall need one of them to look after our small treasure. So, you see, all of you can make a contribution and I thank you all for being here.'

Jesus paused and looked round at his little flock. He smiled again.

'Don't be afraid or nervous. We shall have many trials and tribulations. There will be times when you will wonder why you began this enterprise with me and you will wish you were at home, or out fishing, or making your baskets or pots, but I assure you that, if you hold fast, in the end it will all be worthwhile. It is true that we shall have to make an effort for God – and that effort may well be immense – but I know that God is with us and will give us the Kingdom. Yes, that's right. In the final analysis, we don't earn the Kingdom by making a big effort. It is God's gift to us.'[4]

Jesus then invited the group to pray. He led their thoughts so gently and smoothly into God's presence, making it seem so natural that they should seek to commune with the Almighty. He always used the term 'Father' for God – God seemed so near. They felt uplifted and confident in him.

They were on the point of retiring for rest when there was a further hammering at the door. Puzzled at being disturbed so late, Simon went rather warily to the door to find three men who were strangers to him. Jesus, just behind Simon, recognised the three he had been hoping to see all day – the blacksmith, his assistant and Thaddeus.

'Now we are all here,' said Jesus happily. 'Finally, we have all the leaders of the twelve tribes!'[5]

The whole group sat round on the terrace. Suddenly nobody was ready for bed. They just had to know the reason for the delay in the arrival of the last three members. Introductions had been made all round, and the potential misunderstandings, with the duplication of names, had been noted and sorted out.

Jesus turned to Simon, the fisherman.

'I think I shall call you Peter,' he said. 'Peter means "a rock" or "a stone". You are going to be an important stone in the new Temple we shall build, a Temple that will be at the centre of the Kingdom that is coming.'

Simon Peter looked puzzled and a little alarmed.

'Don't worry,' said Jesus with a smile. 'You can do it!'

Then, turning to Simon the blacksmith, he said, 'You will continue to be Simon the Zealot – but your zeal will be for the new Kingdom, not for the political aspirations of your friends in the north!'

Simon bowed his head.

'And I think we had better call you "little James",' said Jesus to the blacksmith's assistant, 'because you're much shorter than the other James,' referring to the fisherman, who was quite four inches taller and much broader too.

Thaddeus suddenly made an unexpected contribution. 'Actually, the problem of names might have been worse,' he said. 'My second name is Judas – or Jude. If I used that name, there would be the problem of the two Judases to sort out!'

'It's bad enough as it is,' said Jesus, grinning. 'Evidently I didn't chose you people on the basis of ease of nomenclature! But, come on, we're all bursting to know why you chose to keep us waiting till bedtime before arriving and putting us out of our misery. We've had our little inaugural meeting without you! We had given you up for lost!'

Inevitably, it was the older blacksmith who had to begin the story. His face was very serious.

'We've been in two minds all the week – ever since you left, Jesus. The discussion has gone on every night. At first, we almost decided to come here, then later we wavered and almost decided to stay at Gischala. By this morning, we had still not come to any real conclusion and it looked to me as if we would stay there for no better reason than we couldn't make a decision.'

'It was the easy way out,' chimed in Thaddeus. 'When you don't know what to do, don't do anything!'

'Then, at lunch time, something dreadful happened,' continued Simon in a low voice. 'A detachment of Roman soldiers entered our town, bringing about a dozen bodies and eleven prisoners with them.'

'Zealots?' asked his namesake.

'Yes. It appears that, a couple of weeks ago, the Zealots had mounted an ambush and captured a large amount of valuable material from a caravan coming from the north. So Antipas had appealed to Pilate for help in dealing with the problem, and a cohort of legionaries had been dispatched north from Caesarea. They had hunted down the band of Zealots and – well – the result you know.'

Little James took up the story. 'They crucified all the prisoners – in the square and down the main street of the town. They were merciless – they strung those poor fellows up and left them to die in the sun. They said it was a warning to all of us not to get involved in treasonous behaviour.'

As he broke off, Thaddeus continued.

'As we looked at those dead bodies – terribly mutilated, they were – and saw the crucified men hanging there, we knew that we didn't want to be a part of all that. It can seem quite – well, exciting – to be a Zealot when you're in the comfort of your home, when you don't actually have to engage in battle. But when you see what can actually happen…'

'It's different.' Simon finished the sentence for him. 'I didn't want anything to do with that kind of thing. I felt guilty that I'd even provided the weapons – or some of them.'

'So we decided to come with you, Jesus.' It was little James who finished the account. There was a long pause.

'You've had a terrifying experience,' said Jesus, slowly. 'The sight of death is never pleasant, but violent death must be a hundred times worse.'

Here he paused and looked round soberly at the group gathered in front of him.

'But do not imagine, any of you, that the work we have to do will be free of danger. We do not seek confrontation, but I'm afraid that our message may well be misread, or deliberately misinterpreted, as a threat to the existing order. This may mean that we too become the target for the authorities.'

It was Simon Peter who spoke up next.

'Nobody could possibly want to hurt you, Jesus,' he said. 'You always make it clear that you're against bloodshed.'

'Peter, I know what I believe and what I proclaim, but I have to warn you all that things could go wrong for us. We must go into our work with our eyes wide open. Look at what has happened to John the baptiser. Who did he hurt? But he's in Antipas' prison, by all accounts, and no one knows when he will be let out – if ever.'

Turning to the three men from Gischala, Jesus spoke very firmly to them.

'If you came here because you were afraid, then, sadly, I must say to you that you had better return home again. This mission is not for the faint of heart. It, too, has its dangers.'

'No, Jesus. It wasn't fear,' Simon burst out. 'It was the thought of engaging in a bloodbath – of killing others.'

'I hadn't really taken on board fully the implications of a Zealot's life, till I saw the bodies,' added Thaddeus.

'I understand,' replied Jesus, more softly. 'I'm content, so long as it's clear in your minds what is involved here. Welcome. I shall brief you more fully in the morning, when we've all rested.'

So, at last, they all went to their sleep.

NOTES

[1] Mark 4:3.
[2] Mark 3:3.
[3] Matt. 10:10.
[4] Luke 12:32.
[5] Mark 3:16.

Magdala

The next day, Jesus held a further meeting with all his new followers, particularly bringing the latecomers up to date. He asked them to get used to the idea of working in pairs; obviously, the two sets of brothers would pair off, and Philip and Nathaniel were already old friends. Similarly, it seemed right to suggest that the two blacksmiths, Simon and little James, continued to work together, which left Thomas, Matthew, Judas and Thaddeus. Jesus felt that the two older men might like to work together, which left Judas, the only disciple from the south, working alongside Thaddeus, the young baker from the north. These four agreed to try and see how this worked out. Jesus was pleased; he had natural pairings in many cases, and he had all the younger men, John, little James, Thaddeus and Philip supported by more experienced fellows.

Jesus further suggested that Judas should be appointed treasurer for the group. Each of them put into the common purse such money as they could contribute; everyone had brought something, but the total seemed woefully inadequate for several months of activity.

'Don't worry,' said Jesus. 'You'll be surprised at what God can do with a small amount. As I told you, people along the way will be very generous, especially if we have helped them with their problems. All of you have been generous to me in the past – now you will see how others can treat you similarly.'

By mid-morning, the little band had set out on their first mission. Jesus had decided to move south-west, round the lake, to Magdala, a distance of about five miles. With July almost starting, the sun was very hot and five miles' walk would be quite enough!

Jesus asked Simon Peter and Andrew to lead the way. They were closely followed by their fishermen friends, James and John, while the other pairs tagged along behind. Jesus deliberately split his time between the pairs, talking to each in turn and answering their questions. Jesus explained that he intended to ask the rabbi in Magdala for permission to speak at the Synagogue that night. However, he wasn't sure if Hezekiah, the rabbi at Capernaum, knew the rabbi at Magdala, and if news of the situation they had created in Capernaum had already reached Magdala.

As they reached a small village along the way, it became obvious that some news, at least, had travelled ahead of them. They were walking up to the well in the centre of the village hoping to get a drink, when they were approached by a local dignitary who enquired who they were. On hearing that Jesus was the preacher at the head of the party, the man immediately asked if Jesus would stay for a few minutes and say a few words, once he had gathered together some of the people. This seemed a good opportunity, so the little party sat by the well under some olive trees and refreshed themselves while the locals were summoned.

But it soon became clear why Jesus was being made so welcome. The villagers brought out two people who were infirm – a lame woman and a man, somewhat paralysed in one arm. The preacher realised that, once again, he was faced with the dilemma of whether to heal or preach, and he felt certain that nobody would take in what he had to say if he began with the healing. So he arranged, gently, with the people bringing those who were ill, to keep them to one side until after he had finished his address.

'Then I promise I will speak to both the handicapped people separately,' he assured them.

When the little crowd had assembled, he started to speak. He took as his theme the subject he had so often talked about elsewhere – the coming Kingdom of heaven. Again he introduced them to the idea of an inner Kingdom, one that was non-political, a relationship in the heart between the individual and God, and between individuals and each other.

'The Kingdom exists anywhere where God rules – where God is in charge', he said. 'If you allow God to rule in your life, then the Kingdom is already present and active there.'

But, as had happened elsewhere, there was some confusion in people's minds – they were looking for political freedom. Jesus was asked when the Roman subjugation of their land would end and as usual, he stressed that, though he was sure that it would end at some point, he didn't know the precise date.

'Meantime,' he said, 'you must prepare yourselves by cultivating this inner self. The Kingdom of heaven is a bit like a mustard seed'.[1] Mustard is one of the smallest of all seeds, isn't it? But we all know that when it germinates and grows, it can become, in time, not just a small bush but a real tree, big enough for birds to come and nest in its branches. In the same way, this idea of an inner Kingdom may be just an idea – a simple notion – insignificant, you may say. But I tell you that if you take hold of this idea and live by it, it will grow into a transforming experience in your life. Indeed, it will become the biggest element in your existence – and it will eventually shelter within it others who need your protection and care.'

The listeners were quite attentive while Jesus was speaking and there was an encouraging buzz of comment and chatter when he had finished. But the crowd did not disperse. Evidently, they knew that Jesus had been asked to heal some of their neighbours and their curiosity had got the better of them – they just had to stay to see what would happen.

Jesus first approached the man who was partially paralysed. He began by talking to the relations who had brought him, commending their trust in him. As in the earlier cases, he was able to give the man the confidence to try moving his arm and, as before, the man found that he could do far more than he previously thought. He left the little square swinging his arm and gripping and re-gripping his hand in delight. Similarly, Jesus spoke quietly to the lame woman, encouraging her to believe that she could move her left leg more fluently, urging her to forget the years of limping, and step out with assurance. Once again, the cure was effected; the woman left the square walking unaided and with scarcely a limp.

Eventually, Jesus and his party managed to get away from the village and set out for Magdala again. Some of Jesus's new friends, who had not seen his miraculous healing skills in action, were anxious to discuss these tremendous events with their partners. They pressed Jesus for explanations when he walked with them, but he smiled and said that they, too, would heal one day, if they followed his way.[2]

'It's a matter of prayer and believing,' he said. 'God provides the power. All I or you can do is provide the channel for the healing. Of course, not everyone can be healed; after all, we all have to die at some point. Also, there are some conditions which are better dealt with by conventional practice – the local doctor knows well enough how to bind up a broken bone, for example. But there are other conditions that I – and you – can heal, with God's grace. We have to be sufficiently in tune with the will of God, so that we know when our intervention as healers is appropriate.'

They had gone scarcely a mile down the road when they were suddenly faced with a ragged man who jumped out at them from behind a large clump of bushes. Simon Peter, in the lead, drew back sharply, as he saw that the man was covered in skin sores, which affected his face and both arms.[3]

'He's leprous!' cried Peter, frightened. 'Stand back.'

Jesus came up from the rear, where he had been speaking to Judas and Thaddeus.

'What's the matter?' he demanded, then broke off as he saw the man standing in the road, barring their way.

'You are Jesus?' asked the man.

'I am,' replied the preacher, going up to him. 'You are looking for me?'

The man immediately flung himself at Jesus's feet.

'Yes, Rabbi,' he said. 'I have heard that you have the power to cure illnesses. If you want to, you could cure me of my leprosy. Please – do you think …?'

Jesus broke in, stifling the man's request and taking his hands. 'If I *want to*?' he asked, incredulously. 'Why on earth should I not want to? I hate to see people suffering unnecessarily. God wants you to be whole again.'

He looked critically at the man's hands and arms, then at his face. Finally, he said in a commanding voice, 'I tell you, you can be cured. Be clean from your disease…'

Jesus stared deep into the eyes of the sufferer, who at first drew back, but then returned his look. It was as if Jesus was pouring his power into him through this concentrated, searching gaze. They stayed in this way for several seconds, then Jesus drew the man's attention to his arm. He started in wonder as the skin seemed to begin to lose some of its inflamed colour.

'Go home and wash thoroughly,' said Jesus. 'Wash away those scabs and ensure that all the skin is clean. Gradually, your skin will return completely to normal. Then go and show yourself to the rabbi and he will certify that you are cured. Don't forget to offer thanks to God, not only with your lips but also with your life. But don't tell everyone how this came to be – just be thankful in your heart.'

'I will!' said the man, joyfully and excitedly jumping to his feet. He looked again at his arms, then felt his face. 'It's wonderful. Thank you, Rabbi – thank you.'

'Go in peace,' said Jesus, 'and remember, not a word to anyone as to how this happened.'

The man departed, almost skipping down the road in his excitement. The followers of Jesus gathered round him, again completely overwhelmed by what had happened. They tried to articulate their confusion and difficulty in believing what they had seen.

'You cured a leper!' blurted out Peter. 'I can't believe...'

'There are many skin diseases that are similar,' replied Jesus. 'With real trust between the healer and the sufferer, many cures are possible. You see, many of the causes of skin problems are in the mind and spirit, rather than the body. Reach out to the spirit and the mind, and the body will respond.'

At last they reached Magdala, and Jesus asked Nathaniel and Philip to go to find the local rabbi and seek his permission for the meeting. Soon they returned, saying that they had been well received and that he had agreed that Jesus could talk to the people in front of the Synagogue that evening.

'So far, so good,' said Jesus, smiling.

*

Mary was fed up. She was frequently fed up – fed up with her mother and the way she was treated; and fed up with life in a culture in which conventions were strict, not allowing a young woman any freedom worth talking about. At eighteen, she knew that she should be married, or, at least, engaged to be married, but she wasn't going to accept anyone chosen by her mother. What did her mother know about whom or what she wanted? But if she even looked at a fellow of her own choice, she was told off. If she ever managed to get a word or two with him, especially if it was on their own, it was considered to be a terrible crime. Life wasn't worth living like that. She flung herself on her bed and punched the cushions with frustration.

In the kitchen, her mother, Nimrah, was likewise seething. That daughter of hers would be the death of her... If only she had a father to discipline her, she might be better behaved, but Jeriah had been dead for eleven years now. She had grieved for him at the time, for she had loved him dearly; but now she regretted his passing even more, having this wilful and selfish daughter to deal with alone. Oh, Mary was pretty enough – quite a beauty, some said – but her temperament! She was impossible.

Mary had always been something of a problem, but the situation had deteriorated rapidly during her teenage years. She was one of those young people who insisted on her own way on every occasion. When she got her own way, she could be charming, even delightful, but if she was crossed… Then, she could, either literally or figuratively according to the situation, stamp her feet and make a real scene. How many times had Nimrah wished that the ground would open up and swallow her – or her daughter – when such a scene had occurred in public! But that wasn't all, for Mary had several times slipped away from the house, unseen, to meet young men of a lower class – farm labourers and the like. The thought was enough to make one's stomach turn! Nimrah just hoped that Mary's story that they were 'just talking' was true, but, with young people left to their own devices, one never knew. Unfortunately, rumours had got around the town, and this certainly did not improve Mary's chances of making a decent marriage.

As Mary had got older, Nimrah had made the usual enquiries concerning a suitable husband for her. Nimrah was a rich women by the standards of the locals. Jeriah had owned a good business processing olives and producing and selling high-class oil all over the area. He had also owned a similar business near Jerusalem, which required him to go frequently to Judaea. In fact, it had been on a journey home from that area that Jeriah had met his end. Unusually, he had decided to journey through Samaria, where he had been attacked and robbed, and had died from his wounds three days later. Those Samaritans! The descendants of Israelites who had married out of the faith with foreigners! No wonder they were hated and despised. They had killed her Jeriah… damn them to hell! Well, he had left them well provided for. There would be a worthwhile dowry for Mary, but none of the suitable families wanted to be associated with a girl of Mary's reputation. None of the decent young men would take her on – with her fiery temperament and doubtful background.

Nimrah called her daughter for a meal. No doubt they would sit opposite one another across the table with nothing to say. There would be no smile, not a flicker of affection. Life had got to be like that.

Just then, her neighbour called in with some news. Apparently, the preacher from Capernaum, Jesus, originally from Nazareth, had come to town and would be speaking this evening, outside the Synagogue. Would she like to come and hear him? Well, Nimrah thought, it would be better than sitting at home, brooding. She'd suggest that Mary came too, but she'd keep a strict eye on her! It might even do her some good – but she doubted it! Mary had seven devils in her, more than any preacher could exorcise.[4]

Jesus stood up to address the assembled crowd, thanking them, and particularly the rabbi, for the opportunity to speak. He had good news, he told them and went on to outline his ideas on the new Kingdom. The speech followed the usual lines, now very familiar to some of his followers, those who had been with Jesus for several weeks. There was the usual mixed reaction from the people. Again, some were sceptical, wanting a more aggressive stance towards the existing order, but many seemed to consider that the notion of an inner regime to guide one's life might be worth thinking about.

Jesus went on to develop the thought a little further.

'Happy are those who are poor in spirit, for they will find the Kingdom of God,' he said.[5] 'Now, at first sight, you may think I've got that completely wrong. Surely, you may feel, it would be better if people were spiritually rich – rich in their knowledge of God, empowered with a vast knowledge of the scriptures, confident in their prayer-life. Yes, to be rich, spiritually, seems better, at first sight. But I say to you that it is those who know their need of God – who know they have nothing adequate that they can offer to God – who have the correct attitude. God's perfection and glory is such that we *cannot* have anything worthwhile to offer him. It is those who have grasped this fact that will be enabled to find the new Kingdom in their hearts. We need to recognise our own inadequacy before we can react fully to God's grace. Then we find, to our intense surprise, that God welcomes even our poorest attempts at pleasing and serving him. He knows our weaknesses and smiles at our poor response to his love, just as you, who are parents, are so pleased at any affection, however little, shown to you by your children.'

Nimrah, standing listening in the crowd with Mary beside her, stole a glance at her daughter. She feared that Mary had probably come to the meeting for the wrong reason, though, in truth, she had to admit that she herself had also come more out of boredom than anything else. She supposed that Mary had probably hoped to see one of her young men… but, in fact, she saw that Mary was intent on the preacher's words. Or was it his words? Was it not, perhaps, the man himself that had caught her attention? Her eyes were fixed on his face and all her body language indicated that she was really absorbed.

Jesus had finished his address. He asked them to think over all that he had said and invited them all to pray with him for guidance and grace. It was a simple prayer, heartfelt and sincere; it was quite unlike some of the Pharisees' prayers which went on and on, and which seemed to have little to do with real life and experience, merely repeating scriptural texts and becoming an excuse for a further sermon. Nimrah felt her own spirit lifting. She knew that she needed to talk to this man and find out more about him and his message.

As the crowd broke up, she made her way forward timidly and tried to catch the preacher's eye. One of his followers came over and asked her what she wanted. She said she wanted a word with Jesus, and the young man invited her to meet the preacher.

'What's the matter, John?' asked Jesus.

'A woman here wants a word with you.'

Nimrah, at first rather hesitantly, asked Jesus if he was staying in the town and if he would grace her table the following night. Jesus responded warmly, thanking her sincerely and accepting the invitation.

'I'd like to invite your followers too,' said Nimrah, hastily.

'That's very kind,' replied Jesus, 'but I think it might be rather overwhelming for your household if I brought my entire party. I will bring a few, if I may – say, three? The rest, I'm sure, will be looked after very well elsewhere.'

And so it was agreed. When Mary found out what her mother had arranged, she was, for once, obviously pleased. Well, that was progress!

★

Judas and Thaddeus had been shopping in Magdala. Although all the followers of Jesus had been invited out for the main meal of the day that evening, some in one house, some in another, they still needed a few provisions to keep them going till then. They had slept the previous night in a clearing just outside the town, and there they returned, full of the latest gossip from the town, to find Jesus preparing his mind for his next sermon.

'You remember that leper that you cured on the road?' Thaddeus began. 'Well, although you told him strictly to keep the matter quiet, apparently it's all over town. He must have blabbed it out to all and sundry – anyone who would listen.'

Jesus sighed and shook his head. He was always despondent when he felt that his mission might be compromised. 'I suppose it was inevitable,' he said, 'but it does make my work more difficult.'

'They were also talking about your healing work in that village we stopped at down the road,' Judas put in.

'But hardly a mention of the message, I'll be bound. Well, I'm due to speak again here tonight. We'll see what happens. I shan't be surprised if we are met by a queue of people requiring healing, but it really mustn't get in the way of spreading the good news. I shall want you all, very gently, to keep any handicapped people to the side until after I've finished preaching, and I'll attend to them later. Please try to explain gently, won't you, so that they understand?'

Simon Peter, Andrew and Thomas, who were also nearby, nodded and said they'd do their best. They had hardly finished speaking when the local rabbi, an elderly, grizzled man, appeared on the scene, asking to see Jesus. He indicated that he wanted a private word, so he and Jesus sauntered off up the hill to be alone.

'I've come to thank you for your work last night,' the rabbi began.

'I'm glad that you are pleased,' said Jesus, but he realised that the old rabbi wouldn't have come this far if that was all he had to say. There was clearly going to be something else – probably bad news!

'I gather that you have accepted an invitation to dine with Nimrah tonight?'

'That's right. She graciously invited all of us, but I thought that it was better to restrict the party to just four, so as not to overwhelm her hospitality. The rest of my companions are going to eat with others in your congregation who were equally generous.'

The rabbi pondered.

'Well, it's a little unusual to go to the home of a widow, but I suppose she might benefit from talking to you. Obviously, it is necessary for you to take someone with you.'

The rabbi was still hesitating. He pulled at his beard and looked down at his hands as he spoke.

'Look here, I think I should warn you that Nimrah's daughter, Mary, has attracted some notoriety in the town. She's a very beautiful girl, and several of the local ne'er-do-wells have obviously noticed! Unfortunately, there have, apparently, been occasions when she's been out alone with one or more of them and, not surprisingly, tongues have wagged. She seems to be quite a loose young woman; to put it bluntly, some round here have said that she's no better than a prostitute. She's hardly the sort of girl that you, as a preacher, should be associating with.'

'I see,' said Jesus, thoughtfully. 'What does Mary say about herself?'

'Of course, she says that there's nothing in it – she was just talking and laughing with the lads – but then, she would say that, wouldn't she?'

'What does Nimrah think?' Jesus asked.

'Frankly, she doesn't know what to think. She'd like to believe her daughter, but, knowing how young people are at that age—'

'Not just at that age!' the preacher cut in. 'Anyway, thank you for telling me.'

The old rabbi looked at Jesus, puzzled.

'But are you still going tonight?' he asked.

'Oh, yes. I must go. I've promised.'

'Well, it's up to you, of course, but I wouldn't care to risk my reputation in that house in the circumstances. It's a little unusual to accept an invitation from a widow, but that could perhaps be overlooked. It's that girl – why, she might well be able to get you on your own somehow, and then your own standing in this community would really be at risk. Don't say I didn't warn you.'

'I shall be with my followers at the meal and in no danger.' Jesus smiled broadly. 'After dinner, I'll be careful! But, you know, really I have to think of repairing Mary's reputation more than worrying about my own.'

'Be it on your own head then,' replied the rabbi, obviously offended. 'You younger men will never learn!'

So saying, he turned petulantly away and walked down the hill to the town.

That evening, as the sun was starting to go down and all work had ceased, Jesus walked into the town to address the assembled townsfolk again. Tongues had evidently been wagging furiously, mainly about the healings, but to some extent about his speech of the previous evening, so that there were easily double the number there had been the night before. However, as Jesus had predicted, a half-dozen sick people had been carried into the square in the hope that he would cure them. They lay there, helpless, almost hopeless, with a variety of complaints and problems. Simon Peter, Andrew, Thomas and Matthew had shepherded them to one side and explained that their leader would speak to them later. They looked doubtful, expecting, as usual, to be ignored. Their friends and relatives looked downcast and suspicious.

'It was just a story,' said one to his neighbour. 'He either can't heal, or he'll forget and not bother.'

Jesus stood up in front of the Synagogue and smiled round at the assembled crowd. As he did so, their chatter died away and silence fell.

'Tonight,' he said, 'I'd like to start by telling you a story.[6] We all like stories and I hope you'll like this one. It concerns a rich man, a landowner, who had two sons. The man was getting on a bit and needed to look to his sons for their support. The elder son had always worked hard for his father, supervising the work on the farms, making sure that the animals were well looked after and the crops were properly sown, tended and harvested. Thanks to him, the farms remained profitable and his father's reputation was maintained and enhanced. The younger son, on the other hand, was a bit of a rebel. He took no interest in farming. He did what he had to with rather bad grace, and, as soon as possible, most evenings, took himself off to the local town with his friends.

As soon as he became twenty-one, he confronted his father and said, 'Father, you know I'm no good at farming and I can't get interested in it. I'm really a bit in the way here – I'm much more at home in the town. Wouldn't it be better to divide your property now between us, your two sons, and let me take my portion and get on with life in my own way?'

Not surprisingly, the father wasn't very happy about this. He knew that his son might well misuse his inheritance, but because he strongly believed that children should learn to handle their own affairs, he reluctantly agreed. He apportioned all he had between the two boys. The elder son merely noted the new arrangement and continued to work the farms, but the younger one quickly sold up his share and took himself and the money off to a distant town. There, he spent his time in riotous living, drinking, gambling, whoring and generally having what he perceived to be a good time. He had a lot of friends who happily kept him company while he was prepared to fund their pleasures; but, of course, this could not last.

'After a few months, the money started to run out and his friends began to drift away. Ultimately, he found himself bereft of both money and company – nobody wanted to know him. He was left with nothing and nobody. In desperate need just to keep body and soul together, he got a job with a farmer, who sent him into the fields to mind the swine. At night, when he fed the animals, he was highly tempted to eat the meagre food provided for them, he was so hungry. Nobody would give him anything, for everyone was short of food, as a famine had struck that region at that time.

'After sticking this for several days and growing daily more hungry, the lad began to realise how stupid he had been. He was lying in the straw with the pigs at the end of the day, feeling sorry for himself, when he saw just how ridiculous the situation was.

'There are many employees working for my father and brother who are feeding much better than I am tonight! he thought. They are only hired hands and I am the son of a rich man – yet I lie here in this mouldy straw, hungry and dirty, while they have more than enough to eat and will sleep in clean sheets tonight. I must have been mad to allow myself to get into this mess...

'He turned over in his mind all he had done and then what he might do to improve his lot. There's nothing for it, he thought. I'll just have to go back to Dad and admit I've been an idiot. I'll ask him to take me back on to his staff. I'll ask if I can become one of the servants in the house. I'm sure – well, I hope – he'll give me a job...

'The next day, he resigned his job with the farmer and started to retrace his steps back to his father's land. His thoughts alternated between hope that he would be tolerated and fears that he might be thrown out into the street. But his father had always grieved over the loss of his son. The boy had been foolish, certainly, but he was still his son, and the old man wished with all his heart that he would return. Every day, he went to his rooftop and looked down the road that the boy had taken to the town, to see if, by any chance, he was returning. Imagine his joy when, at last, he saw his son in the distance. To begin with, he didn't recognise him, because he was so unkempt. His clothes were ripped, his sandals falling to pieces. His beard was straggling and matted with dirt. Was this really his son? Yes: as he watched the scarecrow get steadily nearer the house, he saw that it was indeed his young boy, and he ran down the stairs and out into the road to meet him, flinging out his arms in greeting.

'The boy drew back and insisted on kneeling at his feet. "Father," he said, very quietly, "I have wronged you. I have taken from you and wasted—"

'"Never mind that, now," interrupted his father, pulling him to his feet and hugging him. "You're back home now and that's all that matters. Come in. Come in and let's get you cleaned up a bit."

'So the father led the boy back into the house and insisted on him having a bath and dressing in fine clothes again.

'"Come down as soon as you can and get something to eat inside you," he said.

'Then he sent round a message to his neighbours, inviting them to come with their families to celebrate with them to mark his son's return. His servants prepared a superb meal and, within a couple of hours, there was quite a party going on, with wine flowing and people feasting, a little group playing music and some dancing, all in celebration of the return of the lost family member. The father kept saying to anyone who would listen, "This, my son, was dead, but now he is alive again!"

'Towards the end of the afternoon, the elder brother, who had been working away from the house in a more remote part of the farm, returned and heard music coming from the house. He called one of the servants over and asked what was going on and the man told him. The news made the elder son very angry.

'Dad never gave me a party with my friends, he thought to himself, not so much as a kid to share with them! Yet this wastrel comes home and immediately he gets the very best of everything.

'He was really upset and determined not to join the party, preferring to sulk in the privacy of his own room. Fortunately, the servant who had seen him arrive went to tell the father what had happened. The old man immediately left the party and went to his son's room. Straightaway, the surly man broke into angry recriminations. The father let him have his say, then he sat on the bed by him and said gently, "Listen, my boy, I understand how you feel. You have been with me and worked for me all these years. I really do appreciate all you have been and done. Everything I have now will belong to you some day. But that does not mean that, when your brother comes home from afar, we should not be glad to see him. I know he has done wrong. He knows it too. I'm sure, however, that he has learnt his lesson. This son of mine was dead – and he's alive again. He was lost and now he's found."'

Jesus looked round the crowd.

'That story gives you a picture – an illustration – of how God loves us,' he said. 'It doesn't matter how far we have strayed from him, how much we have disappointed him, when we turn to go back to him, he will come to meet us and receive us and forgive us.'

He smiled at his congregation. 'Yes, God will welcome you, whoever you are.'

Here Jesus's face changed and became more serious. 'But if you are one of those who have never strayed, if you are like the elder brother who worked hard for the father all his life, don't sulk when someone who's a bad lot makes good. Welcome him, or her, back into the family of God, just as God himself does.'

There was a long silence when Jesus finished speaking. He then offered a short prayer and blessing. But Jesus had not forgotten to attend to the sick people gathered on one side. Despite the best endeavours of the disciples, the crowd stayed to press in on Jesus, hoping to hear what he said and did, and see what happened. As before, Jesus was able to comfort and improve the lot of all the sick brought to him that night and the people departed, all buzzing with astonishment.

Jesus then made his way to Nimrah's house, accompanied by Simon Peter, Matthew and Nathaniel. He had deliberately chosen three older men, from different pairs, so that the others would be better informed of anything that might happen.

They were cordially welcomed by Nimrah's servant, who offered to wash their feet for them before the meal. They were then shown on to the terrace at the back of the house, where a table was beautifully laid ready for them. It was a lovely evening. The air was warm, though rather humid. The stars shone bravely and, as usual, the cicadas were making music, of a sort, in the trees. In the distance, a scops owl hooted and occasionally a tree frog added to the orchestra.

Nimrah soon appeared, followed by Mary. The older woman was still very attractive; she carried herself with quiet dignity, her entire bearing indicating a quiet self-confidence. Her face was hardly lined. Her full lips frequently widened, displaying beautiful white, even teeth in a flashing smile.

When the men saw the younger woman, however, they caught their breath, for she was indeed a beauty. Her long black hair hung down over her shoulders nearly to her waist; although it was straight, it was glossy, shining in the oil lights' glow. Her dark brown eyes glowed. She had inherited her mother's smile, pearly white and radiant. She too carried herself with poise and pride, with a perfect figure. One would have thought that her mother was bound to be really proud of her. But Mary's looks were not the only thing that caught the men's attention that night. The girl positively radiated charm and hospitality all the evening, listening attentively to the conversation and contributing a comment occasionally, when appropriate. There was no hint here of the selfish, surly, defiant girl of which Jesus had been told – and which he had warned his disciples about.

After the meal, when the women had left the table, leaving the men to sip wine and chat, a servant approached Jesus and asked him if he would spare Nimrah a moment alone. The preacher agreed, left the table and followed the servant into the house. He found Nimrah sitting alone, twisting her hands nervously together.

'Jesus, I have something very – awkward – to ask you,' she said, with her eyes dropped, not able to meet his.

'Don't worry,' replied Jesus. 'Just speak up. I shan't mind, whatever it is.'

'Well, it's – Mary,' replied Nimrah, managing now to look up at him. 'She particularly wants to talk to you. She doesn't want me present – or anyone else. I know it's hardly the thing for you to…'

'There's no problem,' smiled her guest. 'She and I can surely speak together without—'

'But you don't understand,' his hostess broke in. 'I'm afraid for you. Mary has been very foolish, and people have even said …'

'I know.' Jesus caught her hand and held it. 'I know all about Mary's reputation. Perhaps she will tell me the truth and be able, gradually, to lose her stigma. In any case, if she wants to talk, I think we had better let her. I suggest that I go a little way down the garden, where I saw a garden seat. I'll wait there for her and she can come to see me and say what she wants to. We'll be in full view of the terrace where the men are sitting – you can go there too, if you like – but Mary and I can talk without being overheard. How does that sound to you?'

Nimrah looked relieved. 'That sounds fine,' she said. 'Surely, nobody could …' She trailed off into silence.

'I'll walk down to the garden seat, then. You tell Mary I shall be there if she wants to see me.'

So it came about that Jesus and Mary had a long chat together, sitting in full view of the others so that there could be no breath of scandal, but at the same time giving them the opportunity to converse privately. Neither of them ever told anyone else what passed between them during that conversation. All anyone else knew was that Mary, from that time on, to a large degree, dropped her sullen ways and became much more manageable. It was as if the prodigal daughter had come home to become a loving child again. Everyone could see that Mary adored Jesus; her eyes would light up as soon as he appeared. But there was more to it than the usual 'crush' that a young woman often has for an older man. She seemed to have caught hold of his essential characteristic – that ability to see things from the other person's point of view, to put herself in their place and treat them accordingly. She seemed now to understand how her mother felt, and that knowledge restrained her from her former rebellious ways.

Jesus also had a word with Nimrah, pointing out to her that she needed to trust her daughter now. He was convinced that Mary wouldn't let her down again. Nimrah, for her part, was so relieved that she had the opportunity to have a good relationship with Mary, something which had been sadly lacking for so many years.

As the little party left that night, Nimrah slipped a bag of coins into Jesus's hand.

'This is to help with your mission, Rabbi,' she said. 'I'm sure you'll need some financial support. Let us know if you need more.'

'Thank you, Nimrah. God bless you.'

NOTES

[1] Mark 4:31.
[2] Mark 6:13.
[3] Mark 1:40.
[4] Luke 8:2.
[5] Matt. 5:3.
[6] Luke 15:11.

Cana and Nazareth

Jesus and his little band set out the following day, heading south-west and inland towards the town of Cana, a distance of about eight miles. It was hot again and the men sweated freely as they plodded along, gradually gaining height as they climbed into some low hills. Fortunately, both the temperature and the humidity dropped a little as they climbed, which was some relief. They stopped at about halfway for a rest and refreshment at one of the few streams still running at this time of year. The fresh water emerging from the hillside was a welcome treat, and the men let the cool water trickle over their tired feet. Overhead, the relentless sun beat down out of a hard blue sky, with not a cloud to be seen. Except for the area immediately adjacent to the stream, the grass all round them had long since turned first yellow, then brown and had finally withered and disappeared into the dust. It seemed that the vegetation could never recover, but the men knew well that, as the temperatures dropped in the autumn, and especially when the first rains came, the green shoots would appear again, as if by magic, carpeting the dusty surface. For the next few months though, there would just dust and stone, except for the occasional more deeply rooted trees, bushes, a few thistles and similar thorny species. The thistles were already eight feet into the air and would easily make ten before the summer was out.

Across the valley, they could see a shepherd, leading his flock out to see if they could find anything to forage. It was a mixed flock of sheep and goats. The goats, the men knew, could live on virtually anything that grew, but the sheep would have a harder time of it.

Jesus looked round at his small company, smiling with a feeling of delight in these fellows who had left so much to come with him – homes, wives, jobs, careers. They were all embarked on an adventure of which nobody knew the ending. He stared at the mixed flock across the way for some time, and then he said, 'Gather round. I want to tell you a little story.'[1]

His followers looked up from washing their feet. Some, who had been lying back, resting their eyes from the glare of the sun, jerked up to see what he wanted. When he saw that he had their attention, Jesus went on.

'Those animals over there have suggested a little story I'd like to share with you. Come and listen.'

Once they were all settled, he began.

'There was once a king, who decided to hold a great convocation for all his courtiers, soldiers and servants. When they had all assembled in his great hall, the monarch entered and sat on his golden throne and called them, one by one, to come and kneel before him. He looked carefully into each man's eyes, and, being a very wise and discerning king, he was able to evaluate their characters for what they really were. Those that he saw were deserving, he told to assemble on the right side of the hall, while those he saw were not worthy, he told to gather on the left.'

Jesus turned and pointed to the shepherd on the hillside, and continued.

'It was rather like that shepherd over there. From time to time, he will need to separate the sheep from the goats – for example, when he is going to take them to market. Anyway, getting back to our story; when the division of his subjects had been completed, the king, with a smile, said to the men who had been placed on the right side, "Come and claim the prize that I have prepared for you. For you have proved worthy and now you will be rewarded."

'The men on the right side of the hall were puzzled. "What did we do which particularly pleased, Your Majesty?" they asked. 'Their king replied quietly, "When I was hungry, you gave me food. When I was thirsty, you gave me drink. When I was cold, you gave me warm clothing. Also, you came to visit me when I was ill or in prison."

'The men on the right looked amazed. "But, Sire, you have never been hungry, or thirsty, or cold, or ill – much less in prison."

'"No, I know, but many others in my kingdom have been, and you looked after them well. As far as I am concerned, that is every bit as good as serving me personally. You certainly deserve your reward."

'Then he turned and walked over to the second group, standing on the left, and, with a serious, cold face, said, "You deserve no reward," he said, "for when I was in need, you were nowhere to be found."

'With hot indignation, those on his left complained that they had never seen the king wanting anything without coming to his assistance.

"Oh, I know that too," said the monarch grimly, "but there were others out there in my cities and in the countryside in desperate need, and you did nothing to help them. As far as I'm concerned, that's the same thing as neglecting me. You deserve no reward, therefore. In fact, you are to be exiled from my kingdom. You can have no part in it."'

The followers of Jesus hardly knew which way to look. They immediately saw what Jesus was driving at. They saw that God might be judging them like the king in the story and they knew that they, like the king's subjects on his left, had often ignored someone in need.

'It's a tough lesson,' said Jesus, 'but it might make you think. You see, while we are none of us worthy of God's blessing – nowhere near good enough to merit God's rewards – that doesn't mean that we don't need to make every effort to serve God, and the only way we can do that in practice is by helping others. We know that God, by his very nature, needs nothing, so we can't serve him directly; but, instead, he wants us to help other people in his place. I tell you, God's Kingdom is about helping and serving, not about being helped and served. Those who respond to God's love as best they can by helping others will find the Kingdom.'

'I don't think I shall ever prove worthy,' said Thomas glumly.

'I'm sure I shan't,' said Matthew.

'You can and you will,' responded Jesus. 'Follow the way that I lead and you will succeed, I promise you. You seem to forget that it is God who is the judge, and he doesn't judge like men do. He can look into your heart and soul and see your intentions, your motives. It is these that he judges, not just your actions. Men see only the outside of you – and sometimes people with the best of intentions fail to perform. God sees what's going on inside you.'

'That just makes it worse!' complained Matthew. 'I am ashamed of the things I think, sometimes!'

'Don't forget God's infinite grace,' was the reply.

Just then, Thaddeus stood up and pointed down the valley.

'There are two men coming up the hill,' he said, straining his eyes into the bright light, 'and they seem to be in a hurry.'

They all stood and waited while two strangers made their way up the slope to them. They were short of breath by the time they reached them. Andrew suddenly realised who it was and went to meet them.

'Matthias – and David!' he cried. 'Fancy seeing you again – and so far from Judaea!'

The two grasped his outstretched hand warmly and then came to greet Jesus. The preacher took Matt's hand and pumped it vigorously. 'It's good to see you again,' he said warmly. 'How are you?'

'I'll be fine when I've got my breath,' replied the other. 'Meet my friend David – another of John's followers. We've been looking for you. We heard you were on this road and have been hurrying to catch you up – in this heat, too!'

The others got them water from the stream and gathered round to hear what they had to say.

'How is John?' asked Jesus.

'Not so good, I'm afraid,' said Matt. 'He's been in prison for several weeks now. There seems to be no end in sight to his captivity.'

'But they let you in to see him?' asked Andrew.

'Yes. We're let in – us two – and one other – you met Jonathan, didn't you, when we were all down by the Jordan? We're let in occasionally – say, once or twice a week – to see John and bring him some food. They give him very little, but we take him something. He's very despondent, I'm afraid.'

'It must be terrible for him,' said Jesus. 'Please give him our warmest greeting and our hopes that soon he'll be freed. Tell him we are thinking about him and praying for him. But why have you left him and come all up here in such a hurry?'

'Well, as I said, we heard that you were in the area, and John asked us to find out how your mission was progressing. He said it would make his life bearable if he knew that you were having a successful ministry. He even asked me to ask you, straight out…'

Here Matt's voice faltered. Jesus waited for a second, then he said gently, 'Go on, Matt. We're all friends here. What was it that John needed to know?'

'He said that I was to ask – are you the Messiah – or should he be looking for someone else? You remember that when we met before, at the house of John barHelez, we told you that he had said that he was sure that he had baptised you as the Messiah…'

Jesus paused, looking at the ground. Then he straightened up and said, 'Go back and tell John that the lame are walking again, lepers are being cleansed, those who were blind can now see and the poor are hearing the good news. He will, I am sure, know the prophecies of the great Isaiah.[2] He must make his own mind about the answer to his question on the basis of this evidence.'

There was a pause before anyone spoke. Then David, the other follower of John, said, 'We'll tell him. We have heard about the people you have healed; the news is everywhere in the district. We have also heard of the way the message is being preached…'

'We'll be sure to tell John.' Matt reached out to take Jesus's hand again.

'Must you be off straightaway?'

'Yes. We must get back to him. He's so down. It'll do him good to get your message from us.'

The thirteen solemnly shook hands with John's two men, wishing them well. Then they were gone down the hill. Jesus watched them descend the slope.

'John, their master, is a great man,' he said. 'He really opened the door on my ministry – waking the people up, sounding a clear trumpet call. He's really done as Isaiah promised.'

He turned and indicated it was time to go. As they continued on their way, the disciples, in their pairs, discussed the strange encounter they had just witnessed. Had Jesus really answered John's pointed question? Was he really claiming to be the Messiah? Could they believe it? It was true that Jesus did wonderful things, but… they shook their heads and wondered.

★

Eventually they made it to Cana. Nathaniel and Philip were again entrusted with the task of seeing the rabbi to seek his blessing for a meeting outside the Synagogue that evening, while Judas and Thaddeus went and did the shopping, so that they could all eat that night. The others sought a suitable site to sleep, just outside the town. Jesus took himself to the top of a knoll to reflect on what he intended to say that evening.

As at Magdala, permission was readily granted for the meeting, and so everybody assembled a little before sunset to see what Jesus would have to say. As usual, Jesus started with the topic of the coming Kingdom. As before, he described his idea of God's Kingdom as being very different from the kingdoms of the earth. He explained that old habits of 'looking after number one' and 'devil take the hindmost' needed to give way to caring for and sharing with others. When that truth had been found and grasped, however, Jesus assured his hearers that it would be an experience of infinite worth.

'It's a bit like the experience of a merchant who was always on the lookout for jewellery for his shop,' he explained.[3] 'This trader had bought and sold jewels regularly all his life and made a reasonable living out of the trade, but one day, he saw a pearl which outshone all the others he had ever seen. It was perfect, absolutely brilliant in its beauty and iridescence, but, of course, it was extremely pricey. The merchant had to sell everything he owned – his house, his lands, his stock, everything – to scrape enough money together to afford the wonderful pearl.

'"But," he said to himself, "it's worth it. This one jewel is worth all the others put together and some more."'

Jesus looked round at his audience, smiling.

'The Kingdom, too, may cost you much,' he said, 'but it too is worth it! It's worth everything else put together.'

Then he continued.

'In seeking this Kingdom that I have described, you have to be ruthless in giving up anything that prevents you from attaining your goal. If you find that something – anything – in your life prevents you from reaching out to those around you who need your help, then that thing, whatever it is, must be sacrificed. Supposing you had a problem with your eye and you went to the doctor and he told you that it was poisoned and must be removed if you were to have any chance of continuing to live.[4] What would you do? You would have no choice, would you? Unpleasant though it would be, you would have that eye taken out, rather than lose your life altogether. Similarly, if your hand was poisoned and needed to be removed if you were to avoid death, you'd agree to the operation, wouldn't you, rather than lose life altogether. In exactly the same way, we have to be ruthless in rooting out anything that prevents us from grasping this "kingdom of right relationships".'

Jesus again looked round and smiled.

'I know it sounds hard, my friends, but it is so rewarding when you try it. And when you fail and lapse back into selfish ways – and you will fail from time to time – remember that God is always willing to forgive you. He will pick you up from where you have fallen, dust you down, bandage any broken skin and set you off on the high road again.'

Someone from the back of the crowd shouted out, 'I don't know what you're talking about! I keep to the Law. I'm a good Jew – well, as good as most round here – and that's all there is to it. I don't hold with all these newfangled explanations.'

'You keep the Law, do you?' asked Jesus. 'Are you sure? Can you really say that you keep to every part, consistently?'

'I do better than some – and as well as most.' The heckler was defiant.

'And what is the Law? Remind us of the two great commandments, please.'

Jesus could hold his own in any argument.

The man at the back muttered sullenly, 'Love the Lord with all your might, and love your neighbour as yourself.'

'Just so – and isn't love precisely what I have been advocating?'

'Well, yes, I suppose so, but you don't have to go on so. It's really quite simple. Just do as the Law says.' The heckler was determined to stand his ground.

'Indeed that is right, in theory,' replied Jesus, 'but in practice it requires infinite attention. You can't keep a law of love like you keep the law on taxation. In the latter case, you can count out exactly the amount that is owing and, having paid it over, know that you have fulfilled everything required of you. But the law of love goes much further. It requires compliance with the *spirit* of the law – not just the letter. Because love is infinite, you can never say that you have done everything required of you.'

This silenced the critic, so Jesus finished the meeting with prayer and the crowd started to drift away. Just as they were leaving the square, however, the local rabbi, together with couple of local Pharisees, approached him and asked for a word.

'We think that you're giving an unfortunate impression,' the rabbi began.

'Oh?' replied Jesus. 'How do you mean?'

'Well, we have been teaching the folk round here for years now,' responded the rabbi, 'and we find that getting them to comply with the Law is, in practice, the best way. Your sermon was all very well, but it's airy-fairy – there's nothing cut and dried about it. People need to know more precisely where they stand, and they know that when they have followed the more precise laws we give them.'

'Well,' said Jesus, 'I don't know what more I can say. Loving cannot be a matter which is precise and cut and dried. By definition, there can be no end to it...'

'Look,' one of the Pharisees burst in, 'we know what's best for our people. Moses knew what was best.'

'I have no quarrel with the Law of Moses.'[5] Jesus's voice was icily serious. 'But I am saying that the whole Law has never been fulfilled – one needs to go beyond the written Law to the spirit behind it.'

The rabbi snorted loudly and shook his head.

'I think you had better leave,' he said. 'You seem to think that you know more than Moses, and more than we do. We have worked with these people for years. We know what they're like. They need specific guidance. I think you had better take yourself off elsewhere.'

Jesus shrugged his shoulders and pursed his lips.

'Very well, Rabbi,' he said. 'We shall be gone in the morning.'

★

They made their way further south-west to Nazareth. This time, Jesus said he himself would see the rabbi, whom he had known for years, and then go on to see his family. The disciples could busy themselves finding and preparing a site where they could eat and sleep that night.

The old rabbi was overjoyed to see the carpenter, whom he had taught as a boy and young man. However, he was surprised when Jesus said he wanted to preach outside the Synagogue that evening. He paused as he considered the matter. Eventually, he said, 'Well, if you think you can handle it, my boy, I suppose it'll be all right. I had heard something about you turning preacher, but I didn't give it much credence. You must forgive me; we still think of you as the local carpenter and builder!'

'Since I left home, I've studied in Jerusalem and elsewhere. I believe that I have something important to say.'

'Very well, then. Let us hear you tonight.'

Jesus thanked the rabbi and then went to see his mother and the family. Of course, they were all very pleased to see him and insisted on him staying for lunch with them, while they plied him with questions. They had heard that he had been preaching, but they needed more detail. Where had he been? What sort of crowds did he draw? Was there any truth in the rumours about him healing cripples?

Jesus did his best to answer their questions, but, since James, the next eldest brother, was the only one who had ever ventured out of Galilee, it was difficult for them to comprehend that their own brother had, indeed, been learning and even teaching in the great Temple in Jerusalem, far away in Judaea. Jesus turned the conversation away from himself to their situation.

'How have you been, Mother?' he asked.

'Very well, really,' replied Mary. Now in her mid-forties, Mary was still a very attractive woman. Her hair was losing the intense blackness that had made her such a beauty in earlier times. Jesus was reminded of Mary of Magdala and her beautiful dark hair and tried to imagine his mother when she had been eighteen. There must have been marked similarities, though the older Mary was much shorter in stature.

'How is business?' he asked James.

'Pretty thriving nowadays, actually,' said his brother. 'We are all able to work – Joseph, Simon, Jude and myself – and there's plenty to do. We keep the family fairly well off – much better than when you and I, as raw beginners, first took over when Dad died! Those were the days – we had to struggle then!'

'I remember.' There was a pause, then Jesus asked, 'Will you all come to hear me preach tonight?'

'I'll be there, my son,' said Mary, straight away.

With varying degrees of reluctance, the rest nodded their heads in agreement. 'Can't let the family down,' they said. 'We'll be there.'

They kept their word and went to the meeting, together with virtually all the townsfolk. Word had quickly got around that the ex-carpenter was going to preach and everybody wanted to find out how he would get on. Then there were those rumours about him healing... They were all there at the appointed hour.

Jesus turned up with his followers and introduced them to his family. His mother was kind as usual, but the disciples noticed some reserve in her greeting, which was echoed by the rest of the family. However, since Jesus needed to begin his address, they all put their slight perplexity to the back of their minds.

Jesus began, as usual, by thanking the rabbi for his permission to preach. He went on by outlining to them his main thesis on the coming Kingdom – that inner relationship with God and, for his sake, with all those round about. He was able to illustrate what he was saying by reference to the family and the need to see everyone as part of one's own family.

'If God is father and mother to all of us,' Jesus argued, 'it must be the case that we are all brothers and sisters. Now, I know most of you and your families. I know how tightly knit are your homes and families, how you depend on one another within the family. Now, the Kingdom is like that – one great big family – where everyone is bound together. It is my mission to tell you and everyone about this coming Kingdom. To do this, I must release people from the misery of their imprisonments – some are imprisoned at present by their fears or prejudices, some by their guilt or ignorance. They cannot accept change in their lives. They cannot admit a new situation like the Kingdom into their existence. Some people are literally blind and look for healing; but many more are blind in understanding – blind to the truth – and they too must be helped to see properly. It is all going to happen – starting now.'

Then, taking up the scroll containing the writings of the prophet Isaiah, Jesus started to read to them.[6]

'"The spirit of the Lord is upon me because he has anointed me; he has sent me to announce good news to the poor, to proclaim release for the prisoners and recovery of sight for the blind; to let the broken victims go free, to proclaim the year of the Lord's favour."'

Jesus looked up from the scroll and smiled at his audience.

'Today, now, this prophecy is being fulfilled. This is what I have come to do,' he said.

There was silence for a few seconds and then someone at the back called out, 'Just a minute, Jesus. You talk about this great Kingdom and it sounds all right, but what makes you think you can bring it about? You're only a carpenter, when all is said and done.'

'That's right,' said another, 'we know where you came from – we know your family – they're all here – just ordinary people like us!'

'I was ploughing the fields when you were still in nappies,' said an old man. 'Why should I listen to you and your highfaluting ideas?'

Jesus tried to make himself heard above the hubbub, but the more he tried speaking, the more the critical voices shrilled at him. Soon the criticism became rather threatening, and Simon Peter, in the front row of the crowd, started to look round anxiously for the rest of Jesus's followers. Having got their attention, he edged forward to be near Jesus. It was lucky for them that the crowd had no natural leader, for, while some were calling for Jesus to be taken out in the street and beaten up for his cheek, others had rather more drastic measures in mind.

Peter moved in to take the preacher by the arm and, with the other followers quickly surrounding him, they all edged away from the crowd and down the road to the open countryside, where their little camp was set up. The crowd followed them to the edge of the village, shouting their abuse, but eventually gave up and turned back. There was nothing to be seen of Jesus's family. Perhaps they had slunk off for fear that they might also be blamed for Jesus's ideas.

'Perhaps discretion is the better part of valour on this occasion,' said Jesus. 'Let's pack up and move away from here, now, tonight. It's ironic, isn't it – a prophet has the least chance of honour in his own town – and even among his family and his own kin.'[7]

So the little troop were on their way in the dark, away from their leader's home town as quickly as they could. A mile down the road, they stopped to catch their breath and take stock, but it seemed as if the Nazarenes had no thought of pursuing them once they had left the immediate environs of the town, so they decided to set up camp again and get some supper. Nevertheless, Peter suggested that they leave a couple of their number a short way out from the camp as 'sentries', just in case of further trouble. Thaddeus and Philip volunteered for this task, but nothing untoward occurred.

After a brief supper, Jesus held a council with the whole group.

'Thank you for looking out for my interests tonight, my friends,' he said. 'That could have been a very nasty experience, but you acted very promptly and efficiently to outwit a potentially dangerous mob. I must admit that I didn't expect to get quite such a hostile reaction in Nazareth, though I probably ought to have foreseen it. But the fact is that we seem to be running into trouble everywhere. Well, I predicted that we should generally get the cold shoulder from the rabbis and the Pharisees once the message was out, and that's exactly what is happening. I've upset some by seeming to offend the laws regarding the Sabbath, by healing people then. I've upset others by seeming to discount the Law altogether – which isn't true. I've upstaged some teachers, especially in Jerusalem, which they didn't like. I've talked with women, which isn't quite the thing, many think, especially if they are of doubtful reputation, like Mary Magdalene.'

Then, with a smile at the appropriate members of the band, he went on. 'Finally, I've upset several religious people by hobnobbing with undesirables like Matthew, here; and no doubt, I'd be in trouble with others if they knew we had some of those dreadful Zealots in our midst!'

The offending ne'er-do-wells grinned as Jesus referred to them. Yes, they had been outcasts, but now, in spite of their difficulties, they felt that life was better for them, not worse. They were the ones who were on the right track.

'Well, I can't change the message,' continued their leader, 'so we have to change the tactics. I propose to preach, therefore, much more in the countryside. I'll get you fellows to whip up the crowds and bring them to me. The ordinary people, in the main, are receptive – Nazareth was the exception, and we know the reason for this. It'll be up to you, in future, to get the people to come to me. Early tomorrow, we'll move away from here smartly and we'll start again elsewhere. I'll give some thought to exactly where overnight and we'll be away first thing. I'm afraid the easier part of our work is now over. Things are going to get more difficult from here on.'

The disciples received this news with some trepidation. They cast some sideways glances at each other, and, after Jesus had retired for the night, there were several muttered conversations between pairs, as they mulled over all that had happened, what might have happened and, above all, what might be in store for them in the future. Opinions varied. Peter, in conversation with Andrew, was, as usual, sure that things would turn out right. Thomas, talking to Matthew, was the pessimist – though he called it realism. Matthew was more sanguine. John, in conversation with his brother, said that he was sure that Jesus was right, whatever he said. In the end, they all took that view: Jesus knew what he was doing. They'd put their hands to this particular plough, and there was no going back now!

NOTES

[1] Matt. 25:31.
[2] Isaiah 29:18; 61:1.
[3] Matt. 13:45.
[4] Matt. 5:29.
[5] Matt. 5:17.
[6] Luke 4:16; Isaiah 61:1.
[7] Mark 6:4.

More teaching – and more trouble

The disciples woke the following morning to find that Jesus had been up well before them. He had already had his quiet period and was busy getting a fire going by the time they struggled up. They had a hurried breakfast, washed and broke camp.

'We'll go east towards the south end of the lake,' announced Jesus. 'There are many small villages in that area but there are no large towns. Perhaps' – and this he said with a rueful smile – 'news of the trouble we've caused won't have preceded us there! Anyway, as I said last night, if I am not made welcome by the village leaders, you'll have to go and persuade the ordinary people to meet me in the countryside.'

They set off, walking in pairs as was their custom, with Jesus walking first with one pair, then another. They were losing height gradually, which made the walking quite easy, though, as the sun got higher in the sky, they began to sweat profusely. They had covered about five miles when they came to a small hamlet, tucked away in a fold of the hills. There they managed to get a drink and arrange for a meeting that evening in the village square. Evidently, the people there had no knowledge of who Jesus was.

They set up a little camp just outside the village. It was rather primitive, but adequate for their purposes. The little stream in the valley had long since dried up with the heat of summer and all their water would need to be collected in skins from the village, but it couldn't be helped. At least there was some shade and an area of reasonably flat ground on which to sleep.

As the sun was sinking towards the horizon, they walked into the village. Jesus began his talk by telling a little story about two men at prayer in the Temple.[1] One was a Pharisee, who liked to pray standing in the main courtyard where everyone could see him. His prayer was a prayer of thanksgiving, in which he thanked God that he was better than those around him; he was not greedy, dishonest or adulterous like tax gatherers and suchlike. He went on to remind God of all the worthy things he did – fasting, praying and tithing regularly. Jesus contrasted this man with the other, who was a tax gatherer. He stood meekly in a corner of the courtyard, out of the way, hardly daring to raise his eyes to heaven, wringing his hands and beating his breast with remorse. All he could find to say was, 'God be merciful to me, a sinner.'

Jesus looked round the little crowd who had gathered to hear him. 'Which prayer do you think found God's favour that day?' he asked.

There was silence. Everyone knew which man Jesus would commend, but none could bring themselves to say so, with a small group of Pharisees standing on the side of the crowd. However, Jesus had no such inhibitions.

'I tell you, it was the second man who went home at peace with God that day. He knew his need of God, his need of God's grace. The first man was puffed up with pride. He thought he could win his way into God's favour by his fasts and prayers and tithes.'

Jesus went on to describe the idea, now well known to the disciples, of God's Kingdom of inner peace, brought about by a recognition of God as Father and, for that reason, a recognition of the need to serve other people, as sisters and brothers.

'People like the Pharisee in the story will never be prepared to serve others. They are too full of their own importance,' he said. 'On the other hand, the tax gatherer, who knew his own inadequacy, has a chance of responding to God's grace and serving other people as part of that response. In this Kingdom of heaven, those who exalt themselves will be humbled, but those who are prepared to humble themselves will find their true value as people.'[2]

The crowd on the whole were fairly receptive to Jesus's message, but, as he expected, a couple of the Pharisees came to see him after he had finished, complaining of his inclusion of a Pharisee in the story.

'How dare you say that Pharisees are really like that!' they demanded.

'Look, it's only a story,' replied the preacher. 'Do you agree that if things happened that way, then the outcome would be as I proposed? Wouldn't God accept the tax gatherer's prayer in preference to that of the Pharisee?'

Grudgingly, the Pharisees muttered their assent. 'But it makes the people think that Pharisees are like that in reality,' they grumbled.

Jesus paused and looked them full in their faces. 'And can you truly say that none of your sect has any of the characteristics of the man in the story?' he challenged.

There was silence.

'Is there not a lot of hypocrisy in some of the people who are supposed to be most religious – those who ought to be giving the best example to those around them?'

Again, silence.

'Do you not agree that religion ought not to be a matter of 'show' – of doing certain things and following certain rituals – but actually serving those in need, as required by the two great laws of love?'

The conversation soon petered out. The Pharisees went off muttering in their beards, by no means won over, yet unable to fault Jesus's observations.

Jesus had already been invited to supper with one of the village leaders, himself a Pharisee, called Simon. Jesus took Simon Peter, Nathaniel and Matthew with him on this occasion. When they returned, several hours later, they were accompanied by their host, who said he would come with them for a breath of air. When he saw the campsite, he looked horrified.

'How can you wash everything properly?' he asked. 'The Law is very clear on how things have to be washed. It's impossible to wash things adequately here. I'm surprised at how you, a self-styled holy man, can allow your people to carry on in this fashion.'

Jesus shook his head. 'You have been kind to us tonight, Simon, and I'm truly grateful,' he said, 'but you seem to have missed the whole point of what I have been trying to say. Surely, the real test in life is not whether your pots and plates – or even your hands – are clean ritually, but whether your hearts are clean.³ You Pharisees are meticulous about the hygiene of pots; you clean the outside of the dishes. But what about your own inner lives? The prophets taught years ago that justice and mercy were much to be preferred to mere ritual! The real test is whether you are prepared to serve others in response to God's goodness to you. Don't you see how hypocritical you seem to those who observe you? People see you wanting the best seats in the Synagogues and making much of your place in society, but they don't see much care for the poor and needy.'

Perhaps not surprisingly, the Pharisee went off, greatly offended.

'It's no good,' said Jesus sadly, after he had gone. 'I must speak the truth.'

The next day, the little group found that they were not welcome in the village, certainly not by the leadership. The word had clearly been put round that this strange preacher was not to be encouraged. Jesus decided that they had better move on again, further east and find a new place to camp. They tramped on another few miles and set up near a small village about three miles away from the lake. This time, however, the village was on quite a well-frequented route from the north, and it was clear that news had already reached the villagers about Jesus's healing exploits in Capernaum, Magdala and the surrounding district. People clustered round them as they entered the place, wanting to know where they would be staying. They had hardly concluded their shopping, however, when the local rabbi, accompanied by a couple of village leaders, buttonholed Jesus and told him quite clearly that he was not welcome in their midst.

'We are told that you preach without reference to the Law,' the Rabbi began, 'and you don't keep the Sabbath.'

'You've upset plenty of people elsewhere, and we're not having it here,' said another.

'You have all sorts of riff-raff in your company – and we don't want them here. We've heard that one of your number is a tax gatherer!'

Jesus saw that it was no use talking to them. They'd be even more incensed when news of his encounter the previous evening reached the village.

'We'll retrace our steps a little,' he said to his followers. 'We'll move back on the little ridge behind the village, out of sight, but not too far away. I fancy the people in the last village may come to hear me again, and these people here may too, if we can prize them from under their leaders' noses!'

★

So they set up camp out in the open countryside. They found a spot underneath the steep side of a hill where they had some shelter from the sun and where there was a natural amphitheatre in which the crowd could sit round, while Jesus stood on a large boulder, seen and heard by all. There was no running water, of course, but Jesus was, on the whole, delighted with the site. During the rest of the day the disciples set off in small groups to the surrounding villages, including the two they had recently visited, to put the word about that Jesus would speak that night at the campsite. Only a couple of dozen people bothered to make the journey that evening, but Jesus did not seem to mind.

'Think of the mustard seed,' he said. 'Remember how it grows! Our crowds will grow too, if we serve the people well.'

He decided to retell the story of the prodigal son and his elder brother. The crowd listened entranced. Jesus could see, as he finished, that some identified with the younger man who ran off and spent his father's money recklessly but came home repentant, while a few smiled grimly as they realised that the religious people were being criticised through the story of the elder brother, for their stiff-necked attitude to repentant ne'er-do-wells. Jesus closed with a short but sincere and simple prayer. He then invited them to return next evening and bring their friends.

During the day, the disciples again fanned out in all directions and let it be known in the surrounding village squares that Jesus was speaking again that evening. This time, there must have been sixty or more to hear what he had to say. But someone came carrying an elderly woman on a stretcher and Jesus knew that his usual dilemma over the sick had recurred.

'I'll be happy to see you later,' he told the two sons who had carried their mother on a stretcher. 'Please wait until after the meeting finishes and I promise I will see your mother.'

Jesus was, as ever, prepared with a story to catch the crowd's imagination. He retold the story of the good shepherd, which Matthew remembered so well. It had riveted his attention as he had sat in his booth receiving the taxes, and it had a similar effect on many others as they listened.

One man cried out, 'Is God really like a good shepherd? Can I really believe it? It's too good to be true. We've always been told that God only looks after those who obey him.'

Jesus replied, 'Of course God wants you, for your own sake, to keep his laws. He knows that if you follow the path of love you will have a happier and more worthwhile existence. But he also knows how frail human nature is and how selfish men and women are, how prone they are to taking their own path in life. He knows that this common trait will catch us all out sometimes. He will forgive our inadequacies – and go on forgiving. He wants us to return to him and be sheltered within his sheepfold. He wants us all to dwell in his home under his protection. I call this protective shield "the Kingdom of heaven".'

Here Jesus went on to describe again his ideas of what the inner Kingdom could be for anyone who wanted to live in it. As usual, he was questioned by those who sought a political kingdom, those who sought a confrontation with Rome. Their questions and Jesus's answers were in full swing when three more people arrived and joined the rear of the crowd. After a few moments, Andrew, who was near the back, realised that the newcomers were Jesus's mother and his two elder brothers, so he edged over to them, to enquire how they were. The men told him, quite gruffly, that they must speak to Jesus immediately. He moved forward and caught Jesus's eye, and the preacher paused and asked the crowd's pardon while he dealt with the point Andrew wanted to make. He bent close to Andrew to confer privately.

'Your family is here, Jesus – your mother and two brothers,' whispered Andrew.[4]

'What do they want?'

'I don't know – but they seem rather upset. They want to see you now.'

'Well, I'm sure they can see I'm fully taken up here for the present. I can't just leave this crowd – and I have to see a sick woman as well.'

'I'll tell them, of course, but I don't think they're going to like it. They are your family, after all...' Andrew looked pained.

'Just at the moment, these people here...' Jesus spread his arm round to indicate the crowd... 'are my family. They need my attention. Ask them to wait and I'll speak to them as soon as I can.'

Andrew went back to see Mary and her sons, knowing that they were going to be upset that Jesus wouldn't interrupt his meeting for them. They looked pretty miffed, but said little.

'We'll wait here,' they said and wandered off a few paces and sat down under an olive tree.

Andrew did his best. 'Can I offer you some refreshment? We have some water here.'

'No, thank you,' said James, Jesus's brother, still rather grimly. 'We're all right.'

But they looked rather stern. Andrew hung around, just in case they needed anything. It took another forty minutes before Jesus finished dealing with the people's questions, closed the meeting, saw the crowd away and then dealt with the sick woman. But, at last, Jesus was able to get away and join his family. Once he arrived, Andrew left them to talk privately and he warned all the others to give their leader a little time to speak with his folk alone. They saw from a distance that the conversation was rather animated – clearly there were some fairly emotional feelings in the air, and things were not all as they should be. After about twenty minutes, the family took its leave and started off up the path towards Nazareth. It would be a long walk back for them. It would be very late before they would be in their beds. Jesus came back into the group of disciples looking very distressed and tired.

'I'm sorry,' he said to his friends. 'I've held you up when you were waiting for your supper.'

'Are you family all right?' asked John. 'Wouldn't they stay for supper with us and sleep here overnight?'

'No, they were determined not to stay,' replied Jesus. 'I fear that I have upset them very much, but it can't be helped. You see, they think that I'm doing everything wrong, by coming out here in the countryside to preach. They know that I've upset the religious authorities – and they're uncomfortable about that. They just want me to come home to Nazareth and settle down again to an ordinary life, and not go about stirring up trouble for myself and everyone else, and living like this, like some outcast or tramp, out in the middle of nowhere.'

'What did you say to that?' asked Peter.

'What could I say? I'm committed to following the path laid down for me by my father – that I have to do. Bless you; you have agreed to join me. Together we are spreading the good news to everyone who will listen. That just has to take precedence even over family ties. I'm sorry, but there it is. Of course I love my mother and family; I had hoped that they would support me in my work, but I can't stop just because they don't feel they can.'

The disciples muttered their sympathy for Jesus in his dilemma. They sat down to their suppers and ate mostly without talking. It was rather a sober party that night.

★

The next morning spirits revived. Jesus had been up early, as usual, and had again prepared the breakfast before some had even woken up. Arrangements were made over the little meal for most of the disciples to go off to the villages to drum up support for the evening's meeting, while others stayed to do some chores round the camp. Since the place seemed so suitable, they decided that it was worthwhile to make some more permanent arrangements – some more shade could be erected for relief from the burning summer sun, the pathway could be widened and cleared for better ease of access for the people, cooler places could be found for storing food and water and so on. Philip, Simon the Zealot and his partner, little James, were practical men and could deal with all these matters. However, it was agreed that everyone should be back for a midday meal, and, after the traditional siesta, Jesus would give them some more instruction on prayer.

'Nathaniel was asking me the other day to give him some teaching on that topic,' said Jesus, 'and I thought you might all like to share in that one.'

So it was agreed. Once the worst of the heat of the midday sun had past, the disciples roused themselves and gathered in the shade round Jesus.

'I'm sure the best place to begin is with a decision on how to address God,' he began. 'Our ancestors, Abraham, Isaac and Joseph, knew that God was their God – the God of the people of Israel. They thought of him as a dread God – one to be feared and worshipped. He demanded obedience and in return he watched over the people of Israel and cared for them. He brought them to Egypt in the time of the great famine, but later, when the Pharaoh enslaved them, he delivered them and brought them out again, after much tribulation – back to "the land flowing with milk and honey". This he did under the leadership of Moses, to whom he gave the written commandments, which later became expanded into the Law as we know it in the Torah. All through the history of the nation, under first judges, then kings, and through the ministry of priests and prophets, God revealed himself more fully. The people gradually came to realise that God was not just the God of Israel, but the one God of all the nations, the creator of all things, everywhere. So, while we still believe that the Jews are God's chosen race, for we were chosen to be the ones to whom God first revealed himself, we now realise that God is the only God, and that all nations must ultimately come to recognise and respond to him. Gradually we have realised just how great and wonderful our God is; he is the creator and sustainer of everything.

'But it wasn't until comparatively recently that we began to see God, not as a dread sovereign and wondrous creator, but as a loving father. He is our great and sovereign Lord and maker of all, but his real greatness lies not in his wondrous glory but in his loving kindness, his fatherly presence, the benign shadow that he casts over and round about us.

'This gives us the clue as to how we should address God. Although he is holy and glorious and almighty – well beyond anything that words can describe – more than everything else, he is, first and foremost, our father; and, as I told you once before, I think, he has also all the characteristics of the best mother. His presence pervades all creation and, even more, all mankind, undergirding and supporting us all. He is within us, among us, part of our very being. Creation is shot through by the creator.

'So, I think the best way to start your prayer is simply, "Our father", or "Our heavenly father", or "Our father in heaven".[5]

'Next we have to think about what we mean when we talk about "heaven". Perhaps, instinctively, we think about heaven as a place, far away, where God lives in glory, worshipped continually by angels, cherubim and seraphim. Or perhaps we feel that heaven is like the Temple in Jerusalem – but far grander, too wonderful to contemplate. But do either of these pictures represent the truth? If God is not only our great creator, but our father and therefore very close to us, surely heaven must be close to us also. In fact, wherever we go, God is still there. We cannot escape him.

'The Psalmist knew that, for he said, "If I take my flight to the frontiers of the morning or dwell at the limits of the western sea, even there thy hand will meet me."[6]

'The truth is that God is in all and pervading all things. He undergirds all we have and are. "Underneath are the everlasting arms."[7] Heaven, therefore must be everywhere, if we can but find it.

'Having addressed God and recognised his nearness, you also need to go on to attempt to recognise God's greatness; so you might say, "Hallowed be your name" or "Glory be to you" or something similar. As I said before, these words are bound to be inadequate, but we need to remind ourselves that God is not a person, as we are. He has the characteristics of a person – that is, we can relate to him as people – but he is infinitely greater than we are. He is God, with all that means in terms of his power, wisdom and holiness. He is, in the end, an infinite mystery.'

Jesus paused for moment to allow his words to sink in, before continuing.

'Next, I think, you should pray for the coming of the Kingdom, of which I have spoken so much, first of all in your own life, but then spreading to every corner of the world.'

James the fisherman burst in, 'Are you now talking of the final rule of Israel over the whole world, when you talk of the Kingdom?'

Jesus smiled, shook his head slightly and replied, 'I have explained many times before that, ultimately, God must rule everywhere. I have no doubt about that, but, as you also know, I do not know when this state of affairs will come about. As we have seen, God has always moved in history, gradually revealing himself. God is certainly moving today in us, as we preach and teach; but how and when we will reach the final stage in this process is a matter only for him. We must simply wait and do what we are called to do, and pray that one day God's purposes will be done on earth, as they are already done in heaven.'

Jesus looked round at his little group. He could see all the emotions – love for himself and trust in his judgement – but also some confusion and perplexity. They could not bring themselves to think of things in the timescale of God, for whom a thousand years could be just a fleeting minute. They wanted things to happen now! Well, things were happening now and more was going to happen soon, but not perhaps always the things they would want or expect.

'Don't forget to thank God and ask him for the ordinary things of life – but don't be greedy. Don't, for example, pray for sagging tables, weighed down with sumptuous feasts, or rivers of wine and oil. Just be content with enough food for today. "Give us enough bread for today" might be suitable prayer, for instance.

'Then you must always acknowledge your inadequacy to God. Of course, he knows already how you have failed him, but you must be prepared to admit it and constantly ask to be forgiven. God will forgive you, you can depend on it, but remember that there is no real forgiveness possible – no mending of the relationship – unless you, in your turn, have forgiven anyone else who may have wronged you! There needs to be a full healing of the situation. You must be reconciled with your neighbour before it is really possible to be reconciled to God.'

'How many times should I forgive my neighbour if he wrongs me?' asked Peter. 'Would seven times be suitable?'[8]

'It's not a question of counting, Peter,' replied his teacher. 'Just as God goes on forgiving you, just as often as it proves necessary, so you, too, must do the same. The law of love cannot be reduced to a numerical formula!'

Peter looked crestfallen.

'Remember how I told the Pharisees that they had to stop thinking that a law could be set within quantifiable boundaries? I tell you the same. There must be no end to your love or forgiveness. You should be delighted about that, for there is no end to God's love and forgiveness either! Ask God to keep you from falling and guide you in the right way. He will not allow you to be tested more greatly than you have the strength to face.

'There's another matter where your attitude to others is related to the way you will be treated yourself. I might as well cover that now. Just as you need to forgive people, before you yourselves can be forgiven, so too you must avoid judging people if you wish not to be judged yourselves.[9] You know how it is; you see something going on, and, if you are not careful, you may come instantly to the conclusion that so-and-so is to blame. Or you hear of a problem, and, again, without even knowing the full facts, you rush to condemn someone who seems to be responsible. Why? Why do we always have to find someone to blame? The fact is that, if you are like that, others will certainly treat you in the same way – and you will be the worse off for it. Less still would you like it if God judged you like that.'

Thomas grimaced and shook his head.

'I feel totally inadequate,' he said. 'I find myself failing to live your law of love, Jesus. I sometimes get cross with some of our friends here, or fail to do my bit to help in the mission, or even round the camp with the chores, and I find myself criticising others, at least to myself, if not to others. I feel a failure in so many ways!'

'The fact that you acknowledge your failures means that you have already started on the road towards dealing with them. You know you have God's forgiveness for any failure – and I'm sure you have ours, insofar as we are aware of any failure on your part. Don't give up. God will not over-test you or give up on you!'

Jesus paused and looked from one face to the next. What splendid fellows he had chosen. Ordinary men, of course, yet with such good hearts. They may be confused and often feel failures, but he knew they wouldn't give up. He concluded his little talk on prayer with these words:

'Finally, always finish your prayers by again recognising God's place in the creation and in your own existence. For instance, "Yours is the Kingdom, the power, and the glory, for ever" might be a good way to finish.'

There was silence, so, after a little pause, Jesus asked them to bow their heads just where they were and pray with him. He repeated the prayer he had just outlined, and then prayed for them to be strengthened and enlightened. They rose feeling refreshed and invigorated for service.

That evening, an even larger crowd, more than a hundred, turned up to hear Jesus speak, and the disciples saw, with some trepidation, that a few of their leaders, a lawyer and a couple of Pharisees, had also made the journey. Not only that, but, predictably, the news that Jesus could heal had spread, in spite of all that Jesus had done to try to prevent it. The disciples knew by now to lead the sick to one side and ask them to wait until after the meeting had finished, but many in the crowd knew about the presence of those who were ill, and were all agog to see if Jesus would heal them.

Jesus, however, made no mention of the sick people when he started to speak. He spoke, as ever, of the Kingdom of God, that inner Kingdom which all could have; that inner conviction that God was Father and therefore everyone else must be either a brother or sister.

When he had finished speaking, the lawyer in the crowd, seeking to test Jesus, asked him what he should do in order to inherit eternal life. Jesus simply turned the question back on him, knowing that the lawyer would know the correct answer.

'What does the Law say?' he asked.[10]

'The great commandment says that you should love the Lord our God with all your heart, soul, strength and mind.'

'Absolutely right,' said Jesus. 'What about the other great commandment?'

'You should love your neighbour as yourself,' came the response.

'Right again,' said the preacher. 'If you fulfil both of these laws, you already have the secret of eternal life.'

'Yes – I understand that… but how do you define my "neighbour"?' asked the lawyer quickly.

Jesus smiled and shook his head slightly, aware that the lawyer knew the answer well enough too, but was just trying to justify his original question.

'Let me answer that by telling a little story,' he said, and he raised his voice so that everyone could hear what he had to say. 'I expect many of you have been up to Jerusalem for Passover, or one of the other great feasts – perhaps Pentecost or Tabernacles. No doubt you went by the usual route, down the Jordan Valley to Jericho, then west, climbing gradually up to Jerusalem. If you have done this, you will know just how dangerous is that stretch of road between Jericho and Jerusalem. The road winds between high cliffs and there are many caves and crevices in the rocks where bandits can hide. They can suddenly leap out at the unwary traveller and rob him of all he has. It is always wise to travel along that stretch of road in a crowd, or at least in pairs.

'Well, there was once a man who travelled that road on his own and he was unfortunate enough to be ambushed by a gang of bandits, who beat him up, robbed him and made off, leaving him for dead. But he was not dead, quite – though he was badly wounded. After a little while, a priest came along the road; he also was risking his life, travelling alone. He came to the spot where the man lay wounded, but when he saw the man, he decided to get quickly on his way before something similar happened to him. A little later, a Levite came to the spot. He went over and looked at the man, by now lying in a pool of his own blood, but he too decided not to get involved and went on his way. However, before long, a Samaritan who was on the road came upon the unfortunate traveller and he immediately stopped. He saw that the man was in great need and straightaway went to his aid. He cleaned his wounds and bandaged them. Then he put the man, as gently as he could, on to his donkey and took him to an inn in the next village along the road. There, he looked after the wounded man, giving him food and drink.

'The following morning, before he left, he gave some money to the innkeeper saying, "Look after this man for me, please. If this is not enough money to cover your expenses until he is well again, I will pay the difference on my way back".'

Jesus looked at the lawyer and said, 'Which of these three, do you think, proved to be neighbour to the unfortunate man who was robbed and beaten up?'

The lawyer looked very embarrassed, knowing full well why the story had been told. He muttered, 'The one who showed him kindness, I suppose.'

'That's right. Now, just you go and do the same.'

The lawyer and his friends left the meeting, looking for all the world like dogs who had been chastised for eating the children's meat. Jesus looked after them with a slight smile on his face. Then he turned to the crowd and continued.

'You'll notice, my friends, that, in my story, it was the religious leaders who failed to be good neighbours. The test of one's religion is not whether you go to the Temple or the Synagogue regularly, but whether you care about those in need. Notice, too, that the hero of my story was a Samaritan, who did the right thing by the unfortunate man. Now, we Jews have all been brought up to despise the Samaritans – they are a mixed race, half Israelite, half foreign – left over from the time when the Northern Kingdom of Israel was crushed and their leaders were carried away into slavery, centuries ago. People from Assyria, the conquerors, came to populate the lands vacated by those who were carried off into captivity, and, in time, this mixture of peoples intermarried and became what we now know as Samaritans. Yes, we've been taught to despise them, because they compromised their Jewishness – but that is certainly not the fault of those who are alive today. We ought not to blame the Samaritans of today for the sins of their fathers and mothers. In any case, it is stupid to hate your enemies, for it only prolongs the animosity. Try loving your enemies, and the wounds can then be healed.'[11]

Finally, Jesus closed the meeting with a short simple prayer and wished the people goodnight, but most of them didn't move away. They wanted to see if Jesus could cure the people who had come with handicaps. Predictably, Jesus did cure them, but afterwards he was again in two minds about it. He was happy for those who had been cured, but it discouraged him that people might not really have wanted to bother with the message, so much as to see the people healed.

'In a day or two, I should like to move on,' he said. 'By now, most of the people who are going to come will have been, and it's time to seek new pastures.'

And so it went on, all through the long, hot summer. Jesus and his disciples moved from place to place in the area of southern Galilee, stopping only a few nights in any one place, then moving on, either when confronted by irate village or Synagogue leaders, or when overwhelmed by people just wanting to see what they believed were 'tricks' of healing.

Now that they were operating outside the towns and villages, invitations to meals became few and far between. Fortunately, some people brought gifts of food with them, which were gratefully received. The tradition of the hosts supplying the visitors just had to be abandoned – it was the visitors who brought their own meals, and often some for the hosts as well! Once, when a crowd of about five thousand people had turned up for a meeting, which lasted all day, the disciples had wondered how there could possibly be enough for such a crowd; but Jesus had met the situation with his usual calm, and it turned out that there was not only enough for everyone, but plenty left over for their food store in the camp – in fact, twelve baskets full![12]

Sometimes, though, their funds ran dangerously low. Judas would come to Jesus with a worried frown and report that things looked precarious. So often, though, just as things were getting really grim, someone would come to the meeting and, taking Jesus on one side, would slip money into his hand. Once, however, a man came and started to make a big show of offering Jesus money for the mission. Although the missionaries could really have done with the money, Jesus politely but firmly refused to take it. The man was very surprised and rather miffed. He stuck his nose in the air and stalked off the site very haughtily. When he had gone and the crowd had disappeared, Jesus called his followers together to explain his actions.

'When people give charitably, they shouldn't make a show of it,' he said.[13] 'When they do, the only reward they will get is the passing regard of the unworthy people round about. No – that's not the way. When you give, do it secretly, without anyone knowing. Don't even let your left hand know what your right hand is doing! Then God, who sees everything in secret, will reward you.'

NOTES
[1] Luke 18:9.
[2] Matt. 23:12.
[3] Luke 11:38.
[4] Mark 3:31.
[5] Matt. 6:9.
[6] Psalm 139:9.
[7] Deut. 33:27.
[8] Matt. 18:21.
[9] Matt. 7:1.
[10] Luke 10:25.
[11] Matt. 5:44.
[12] Mark 6:43.
[13] Matt. 6:1-4.

The end of the first mission

The work continued in this way for many weeks. Larger and larger numbers of people came to the meetings, as knowledge of Jesus and his remarkable powers, both of healing and speaking, became more widespread. The disciples had more and more to do, organising the crowds, caring for the handicapped and trying to protect Jesus from the worst of the pressures. Inevitably, however, the leader was feeling the strain. He had to prepare his thoughts each day, preach at least twice, often more, and frequently deal with hostile questions, as well as heal, counsel and comfort those in particular need. When time permitted, Jesus gave his followers more detailed teaching, but often there was too much else to do. Even Jesus's formidable resources were fully stretched.

So, at last, he decided that the time had come for a short respite. It was now mid-September and the worst heat of summer was passing. There were still several weeks of good weather to come, but gradually the climate was cooling and everyone felt a sense of relief. Jesus told his followers that he had decided that it was time to go back to Capernaum for a few days' rest before heading north.

They set up their camp one night just to the west of Tiberias. There was no question of going into the built-up area – Jesus had no liking for large towns, especially Antipas's seat of government! However, much to their surprise, someone paid them a visit. It was Matthias, who came alone this time.

'However did you know where to find us?' asked Jesus.

'It would be difficult for you to move anywhere in Galilee without it being reported back to Antipas,' said Matt, 'and because I have been visiting John the Baptist in prison regularly, I've become known at the palace – to the servants, of course – and they have kept me in touch with your progress.'

'I see,' said Jesus, thoughtfully. 'I hadn't realised that we had caused that much of a stir.'

'Antipas needs to know what's going on in Galilee; he has his spies everywhere. But I'm afraid I have to give you some sad news – dreadful news, in fact – and warn you to be very careful in the future. My master, John, has been killed by Antipas – executed on a whim.'[1]

'What?' Jesus could hardly believe what he was hearing. 'What on earth happened to provoke Antipas to such an extent?'

'Well, of course, I only heard the story at third or fourth hand, but it seems that they were having a party or banquet or something similar – I gather it was the King's birthday. Anyway, lots of important guests were there, and Herodias's daughter, Salome, danced for the King and his guests. It seems he was so pleased that he promised her anything she wanted – even half his kingdom! Well, Salome asked her mother what she should ask for, and Herodias told her to ask for John's head on a platter!'

'How gruesome!' said Andrew, his face wrinkled in disgust.

'Why was Herodias so incensed with John?' asked Thomas.

'Well, you remember that John was very critical of the marriage between Antipas and Herodias – since both had been married before – and it appears that Herodias has never forgiven him for what he said. This was her opportunity and she took it. The King was, no doubt, half drunk when he made his promise to Salome, but couldn't lose face in front of all his important guests. He just had to order the execution.'

'It's a truly sad end to the life of a fine man,' said Jesus solemnly. 'I'm sure we all grieve for him. Thank you for coming to tell us – and for your warning. We shall be careful. As a matter of fact, we are on our way north, further away from the centre of things. It's perhaps just as well.'

'I'd say it was a very wise thing to do,' replied Matt. 'Stay out of the way of Antipas, at least for a while. He's certainly having you watched. If I were you, I'd be leaving Galilee altogether.'

'No,' said Jesus slowly, 'we'll stick to our plan, at least for the time being. In three months, it will be too cold and wet to live out of doors and we shall go to ground anyway'.

'Well, good luck.'

'What will you do now?' asked Jesus.

Matt shrugged his shoulders.

'Oh, I don't know,' he said. 'All the rest of John's people have already left for their homes. I guess I shall do the same and make my way to my village – Bethphage, just outside Jerusalem on the Mount of Olives. My work is finished here. John too knew that he had done what was required of him and he could leave everything safely in your hands.'

'He said that, did he? That's interesting. Well, I shall certainly look you up when I next come to Jerusalem – you must let me know where I can find you. I'll be down at the end of the year.'

Matt stayed with them overnight and set off south next morning. The rest moved off north to Magdala, making camp just outside the town. Jesus went with Judas and Thaddeus into town and, while his disciples attended to the shopping, he went round to Nimrah's house and enquired of her servant whether she would receive him. Almost immediately, Nimrah appeared and insisted that he come through on to the terrace for some refreshment. They settled themselves on comfortable chairs and ate a few fresh grapes.

'How are things with you, Nimrah?' enquired Jesus.

'Very much better than they were on your last visit, thanks to you. Mary is a different girl. Oh, we still have our moments, but taken all round life is so much sweeter now. We've come to trust one another again and love one another. No, that's not right... I never stopped loving her... I just couldn't show it. I'm sounding terribly muddled – sorry...' Nimrah broke off, flustered.

'I understand,' said Jesus, smiling. 'I'm glad things are so much better for you. I hope Mary feels the same way...'

'I think so. She's here and will be delighted to see you,' replied his hostess. 'I'll call her.'

She called a servant and told her to find Mary and ask her to come to the terrace. Mary was, indeed, pleased to see Jesus, flushing with joy and smiling winningly. There was really no need to ask her how she was – it was immediately apparent that here was a happy spirit.

'You do look tired, Jesus,' she said. 'How have things been with you?'

Jesus briefly related the main happenings since they had left Magdala on their way south.

'So the people do listen to you and accept your message?' asked Mary. 'I was sure they would.'

'Yes,' answered Jesus slowly. 'Yes, they listen, some of them. Some argue and dispute. Often it is the religious people who can't accept what I have to say. They already know what they believe and won't be told. They can't accept anything new – they can't change or enlarge their ideas. On the other hand, the ordinary folk often seem to warm to what I say, but the trouble is that they are so often distracted from the message by the healing.'

'Then you are still healing – that's wonderful,' cried Mary.

'I heal those who come to me, yes,' replied the preacher, 'but, as I indicated, the healing distracts the people from thinking about what I say. They get so excited...'

'Surely it is to be expected,' said Nimrah, 'but they will honour you for your healing and believe what you say more readily.'

'Perhaps,' said Jesus. 'I sometimes wonder, though.'

The conversation drifted on happily. Mary was so pleased to have some time with Jesus, for whom, evidently, she had developed tremendous regard. Nimrah, seeing her with him, wondered whether she was not being carried away by this charismatic preacher. She wondered how it would all end. Well, anything was preferable to the infighting that had gone on between them prior to Mary's encounter with Jesus! Of course, before he left, she invited him back to supper, with some of his friends. This time, Jesus chose the younger members of his party to accompany him – John, Thaddeus, Philip and little James. These were all delighted to be asked, having seen from afar a little of the beautiful girl who was to be one of their hostesses. The meal was a great success, enjoyed by all. The disciples were encouraged to talk of their lives on mission, speaking not only warmly of Jesus's sterling work and the marvellous effect he had on so many, but also of some of the amusing or hair-raising incidents that had occurred. For instance, there was the time that Thaddeus had almost let the campfire get out of control and nearly succeeded in burning down an entire village.

'It turned out all right in the end,' said the young man, 'but, for a moment or two, I thought that that fire had got away. You know how careful you have to be in the summer, when everything is so dry. I'd just gone away to get a few more logs and a spark must have blown over and caught on some dried up grass and, in a minute, the fire had blazed up and nearly caught the leaves on a nearby bush. If the bush had gone up, then the tree next to it would have caught, and pretty soon the whole valley would have followed. The village nearby might well have been burnt to the ground. It was a near thing!'

'We always left some water near the fire after that,' added James, 'just in case!'

'Then there was the time old Nathaniel sat on his water skin and it burst under him!' laughed John. 'You can imagine how precious water is, when you have to lug it all from the nearest village. Well, he'd just got back to camp with two skins full and, exhausted, he flopped down and landed right on one, and that was that. You should have seen his face – and his robe!'

'He was able to get some more water, though,' said Jesus. 'That's part of life – fetching water. However much you are able to drink today, you'll always need to replenish your stock tomorrow; but, in contrast, think for a moment of the pure water of God's message – the living water that flows from the Father, which, once received, is yours for ever and needs no replenishment.'[2]

The company received this truth more soberly. But Jesus didn't pursue the idea and soon had them all laughing again with a story of his own. Mary thought he was wonderful – able to be profound one minute, yet light-hearted the next. What a man!

Just as Jesus indicated that they should be leaving, Mary suddenly surprised them all by asking if she could go with them on the mission.

'I'd make myself really useful,' she said. 'I can cook, mend and tend that fire for you. I could wash clothes…'

'It sounds delightful,' replied Jesus, smiling, 'but I think your presence would outrage too many people – more even than we have already offended.'

Mary's face dropped. 'I don't see why…' she started to say, but her mother cut in firmly.

'I'm sorry, Mary, but it's quite out of the question. Of course, we know that you would come to no harm with Jesus and his men, but imagine what people would think – and say. A young woman, alone with thirteen men! Even you must surely see that it's totally unacceptable.'

Mary gave up. There was clearly no way. Reluctantly, she bid farewell to the visitors, with a particularly long glance at Jesus as he left. She was smitten, there was no doubt of that! Nimrah managed to slip Jesus some more money towards his work. Jesus smiled and thanked her warmly.

'What should we do without you?' he asked.

'More to the point, what should we have been without you?' was the reply.

★

Jesus decided that they should delay their departure the next day so that they would arrive at Capernaum after dark.

'If we are to have a few days' holiday,' said Jesus, 'we had better keep out of sight! I certainly don't want the local rabbi or the Pharisees to know that I'm around; nor do I want to have to speak to anyone for a few days. In addition, it might minimise the information being passed to Antipas.'

When they arrived at Peter's home, of course, the big fisherman and his brother were welcomed ecstatically by Ruth and Abigail. They had both kept well during the men's absence, but they had missed them sorely. The men's mother, too, had been lonely without seeing them. James and John found their parents in good shape, but Zebedee was still grumbling that he had been left to keep the business running alone.

Jesus and Judas were taken in readily, the former lodging with Peter, the latter with James and John. The other disciples were anxious to press on to their own homes to the east and north. It was arranged that they would all meet up again in Urta, at Thomas's home, in a week's time. That would then give them six or seven more weeks until the rainy season started and they would have to suspend operations until the spring.

★

Thomas and Rachel made them all very welcome at Urta a week later. Rachel had been overjoyed to see her husband, even if it was only for a few days on this occasion. Her sister-in-law's confinement had gone well and both mother and baby – a son – were doing well. Rachel had managed to join in the celebrations with hardly a tinge of jealousy this time.

It was surprising how a few days' rest seemed to have revived all their spirits and given them new zest to continue the mission. Jesus, particularly, seemed completely refreshed. He had spent many hours resting and reflecting on the roof of Peter's house, out of sight and free from worry or disturbance. Peter and Andrew, after a day or so, had returned to fishing. 'A change is as good as a rest,' Peter had said – 'and it will help with the finances!' And so it proved. James and John saw that their father had a few days off while they returned to the lake; not that Zebedee was very grateful. 'You'll be off again in five minutes, no doubt,' he had complained.

It was true. The week had soon flown by.

'We'll be home again before long,' James had reassured him, but the old man liked to grumble. The fact was that the hired men did most of the work – they had all been working for Zebedee for so long that they could carry on perfectly well without him!

Judas had spent some of his time enquiring about employment for the winter period, which he hoped to spend in the Capernaum district. He had returned to Peter's home one day much encouraged. One of the bigger traders in the town had offered him employment as a bookkeeper and scrivener, which would keep him for the winter.

The three men from Gischala reported back with cheery faces. There had been no more trouble from the authorities after they left; the Zealots had retreated into the hills and kept out of sight and everything had calmed down. The townspeople had been greatly shaken by the mass executions, of course, but even that awful memory had faded a little and life had returned to something like normality. The other blacksmith in the town had done roaring trade in Simon's absence and was rather half-hearted in his welcome when they met, until he learnt that Simon was due to leave again in a week!

Matthew had had a frosty reception when he returned to Joanna. After only a couple of days with her, and with the situation not showing any sign of improving, he had gone early to Urta, where his partner, Thomas, had taken him in. These two were becoming good friends. Although they were from very different backgrounds and with different skills, they complemented each other temperamentally; Thomas was inclined to be pessimistic – or, on his own definition, 'realistic' – whereas Matthew was the eternal optimist. But, together with Peter, James the fisherman, and Andrew, they brought a good deal of common sense to the group – a contribution born out of years of life experience. This balanced the more exuberant spirits of the younger fellows – Philip, Simon, Thaddeus, little James and John. Nathaniel, of course, brought the wisdom of a grandfather and was respected for that. Judas – well, he was a bit of an enigma. He was by far the best educated of them all, but sometimes he seemed to be lacking stability of character. He was a bit like a grasshopper, hopping quickly from topic to topic and from mood to mood. Of course he was different – he was from the south! Somehow the others felt vaguely that he didn't quite fit in with them, though the subject was rarely mentioned.

It was good to be together again, however, and share a meal. The conversation flowed freely, with many laughs. Rachel enjoyed mothering them all, in spite of the way in which her normally immaculate house was inevitably disturbed by so many visitors. When the meal was coming to a close, as they sipped their wine and picked at a few grapes, Jesus called them all to some kind of order.

'My friends,' he began, 'we have all had a good rest and should be ready for several more weeks of mission in the north. As you know, the people there have a fierce reputation for independence. They want to live in a free Israel again; well, wouldn't we all like that? It gives me no pleasure to know that we are governed by Rome, through their puppet King, Herod Antipas, but that is the situation we have, and, as you know, I have no plan to try and change it. God will change it in his own time.

'Our mission is to give the people hope that their lives are not wasted, or even, at any level that counts, much affected by their rulers. I shall continue to push the idea of the inner Kingdom, one that neither Tiberias Caesar nor

Herod Antipas can influence. Whenever we are faced with the political question, I urge you to duck it. It is an irrelevance to our work, which is to bring love, freedom and inner strength to individuals and thereby enhance the life of the whole community.

'We shall do here in the north the same as we did in the south. I will preach in the towns when we are welcomed, but in the countryside when we are not. I will invariably tend to those who come for healing, but I hope that the main emphasis will always be on the message. I will give whatever time I can to teaching you as a group. Towards the end of our season, I shall expect you to go out in pairs to preach yourselves – you've heard the message many times now and know well enough by now what to say.'

The disciples exchanged some anxious looks.

'I'm not sure that I'm ready for that,' said Peter.

'Nor I.' This came from several others almost at once.

'You are ready – because God will speak through you. Do not worry.' Jesus could persuade anyone!

And so, next day, they set off on their task, finding initially that they were welcomed in the towns, but, as before, as soon as the Synagogue authorities realised how different Jesus's emphasis was, they found themselves living and working out in the open countryside. After another slow start, however, they found that the people came readily to hear Jesus. Inevitably, the healing ministry was sought. Jesus only had to heal a few people for his reputation to go before him, and his strength was tested yet again.

★

One night, Jesus had, unusually, been invited to dine at the home of a Pharisee called Simon, in one of the villages in the far north of Galilee, near the Phoenician border. Simon had attended a meeting in the village square and had invited Jesus and a couple of his followers to supper immediately afterwards. Jesus had asked Philip and Nathaniel to join him on this occasion. The meal was very pleasant, if not particularly grandiose, but the travellers enjoyed eating round a table, instead of roughing it on the ground as they had to do so often in the camp. The conversation flowed freely. Simon seemed to be in sympathy with much that Jesus had been saying, but, inevitably, being a strict Pharisee, there were some points which he quibbled over, and Jesus eventually became frustrated by his attitude.

'I really don't know how to please you Pharisees,' he said. 'You seem to find something to argue about no matter what I say or do. It was the same when John the Baptist preached. You Pharisees criticised him for being a bit of a killjoy – he lived in the desert; he didn't drink and he fasted often. Yet when I come, eating and drinking and enjoying company, I am accused of being a wine-bibber and a glutton!'[3]

Simon didn't reply for a moment. Then he said quietly, 'My trouble – and

I'm sure it's the same with many of my colleagues in the sect – is that you come with such a different approach to the religious life. We were brought up to follow the Law – keep to the rules which have been laid down. Follow the beaten track, where there is safety. You come, it seems to us, without any rules. You bring a fresh look but…'

'I don't quarrel with the Law – the principles behind the Law,' replied Jesus. 'I try to fulfil the essence of the Law, which is to give pride of place in life to God and to helping others. Anything that fits with that principle, I do. Anything that conflicts with that, I avoid.'

Just then, there was a knock at the door and a servant came in, saying that there was a woman at the door who wished to speak to Jesus. Simon looked in amazement at his guest, and asked him if he knew who she might be.

'I've no idea,' said Jesus. 'Naturally, in the course of my work, lots of folk see me and hear me, and sometimes they try to get a word with me later if they have a particular problem in their lives. Perhaps we came away from the meeting rather quickly tonight for supper with you and she missed out.'

'Ask her to come in,' said Simon to the servant and, a few moments later, he returned followed by an unmarried woman in her mid-twenties who was carrying a small flask of oil. She looked around the table and then, seeing Jesus, she quickly made her way to him and fell at his feet, weeping.[4] Amazed and puzzled, the men weren't quite sure what to do; they looked at one another, unsure and astounded. Meanwhile, the woman had uncorked the bottle and began to anoint Jesus's feet with the precious oil it contained, and wipe them with her beautiful, long, dark hair, which flowed over her shoulders almost to her waist. Her tears fell on his feet and she kissed them and wiped them with her locks. After a moment or so, Simon recovered his tongue, and began to rebuke the woman, but Jesus silenced him with a small gesture. The woman continued to wash the preacher's feet and, when she had finished, she spoke softly to him. The disciples next to Jesus could only just hear her voice, so softly was it delivered.

'Rabbi, I want to thank you,' she was saying. 'You have, tonight, rescued a soul from itself. There were so many things in my life which I had got wrong – I thought I had drifted for ever away from an acceptable life. But you told me that God would still welcome me. Even me. I just want…'

'Don't fret, my daughter,' Jesus broke in, also very softly. 'If you have been found by the great shepherd and brought back to the sheepfold, then I rejoice. I welcome you in his name. Your past is forgiven. Believe me – it is all a thing of the past, now. Go home and begin a new life among the faithful sheep.'

'But will they welcome me too?' The woman was still weeping.

'I cannot say,' replied Jesus, kindly. 'I hope and pray they will, but you will have to face up to whatever comes and make a way for yourself in harmony with God. This is the only way to inner happiness. Go now and don't make the same mistakes again – and thank you for what you have done for me tonight. It was a beautiful thing to do.'

Slowly, the woman rose to her feet, taking the empty bottle with her. She looked for a long moment at Jesus's face, deep into his big, brown eyes, then, with a long sigh, she walked from the room.

There was an embarrassed silence after the door slammed behind her until, at last, Simon looked at Jesus and said, 'You know what that woman is, don't you?'

'I have a good idea,' replied the preacher. 'You only had to look at her clothes and general appearance to get the message...'

'She is a prostitute!' said Simon, with fierce disgust. 'And you encouraged her to stay in my house. You let her touch you and wash your feet in a quite unseemly manner. I am appalled – scandalised. And in my house...' He broke off, evidently beyond speech.

Jesus allowed him a few seconds before replying.

'Simon,' he said, 'I will be quite frank with you. You were kind enough to invite my friends and me to your house tonight and give us a good meal, for which we are very grateful. But your servant did not wash our feet for us when we arrived, in spite of the fact that we have been out in the dust all day. You did not kiss us to welcome us here. You certainly didn't anoint us with oil. This woman, whom you despise so much, has done all three for me. Evidently, she feels that I have done something for her tonight and she wished to repay my kindness in the only way she knows. Why do you despise her gifts?'

Simon shook his head, evidently still displeased. Jesus leaned towards him, his hands outstretched.

'What did I do for her?' he said. 'You were at the meeting, so you know. I simply told you all a little story of a shepherd who lost one of his sheep... and he loved that sheep so much that he went out into the desert until he found it. She saw herself mirrored in that simple story; she believes now that God loves her like that, no matter what she has done. Can't you rejoice at that? Can't you hope with me that she will find a new and better life?'

'But she is a fallen creature!' Simon's voice was shrill. 'Surely she is beyond recall. She certainly shouldn't come here making a spectacle of herself and embarrassing us both...' His face was still filled with disgust.

Jesus shook his head. He pulled at his beard before replying.

'Nobody is beyond recall,' he said. 'Let me tell you another little story. There was once a moneylender who had two men in debt to him. One owed five hundred silver pieces, the other fifty. Both were quite unable to pay, so, being in a benevolent mood, the moneylender decided to cancel both debts. Now, which of the debtors will be more grateful, do you think?'

'Well, I suppose the one who owed more,' replied Simon suspiciously, wondering what was to follow.

'Exactly,' replied his guest. 'In the same way, this woman has been forgiven much and is very grateful. We have to find it in our hearts to accept her, just as God has done, not reject her. You have lived a righteous life and need less forgiveness – but this should not result in you being less loving.'

The Pharisee sat for several seconds looking doubtfully at his hands. Finally, he said, 'I don't know. I really don't know about you, Jesus. You disturb me. What you say sounds right, but I just can't accept – still less love – this kind of person.'

He paused for second, then, with renewed vehemence, he cried, 'Nor was it right for you to tell her that her past life is forgiven – that is God's prerogative, not yours!'

Jesus looked at him kindly, then, with a slight shake of his head, he said, 'But God is always willing to forgive. Even before the sinner has repented, he wants to forgive. I know that he has forgiven that poor woman, just as he will forgive you for your unkind treatment of her.'

There was silence. Then Simon got to his feet.

'I think that it is time that you went, Jesus,' he said. 'I have tried to befriend you, to understand you and even agree with you, wherever possible, but you simply have got things wrong. We cannot agree. You'd better go.'

And so the evening ended on a sour note. The three friends departed as quickly as they could and made their way with some regret to the camp. The next day, they moved on elsewhere.

★

The religious authorities may have been critical of Jesus, but the attitude of the general populace was quite different. So many said to Jesus, or to his followers, after the meetings, how much they appreciated his straightforward approach to life, his lack of petty rule-making and his assurance that God was really like a kindly father, rather than a stern judge or fierce king.

'What I like is that Jesus talks with a real knowledge of God,' said one man to Thomas one day. 'But how does he know what God is like?'

Thomas reflected for a moment before replying.

'He seems to have a special relationship with God – he seems almost instinctively to know just how God thinks and feels,' he said. 'Of course, I know that God isn't human and doesn't think and feel like a human being, but Jesus somehow makes us feel that he really cares as if he were a human father. How Jesus knows, I can't tell – but he does. We all feel it. It is almost as if, when we look at him, we see something of God himself.[5] We have come to believe that his purpose, his hopes and his attitudes are all identical with God's.'

'Can a man really be that close to God?' asked another.

Matthew, who was also present, burst in, 'He really seems to be. To me, it is as if he is a window into the heart of God – if that isn't blasphemy.'

The disciples often discussed their feelings about Jesus when he was away on his own, preparing his mind for the next meeting with the people.

'Do you think he is really the Messiah?' was the question they often pondered. 'What about his wonderful healing miracles? Don't they show that he is special?'

'Others have been healers,' someone would point out.

'On this scale, though?'

Nobody really knew – what they knew about the other healers was all hearsay. So the discussions went on. Often they talked about the coming of the Kingdom – not just the 'inner Kingdom', that Jesus so frequently referred to, but the final Kingdom, when God would reign supreme, as foretold by the prophets. If Jesus was really the Messiah, why didn't he know when the Kingdom would come? He had referred to them, his twelve followers, as the leaders of the twelve tribes – what did that mean? Everyone knew that ten of the tribes had been lost six hundred years ago. Would God recover them? Did Jesus really believe that God would 'break through' one day? How would it happen? It was all very puzzling.

If the followers of Jesus were confused, the people were even more uncertain. They followed him about from place to place, hearing his homilies day after day, yet understanding only a small proportion of what they heard. They seemed to have selective hearing, taking in only what they wanted to hear. They heard about the coming Kingdom, and, being Northern Galileans, they thought instinctively of deliverance from political oppression, rather than freedom from the evils that spoil daily life. One day, after Jesus had been talking of his hopes for the Kingdom, the people started really pressing him to declare himself and lead them to the new life.

'Let's have Jesus as our king,' someone shouted.

The cry was immediately taken up by scores of others around the crowd.

'Lead us to glory!' shouted another.

'I have come to lead you in the right path, but…' Jesus started to say.

'Hallelujah!' shouted someone else. 'Lead us! Lead us!'

'Jesus for King!' There was the challenge again.[6]

'I am not your king,' said Jesus. ' I have no wish to be an earthly king. I'm not here to lead you on the battlefield, like an earthly monarch. God doesn't want to see his people fighting and dying…'

'You can do it! Down with Rome…'

Eventually, Jesus managed to calm the crowd enough to get them to leave. When they had gone, he conferred with his followers.

'This isn't at all what I want,' he sighed. 'They just won't understand that political freedom isn't the issue. They must wait for God to release them from Rome. Meantime, they must accept his offer of freedom from their worst selves. They must learn to love…'

They were about to turn in for the night when they were disturbed by two men who stole into the camp, asking to talk with Jesus. The leader was a very tall man, sporting an enormous beard. The other was a small, ferret-like creature, who had narrow slits for eyes and looked distinctly unpleasant. The preacher pulled himself from his blanket and, rubbing his eyes, sat by the dying fire and asked what the men wanted.

'We've come to make you an offer,' said the leader, who declined to give his name.

'Oh? What kind of offer?' Jesus was puzzled.

'We were at your meeting earlier this evening and we could see that the people are ready to follow your lead, wherever it goes.'

'Yes, I know. They got carried away. They're very confused. I've been trying to tell them—'

The big man leaned towards Jesus, interrupting him. 'You have to grasp this great opportunity, Jesus,' he said. 'It's time you stopped messing about with vague thoughts about freedom from sin, or self, or whatever, and devoted yourself to the real issue. The real issue is freedom from Rome – freedom to live in our own country, under our own ruler. And you can be that ruler. You know you can. They'll follow you. So will we…'

Jesus shook his head vigorously. 'But you know that I don't have any pretensions…' he started to say.

'You're a Jew, aren't you? Then you ought to want to be free. You ought to want to get rid of Rome, and Antipas… You can, you know. We have many men hidden away in the mountains, ready to take up arms as soon as the moment arrives – as soon as you give the word and bring the mass of the people in behind us. It's all there for the taking. Now, what do you say?'

Jesus paused for just a second and then said, very firmly, 'I have said no, and I meant it. I will go on saying no to all thoughts of violence. It is for God to act – and he will, very soon. Whether his action will release you from Rome, I don't know, but salvation – personal freedom – will come soon. I know it. All you have to do is watch and wait for it and be ready to receive it when it does come. Open your hearts to God and allow him into your lives… I've said it all so often.'

The smaller man stood up impatiently.

'It's useless to argue with him,' he sneered. 'He's only interested in his religious beliefs and can't see that politics and religion are inseparable in this part of the world. We know that God helps those who help themselves. Let's go.'

More reluctantly, his companion got to his feet too.

'You just think over what we have said,' the tall man told Jesus. 'We'll wait for a while. We can wait. We'll see you again and see if you haven't changed your mind. You'll come round.'

As they started to leave, Jesus called after them, 'Don't wait for me. I can be as stubborn as you are, you'll see!'

When the men had finally departed, Jesus called his followers round him and told them, bluntly, 'We're out of here tomorrow, early. Up with the sun, and on our way. It's too dangerous to stay here longer.'

★

They set up camp again a few miles to the south, in an area they hadn't visited before.

'It's your turn, now,' said Jesus. 'I want you to go out, in your pairs, and talk to the people telling them the same good news as I've been preaching for the whole season.[7] Don't worry. I'll go over with you everything I want you to say before you set out.'

The disciples grimaced and looked at each other, but they reluctantly accepted the idea. All day long, they sat in their pairs, preparing their minds and hearts, with Jesus moving between the pairs, offering advice and guidance.

'Don't worry about taking a lot of stores and money with you,' he said. 'You'll find people very generous, especially if you serve them.'

The next day, they set out. They were due to be away from Jesus for just a week, then come back to report to him on their progress. In fact, they found that, just as Jesus had predicted, they were able to speak, albeit haltingly to begin with, but, with practice and increasing confidence, with greater and greater clarity and authority. By the time they returned to Jesus, they were surprisingly upbeat about the idea of speaking for themselves. The terror of standing up and opening their mouths had gone, if not completely, at least to a large extent.

'Next year, you'll do even better,' said Jesus, smiling, 'but I think that the weather will soon be closing in on us, and we should make our plans for the winter.'

Most of the followers opted, of course, for home. Even Simon, little James and Thaddeus thought they would be all right in Gischala, provided they steered well clear of the Zealots. Matthew decided to stay with Thomas in Urta and Judas had a job lined up in Capernaum, staying with James and John, the fishermen.

'What will you do, Jesus?' asked Peter.

'I have to go to Jerusalem,' he replied. 'I have friends to see there and I want to be in the Holy City for the Feast of Dedication. After that? Who knows? I shall be all right.'

'When shall we all meet again, then?' Andrew was keen.

'That's what I wanted to arrange with you,' replied Jesus. 'I want you all to be in Capernaum, at Simon Peter's house, for Passover next spring. It is unfortunate that we shall have to miss the feast in Jerusalem on that occasion, but I can see no alternative – we just have to get on with the ministry. By then, with any luck, the weather should be good enough for us to sleep outside without difficulty. I'll see you all then. Have a restful winter, and come back prepared for hard work!'

NOTES

[1] Mark 6:28.
[2] John 4:14.
[3] Luke 7:34.
[4] Luke 7:38.
[5] John 14:9.
[6] John 6:15.
[7] Mark 6:7.

Winter in Jerusalem

Jesus made his way south to Jericho. There was no need to hurry; he could take the long journey reasonably gently. The weather was much cooler by now, which helped, but a few short, sharp storms halted progress temporarily. As usual, the rain, once it came, came down in buckets. Fortunately, there were plenty of trees along the Jordan Valley – figs, carobs, dates, apricots, olives, pomegranates, citrus and many others – so shelter was easily found. On a couple of occasions, however, when the storm was accompanied by brilliant lightning and deafening thunder, Jesus preferred to risk getting wet, crouching near a wall. After the storms, walking was often seriously impeded by the state of the path, which became a sea of mud in many places; but the sun soon returned and before long everything had dried out again. Unless the ground was wet at night, it was still possible to sleep out in the open, but, on a couple of occasions, the ground was soaked and Jesus had to take a bed at a wayside inn.

After seven days walking, he reached the ancient city, and found his way to the house of John barHelez. The old servant grinned broadly when he saw who had arrived and welcomed him into the spacious hall.

'Come in, sir,' he said. 'The master's here, having finished his term of service at the temple. I'll tell him you are here. He will be pleased to see you. He often speaks of you.'

He showed Jesus into the living room and seated him, and very soon he was joined by his friend. Jesus rose and the two embraced each other warmly.

'It's so good to see you, Jesus,' said the priest. 'I've been wondering how you were getting on.'

'We'll have a long talk over supper, if I can stay,' replied Jesus, 'and you can tell me how things are progressing with you.'

'Of course you can stay – and welcome.'

In fact, they talked well into the night. Jesus told John all that had happened since they had last met in midsummer. He described his newly found friends and his opponents, the successes and the difficulties. He was always at ease with John, even though they so often differed, so he could tell the story very frankly.

John mentioned that he had heard some reports of Jesus's activities through the High Priest's office, but the details were rather vague. What went on in Galilee was not of the greatest concern to the High Priest, since he was not politically responsible for the area, as he was in Judaea. Nevertheless, anyone claiming to give a lead in religious matters anywhere in Jewry was bound to be of some interest to the Temple authorities.

'What are you planning to do in Jerusalem this time?' he asked, rather anxiously. 'Do be careful. Here, as you know, the High Priest is very powerful – second only to the Roman Prefect, who expects the Temple authorities to keep the province quiet and subservient.'

'Don't worry.' Jesus smiled. 'I'm here primarily for a rest and in order to earn a little money so that we can carry on the mission next spring. I shan't be in the Temple very often – mainly just for a few days at the time of the festival. I'll behave – I promise!'

'It's all very well for you to grin,' replied his friend, rather sternly. 'It's clear that you've caused quite a bit of a rumpus in Galilee. If you did that sort of thing in Judaea, worse still in Jerusalem, I wouldn't give a fig for your chances of a long life.'

'It's not as if I've done anything very terrible,' complained his friend. 'All right, I've broken a few minutiae of the Pharisaic law – I can't get too upset about washing pots and so on. Also, I've broken the Sabbath occasionally, by their very strict interpretation. What else?'

'You've challenged the existing order, Jesus. You've hobnobbed with some pretty questionable characters, by your own admission. You've got a former tax collector and a couple of former Zealots in your party. You've been seen with some women of doubtful character. You spend a lot of time with the handicapped, the sick and so on. You know that the sick are regarded as imperfect and shouldn't be accepted into society – they certainly can't enter the Temple.'

'I know – and I think that's terrible. The sick can't help being sick. The lame don't want to be lame. They're still people and need more help, not less – acceptance, not rejection. As for the other disreputable folk, isn't it better to care for them and help them change their ways?' Jesus sounded exasperated.

'You've upset some important people. Often – almost always – they are the senior religious people in the towns – the rabbis, scribes, Pharisees and so on. You can't expect them to like you criticising them and calling them hypocrites.'

'But that's what they are! They've got everything muddled up! They can't seem to see that real religion is about caring, not show. They like strutting about looking important, but couldn't care less about those in need. Religion is about God and people, not following stupid rules.'

'What do you mean – stupid rules?' John sounded defensive.

'Well, for example, the Law says that we must not work on the Sabbath. That's a good principle. I agree with it. But how is it interpreted? Just to take one instance, the Pharisees say that the tying of knots is to be regarded as "work", but they recognise that a woman needs to tie a knot in her shift or her girdle in order to dress, so they make an exception and allow the tying of a girdle on the Sabbath. So what happens? Anyone who wants to tie a knot around the house on the Sabbath – say, to haul up a bucket from the well – uses a woman's girdle to do it! Now what could be more ridiculous! The setting of petty rules soon induces idiotic ways of getting round them.'

'So what do you suggest?' John was not sounding sympathetic.

'I want to do away with the mass and maze of petty rules and get people to concentrate on the principles – and the principle should always be based on love. Love for God and love for one another. What could be simpler or more apt?'

'How can you expect ordinary, uneducated people to work on airy-fairy principles?' asked John. 'It might be all right for people like you and me – we've studied the Law, we can make the right deductions; but the ordinary fellow in the street can't be left floundering around without proper guidance.'

'You underestimate the so-called ordinary fellow,' replied his guest.

'I certainly don't underestimate the reaction of the Jerusalem authorities if you start saying things like that here,' returned John sharply, but he softened his tone as he continued.

'Look, you know that I share with you your dislike of some of the things which go on. I agree that some of my fellow priests and some of the Pharisees are rather ostentatious about their practice of religion, which can give an unfortunate impression, but are you sure that the sick can't help being sick? We have always believed that sickness is a result of sin, if not on the part of the person concerned, then on the part of his father, or grandfather. It's written into the commandments: "I punish the children for the sins of their fathers, unto the third and fourth generation…"'[1]

Jesus shook his head and scratched his chin.

'But the Law does not say that the punishment is to be in the form of sickness,' he said. 'I do not believe that sickness is God's punishment for sin. Sickness may have to do with guilt – I agree with that. But God is always willing to forgive sin.'

'You say so, but on what authority?' John returned to the attack. 'No wonder the Pharisees criticise you when you say you have the authority to forgive sins. That is our job, as priests. We interpret on behalf of God who is forgiven and who isn't. You're not a priest, Jesus.'

'No. There are some things I'm grateful for!' Jesus grinned again. 'Come on, my friend, let's not quarrel. Let's talk about you and where you are in your spiritual quest. Are you happy being a priest?'

John did not reply immediately. He looked away and appeared to be studying the wine in his mug. Eventually, he looked up and said slowly, 'You know I'm not completely happy. I never have been. We were both searching when we met at Qumran. You think you have now found what you want. I didn't find what I wanted then and I am still not sure which is the right path for me now. I worry about many things – some of which we have covered tonight. I too worry about the posturing of some of the religious people, their attitude to the poor and their use of overlong prayers.[2] Also, I still worry about the racket that goes on in the Temple courtyard, of which we have spoken many times in the past. The prices for sacrificial animals in the sanctuary are still exorbitant – the pilgrims now pay more than ten times as much for a pigeon inside the Temple as they would in the local market. Then there's the question of the exchange rates for Temple currency… well, you know all about that.'

'So why do you tolerate all these things.?' asked Jesus gently, his arms outstretched, his palms turned to the ceiling.

'What's the alternative?' replied his friend. '*I* can't change anything. I'm really not made for the life of an Essene, nor for living in the open air, like John the Baptist or yourself. What did John achieve? Nothing. In the end, he was murdered for his beliefs. Where did that get him? More to the point, what use was it to God? The calling of the priesthood may be defective, but it does a real service to God, and that nobody can deny. And it's safe – I know where I am, if I follow the rules…'

Jesus continued to speak quietly. 'But if the rules are wrong – or irrelevant? Will you go for security under those circumstances?'

There was a long silence. Eventually, John muttered, 'I don't know, Jesus.'

Jesus let another long moment pass before saying, 'Look, John, we've been friends a long time, so I think I can say what is in my mind without giving offence. One thing that worries me is that the priests are all living well, while so many others are poor. You have a lovely house here, and I'm grateful to you for putting me up in it. You have servants and much comfort – which you are pleased to share with me – and I appreciate a couple of days of comfort too. But more senior priests have even better facilities and the High Priest lives the life of a king! Now, is it right that God's special representatives on earth should have all this wealth, while so many around them go short?'

John responded with some warmth.

'But why are people going short? Isn't it that they will not work for their living? Many are bone idle. And would you really have the priests exist like the Qumranis – penniless monks, living the life of slaves in the desert? Shouldn't God's priests be seen to be reasonably housed and fed? When faithful people pay their tithe and the Temple tax, part of which comes to us, it's their response to God himself. Shouldn't they give generously to God?'

'It's a question of the amount…'

'We all pay the tithe…'

Jesus shook his head and replied, 'But you know as well as I do that a fixed percentage applied to a lot of money hurts the giver far less than the same fraction applied to a very little. Which is more important in the end; giving to the already bulging Temple coffers, or feeding your children? Rich people have it easy – but, I tell you this, they will find it more difficult to find their way to God than the poor will. I believe it is easier for a camel to go through the eye of a needle than for a rich man to enter the Kingdom of God.'[3]

John sat silently considering this for a while, then he looked up, sadness written across his face.

'I don't know, my friend. I really don't know. For the time being, I must continue to follow what I believe to be my calling.'

Jesus thought it was time to change the subject.

'Tell me, what is Lazarus doing with himself these days?'

'I haven't seen him for some time,' replied the other. 'The last I heard, nothing much had changed. He's still searching for an expression of faith that satisfies him. I saw him in the Temple recently in the distance, but I was busy and not able to get a word with him.'

'I'll look out for him when I'm there for the festival – almost certainly he'll be there somewhere and we can hopefully have a gossip. If not, I'll go out to Bethany specially.'

'How long will you be in Judaea?' asked John. 'You'll stay with me here in Jericho, of course –' this with a smile – 'in spite of my disgusting opulence!'

Jesus smiled that broad, winning smile of his.

'It's really kind of you, John, but I won't stay more than a few days,' he said. 'Please don't take offence. No doubt you'll have duties to attend to at the Temple over the period of the festival, and I want to be nearer Jerusalem then too. In addition, I have to look up some other friends and get myself some employment for a few months, till the spring comes.'

'Then you'll be back on the road?'

'Yes. Back on the road with my followers, though it looks as if we might have to be out of Galilee for much of the time. It's getting a bit too dangerous to stay there for long – Antipas is apparently taking an interest…'

'I'm sure he doesn't like disturbances any more than Caiaphas or the Romans do. The Zealots in the north tend to get stirred up from time to time.'

'I know that all too well, ' said Jesus, shaking his head. 'When we were up in the far north, they even tried to persuade me to become their king!'

'But that's not on your agenda?' John sounded anxious.

'No, of course not, but it is as you have often said – things can be misunderstood, either deliberately or otherwise. Before you know it, you can be in prison, like John the Baptist, and then—?'

Jesus stopped with eyebrows upraised.

'Yes! You must be careful, Jesus. I'd hate anything to happen to you.'

The conversation went on into the night. The pair were happy in each other's company and neither wanted to be the first to suggest retiring.

★

After resting up for a couple of days, Jesus made his way to Jerusalem. The festival of Dedication would be starting in just a few days' time, but there were things he wanted to get done before the main flood of pilgrims arrived. Fortunately, John was going up to town too to attend to his priestly duties and was taking a couple of servants with him, so Jesus had company for the dangerous stretch of road between Jericho and the capital. They climbed the steep hill into the old town and up the immense flight of marble steps into the great Temple, which looked majestically down over the Kedron Valley. There, Jesus arranged to meet John later in the day, before going to see if he could borrow some scrolls of the great prophets for study in the Temple library.

He worked for the rest of the morning without interruption, but, just as he was about to leave the Temple precinct to seek lunch, he heard a familiar voice hailing him. It was Lazarus, grinning with delight at seeing his friend again. They enjoyed a brief meal together, exchanging some domestic news, and agreed that they should meet again for dinner in Bethany a couple of days later. Jesus would then stay over in the village.

'We can then share all the news at leisure,' said Lazarus, 'and you won't have to repeat it all to the girls.'

'That's excellent,' replied his friend. 'I'll see you then.'

That settled, Jesus made his way to his rendezvous with John, who had said that he knew a good place for Jesus to stay, if he was determined to remain in town.

'Justus keeps a good house and doesn't charge exorbitant prices. You'll be fine with him – if he has any room available. You're ahead of most of the pilgrims, so you should be all right.'

They pushed their way through the narrow, crowded streets till they came to the inn. The landlord greeted them affably enough and confirmed that he had enough room to accommodate Jesus. John took his leave reluctantly.

'We must meet again before you go back north, Jesus. Promise me. You're good for me. You make me think.'

'Of course I'll see you. We'll see each other many times while I am in town. I'll leave a message at your office in the Temple complex if you are not there.'

They shook hands and the priest was gone.

Jesus spent most of the period of the festival in the Temple, studying, thinking and praying. He did as he had promised John, and avoided any discussions which could become confrontational, being content to listen most of the time. He didn't like some of what he heard and saw, but he held his peace. At night, he chatted with the guests at the inn, but again was careful not to say or do anything that would draw attention to himself. Whenever possible, he talked to Justus and his family – his wife, Gomer, and his children, especially his eldest son, John Mark, a lad of seventeen, who quickly came to regard Jesus as his hero.

During the festival, Jesus's time with the family was rather limited as they were pretty busy, the inn being chock-a-block with pilgrims, but after the visitors had departed, Jesus enjoyed many hours talking to them all. However, he also noticed that there were some parts of the inn that urgently needed refurbishing – the woodwork was rotting badly and needed renewal. He asked Justus if he would like him to fix it.

'Is that your line of country?' asked the landlord, surprised. 'I thought you were a rabbi.'

'I was a carpenter long before I was a preacher,' said Jesus, laughing. 'As you probably know, carpenters in the villages have to turn their hands to all kinds of joinery and building jobs, so, as I need to earn my living through the winter period, I'd be happy to take on any jobs you might have for me.'

'What about tools?' asked Justus.

'I'll have to go and buy some – or, perhaps, hire them.'

'Leave that to me,' replied the landlord.

It didn't take long for Justus, who had lived in that area for many years, to borrow the necessary, and Jesus was soon busy carrying out the repairs at the inn. The landlord nodded his approval when he saw the standard of the work, remarking how well everything fitted and was finished off. Just as Jesus was coming to the end of the work at the inn, Justus came to him and asked if he was interested in some more jobs in the area.

'Of course,' replied Jesus. 'Whatever you can find for me.'

'I have a couple of friends down at the market place who need some help. One's a locksmith, called Cleopas, and the other's Nathan, a cobbler. They have small workshops next door to one another, and the other day I heard them saying that they needed some work doing on the front of their two shops.'

'Lead me to it!' was the reply.

Jesus got on very well with both Cleopas and Nathan. During the hours he spent working at their workshops, rather dingy little places where the two men carried out their trades, he held long conversations with them. They encouraged him to explain his hopes and dreams for improving life for the nation of Israel, and, beyond that, the world. He told them of his ideas for the new Kingdom and the way in which God would have his way, not by force of arms, but by the willing consent of men and women of goodwill coming voluntarily to him and giving their lives in service and love. The three men became good friends.

One thing led to another. Each customer introduced him to another and soon Jesus found himself with more than enough work for the entire winter stay in Jerusalem. He was also able to take some time out to visit Bethany to see Lazarus, Martha and Mary, as he had promised, which was a joy for them all. Lazarus confided in his friend that he was still restless, spiritually speaking, and unsure what he should do to fulfil what he believed to be his calling.

'I don't feel right, just drifting through life like I do,' he explained. 'I try to keep the Law and go to the Temple for festivals as a good Jew should, but somehow that doesn't seem enough. We've tried the life at Qumran – together – and neither of us felt that that life was right for us. John may now be happy as a priest, but I couldn't do that either – even if I had the education. I am beginning to think that I ought to go to one of the other Essene communities – they differ from place to place, you know – and see what they can offer me.'

'Some of them are even more extreme, demanding quite extraordinary responses from their adherents,' warned Jesus. 'Is that really what you have in mind? Real religion doesn't necessarily involve extraordinary lifestyles, you know!'

'I'm not happy as I am,' Lazarus replied, looked very depressed.

'Isn't it possible that God wants your response in and through what we might call an "ordinary life"?' Jesus's voice was gentle.

'But I want to show God that I really care!' cried Lazarus, now quite in anguish.

'You must, of course, follow your own conscience,' replied his friend soothingly, 'but I do urge you to think it through carefully before you do anything rash. Your sisters here need your support, financially and socially. They will find it very difficult to manage on their own. I know they have other relations in the area, but these people all have their own responsibilities – families, businesses and so on. Might it not be your calling to fend for your sisters and serve the other folk in this village in ordinary ways, rather than by doing something more dramatic?'

And so another conversation went on well into the night.

*

One day, Jesus was enjoying a few moments with Mary in the courtyard at Bethany. The girl seemed contented enough, but Jesus wondered whether, under the surface, she was questioning, like her brother, what she should do with her life. Of course, the question of marriage would be well to the fore – for a girl, at seventeen, it was high time. She was pretty enough, but there would be no dowry. Mary, however, seemed more anxious to talk to Jesus about his work and his hopes.

'Tell me about your mission, Jesus,' she pleaded. 'What do you tell the people?'

Jesus outlined his thinking on the Kingdom of heaven – that inner realm of love and tranquillity, open to all who sought it. He found himself talking at some length, because every time he stopped, Mary would prompt him with another question or a sympathetic comment. She seemed to understand his world and enter into his problems and frustrations. He chatted happily on, glad enough to have an attentive ear and responsive mind.

'I'd love to come with you and share in the work. I could be of some use, I'm sure,' Mary said wistfully.

'It's no place for a woman.' Jesus smiled and shook his head. 'We had a similar offer from another young lady of about your age – another Mary, actually – but there's no way. It would really outrage society to have you in our midst – however innocent it was in reality!'

Just then Martha appeared in the doorway.

'Mary! Can't you see I'm busy? There are a hundred things to do, if we're to have supper ready for when Lazarus comes home. Jesus, tell her to come and help, please – I really can't manage on my own.'[4]

Jesus intervened quietly. 'Martha, my dear, you worry too much. You have a lot to do, it's true, but there's not that much rush. Mary and I rarely get a chance to talk quietly together and, perhaps, just at the moment, that should take priority. But you're welcome to come and join us – we'll all talk together – then, later, we can all help with the chores.'

Martha wasn't pleased and went off complaining under her breath. The spell was broken between the other two and pretty soon they too made their way to the kitchen. An opportunity for an in-depth relationship was lost.

★

A couple of weeks later, Jesus took time off to try to find Matthias, as he had promised him he would. He left Jerusalem and crossed the Kedron Valley and climbed the Mount of Olives to the village of Bethphage, just off the summit. He asked around and pretty soon he was directed to Matthias's little house, where he was greeted most enthusiastically.

'It's good to see you, Jesus,' said Matt. 'Come in and sit yourself down. I'll get a mug of beer for you.'

Jesus asked him how his life was progressing since his return from Galilee. Matt shrugged and grimaced.

'Well, I've taken up where I left off. My brother and I are farmers, and we also do a bit of this and that – carpentry and building – that sort of thing. We get by. He's glad enough to have me back, for there's plenty of work hereabouts… How are things going for you?'

Jesus filled in the story since they had last met in September, finishing with the experience in the north of Galilee, where the crowd had wanted to proclaim him a king and leader against Rome.

'Some military leader I'd make!' he added, laughing.

'It isn't funny, Jesus,' replied the other. 'You'll end up dead, like poor John, if you're not careful. Either Antipas will move against you himself, or more likely he'll call in the Romans and you'll finish up on a cross.'

'I'm aware of the dangers, Matt,' said Jesus more soberly. 'I just had to laugh at the idea of me being a soldier! Anyone less suitable would be difficult to imagine. I'm sure that, if I had joined the Zealots, I would have been their leader in name only – they would have expected to control the action in reality. No. No, that's not the way.'

There was silence for a while, then Jesus asked, 'Tell me, how was John in his last days?'

Matt tugged at his beard before replying.

'He was still sure of you. He always thought that you were the one.'

'What did he think I would do – exactly?'

'I'm not sure – I don't think he really knew. I think perhaps he might have been more in favour of you allying yourself with the Zealots – he was more inclined to see things in political terms than you, I think – but, in the end, I think he would have been guided by what you wanted.'

'I am only concerned with what God wants,' replied his guest. 'Even if a revolt were successful, which I very much doubt, what would that achieve?

The Maccabees revolted against their oppressors nearly two hundred years ago and the nation was free for a little while, but it didn't last. It certainly didn't produce a happy life for the people. The revolution that I propose, the revolution of the heart, brings real happiness and is permanent – nobody can crush it. The human spirit, empowered by God, is indestructible.'

'I understand that,' said Matt. 'I'm sure you must be right, but how are you going to bring about this revolution?'

'Here and there, people are already turning their lives around and seeing things in a different way. The Kingdom is growing already, like the mustard seed grows, and must some day mature.'

'But it's such a slow process, isn't it? You can only talk to a few people at a time – and, of them, many will listen but not hear. We saw that with John's mission. Quite a few were baptised, but I wonder now how many really changed their thinking? How many lives really took fire?'

Matt looked really downhearted, but Jesus smiled.

'You mustn't be discouraged, my friend,' he said. 'God's time works on a different scale to ours. He has all eternity to realise his plans for the world. But I have the feeling that soon I will be called upon to make a really significant step forward in God's purposes. I'm not sure quite what form it will take yet, but I'm inching my way towards an idea. I have been drawn many times in the past few days, when visiting the Temple, to look at a passage in the book of the prophet Isaiah – a passage towards the end of the scroll. There you can read:

> He was despised, he shrank from the sight of men –
> Yet on himself he bore our sufferings –
> he was pierced for our transgressions,
> tortured for our iniquities –
> We had all strayed like sheep –
> the Lord laid upon him the guilt of us all.[5]

'Now, the person referred to in the passage is, I'm sure, the chosen Messiah. If I am he, and I think I am, then I have to make sense of this passage – and I am coming to the view that it must mean that the essential role of the Messiah is to serve and, ultimately, to suffer for the people. Does that sound right to you?'

Matt looking puzzled and alarmed. 'What do you have in mind?' he asked. 'How can you suffer for all the people – and what good would it do if you did?'

'If I suffered by refusing to compromise with evil, it would show, for all time, what God thinks of evil. If I could go on loving men even when they made me suffer, that too would show men God's eternal attitude – how he loves and suffers. He loves us all and hates us to be at odds with him.'

Jesus looked closely at Matt, wondering if he followed the argument. There was a long pause while the other man digested this idea. Eventually, Matt spoke slowly, picking his words carefully.

'You mean that you would, as God's representative, demonstrate in practice

– in history – what God's eternal nature and purpose is. Am I understanding you correctly?'

Jesus's eyes lit up. 'You've expressed it wonderfully well. Yes. That's it in a nutshell. As I said, I don't know yet quite how this could work out in practice. What "service" am I to undertake for the people? What "suffering" is called for? I must wait for further guidance from my heavenly Father.'

'But what does it achieve in practice, Jesus? Don't serve and suffer for nothing – for people merely to walk away.' Matt sounded doubtful.

'Well, I believe that men would respond if they truly believed that I was showing forth God's love. Especially if, somehow, they could be convinced that love was, in the final analysis, the most powerful force on earth – and in heaven – which I really believe to be the case.'

Jesus smiled. 'Thank you for listening to me,' he said. 'It's good to have someone to talk things over with. I have many other friends, of course, but most of them are way up in Galilee at present, and the others have their own problems at the moment. I knew that if John the Baptist chose you, I could depend on you.'

'Of course you can. I am pleased that you feel you can confide in me,' said Matt, and he meant it. 'Anything I can do to help, please tell me.'

NOTES

[1] Exodus 20:5.
[2] Mark 12:40.
[3] Matt. 19:24.
[4] Luke 10:40.
[5] Isaiah 53:3–6.

The second mission begins

It was the middle of April. The wild flowers that had bloomed everywhere since the middle of January would soon be over. The almond trees had long since blossomed; the apricot blossom, too, would soon be gone. Rain came rarely now. When Jesus arrived at Peter's house in Capernaum, most of the rest of his friends were already there. In fact, the three men from Gischala had been there for several weeks, after finding that it was too difficult to stay in their home town.

'The Zealots are still very active at home,' growled Simon. 'There was a lot of pressure on us to support them – if not by actually going up into the hills and joining the military activities, certainly by providing them with goods and services.'

'In our case,' interposed James, 'of course, they wanted swords and arrowheads and the like. They have all the tradesmen under their thumbs.'

'Even bakers!' chipped in Thaddeus. 'The Romans will move in and catch them sometime, as sure as eggs are eggs, and there will be more crosses in the town.'

'So we came back here early,' finished James. 'We've helped out with local tradesmen for the last few weeks. We've even been out fishing with big James and John, Peter and Andrew!'

'You weren't much good on the last occasion,' grinned John. 'There was a bit of a swell and they were all seasick!'

'And how good a blacksmith are you?' retorted little James. 'Everyone to his own trade, I guess!'

Jesus hastily changed the topic and enquired how things were with Matthew. It transpired that he had arrived about a week ago.

'I thought it best to let Thomas and Rachel have some time alone together,' he explained. 'They were very kind to take me in for as long as they did. They made me very welcome, but I'm no good at making baskets! However, they found me some employment in Urta, as a scrivener.'

'Is Joanna still being difficult?' Jesus asked.

'It's best not talked about,' replied Matthew with a wry smile. 'She just doesn't understand – and never will, I fear.'

Jesus left it at that. He discovered that Judas had enjoyed his stay in Capernaum over the winter, and, of course, the fishermen had benefited greatly from being in their home surroundings. Philip and Nathaniel had been welcomed home in Bethsaida and had been quickly back in their old ways – Philip in the pottery, Nathaniel at his duties in the Synagogue. There had initially been some hesitation about Nathaniel's work there, in view of his association with Jesus, but in the end the local rabbi had decided to risk it. Nathaniel and Philip had walked over to Capernaum the same day as Jesus arrived from Jerusalem. As usual, Thomas came in last, just in time for supper. There was a great deal of backslapping and handshaking. It was good to be together again. Everyone had made a little money during the winter to give Judas for the common fund, enough to get them started on the road.

'So are we all ready for the new mission?' asked Jesus.

There was a murmur of assent all round, but Peter, as usual, spoke up louder than the rest. 'Let's go, Jesus. Just give the word.'

Jesus smiled. He was pleased at their enthusiasm, but when he spoke he set a more serious tone.

'I've been thinking a lot over the winter,' he said. 'It seems clear to me that we are going to hit considerable difficulties this year. Last summer, nobody quite knew what to expect from us, so we got the benefit of the doubt from the authorities for some time. This year, they know what we're about, and I expect that pressure will very soon be placed on us to shut us up. We can start out as we did last year, but I will not be at all surprised if we are not forced to move on much more this time – move on, and, indeed, move out.'

There was some surprise at this from most of the disciples. Only Thomas and Nathaniel seemed to have realised that this was likely. Jesus continued.

'Yes, I fully expect we shall be forced to move out of Galilee after just a short time; it'll be too difficult, and even dangerous, to stay. So you must be prepared to travel further and further afield. I shall give more time this year to teaching you, as a group, rather than talking only to the crowds.'

'But we shan't be breaking any law,' said Peter. 'Where will the danger come from?'

'Listen, we are at best an embarrassment to the religious authorities, and at worst a danger to the civil authorities,' replied Jesus. 'If we get the crowd growing restive and demanding a revolution – as happened in the north towards the end of the autumn – then Antipas will certainly want to be rid of us. Things could get nasty.'

Jesus looked serious and it began to dawn on the disciples how things stood, but they couldn't be discouraged for long. They were together again and Jesus would know how to deal with the problems, of that they had no doubt! They enjoyed their first meal together again and then dispersed to the several homes in the district which had offered bed space.

The next morning, as they were making their final farewells to Ruth, Abigail and Peter and Andrew's mother, there came an urgent knock at the door. Peter went to see who it was and came back to Jesus with a perplexed look on his face.

'It's Jairus – the leader of the Synagogue,' he told Jesus. 'He wants to speak to you – at the door. Will you come?'

'Of course,' said the preacher and went quickly with him to see their important visitor. Jairus greeted them with a very worried look.

'It's my daughter. She's very ill. Will you please come to see her? I heard that you had returned to town and I thought that you might be willing to help.'[1]

Jesus paused for just a second. Jairus had clearly been fully involved with getting him ejected from the Synagogue last year, yet now, when his daughter was ill, the Synagogue leader was turning instinctively to him. Jesus looked over to Peter.

'I want you, big James and John, to come with me. The rest of you, stay here please; I'll be back shortly.'

The four left at the heels of Jairus. As they went along the road, Jesus asked about the circumstances.

'What's wrong with the young girl?'

'She was taken ill during the night,' replied Jairus. 'She was a bit off-colour in the evening but we didn't think it was very much. You know how children are – up and down. However, in the night, she suddenly became very hot and feverish, vomited and seemed very ill. Nothing we did could bring her temperature down. The local doctor was sent for and has been at the house now for several hours, but there is no improvement. He's afraid she might die…'

'You mustn't say that,' said Jesus. 'She's very young and young people are surprisingly tough.'

As they strode along, a sizeable crowd was gathering around them. Evidently, news of Jairus's emergency and his appeal to Jesus had got around, and more and more people were realising that the famous healer was once more in Capernaum. So it was that, within a few minutes, something approaching a mob was hurrying along towards Jairus's large house. They had nearly arrived there, when, suddenly, Jesus stopped and turned around, causing many people immediately behind him to stumble and jostle each other as they came abruptly to a halt.

'Who touched me?' asked Jesus quietly.

Peter, who was close behind his leader, answered, rather impatiently, 'Jesus, you can see how many people are following you. Any one of them could have touched you, by mistake.'

'I realise that,' replied Jesus soothingly. 'This was different. Someone touched me who needed help – healing, too, if I'm not mistaken. Who was it?'

He looked round, searching the ring of faces round him.

'I'm not angry,' he explained, still quietly. 'I want to help. Please, whoever it was, say so, and I will help.'

There was long pause and eventually, with head bowed low, a woman of about forty years of age came slowly forward. Jesus stepped forward and held his hands out to her. With much hesitation, the woman took the outstretched hands, saying, 'It was I who touched you. Forgive me. I had no right…'

Jesus smiled at her warmly. 'What were you seeking? Why did you think it was important to try to touch me?'

The woman glanced round at the crowd, now all pushing to hear what was going on. She seemed very embarrassed.

'Don't mind them,' said Jesus. 'Tell me about your problem – just whisper to me.'

Gradually the woman gathered enough courage to confide quietly in Jesus. The preacher told his friends about it later. The woman had apparently been ill for years, suffering frequent haemorrhaging, which left her anaemic and very weak. Year after year she had suffered, feeling low most of the time but sometimes really very ill. She had spent a good deal of money on doctors but nothing they could do seemed to relieve the problem. As they had learned of her problem, her friends had kept away from her, as the culture ruled that people with a blood loss were to be regarded as unclean. She was not permitted to enter the Synagogue, and there was nothing she could do about it. She felt worse every year that went by. Then she had heard of Jesus's healing work, and couldn't believe her luck when she heard that Jesus was actually back in the town. She had come out that morning in the hope of seeing him.

'I thought that if I could just touch your robe, perhaps I would be healed,' she explained to Jesus. 'I didn't mean to interrupt you, or even that you should know that I had touched you. I realise that I am not worthy…'

'Why do you say that?' asked Jesus. 'Of course you are worthy of my help. Everyone is. Don't be fearful. You will find that you will now be well again. Your trust has enabled this healing to come about. Go in peace.'

The woman bowed over his hands and was trying to find words to thank him, when a servant came pushing through the crowd to Jairus. He knelt at his feet and spoke in a broken voice.

'I'm sorry, Master. It's too late,' he said. 'I have to tell you that… your daughter has died. It's too late for Jesus to come now.'

'Don't worry, Jairus,' said Jesus quickly. 'Go on trusting that she will be well. Come on. Let's go in.'

So saying, he strode quickly up to Jairus's door, followed by his three disciples and the hesitant householder. Inside, Jairus's wife, weeping bitterly, met her husband and fell upon his shoulders, clutching him violently. Many of the family and some close friends, similarly distressed, were crying bitterly. It was enough to make any heart break.

'Don't weep, friends,' said Jesus, quietly but authoritatively. 'The little girl is not dead. She is only sleeping.'

Jairus's wife looked at him, hesitating between tears and insane laughter. She cried out, 'How do you know? You weren't even here! You don't know…' And she burst into violent tears again.

Jesus turned to her and said quietly, 'Don't cry. I promise you that what I say is correct. Show me where the little girl is and you will see. I would like just you and Jairus and my three friends to come into the room with me. The rest of the family and friends should stay here, please.'

Jairus said nothing but led the way to his daughter's room. He opened the door for Jesus to go in first, then followed with his wife. Peter, James and John came in last and stood just inside the door. They saw a young girl of about twelve lying prone on the bed, indeed looking as though she was dead. Jesus approached the bed and sat down next to her, taking the apparently lifeless hand.

He raised it gently to his lips for a second, paused and then said, very quietly, but firmly, 'Sweetheart, wake up. It's time to get up.'

For a moment, nothing happened. Then, slowly, the little girl's eyes opened. She looked up, gradually focussing on Jesus's face. Jesus never took his eyes from her.

'You're all right, little lass. You'll be well now. Come on. You can get up.'

Slowly, the girl started to rise from her bed, with Jesus's assistance, and soon she was on her feet and gathered into her father's hungry arms.

'You're well. You're really well!' he cried, joyously. 'I can't believe it.'

Her mother, too, started forward, crying out and reaching to hug her daughter. For several minutes, neither parent would let go of their child. Then, Jairus relinquished his hold and turned to Jesus.

'I don't know how to thank you…' he began.

'She was only sleeping,' said the preacher.

'What can I say?' mumbled Jairus. 'I was among those who wanted you removed from our Synagogue and town last year – and yet still you came when I asked you to and you have restored our daughter to us, alive and well. I can only say thank you.'

Jesus put up his hand to try to stop him.

'There really is no need to thank me,' he said. 'Your little girl has had a fever, but came through it and was sleeping. Now she's awake. Please say nothing more about it. Look at her – she looks hungry. Give her some breakfast!'

It was true. The child looked quite well now and her eyes brightened up at the thought of food! The disciples stood out of the way while the family left the room to be welcomed ecstatically by the rest of the household. Jesus and his disciples turned to leave, but not before Jairus had slipped a bag of coins into the preacher's hand.

'You'll need some help with your mission, no doubt,' he said. 'Please take this. Heaven knows, you've more than earned it.'

★

Jesus and his friends set out from Capernaum walking due west. They hadn't gone very far when they were met by a small knot of people.

'Aren't you Jesus, the healer?' asked their leader.

Jesus smiled and said that his name was Jesus.

'Our friend here,' said the man, indicating one of his companions, 'has always had a limp. Could you help him, please?'

'I will help him, but I want all of you to stay here,' he said to the group. Then, to his disciples, he said, 'Stay with them. Make sure they don't follow. I'd like just Judas and Thaddeus to come with us.'

Accompanied by his two rather bewildered disciples, he took the man by the arm and indicated that they should walk over into a small copse that was growing a couple of hundred paces away. When they were out of sight of the rest, Jesus stopped and faced the handicapped man, asking how long he had been lame.

'The left leg has never been strong,' the man replied, 'but for the last several months it has become much worse'.

Jesus sighed and dropped to his knees.

'Let me see,' he said.

The man fumbled to lift his robe and display his leg. The left calf muscle was noticeably weaker than the right one. Jesus felt gently round the affected area.

'Can you believe that I can and will help?' he asked.

The man hesitated. 'I'm sure you will do all you can,' he temporised.

'You must trust that God can help you in every situation in life,' Jesus said firmly. 'Come along – walk with me.'

Together they set out along the path, leaving the two disciples watching and wondering. Increasingly, as he walked with Jesus, the lame man increased his stride, walking ever more surely. After just a few minutes, Jesus turned him round and they walked together back to his waiting followers.

'See – you can do it!' he said. 'You can walk like everyone else.'

The other turned to his healer and fell at his knees. 'Thank you, Rabbi,' he mumbled. 'Thank you. Thank you.'

Jesus pulled him to his feet and looked him fully in the face.

'If you want to thank me,' he said, 'you'll go home and give thanks to God for your healing, but tell nobody what has happened here.'

The man looked astounded. 'But, Rabbi…', he began.

'Tell nobody, do you hear me?' Jesus was most insistent.

Slowly the puzzled man responded. 'Very well, Rabbi, I will do as you have asked.' And he turned and made his way slowly back to his friends.

'But surely he'll have to tell his friends?' asked Judas, when he was out of hearing.

'He'll have to tell them something, I suppose,' replied his leader, 'but I want as little fuss as possible. You know why – we've been all through this many times.'

'It was good of you to invite us to be here, Jesus,' said Thaddeus, 'but why did you do so?'

Jesus paused for a second before replying.

'I just wanted you to see what happened. If necessary, you can act as witnesses that I used no witchcraft – and I needed your support too, my friends. Thanks for being with me.'

They went slowly back to join the rest of the disciples and, as they continued their journey, Judas and Thaddeus briefly recounted to the others what had happened. Though they had all seen Jesus at work healing on several occasions, they continued to marvel at his healing touch.

It was the same story wherever they went. Although they were often in parts of Galilee that they had not visited in the previous year, Jesus's reputation had preceded him. He was soon recognised. The common people were pleased to see him and brought him all their handicapped family members for healing. It was easy to collect a crowd in the countryside for a meeting, and Jesus was fully occupied preaching and healing.

But one morning, when they moved further south and were a couple of miles west of Tiberias, they were approached by a small party of women with quite a different thought in their minds. It was very unusual to find women travelling accompanied only by a couple of menservants, and so Philip, with whom they spoke first, wore quite a puzzled look when he reported to Jesus, who was up on the brow of the hill, preparing his mind for his next speaking engagement.

'What do they want?' Jesus too was surprised.

'I've no idea,' replied Philip. 'I was completely taken aback to see them, this far out of town.'

'I'll come down and meet them,' said Jesus. 'You'd better come with me to give me some support!'

They went down the hill to join the women, who had, meantime, been found a place in the shade and some refreshment by Matthew. Jesus walked over to the group and introduced himself and the two disciples.

'It's unusual to see ladies this far from anywhere,' he observed. 'What can we do for you?'

One of the women introduced herself as Joanna. She seemed to have assumed the role of leader of the group.

'We've been hearing all about you, Rabbi. Your reputation is well known even in Tiberias and in the King's palace. My husband, Chuza, is one of the King's stewards,[2] and he tells me that you are taking the province by storm, preaching and healing all manner of people. We very much wanted to meet you, to tell you how we admire your work and how interested we are in it.'

'You're very kind,' murmured Jesus. 'Are you sure you have heard correctly, though? Rumour can be so distorted.'

'Perhaps you could give us some of your time and tell us, for yourself, what you have come to preach.'

Joanna looked at him very frankly, so that Jesus felt compelled to smile and agree to her request. He suggested that they all stay to lunch with the disciples and afterwards he would be glad to speak at length with them. Joanna introduced her three friends, Susanna, Rebecca and Lydia. Either they or their husbands worked in the palace in various roles. After lunch, Jesus sat down with them and summarised his main theme – the coming Kingdom, and how it could come to any individual who wished to find it. The women were apparently thrilled, seeing in Jesus's teaching a new and better life for women, who were in so many ways discriminated against.

'How can we help in the bringing of this message?' asked Susanna.

'As things stand, there is nothing you can do for us directly,' replied Jesus, 'but you can each go home and prepare for the Kingdom within yourselves. Start to see life in God's terms – try to follow his law of love – wait for the coming of the final Kingdom, when God will be in all and over all.'

'When will that be?' asked Lydia. 'Will there be a great battle for supremacy over Rome? What will happen to Antipas and his kingdom?'

'I don't know the answers to all your questions,' said Jesus with a smile. 'Only God knows about the end of time. Sometimes I think it might be quite soon, but on other occasions I wonder whether God will let the world continue as it is for centuries yet – perhaps millennia. Only God knows. I'm sure Rome will be swept away at some time – earthly kingdoms never last – but I do believe that something is moving now, preparing the way for men to come to God. I feel that something significant will happen soon.'

The conversation continued for some time. Eventually, the women indicated that they should be getting back, or they would be missed and questions would be asked. Before they went, Joanna insisted that Jesus take a gift from the women for the mission.

'Take it,' she said. 'My husband is pretty well paid and is basically sympathetic with your cause. Of course, he can't say so officially or he'd lose his job, but he follows your work. I'm sure you know that Antipas has his spies out, checking on you, but we don't think the King will seek to move against you unless there is some kind of social disturbance – and, so far at least, you've avoided that.'

'Thank you for the gift and for the information,' replied Jesus. 'We know we have to be careful. At the moment, we're more in trouble with the religious authorities than the civil ones.'

It was true; the religious and village authorities were by now almost unanimous in forbidding him the use of the Synagogues or the marketplaces. News had obviously got around about the strange teachings and practices of this man, and they wanted nothing to do with him, except to try occasionally to trap him into saying something even more incriminating. Indeed, some Pharisees came to see him at the camp one night, and Jesus invited them to take supper with the disciples. They were obviously taken aback at this and hastily excused themselves, saying that they had already eaten, but then they started to criticise the disciples for the way they were preparing their own meal.[3]

'They don't seem to know that they should wash their hands before preparing or eating a meal,' they complained to Jesus. 'It's all in our Law, so why don't they follow what is accepted by all good Jews?'

Jesus was tired after his day's work and could not hide his impatience. He turned on them, saying, 'You really are hypocrites! How can you stand there getting all worked up about a trivial matter, when there so many more important things to worry about? How well did Isaiah prophesy when he said:

> This people approach me with their mouths,
>   and honour me with their lips,
>   while their hearts are far from me
> and their religion is but a precept of men,
>   learnt by rote.[4]

'You pay God lip service – your worship is vain! You prefer your own tradition to the real Law of God.'

The Pharisees were astonished at his outburst, but Jesus continued to embarrass them, saying, 'The Law of Moses states that everyone should honour his father and mother,[5] but you say, in your tradition, that if you pronounce something as "set aside for God" (or "Corban"), then this takes precedence over the requirement to honour your parents.[6] And so often you use this as an excuse just to deny something to your parents. You are just hypocrites.'

Jesus made an impatient gesture, turned away and strode out of the camp. The Pharisees couldn't believe their eyes. They looked incredulously at one another for a few seconds, then, shrugging their shoulders, shaking their heads or pulling at their beards, they beat a hasty retreat. Peter let them get well out of sight, then went to find his leader. Jesus was sitting on a rock, just outside the camp, his head in his hands.

'I suppose I shouldn't have said that,' he said, looking up as Peter approached. 'That'll be one more thing they hold against me. But it's true. They simply haven't got things at all straight in their minds – they have no sense of priority.'

Shortly after this, Jesus decided that the group should give up their work in Galilee and move into Phoenicia, to the west, where they could have a rest from the antagonism and he could concentrate on teaching his disciples for a while, without being distracted by any outside factor. Jesus felt that, with the generosity first of Jairus, then Joanna and her group of women, they could manage financially for a while comfortably enough. So they journeyed west and north, camping a few miles outside the ancient city of Tyre.

NOTES

[1] Mark 5:23.
[2] Luke 8:3.
[3] Mark 7:2.
[4] Isaiah 29:13.
[5] Exodus 20:12.
[6] Mark 7:11.

Retreat to the North

The weather was getting hotter every day. The sun shone out of a hard blue sky, baking the soil hard and liberating more and more dust. The grass had turned yellow and would soon be brown, and all the succulent green plants were dying back, leaving only a few thorny species for the goats to pick at. The little group had found a camping spot with some level ground and shade from a couple of large carob trees, and had made themselves as comfortable as they could. They had to walk a fair distance to the nearest village to draw water from the well and get their kitchen necessities, but otherwise they considered themselves well off. Each day, Jesus would gather them round him for prayer, to explain more fully than before the features of his 'inner Kingdom' and to explore with them in greater detail what 'loving your neighbour' really amounted to.

'Our Jewish Law restricts retaliation to an appropriate response,' Jesus reminded them. 'Anyone who has been wronged is forbidden to use overkill. If someone has blinded you in one eye, then the law states that you may retaliate only in similar fashion – you may not kill or maim for life, or even blind in both eyes. No; the punishment for taking one eye is to take just one eye back, no more. Similarly, you may take just one tooth for one tooth, and no more.'[1]

'Isn't that right?' asked Nathaniel. 'It's fair and just. What could be wrong with that?'

'It isn't a question of justice,' replied Jesus. 'It's a question of love. If you insist on what you consider to be your "rights", all you do is to bring pain and suffering to someone else. You don't repair the wrong done to yourself. After all, nothing can bring back the eye that was blinded or the tooth that was lost. So what have you achieved? All that has happened is that someone else has suffered – which is not a loving response. So I say, don't seek revenge at all. In fact, if someone strikes you on one cheek, the best response is to offer him the other one too!'[2]

Peter looked appalled at that. Several others were shaking their heads in disbelief, but Jesus smiled and continued.

'In practice, very few men will be able to bring themselves to strike a second time on an unguarded face. By your action, you take all the heat out of the situation and the man who started the fight is forced to think again. The violence is halted. But if, on the other hand, you strike back, a brawl soon ensues. The result is chaos, hurt and a breakdown in relationships for a long time.'

Jesus went on to point out that sometimes the offence might not be given intentionally; it was always possible that a person striking someone else had not intended the blow, in which case it was even more important not to retaliate.

'All this is easier said than done,' commented big James. 'If anyone thumped me in the past, I always reckoned it was best to thump them back – otherwise people take advantage of you.'

'You just try it my way,' said Jesus. 'My way brings peace and loving relations. If you insist on justice all the time, then justice will be served on you – and if God were to give us justice, which of us would survive? We need to be grateful that God gives us love, not justice. So, I say that when a soldier commands you to carry his bag one mile for him – and we know that Roman law allows him to make such a demand – offer instead to go two miles.[3] That way, the situation is transformed from a legal requirement to a comradely act. Similarly, if your neighbour wants to sue you for your shirt, offer him your coat as well. Again, the legal battle is changed into a matter of friendship.'

The discussion continued for some time.

'You should remember what I told you before,' Jesus said. 'God knows your thoughts, not just your deeds. The thought behind the deed can be just as important – sometimes even more important – than the deed itself. But this can work in different ways. As we have seen, sometimes the thought may be entirely harmless but can unintentionally give rise to an offence. On other occasions, the original thought can be relatively harmless, but one thing can lead to another, much less innocent. For example, irritation can lead to annoyance, annoyance to anger, anger to violence and violence eventually to murder! So, in God's eyes, irritation can be allied to murder – as the one is the starting point for the other. In consequence, I say that even irritation is worthy of heavy punishment.[4] In a similar way, a lustful look can be the beginning of the road to adultery.[5] Likewise, envy can lead to theft. You need, therefore, to beware as soon as the first evil thought creeps into your mind, lest it leads on to the greater problems.'

'Who can attain that sort of perfection?' asked Matthew. 'I confess that I frequently have evil thoughts, both of anger and lust, but, so far at least, they haven't led to the greater evils you have described.'

Jesus smiled at his frankness, his large brown eyes full of kindness.

'You may be able to control things and not let them develop,' he replied, 'but the potential for development is always there and may, sometime, catch you out. If you can do away with those initial thoughts, then the more serious problems cannot arise.'

Again the discussion continued for some long time, with many disciples contributing their experiences and all trying to focus on Jesus's new way of looking at things. Every day he gave them new insights, but he asked a lot of his followers!

One day, Peter and Andrew were in the nearby village doing the shopping on behalf of the group. Relations between Jews and foreigners, like Phoenicians, were usually very strained, and the men kept a wary eye on those around them. However, after a little while, they were engaged in conversation by a couple of the local women, who were teasing them for having to do their own household chores.

'Haven't you any wives to go shopping for you?' they said, laughing.

'Not here – but I've got one all right, don't you fret!' replied Peter, who never minded a bit of banter with women.

One of them, a big, busty type in her mid-forties, asked, 'You're not from round here, are you? I can tell by your accent. You're from Galilee.'

'That's right. We're making a little trip this region.'

One thing led to another in the conversation and before long Peter let slip the name of Jesus.

'Isn't that the healer who's been doing strange things in Galilee?' asked the big woman.

Peter realised that he had opened his mouth once too often, but it was too late. Without lying through his teeth, he couldn't deny that it was the well-known Nazarene healer that was with the group. Not surprisingly, the news spread round the little village very quickly and that very evening they had a visitor, another woman, who, looking very fearful, came to the camp and fell at Jesus's feet.[6]

'Master,' she began, 'I need your help. Please help me.'

Jesus did not immediately respond in his usual kindly way, but, with a rather stern expression, replied, 'You are a local woman, aren't you – a Syro-Phoenician? Why ever do you come to me, a foreigner – a Jew – for help?'

The woman pursed her lips, as if stifling an angry retort; but, after a pause, she replied imploringly, 'We have heard that you can heal the sick, and my little girl – my only daughter – needs your help. She has the devil in her. Please come and remove this evil presence which is ruining her life.'

'But surely you realise that I must minister first to my own people, Israel?' replied Jesus, still rather coldly, though with the ghost of a smile at the corner of his mouth. 'I should not take their food and give it to the house dogs.'

'I understand that, Rabbi,' responded the woman, gently. 'Of course that's right. But when your family eats at home, surely you let your dogs eat the scraps that fall from the table on to the floor?'

At this, Jesus's face broke into a broad smile. He looked kindly at the woman for the first time and said softly, 'You are right. For that thought, you must be rewarded. Your trust has made this cure possible. When you get home, you will find your daughter better.'

The woman broke down and sobbed with joy, trying ineffectually to thank him.

'Go home now,' said Jesus, 'and don't tell anyone else about this.'

The woman, still crying and trying to articulate her gratitude, made her way out of the camp and over the hill towards the village.

Jesus watched till she was out of sight, then said, soberly, 'I suppose it had to come out. We'll need to be away tomorrow, or else we shall be inundated by people bringing their sick relatives. We'll break camp first thing tomorrow and be on our way. I think we should go east and cross into Ituraea, Tetrarch Philip's domain, well away from here. We'll need to put in twenty miles tomorrow, so you'd better have a good rest tonight!'

★

They started early next morning, to be well on their way before the sun was too hot, but by mid-morning the temperature had risen to an uncomfortable level. Nevertheless, they struggled on, using the goat tracks which crossed the craggy countryside, until they came at last, dusty and tired, to the Jordan. The river is only a small stream this far north, gushing down from the hills of Syria towards the Sea of Galilee, more than twenty miles to the south. Here, just three miles short of Caesaraea Philippi, Jesus suggested that they make camp. They were to camp there for many days. There was shade under the trees, and it was good not to have to drag water from the village each day. The men could drink their fill and bathe their dusty bodies to their hearts' content.

Over supper one night, the conversation turned to the religious authorities and their attitude to Jesus and his message, and Jesus's quite fierce condemnation of them.

'It's funny,' said Thomas. 'All my life, I always had a sneaking feeling inside me that the rabbis were – well – off the right track; and yet, as a boy, I'd been told to respect the rabbi and the scribes and suchlike, so I thought it must be me that was wrong!'

Nathaniel agreed. He'd had a lot to do with the rabbi in Bethsaida, and had found Jesus's views of the religious hierarchy hard to take at first; but, as he thought it through, he realised that Jesus was right. Being in charge at the Synagogue, or even being the High Priest in the Temple in Jerusalem, didn't automatically put you in the right. You had to be judged on your life.

'Beware of false prophets who come to you looking like sweet little lambs, but who are actually ravenous wolves, dressed up as sheep,' warned Jesus.[7] 'They'll gobble you up as sure as day follows night, if you allow them to. Instead, look at their lives – their actions – how they treat people. You will know what they are by the results you see! You don't pick grapes from briars, do you – or figs from thistles? Of course not. Grapes come only from the vine – and nothing of value ever comes from briars or thistles!'

Each day, Jesus led them in prayer and continued his teaching. The topics covered were many and varied. One day, the disciples asked him about which foods were allowed, and which were to be avoided.

'There are many foods that the Pharisees forbid,' said Andrew. 'What do you think, Jesus?'

'The food laws are very complicated,' agreed his leader. 'We Jews have always been taught to avoid pork, for example. Certainly it is a meat that very often quickly becomes unfit for human consumption in the heat of summer, but, actually, there is nothing that God has made that is intrinsically evil. No. All foods are clean.[8] It is not the things that are taken into a man that are evil, it is the things that come out of him: thoughts and deeds like murder, greed, adultery, fornication, envy, slander, arrogance and suchlike. All these evils arise from within men. Evil thoughts become evil deeds and are let loose into the world, contaminating it for everyone. These are the things to be wary about, not what you eat!'

They had been encamped near Caesarea Philippi for nearly a month, when, just after he had finished his morning prayers, Jesus gathered all his friends around him and announced, 'We have come to a crucial point in our ministry. We spent many months last year and some time early this year proclaiming the message in Galilee. Many people heard it and responded. Some heard it, but were distracted from considering it properly by seeing the healings. Others heard the message and promptly forgot it. Some were antagonised by it. We upset some important people in Galilee who were too entrenched in their present views to change and were threatened by the message. But for the last month or so, we have been away from the mission field, gathering our strength, spiritually – we have had considerable time for discussion and prayer together.

'We must now decide how to proceed further. My feeling is that we must move into Judaea and open up the mission there. It may well be that we will have similar results – that is, some success, but some trouble – and I'm certain that the Temple authorities there are likely to be even more upset than the religious people in Galilee, because, as you know, they represent both the civil authority as well as the religious life of the nation. Although the Roman Prefect is, obviously, formally in charge, in practice, most of the day-to-day administration is left to the High Priest and the Temple authorities. I have influential friends in Jerusalem, people near the Temple hierarchy, and they have warned me to be very careful when working there. Judas has worked in the Temple and I'm sure that he, too, knows the problems from first-hand experience.'

Judas agreed readily. 'You're quite right, Jesus – unfortunately.'

'Then why take the risk?' asked Peter. 'Why go into Judaea if there's likely to be trouble?'

'Because Judaea, and particularly Jerusalem, are at the heart of the Jewish nation. I cannot fulfil what God wants me do unless I confront the centre of the nation.'

'But we could all be thrown in jail.' Thomas looked worried. 'Why take that risk?'

Jesus paused before he put his next question and he drew a deep breath. 'Look. This is the crucial point – and I need an honest answer to this question. Those people who have responded to the message, so far – who do they think I am?'

Nobody answered for a second or two, then Andrew replied, 'Some say you must be John the Baptist, returned from the dead.'

Nathaniel suggested, 'Some think you might be the great Elijah returned to earth.'

'I've heard some say you are a second Jeremiah – or some other prophet.' This from Philip.

There was an uncomfortable pause until Jesus asked, quietly, looking at the ground, 'And what do you think?'

It was Peter that spoke next, in that impetuous way of his. He said, 'You're God's Messiah, the one who has been promised for so long.'[9]

Jesus looked at him and smiled. 'What a good fellow you are, Simon,' he said quietly. 'I renamed you well when I called you Peter, the rock. You will be a cornerstone in the new community of those who follow my way.'

Andrew quickly backed his brother up. 'John the Baptist recognised you when you were baptised. He was sure, that day, that you were the one, and I feel sure he never lost that belief. That's what I understood Matthias to say, when we last saw him.'

Jesus nodded, again smiling that winning smile of his.

'Yes. I had the same message from Matt when I saw him at the end of last year – after the Feast of Dedication. It is very reassuring that a few people, at least, believe this to be true. I have felt myself to be Messiah for some time now – since just prior to my baptism – but I needed to hear it from you, to confirm my belief.'

The other disciples were nodding vigorously and smiling too, growling their agreement with what was being said.

'You're the one, Jesus,' said John. 'We've always felt it.'

'Well, my friends, we will proceed on that assumption, since we all seem to be agreed,' said Jesus, 'but this is strictly between ourselves for the present, do you understand?'

He looked round the group, waiting for each to nod his assent.

'So now we have to ask ourselves what the Messiah should do in this situation,' he went on. 'As I said earlier, I have come to the conclusion that the Messiah should, and must, be recognised in Jerusalem. Even if the whole of Galilee acknowledged me, it would amount to nothing if Judaea and Jerusalem didn't share in that belief. We have to go south and work there. That is where the decisive battle must be fought and won.'

'I'm not sure what you mean by "the decisive battle" – what does that imply, exactly?' asked big James.

'I'm still pondering on that question myself,' replied his leader. 'I have been thinking for many weeks now about a passage in the prophet Isaiah, in which he speaks of the work of the Messiah in terms of service and suffering.'

'*Suffering*?' Peter could not believe his ears. 'You? But if you are Messiah, surely you are not called to suffer? This must never happen.'

Jesus's face suddenly grew quite stern. He turned to Peter, saying, 'You're quite wrong, Peter. You're thinking like the world thinks. You think that a leader like the Messiah should be a king who rules in splendour, to be waited on by servants and toadies, but that's not God's way. Isaiah prophesied that the Messiah would serve and suffer for the people, and if that is what God wants, then that is what I must do. After all, all through our history, many prophets have been rejected by the nation and made to suffer. Often they have only been recognised as prophets long after their death.'

'But, Jesus …' Peter broke in.

'No "buts" about it, Peter. My mind is quite clear on this point. The only question is quite how and where this service and suffering may come about. We must go to Judaea and see what transpires.'

Seeking to change the subject, Andrew asked, 'Jesus, now that we have – well, between ourselves – recognised you as the Messiah, how should we address you? I mean – you are – well, you are the anointed one…' He ground to an embarrassed halt.

Jesus smiled at him and clapped him on the shoulder.

'I'm still your friend Jesus,' he said, 'and I hope I always will be. But it is interesting to consider what the Messiah has been called in scripture. All sorts of titles have been used, but the one I like myself is "Son of Man".'

'"Son of Man"?' queried big James. 'What does that mean?'

'It is enigmatic, isn't it?' replied his leader. 'That's part of its charm. Above all, it identifies the Messiah with the people – with the whole of the nation. He is to be part of mankind. It was this term that the great prophet Ezekiel used many times of himself.[10] I like it. But the term also occurs in the writings of Daniel, where he talks about "one like the Son of Man coming in the clouds of heaven". This Son of Man is close to God – he brings the nation through adversity to God and is himself vindicated by God.'[11]

'Would it not be more fitting for the Messiah to be addressed as the Son of God?' asked Nathaniel, who was always among the more deep thinking of the group.

'We are all sons and daughters of God,' replied Jesus. 'Everyone of us can acknowledge God as his father, so we must all be his sons or daughters. At the same time, it must be the case that the Messiah is, uniquely, his son – his first-born, if you like. For my part, though, I still prefer the title "Son of Man".'

There was a pause, and then Jesus went on.

'However, as we have just agreed, all this is just between ourselves for the time being. People must come to recognise me for themselves – as you did. I didn't force my claim on you – you came to that decision for yourselves, as John the Baptist did. Others may come to the same conclusion – I hope they will – and then they too will follow my way and find the salvation that God gives through me.'

'What does that mean – "find salvation"?' asked Thomas.

Jesus smiled. 'That's another enigmatic phrase, isn't it?' he replied. 'I think it's best described as "to find life" – and the meaning to life. It means that we are to be free of all worldly ambitions. Instead we want only to do God's will, which is to love. It allows us to experience life in all its fullness and abundance.[12] You should know by now what I am talking about – it is the life that we have been sharing together for the past year and more; but, as I have said, it may also involve service for others – and suffering, if necessary.'

'You are determined to involve suffering!' observed Thomas, shaking his head sadly. 'Why must you suffer?'

'We must all serve and suffer, while there are those who don't know the truth and follow the way of life,' replied Jesus, 'but perhaps the Son of Man must suffer uniquely, to show everyone just how the mind of God works and how the heart of God suffers while man is estranged from him. However, I believe that God will somehow finally demonstrate his victory over suffering. In the end, he will be seen to be supreme. We must and will find his purpose together. Tomorrow, we'll break camp and move south. We'll briefly visit all our homes on the way south, so that you can have a few days with your folks, but I'd like to be in Judaea within a couple of weeks.'

They followed the leader's directions and started out next morning early. They set out for Gischala, so that Simon, Thaddeus and little James could see their families. They followed the river south for about ten miles, before turning south-west into the hills. It was slow going, for the terrain was extremely difficult. There wasn't a patch of level ground anywhere along the route, and the men had constantly to battle with slopes composed of loose stones, which made footwork very tricky. The sparse vegetation was inevitably covered with prickles or spines, making it useless for handholds. They had gone about three miles from the river and were picking their way through a little gorge, when, suddenly, two big men, carrying swords, emerged from the rocks strewn along the way and stood in their path.

'Stay where you are!' they demanded. 'You're surrounded, so don't try anything.'

They looked round and saw that it was true. About a dozen armed men were emerging from behind boulders and crevices in the rocks in the gorge above and behind them, all carrying arms. Jesus held out his hands in a gesture of peace, showing that he had no weapons.

'Greetings,' he said quietly. 'What can we do for you?'

'Who are you? What is your business in this part of the country?' was the harsh reply.

'I am a preacher and these are my followers. We travel round bringing our good news to anyone who will listen.' Jesus kept his voice calm and reassuring.

'What is your name?'

'I am Jesus, from Nazareth. I and my party were preaching in this part of the country last autumn. We've come back for a quick visit.'

At this, the men conferred quietly and briefly. Then their spokesman said, 'You'd better come with us – and quietly. Make no trouble or else it'll be the worse for you.'

They were led away through the hills and eventually came to a camp in a secluded spot, where a small stream bubbled up out of the hillside. Here, they were told to sit while their captors consulted with a large man who appeared to be the group's leader. He was a very tall man, with an enormous beard and long unkempt hair. Next to him was a small man with a ferret-like face. After a few moments, the tall man came over and addressed himself to Jesus, who stood as he approached.

'We've met before, haven't we?'

'Oh, yes,' replied the preacher. 'We've met.'

'When we met last, I suggested to you that we could work together. It's a bit of good fortune that we've met up again. We thought that you were new recruits coming to join our unit – they're coming in all the time – but you would be especially welcome.'

Jesus smiled briefly and replied, 'I'm sorry to disappoint you. We haven't come to join your cause. We were just passing through on our way to Gischala. I have to tell you that I haven't changed my mind at all since we last met. You Zealots are brave fellows, I'm sure, and no doubt doing what you think is right for the nation, but I cannot agree with you. In some ways, I wish I could – it would be good to be in alliance with so many strong fighting men – but violence is just not our way...'

'It's the only practical way,' the tall man broke in. 'It's the only way the Romans will understand. No doubt you preachers mean well, but nothing will ever happen if it's left to you. But together, with your words and our weapons, we could take this country by storm and get the whole nation to rise against the oppressor—'

It was Jesus's turn to break in, but he did so quite quietly.

'It's no use, my friend. We shall never agree. I cannot be a party to violence. I'm sorry.'

There was a pause. Then the tall man spoke again, urgently. 'There really is no other way. If we want freedom we have to fight for it!'

He paused and took a long look at Jesus, who returned the stare with a question in his brown eyes. Eventually the Zealot spoke again.

'I'll tell you what I'll do. I will give you till tomorrow to think it over, then we will talk again.'

Jesus shook his head. 'It'll be no use. I shan't change my mind.'

'You will! Wait till you see what we will offer.'

He pointed over Jesus's shoulder to a small mountain, a couple of miles away, rising well above the surrounding hills.

'I will meet you on the summit of that hill over there, at about noon tomorrow. Bring no more than two or three of your men. I will be there with my friend here and we'll make you an offer you can't refuse. Make sure you are there. We will be watching you in the meantime, Jesus, to make sure you don't leave the area. The rest of your party can leave as soon as they like.'

With that, the Zealots signalled that they should go. They walked away as quickly as the rough ground allowed, feeling glad to be away from a place which bristled with so much malevolence. The atmosphere in the Zealots' camp had been one of apprehension and watchfulness, in great contrast with their own, with its tranquillity, fun and peaceful contemplation.

They found a place to make camp for the night a half mile away. John pointed out to Jesus, with some apprehension, that a couple of men could be seen on the skyline, overlooking them from the top of the hill. They made their meagre supper and fell to discussing the situation facing them. Jesus was adamant that, no matter what they said or offered, he would have nothing to do with the Zealots. He understood them and their desire for the nation's freedom, but had no intention of forming any kind of alliance with them. Little James spoke for several others when he asked Jesus, 'But if you don't agree to cooperate with them, what might they do to you – or to us?'

'What can they do?' replied the leader. 'They won't want us as prisoners. They won't want to guard us, feed us, and so on. I don't see what they gain by killing us or hurting us – that would only antagonise the people we have influenced positively around the country. No. They will have to let us go. They have no real choice that makes any sense.'

Philip broke in, 'I think we ought to beat a hasty retreat now, while we have the opportunity – and we're all still together.'

'We couldn't manage this countryside in the dark.' This came from Simon, who knew the terrain better than any of them. 'It's the same rough, hilly ground all round Gischala, one or more of us would have a sprained ankle or worse long before we reached town.'

'Well, we ought to be off at first light then,' suggested Philip.

'Don't forget the guards on the hilltop.' John reminded him.

'We could silence them – there's only two of them,' growled Simon.

'There'll be no violence,' said Jesus quietly. 'In any case, these fellows aren't stupid. I'm pretty certain they'll have other scouts out farther down this valley. They know we're heading for Gischala – they'll have the route covered. No. I think we must go through with it and see what they have to say.'

Peter wasn't so sure. 'I don't trust that second in command,' he said. 'His face strikes me as more like a rat than a man! And you can't trust a rat.'

'He can't help his face,' said Jesus, laughing. 'Perhaps he may not care much for yours!'

Several others in the band thought that rather likely – at least they said so, trying to lighten the atmosphere. Eventually, they all had to accept that Jesus was probably right in his assessment of the situation. So it was agreed that the main party should break camp in the morning and push on to Gischala, while Jesus, Peter, big James and John would go to the appointed rendezvous and seek to disengage finally from the Zealots.

★

It took the four friends three hours to climb the steep slope from their camp to the summit of the mountain. When they eventually arrived, they found that they were there ahead of the Zealots. The sun was hot, even at that altitude, and, after their stiff climb, they felt sleepy, particularly as the disciples had not been able to manage much in the way of sleep, with the uncertainty of the situation preying on their minds. Only Jesus seemed unperturbed.

'We've analysed the situation,' he said, 'and decided on a course of action. Why bother to worry further? We are in God's hands – he will have directed our thoughts. I'm content to leave it to him now.'

They shared the small package of food that they had brought with them, drank a little water from their wineskin and settled down to wait. As there was no shade, the men erected a makeshift tent, using their walking sticks and their outer robes. Eventually, one by one, the fishermen drifted off into a fitful dose.

When Peter awoke, he saw that Jesus was no longer with them in the shelter. He looked out and saw him standing about fifty yards away, across the summit of the mountain, talking to the two Zealots. To his amazement, he saw that Jesus was wearing a fine white robe, that reached to his ankles. The edges were trimmed with what looked like gold. On his head there was a circlet of gold and round his waist was a golden belt, apparently encrusted with jewels. Peter could hardly believe his eyes – he thought he must be still dreaming. He awakened his comrades, who started uncertainly from their sleep.

'Look over there,' whispered Peter to them.

Jesus was still standing talking to the two men. He looked splendid, thus clad – almost like a king.[13] The sun, blazing down behind him, shone on the gold, making it scintillate.

'Whatever does this mean?' whispered John. 'Whatever is happening?'

'Search me,' replied Peter. 'I thought at first I must be dreaming, but – I'm not, am I?'

While they were watching, Jesus was removing the regalia and the white robe and handing it back to the tall man with the large beard, who seemed most reluctant to take it. A fairly animated conversation followed; the disciples could see Jesus shaking his head, while the others were evidently pressing him with arguments.

'Should we go over?' asked James.

'I'm not sure,' replied Peter. 'I think we'd better wait. He'll call us if he needs us.'

'He might think we're still asleep, though,' said John. 'He may need us. I don't like the look of those two – they're getting quite cross now, I think. Look at how they're gesticulating.'

However, before they could reach a decision, they saw that Jesus was offering to shake hands with the two men, and, after a lengthy pause, the others took his hand and walked away, taking the regalia with them. Jesus watched them start down the hill, then turned to go back to the little shelter.

The disciples emerged fully into the daylight and met him part-way across the summit.

'Whatever was going on?' asked Peter, anxiously. 'We didn't know whether to come to join you or simply watch.'

'You did right not to interrupt,' said Jesus. 'How much did you see and hear?'

'I saw you all dressed up – almost like a king,' replied the big fisherman. 'What on earth was happening?'

Jesus smiled grimly. 'The Zealots are still desperate for me to join them as their King – and potentially the King of a free Israel,' he said. 'They still think that with my preaching and their arms, a revolution can be raised that will rid the country of the Romans. They want me as a kind of rabble-rouser! They actually offered me quite a substantial quantity of money. They obviously don't know me! They claim that the regalia was worn by the last Hasmonean King, who was deposed by the Romans – oh, nearly a hundred years ago. Since then, as you know, we've been ruled by Rome, or their puppet kings – the Herods. They insisted I try the robes on!'

'Do you believe they were really worn by the last Hasmonean?' asked John, amazed.

Jesus shook his head slightly and replied, 'It was not worth arguing the point – but I doubt it very much. Why would a couple of ruffians in Northern Galilee have access to the genuine articles? Where have the robes been for the past hundred years? No. The story doesn't hold water. It was just a good yarn, that might take in someone who wanted to believe it.'

'But whatever made you try on all the regalia?' asked Peter. 'Surely you had no intention of—'

'No. No – none at all,' Jesus broke in. 'But I thought they would be more convinced by my refusal if I let them go through with their little charade. If I still refused after standing there for a moment in glory (so to speak), I thought they would know for certain that I really wouldn't agree to play that role.'

'And were they convinced?' asked James.

'Not really – or, if they were, it was very reluctantly,' replied their leader. 'Anyway, I got rid of them, and I hope that that is the last we shall see of them. In any case, I don't intend to stay in this district for long, in case they try again. Come along, let's be on our way.'

★

When Jesus and his three friends finally reached Gischala just before sunset, they found the rest of their group surrounded by a crowd of about twenty locals in the village square. In the centre of the mob, a boy of about twelve years of age was sitting. He had a strange, vacant look about him, as if he was only semi-conscious, yet his eyes were open and he was looking around him with his mouth hanging open. His father was standing over him, talking earnestly with Simon, as Jesus came into the square. Immediately the locals saw him coming, they called out to the father that Jesus had arrived and he hurried over to the newcomers.

'Rabbi, I've been asking your disciples to cure my son,' he said. 'He's got an evil spirit. Look at him – he's not with it at all. He can't speak – he's like a child of two! But worse than that, from time to time, the spirit makes him shake all over and he crashes to the ground, foaming at the mouth and as rigid as a tent pole. We're at our wits' end, trying to cope. Please help us. I asked your disciples here, but they couldn't do anything.'[14]

Jesus stood rooted to the spot, evidently nonplussed for a moment. Then he said quietly, 'They just haven't the faith yet. Bring the lad here to me.'

The father went back to the boy and took him by the hand. Slowly he got to his feet and staggered towards Jesus, but suddenly he was seized with a fit and fell to the ground at Jesus's feet, shaking uncontrollably. Immediately, Jesus stooped down to hold the lad, hugging him tightly to himself.

'How long has this sort of thing been happening to him?' he asked.

'Ever since he was child,' replied the father, deeply distressed. 'Once he nearly fell into the fire, and several times he's fallen into the stream and nearly drowned. If you can, please do something to help him.'

'If I can?' commented Jesus wryly. 'It's a question of faith, my friend.'

'I have some faith.' The father's voice was pitiable. 'Help me where my faith falls short. Look at him!'

The boy was indeed in a terrible condition, foaming at the mouth, shaking and trying to free himself from the loving arms of the preacher. Jesus looked down at the epileptic's face, his brown eyes boring into the eyes of the suffering boy. He shook his shoulders and cried out, '*Come out of him*! Whatever it is that is torturing this boy, be gone and never return.'

The boy slowly stopped shaking and became limp in Jesus's arms. After a few moments, he slumped down on the floor in a dead faint, so that one of the bystanders shouted out, 'He's killed him!'

But Jesus caught hold of the lad's hands and pulled him gently into a sitting position. After just a short time, the boy opened his eyes. The look he gave Jesus was no longer vacant, but quite normal. His eyes focussed on Jesus's lovely face and a small smile formed on his mouth.

'Come on, lad,' said Jesus quietly. 'Stand up.'

The boy slowly staggered to his feet, with Jesus supporting him. The preacher turned him to his father, who was standing amazed and overcome with thankfulness.

'How can I thank you?' he breathed.

'Give thanks to God for your boy's health and live a life of thankfulness,' returned Jesus.

The father clutched at Jesus's hands and mumbled his thanks. Eventually, he moved away, holding his son round the waist, as he led him down the road to a home he had never recognised in the past.

After the crowd had dispersed, Jesus and his friends made their way to Simon's smithy, where they crowded into the little dwelling and found space to stay overnight. After supper, Simon summoned his courage to ask Jesus the question that had been on all their minds.

'Why couldn't we heal that poor boy, Jesus? We did very much like you did, but he didn't respond.'

Jesus paused before replying.

'You must not be impatient. You need more faith. It will come. It will take more time and much more prayer. You will do it – don't despair.'

NOTES

[1] Matt. 5:38; Exodus 21:24.
[2] Matt. 5:39.
[3] Matt. 5:41.
[4] Matt. 5:22.
[5] Matt. 5:28.
[6] Mark 7: 25.
[7] Matt. 7:15.
[8] Mark 7:20.
[9] Mark 8:29.
[10] Ezekiel 2:1; 3:1; 4:1, etc.
[11] Daniel 7:13.
[12] John 10:10.
[13] Mark 9:3.
[14] Mark 9:18.

The mission to Judaea

For the most part, the disciples enjoyed their few days' respite with their families. Jesus had decided not to visit Nazareth, fearing that his presence would only make more trouble. Instead, he preferred to stay quietly at Peter and Ruth's house, out of the way, spending a good deal of time on the roof, reflecting and praying. Sometimes, he, Judas and the fishermen walked along the lake side after dark, enjoying the balmy air of the evening. Once, to please the fishermen, they all went fishing at night, but caught very little.

Matthew had tried again to make things up with Joanna, but without success. His wife simply couldn't reconcile herself to the loss of her status and income, and remained bitter. Consequently, Matthew had been the first to arrive back at Capernaum, where he spent some time with Judas, the only disciple who did not have family in the area. The two accountants relaxed comfortably together, enjoying the leisure and one another's company. One evening, just after supper, as the sun dipped below the horizon in a blaze of orange and pink, they were walking along the lake shore and fell to discussing the mission. Judas was in a confidential mood.

'I have the greatest respect for Jesus, of course,' he began, 'but sometimes I wish he was a bit more – well – assertive – even militant.'

Matthew was very surprised. He had never heard any of the other disciples question, much less doubt, anything Jesus said or did.

'You don't really think we should have teamed up with the Zealots, do you?' he asked, incredulously. 'Surely that would have been a mistake.'

'No, I didn't mean that!' Judas replied slowly.

Matthew wasn't quite convinced that he meant it. He scrutinised the man from the south carefully as Judas continued, 'No, I don't think that would be right, but I sometimes wonder whether we ought not to be, well, somehow – ah – forcing things along a bit harder.'

'What do you mean?'

'Oh, I'm not at all sure.' Judas pulled at his beard. 'I just want something to happen… We seem to me to be rather stuck in a rut.'

'Will you be happier when we're in Judaea?' Matthew sounded doubtful.

'Oh, yes – I think that will help. I want to go south. I understand the Judeans better than the Galileans.' This time Judas seemed more convincing.

Matthew persisted. 'What's the difference? It'll be the same message; Jesus won't change that.'

'No, but the Judaean is more sophisticated than the Galilean.'

Judas suddenly realised what he had said. 'Oh, no offence, old chap – I realise that you are also a Galilean, but you're an exception, of course. You're educated, whereas most Galileans aren't.' Judas could be quite a snob at times!

Matthew reacted predictably. 'You'd better not say that to the others,' he said. 'They're sometimes rather – well – ashamed of their background. Apart from Nathaniel, who can read and who has some real education, certainly in the scriptures, the rest of our friends are just common tradesmen – fishermen, a potter, a basket maker, a couple of blacksmiths and a baker! But, you know, as companions, you really couldn't have nicer guys. I've really enjoyed their company and learned a lot from them. Especially Thomas – he's a splendid fellow!'

Judas nodded. 'Oh, I agree. He can sometimes be a bit – surly, but he'd be good in a crisis, I think.' But he didn't sound too sure.

They walked along in silence for a while, looking across the lake, noticing the first of the fishing boats pulling out for the night's work.

'What do you want Jesus to do differently, then?' asked Matthew. He had obviously been turning everything over in his mind.

Judas screwed up his face in perplexity. 'I'm not sure,' he said, eventually. 'I just feel that we need a new initiative. Perhaps in Judaea it'll come naturally. The people there will react differently.'

'We'll soon see.'

They left it at that, but Matthew wondered later, from time to time, what it was that the man from Gaza was considering. When the disciples met up again, however, all such thoughts were banished. It was so good to be together again! The little house rang with much merriment and more than a little leg-pulling. Jesus was on top form, listening to all their news and making some wry comments of his own.

However, just before Ruth was due to serve the evening meal, there came a forceful knock at the door. Peter went to answer it and was surprised, and more than a little dismayed, to find a Roman Centurion standing there.[1] The man was formidable, made even taller by his high-plumed helmet. Unusually, the big fisherman was temporarily lost for words, but the officer soon put his mind at rest. Instead of barking in the usual harsh commanding voice of the military, he used a quite gentle, but persuasively urgent tone, as he asked for Jesus.

'I understand that Jesus, the healer, is staying with you,' he began.

Peter was quite taken aback, as Jesus had been at pains to keep his presence in the town quiet. Evidently, somehow the word must have got out. Rather grudgingly, Peter acknowledged that this was true.

'Could I speak to him, please?'

'Please' was such an unusual word coming from a Roman, especially a soldier, that Peter found himself agreeing before he had really thought whether it was wise to do so, but when he called Jesus and told him who was waiting at the door, the preacher seemed entirely at ease.

'He's a man, just like the rest of us,' whispered the Nazarene as he went with Peter back to the door. Then, to the visitor, he said, 'What can I do for you?'

The Centurion came to attention and saluted as Peter introduced Jesus.

'It's very good of you to see me,' he began. 'I appreciate it. I have a servant, a slave, whom I value greatly. He's served me faithfully for years. He's very ill. Someone told me that you are a wonderful healer and that you were visiting Capernaum, and so I wondered… if you wouldn't mind…'

'I will come,' said Jesus, without waiting for the man to finish.

'Oh, no, there's no need for that,' replied the centurion hastily. 'Please don't trouble yourself with coming all the way to my house – though, of course, you would be very welcome. No: I am used to giving orders myself: if I tell a soldier to go, he goes. If I tell my servant to do something, he does it, and so on. In the same way, please just say the word and I'm sure that my servant will be better.'

Jesus turned to Peter, a look of wonder on his face.

'That's real faith,' he said quietly. Then he turned back to the officer.

'Go in peace,' he said. 'Your trust has ensured that your servant will be cured.'

The soldier smiled with relief and thanked Jesus warmly before leaving.

'That was real faith,' repeated Jesus, obviously touched. 'Amazing. I don't think I've come across faith like that anywhere we've been so far! I tell you this – it won't just be Jews who find their way into the Kingdom! Some Gentiles will come to feast with the chosen, while many Jews will be excluded.'

★

The group started south the following day. Jesus's intention was to walk, as usual, down the Jordan Valley, but turn west as soon as they were south of Samaria. They could then visit the many Judaean villages in the north of the province, before turning south towards Gaza. Finally, they could turn east again and head towards the Dead Sea. For the time being, Jesus felt that they should avoid Jerusalem itself – that must be their final destination.

The work was conducted in much the same way as had been carried out in Galilee, though with less difficulty to begin with. The village rabbis had not heard of Jesus and his teaching, so he was allowed to conduct his mission in the villages again, instead of being banished to the open countryside. No news of Jesus's fame as a healer had yet reached the south, so Jesus found that he could concentrate on preaching. He re-used his best parables; he told and retold the stories of the costly pearl, the good shepherd, the woman's lost coin, the prodigal son and his elder brother, the good Samaritan, the sower, and the sheep and the goats, as well as telling some new ones. His disciples were particularly intrigued with the one he told about the great feast.[2]

'There was once a rich man who decided to give great dinner party,' he said. 'He invited all his family and friends but, when the supper had been prepared and they were called to the feast, one by one they all excused themselves, claiming to be too busy to come. One said he was buying some land and had to view it and finalise the sale. Another said that he had recently purchased a team of oxen and had to try them out. A third excused himself by saying that he was about to get married. All the others made similar excuses. Naturally enough, the master of the house was very disappointed, so he called his servants together and ordered them to go into the streets nearby and call in all the poor people they could find to the feast – not forgetting the crippled, the blind and the lame. This they did, but they found that there was still some room at the supper. "Go out again," said the host. 'Go into the countryside – search along the roads, looking under the hedges for those rejected by society. Persuade them to come too. I want my house to be full, with every place at the table taken. They shall all come in, but not one of those originally invited will be here!'"

The followers of Jesus were not certain what Jesus meant by this story, so they asked him later.

'I had hoped that it would be obvious,' the preacher replied, smiling. 'You have seen it happening in practice during our mission so often. The people who appear to be religious – the people you would expect to be invited by God to his great celebration, folk like the scribes, the Pharisees, the lawyers, and suchlike – cannot find it in their hearts to accept what God is giving them. It does not fit their idea of what God should be offering. The feast that God has actually prepared – the Kingdom of which I have spoken so often – does not appeal to them. Instead, it is those who often appear unworthy – the poor people, those who are handicapped and those who are outcasts – who find their way to the supper and are glad to do so. They come with no preconceived notions, simply taking God at face value, responding to his fatherly goodness and love.

'We could maybe go further… and say that if God's chosen nation, the Jews, reject him, God may well send out into the rest of the world and offer his loving Kingdom to other nations. Remember what I said about the woman who came to see us in the camp outside Tyre? Think about the Roman soldier who visited Peter's house just before we set out for Judaea. Neither of these were Jews, but they showed faith far in excess of many of God's so-called chosen people. Perhaps God is calling those whom we Jews have always rejected. They have shown that they can certainly respond to his grace. It makes you think.'

This last idea staggered the disciples. They had always thought in terms of God in relationship with the Jews. For centuries, God had kept his covenant with his people, beginning right back at the time of Abraham, the father of the nation.[3] Was it possible that the covenant would be extended, or even transferred, to the despised Gentiles? Could there be a new covenant with the Gentiles? It seemed unthinkable…

Jesus told another parable when a man from the crowd asked Jesus to arbitrate in a dispute with his brother over an inheritance.[4] The preacher was quite incensed.

'My good fellow, who appointed me as a judge or arbitrator?' he asked. 'As a matter of fact, I'm not particularly interested in such matters. There's far too much emphasis on possessions and what folk earn and own.'

Then, raising his voice so that everyone could hear, Jesus continued.

'Beware of greed and envy, for even when a man has more than enough, he still hasn't found real life. Listen to this little story... There was once a rich farmer whose fields were particularly productive, the crops being more abundant than ever before. Indeed, the farmer started to worry about how he could possibly store his bumper harvest. Finally, he said to himself, "I'll just have to pull down my existing barns and build bigger. If I do that, I'll be able to retire and live a life of ease and luxury, eating, drinking and enjoying myself." But the very night he laid his plans, God said to him, "You stupid idiot! Tonight you're going to die! So much for your money, your harvest and your barns! Who will get them all? Not you, for sure!" It is the same with those who amass riches in this world – what does it really profit them? If they have neglected to relate to God and their fellow men, they haven't found real life.'

Jesus went on to expound this idea more fully.[5]

'It is quite wrong to worry constantly about the material things of life. God knows you have to eat and to have clothes and a home, but the real thing is the Kingdom. God will feed, clothe and house you, just as he feeds the wild birds and clothes the wild flowers in the hedgerow. You have to keep a sense of proportion – what's the sense of worrying about things of secondary importance? You might as well worry about growing taller – it doesn't do you any good! No. Concern yourselves first and foremost with finding the Kingdom of God – that inner peace of mind and spirit that comes from being right with God and your neighbour! This Kingdom is God's gift to you, if only you will receive it!'

Quite a number of people in the crowds who listened did seem to appreciate the message. Many went home saying that they understood and would try to embrace Jesus's ideas. A few went further and actually wanted to join the mission itself, but when they saw how the disciples had to live, sleeping out in the open, washing when they could, sometimes being invited into homes to eat but more often cooking over an open fire, they backed off.[6] A couple said they would come when they had finished their business, but Jesus was not prepared to wait – he needed their full commitment straightaway. He had to move on and cover as much ground as possible. He knew very well that discipleship was costly and was likely to become even more so. Once, he told the crowd that if anyone wanted to follow him, he would have to be prepared to leave everything and everyone – mother, father, wife and children, and even that he had to be prepared to die for the Kingdom's sake.[7] He therefore warned people to think carefully before enlisting in his service, in the same way as an engineer thinks, plans and calculates carefully before attempting to build a tower, or a general thinks carefully before going to war, making sure that his army is large enough and well enough equipped to have a real chance of victory.

'Think how foolish you would look trying to build a tower with insufficient bricks!' he said. 'How people would laugh at you if you ran out when the building was halfway complete! In the same way, you will look ridiculous if you start on this mission and turn back a couple of miles down the road!'

*

One day, they were just planning to break camp and move to a new location when a small party of horsemen rode up and dismounted. The leader, a tall young man, richly dressed, approached and asked Andrew where he could find Jesus.

'I'll just fetch him for you, sir,' said the fisherman and went over to where Jesus was busy tidying up his few belongings.

'I'll come,' said the preacher, and he strode over to the good-looking newcomer with hand outstretched. But the young man didn't take the proffered hand. Instead, to everyone's surprise, he knelt at Jesus's feet. Then, looking up at him, he said, 'Good Master, what must I do to be acceptable to God and live for ever with him?'

Jesus reached down and pulled the young man to his feet.

'There's no need to kneel to me! And why do you call me good? There is none good, except God himself.'[8]

'I have heard how good you are to everyone,' replied the visitor. 'Your reputation is that you are close to God yourself and that you can help people to find him and live with him eternally.'

'There's no secret about finding God,' said Jesus, smiling. 'You know the commandments, I'm sure: do not murder, do not steal, do not give false evidence, do not commit adultery, honour your father and mother and so on...'

The young man spoke eagerly. 'I've kept all these since I was just a boy. Do I qualify?'

Jesus looked at him closely. He was a very good-looking man, well dressed – seemingly advantaged in every way. Round his neck was an expensive-looking medallion. Across the way, Jesus saw his friends and servants, all well dressed. The horses wore expensive harness, edged with silver. He felt sad, for he suspected that what he was about to ask would prove to be impossible.

'There's just one thing,' he said. 'You have to adjust your priorities. Give up this rich style of life with all its finery. Sell your excess and give the proceeds to the poor. Give it away, I say, and come and join us in our mission!'

The young man looked stunned. He drew back from Jesus, his nostrils flaring.

'I can't do that,' he snarled. 'You must be out of your mind. Don't you know who I am?'

'I've no idea,' replied Jesus, evenly. 'Whoever you are, my answer remains the same. You are a good-looking man, with much to offer the world, if only you will do so. Why is my advice so ridiculous?'

'My name is Joseph, from Arimathea. I am the Prince of that region. I can't throw everything up at a moment's notice, leave all my responsibilities to follow you and live like a scarecrow!'

'Then there is nothing more to be said.' Jesus looked sadly at the man. 'You have so much to offer. As a Prince, you have influence that you could use for good; but I can see that you cannot bring yourself to change. Goodbye.'

With that, the preacher turned away and returned to his packing. The young man watched him go for a moment, then he also turned and stalked off to his horse. The party mounted and rode away in haste, stirring clouds of dust behind them.

If Jesus was sometimes severe with adults, this was in marked contrast with his attitude to the children. One day, when Jesus was resting after preaching all the morning, some mothers tried to bring their children to Jesus. They were, no doubt, hoping that he would tell them some of his incomparable stories. Philip and Nathaniel were preparing the midday meal over the fire when the little group of mothers came to the camp asking for him.

'I'm sorry,' said Nathaniel. 'Our leader is resting now. He's had a very busy morning.'

The women were obviously disappointed and tried persuading the two disciples, until they had to get quite gruff in their refusal. Peter, hearing the argument, came over to try to find out what was happening, and soon started adding his loud tones to the refusal. Before long, between them, they roused Jesus, who appeared on the scene and, to the disciples' amazement, immediately took two of the smaller children in his arms and led them all over to a little patch of shade, where, sitting down, he started to talk to them. He was at his best with children, telling them stories, answering their questions and laughing at their antics. They adored him. The little ones insisted on climbing on his knee and everyone crowded near so that he could cuddle them. After nearly an hour, the mothers decreed that they had to go on their way, but before they did so, Jesus insisted on blessing each child in turn. They departed with much hand-waving and a few tears.

When they were out of sight, Jesus called to all the disciples and was really quite indignant about the way they had received the little group.

'Never turn children away,' he said, shaking his head, his brown eyes flashing.[9] 'I am never too tired to see the children! They will most easily find the Kingdom, for their lives have not been complicated with all the business and temptations that adults have taken on. I have told you before – we all have to become like children before we can accept the Kingdom.'

The disciples weren't quite sure what he meant, but they were not disposed to ask questions while he was so displeased. Philip, particularly, was downcast that he had apparently upset his leader so much, and Peter and Nathaniel were also quite put out.

'He's so rarely upset – especially with us,' commented Peter to the older man. 'He's usually so patient; he must feel very strongly about the matter.'

Nathaniel agreed. 'He usually reserves his strictures for the Pharisees and scribes. He lays into them fairly often, but it's rare for him to have a go at us! We'd better keep out of his way for a while, I think!'

Jesus had indeed clashed again with the Pharisees, who were more numerous in Judaea than in Galilee. It hadn't taken long for them to become aware of his teaching and they had increasingly come to his meetings to see what it was all about and criticise. They had boringly raised the same issues as had surfaced in Galilee – the keeping of the Sabbath, the routine of washing both hands and pots at meal-times, the giving of tithes, and sundry other minutiae of the law. Jesus was scathing about their attitude, referring to them as 'whitewashed tombs', looking beautiful on the outside, but actually full of bones and filth.[10] He criticised them for piling their legal requirements on others, while not lifting a finger in charity for the poor and destitute.

'They look after themselves all right,' he scoffed. 'They live well and like to be seen to be important. They want the best places in the Synagogues and all the social kudos. They love money and all that it brings, but the fact is that you cannot love money and also love God. You just cannot serve two masters![11] You have to choose.'

Jesus shook his head and pulled at his dark brown beard. He continued, 'The Pharisees and scribes have lost all sense of the real message of the prophets. The prophets talk of justice and mercy.[12] These religious folk seem to know nothing about all that! It has always been the same – the religious establishment has been at the forefront of those wanting to persecute the prophets – and no doubt they'll be after me too! They're nothing but a nest of vipers!'

It was clear that the problems were growing again. It was not long before it was not just the local Pharisees and rabbis who were attending and criticising; increasingly, the religious authorities were coming from Jerusalem itself. Jesus knew that things must be hotting up for him in the Temple precincts, and the disciples began to wonder what lay in store for them if they continued in this manner.

Things grew even worse one day when Jesus came across a man who was said to have a devil in him. The preacher had walked into a village, on his way to address a large crowd in the village square, and seen a little man lying in the road, shaking all over and frothing at the mouth. Nobody was nearby. Nobody seemed to be caring for the poor chap, so Jesus went over to him, held him tightly to himself and spoke quietly, but authoritatively, in his ear.

'Have no fear, my friend,' he said. 'Whatever it is that troubles you, put it behind you. I assure you that there is nothing that can corrupt you like this permanently. Trust me.'

The man became limp in Jesus's arms, and, after a few moments, started to recover. He looked in a puzzled way at Jesus.

'It's all right,' said his healer. 'You're quite safe and well now. Don't fear.'

The man struggled to his feet, still visibly shaken, but obviously looking better. He struggled for words.

'I feel so well…' he said at last. 'Thank you… thank you…'

'I'm so glad you are well, my friend,' returned Jesus. 'Don't thank me – thank God and go and live a life of thankfulness. If you want to help me, don't tell people about this meeting of ours. I'd really prefer to keep things quiet.'

'But…'

'Just do as I say,' emphasised Jesus.

But the word must have got around, because later the same day Jesus was challenged about the cure by some Pharisees, who came to see him after his evening meeting.

'We hear that you have been driving out devils,' one said, challengingly. 'We talked earlier to a man that the whole village knows was possessed – has been for years – and now he's as sane as any of us. He told us that it was you that cured him.'

Jesus paused for several seconds, wondering how best to answer. But before he could say anything, the leader of the Pharisees continued accusingly, 'You cast out devils because you are a devil yourself – in league with Beelzebub, Prince of Devils. That's where the power comes from – the Evil One himself.'[13]

'Yes. He's in league with the devil,' said another. 'A devil in our village – it's unthinkable.'

'Just a minute,' replied Jesus, quietly. 'Just talk sense. Is it at all likely that the devil would work against himself? Why on earth would Beelzebub cast out another devil? No kingdom works against itself – that would be a certain way to its destruction! Why, some of your own sect have cured people of their devils, but you don't accuse them of being in league with Satan! Go and ask them how they effect their cures. They will tell you that health and healing come only from God.'

The Pharisees left, shaking their heads and muttering, but it was another warning that things were getting worse for Jesus and his followers. However, the season was by now advancing into autumn. The days were getting shorter and cooler. September was drawing to its close and Jesus decided that it was time to send the disciples out on their own again, while he had a short break. He called them all together one evening and told them to prepare for going out in pairs again, as they had done in Galilee. He was pleased that, this time, there was less apprehension. The men seemed to believe that, with his help in preparation, they could manage to conduct a mission on their own for a couple of weeks. They dispersed a few days later, some to revisit areas where they had been well received, others to press on to new areas, as yet untouched by the mission. They agreed a time and place to meet up again.

Jesus himself turned towards Bethany. There, he knew, he would find rest and refreshment at the home of Lazarus and his sisters. It had been a difficult few months, and he needed a break from the constant attention of the people who needed his ministry and the opposition of the religious hierarchy. He arrived at the village house just as the sun was setting and knocked at the well-remembered door. Mary came to let him in and was predictably delighted to see him, kissing him on both cheeks very warmly, with loud exclamations of her joy at seeing him again. Martha, too, in her much less demonstrative way, welcomed Jesus.

'Sit you down,' she said. 'I'll get some fruit juice – or would prefer beer?'

Jesus slumped in a chair on the terrace at the back of the house and enjoyed being pampered by the two women.

'How's Lazarus?' he asked.

Mary's face fell and Martha rolled her eyes upward.

'He's – um – well, he's very...' Martha stammered and came to a standstill.

Mary intervened.

'He became very morose and peculiar,' she said. 'You know as well as anyone how hard he has tried to find spiritual rest. He wants to serve God but doesn't know quite how to do it. Now he's left home again – to join one of the more eccentric Essene communities, way out in the desert beyond Jordan. We haven't seen him for – what – two months, or more?'

'It must be at least that,' agreed Martha.

'I shall be sorry to miss him.' Jesus spoke in a low voice. 'I had hoped to have convinced him that he was serving God by staying here with you, but apparently I failed...'

The evening meal was overshadowed by the empty chair at the end of the table. The three enjoyed each other's company but each was aware that there was one missing from the familiar group. It wasn't quite the same. The sisters insisted that Jesus stayed with them just as long as he wanted. He could sit in their back garden and rest, or, if he preferred, prepare his mind for what was to come when he returned to the mission. The preacher was glad to have that opportunity – it had been a long hard summer and the difficulties seemed to be mounting. He needed time to think and pray quietly alone. After three days, however, he told the sisters that he intended to move on, but he would return briefly later on his way back to the mission. He decided to walk over to Bethphage to see if Matt was around. He found him in his courtyard, chopping wood for the coming winter.

'It's good to see you, Jesus.' Matt's face was alight with joy. 'Come in and tell me all your news.'

When they were settled with a mug of wine each, Jesus insisted on hearing the other's news first.

'There's little to tell. We've been busy enough to keep our meals coming on to the table, which is all one can ask these days.'

'You don't believe that,' replied Jesus. 'Life isn't just about keeping bread on the plate. When you were with John the Baptist you knew better than that!'

'Yes, that's true,' returned the other. 'I meant that I am content – but I agree that life seems to be dull and lacking purpose now. Perhaps, some day, I shall find a new company in which I can serve.'

'One day I shall need your help, Matt,' Jesus said, looking keenly at him.

'I'm always at your service – you know that.'

'Things are getting increasingly difficult for us,' explained his friend. 'We have travelled widely both in Galilee and Judaea and it is clear to me that, although many of the common people appreciate my message and some make an attempt to respond, the religious authorities are adamantly against me and all I stand for. I believe that before long there will be some sort of climax – but I feel that I must make sure that it occurs on my terms not on theirs. That climax must occur in Jerusalem, for that is the centre of our faith…'

'I'm here when you need me, Jesus. I realise I haven't been through the heat of the battle with you so far – others have carried the burden – but maybe I can help you when you reach Jerusalem.'

'Thank you, my friend. I will have need of you. There are others in Jerusalem too and I shall be seeing them before rejoining the Galileans in the mission field. We shall have to plan our next moves very carefully.'

Jesus stayed with Matt overnight. He had come to like and respect Jesus very much by this time and was beginning to regret not throwing in his lot with the Nazarene earlier, but he determined to do what he could in the future. It was with real regret that he bid Jesus farewell when he left the following morning.

The preacher started down the Mount of Olives towards the Holy City, past the Garden of Gethsemane, across the Kedron Valley, then up the steep slope to the city gate. Above him reared the vast bulk of the great Temple, its golden pinnacles flashing in the sun. The smoke from the fires consuming the daily sacrifices hung in the air. The sound of the priests' chanting echoed from the interior. Jesus paused and took it all in, before making his way to Justus's inn. He found the landlord busy in the kitchen preparing for the evening's trade, surrounded by his wife and several serving girls.

'I'll leave you to it,' Justus told his wife. 'I must get Jesus's news.'

He fixed some refreshment and they sat in the courtyard, enjoying the autumn sunshine. Jesus briefly recounted what had happened since they had last met and found that, as at Bethphage, he had a ready ear and an offer of help, should he need it.

'I appreciate your kindness,' Jesus told Justus. 'You and your family have been very kind to me, and I fear I shall need to count on your kindness more in the future.'

'There's really no problem,' said Justus, grinning. 'We'll do anything we can – you know that.'

'Well, you can start by putting me up for two nights, if you would,' replied the preacher. 'I want to go the Temple tomorrow for a few hours…'

'It'll be pleasure,' replied Justus. 'There's no difficulty for a day or two. There's no crush until the festival of Trumpets comes along in a week's time.'

'I'll have to be on my way in a couple of days.'

★

The following day, Jesus went up to the Temple. He sat studying the scriptures for three hours and then went to pray in the court of the Jews. It was reasonably quiet in there, quite unlike the noise of the outer courtyard, where the business of the Temple was conducted. There, as usual, numerous animals were on sale for sacrifice and the money changers bawled their prices and exchange rates at every passer-by.

After prayer, Jesus started across the noisy courtyard on his way to get some lunch when he saw John barHelez emerging from one of the Temple offices. The two friends greeted each other warmly as usual.

'I didn't know you were in town,' said John, rather as though he thought he ought to have been told. 'I heard you were out in the villages, down south.'

'I have been,' replied his friend, 'but I decided I needed a few days' rest. I've left my followers to continue the good work while I visit a few friends in and around Jerusalem. Naturally I would have looked you up at some point.'

'I should think so too!'

The conversation was cut short by John's need to prepare for his next service within the Temple. The two agreed to meet that evening at Justus's inn and share a meal. Jesus spent some more time in the Temple, but also found time to drop in on Nathan and Cleopas, who were delighted to see him and dropped their work to have a chat. The two shopkeepers were extremely interested in the progress of the mission and excited to hear that things were happening nearer to Jerusalem.

'When will you preach in the Temple?' asked Cleopas. 'We want to hear you here, in the Holy City. That's where all great prophets operate!'

'I know,' replied Jesus. 'I realise that I must challenge the city and the Temple one day. It won't be this side of the winter, but soon, I promise you. Most likely next Passover, I think.'

'We shall look out for you, Jesus.' Nathan's eyes were shining.

John and Jesus met just after dark and found a place in the corner of Justus's inn where they could talk undisturbed. It was not long before John started to warn his friend that he was heading for trouble.

'The Temple police are reporting that the populace is showing more and more interest in your activities,' he said. 'The High Priest is having you watched very carefully. I gather that some of our people – Temple scribes and lawyers – have clashed with you on a number of occasions. I don't think you can expect to be allowed to go on like this for much longer.'

'It has never been against Jewish Law to preach and discuss theological matters. All right, I have broken some of the minutiae of the code laid down by the scribes and Pharisees, but I have upheld the Torah and encouraged everyone else to do the same. The High Priest, as a Sadducee, doesn't recognise the Pharisaic law himself, so he can hardly complain if I don't either!'

'So far you've avoided any popular movement – any suggestion of a riot or disturbance,' said John. 'That's the important thing. If there were any disturbance of the peace, that would trigger an immediate response on the part of the Temple Guard. I've told you before, it is from the High Priest as a politician that you have most to fear. He has to keep in with Pilate, the Governor.'

'You know I haven't any political ambitions, John.' Jesus shook his head. 'I don't want any part in rioting or disorder.'

The two men talked on well into the night. The distance between them, theologically, could not destroy, or even weaken, the warmth of genuine regard that each had for the other. John was at pains to make clear to his friend his support for him, as far as his priestly duties allowed.

'One day, you will be invaluable to me and my cause,' said Jesus. 'I know I can rely on you.'

'Of course you can.'

The two parted regretfully. Jesus took himself off upstairs to his bed space and began preparing for the night. However, he had hardly washed his face when Justus came into the room in some haste and asked him to return downstairs.

'There's quite an important-looking man waiting downstairs for you, Jesus,' said Justus. 'I've no idea what he wants. Will you come?'

Jesus complied, puzzled. When he arrived, he found a very well-dressed man, of middle age, waiting in the room, pacing up and down in some agitation.

'Sir? What can I do for you?' began Jesus.

'You are Jesus, the preacher?' enquired the newcomer. 'You're the man who has been preaching both in Judaea and earlier in Galilee?'

'Yes, I am,' agreed Jesus. 'How can I help you?'

'Have we a place where we can talk privately?'

Jesus quickly arranged with Justus to use a small side room, away from anyone else. The two men sat facing one another across a rough wooden table, neither speaking for a little. Then, the stranger began.

'My name is Nicodemus.[14] You may have heard of me. I am a member of the Sanhedrin, the Central Council of the Jews in Jerusalem, and, as such, I suppose you can say that I have some influence hereabouts.'

'I see,' replied Jesus. 'I am honoured that you should wish to speak to me. What service can I do you, sir?'

'I have heard about your work over the past two summers. I am interested in your message, which I think I understand, but I would like to question you further. Also I should warn you that others in Jerusalem are not in sympathy with your views.'

'I know,' sighed Jesus, shaking his head slightly. 'I have friends who keep me in touch with what's happening in the Temple. They have warned me too…'

'Have they indeed! I wonder who they could be?' Nicodemus paused for an answer, but Jesus did not reply. Eventually Nicodemus spoke again.

'Can you summarise your teachings for me? Please understand that I am not trying to catch you out – I am quite sincere in wanting to know. I accept completely that you must be sent by God, for nobody could do the things you have done without God's blessing. I have heard of your wonderful healing miracles. Even if they have been exaggerated somewhat in the telling, there are too many to be entirely fabricated and such things can only be done by those who are blessed by God.'

Jesus thought for a moment, then spoke softly.

'It amounts to this. Every man must be prepared to be born again.'

Nicodemus broke in before Jesus could elaborate. 'Born again?' he cried, staggered by the concept. 'Can anyone enter his mother's womb a second time and be born over again?'

'Please let me finish,' replied Jesus calmly. 'Obviously I didn't mean it literally. I speak a great deal in parables and pictures and this is just another picture. No. I mean that each of us has to be born spiritually, as well as physically. We have to be born into the world of the Spirit, into God's world, or the Kingdom of God, as I like to call it. There, we have totally to rethink our attitude to everything – starting with our attitude to God, as our Father. We have to accept his pattern for our own lives. This will affect the way we treat those around us – we have to recognise each other as brothers and sisters. We have to learn to live for each other, no longer for ourselves. We have to learn to honour each other, just as much as we always honour ourselves. In fact, we must take really seriously the old law about loving your neighbour as yourself.'

'What can bring about this great change in a man's life?' asked Nicodemus.

'I tell you that it is only possible if you trust in God and follow the way I have set out. Seek his Spirit, which is active throughout the world, like the wind itself, blowing everywhere at God's behest.'

'How do I know that I can believe you?' asked Nicodemus doubtfully. 'Forgive me, but you have no great training – you are not a priest – not even a village rabbi. Where do you get your authority from?'

'I am just a son of man, I know,' replied Jesus. 'I have studied, but I am not a priest. Nevertheless, I believe that God has spoken to me – as he did to the prophets of old – and that one day you will see this son of man lifted up so that all can see and respond to him. I believe that God has commissioned me. I am sure that everyone who follows my way will find his way safely into the presence of the Father. I have come to bring light and life – those who follow the light and walk in the light will find true life.'

The two men talked on for some time. At length the councillor rose to leave.

'You have given me a lot to think over, Jesus,' he said. 'You are either a man of God, or a deluded rogue – I'm not yet sure which. But I don't see any harm in you. I shall have to consider all that you have said further. In the meantime, be careful not to stir up any trouble or the Council may well act against you.'

'Thank you for your warning,' returned Jesus. 'Goodnight.'

NOTES

[1] Matt. 8:5.
[2] Luke 14:16.
[3] Genesis 17:7.
[4] Luke 12:13.
[5] Matt. 6:25–30.
[6] Luke 9:57–62.
[7] Luke 14:26.
[8] Mark 10:18.
[9] Mark 10:14.
[10] Matt. 23:27.
[11] Matt. 6:24.
[12] Micah 6:8.
[13] Luke 11:15.
[14] John 3:1–16.

The end of the second mission

The followers of Jesus were pleased to be back with their teacher and together again. On the whole, they felt that their mission had been well received, though some had found preaching easier than others. Thomas and Matthew had struggled a bit, finding it especially difficult to cope with questions. The initial address, well prepared, went well enough, but they were sometimes at a loss when trying to deal 'off the cuff' with points put to them. Judas said that he relished this challenge and felt that things hadn't gone too badly at all, though his partner, Thaddeus, was less sure. Nathaniel had felt the benefit of his vast experience of the scriptures, while Philip had been glad to shelter behind his more experienced colleague. Each had his own story to tell. James and John, the fishermen, had kept very quiet during the debriefing session, but when the others had dispersed to get on with the chores – shopping, cooking and so on – they made their way to Jesus full of enthusiasm and asked him a favour.

'What do you want?' asked the preacher.

James began. 'You know that you said we were to tell the people about the coming Kingdom…'

Jesus looked puzzled. 'Yes, of course. That is the centre of all that I have preached, and I hope that is what you have stressed too.'

John hastened to agree. 'We have been telling the people that they should begin to prepare their minds and hearts for the new Kingdom, and that soon you would usher in the final reign of God…'

Jesus interrupted. 'I have always made it clear that the timing is a matter for God. The final Kingdom may come very soon – I certainly believe that a decisive step will shortly occur – but it is equally possible that the ultimate reign of God over everything may take much longer.'

James continued, 'But let us assume that God does step in soon. We feel sure that, as his Messiah, you will be the one commissioned by God to usher in this Kingdom—'

John butted in, breathlessly, 'And we want – we hope – that you will let us sit on either side of you, when you are enthroned in splendour in that Kingdom.'[1]

It was out – their hopes and ambitions expressed in that one breathless exclamation. They saw almost at once the disappointment in Jesus's face. He shut his eyes, pursed his lips and kept silent for several moments before replying, his voice full of disappointment.

'My friends, it seems to me that you have misunderstood all that I have been saying to you all this time. In the first place, as I have just said, I don't know God's timetable. You must remember that God's view of time is very different from ours. A millennium is just a minute in God's time. If he chooses to wait for ten millennia, we have to accept that. Why should God not allow more of his children to be born and be welcomed into his family?

'Secondly, even if I knew when the Kingdom is going to be established by God, it is for him, not me, to decide on the actual arrangements. You can share with me in this earthly mission – you are doing so – and we don't know what that may entail before all is done. There may be much to be borne. But, as for the arrangements to occur in heaven, that must be a matter only for God!

'Lastly, and most importantly, you seem to have misunderstood completely the nature of the Kingdom. Haven't you heard me talking often enough about service? In the new Kingdom, each of us serves the next person. Greatness is not to be found in achieving rank or position, sitting on thrones in pomp here or there, but in being prepared to defer to the next fellow.'

So intent had Jesus been on his little discourse, that he had not realised that both Judas and Thaddeus had been within earshot while he had been talking to James and John. As soon as Jesus had moved away, Judas cornered the two fishermen and demanded to know the subject of their conversation. Rather shamefacedly, John had tried to explain. He realised just how inappropriate his request to Jesus had been as soon as he had to articulate it to the other disciple.

'And what made you think that you should be the most important?' demanded Judas, indignantly.

'We've all been involved with Jesus,' chimed in Thaddeus. 'Of course, we know you were with him almost from the beginning, but by now, surely, we're all important to him.'

Other followers gathered round and the situation had to be explained yet again. James and John came in for some heated comments from their comrades, all of whom felt slighted that the fishermen should have wanted to be selected for special treatment. Before long, Jesus himself became aware of the increasingly noisy debate and had to return to intervene and quieten them all down.

'It comes to this,' he said. 'If anyone wants to be first, he must make himself last of all and servant of all.[2] You must become childlike – uninterested in position and rank... how often must I say it? Now, please, can we have no more of this kind of jealous talk? We are all here to serve – this is the role of the Messiah and all who follow him.'

★

The mission continued much as before for several weeks, with the usual mixture of encouraging and discouraging features. They laboured on until they reached the countryside surrounding the town of Bethlehem, where they camped for several days. Jesus spoke to increasingly large crowds, many of whom came from fair distances, including some from as far away as Jerusalem, about five miles to the north.

Three days after they had set up camp near Bethlehem, John was surprised when a young man arrived, asking for Jesus, saying that he had been sent by the women from Bethany.[3] John had met the sisters, of course, when he visited Jerusalem with Jesus during Pentecost eighteen months earlier. He reported immediately to his leader, taking the messenger with him. They found Jesus sitting a little way outside camp, pondering on his message for the coming evening meeting.

'What's the trouble?' he asked.

The messenger, a young lad who lived across the way from Martha and Mary, looked rather serious as he said, 'We heard you were in the district, Jesus. Martha asked me to come to find you. I'm sorry, but I have to tell you that Lazarus has returned home, very ill. He was carried home by a party of Essenes from the community where he was staying and has been ill in his room ever since. It is even feared that he may die.'

'I see.' Jesus also looked serious, yet also slightly puzzled. 'Tell me how it happened and what is wrong with him.'

'Well, that's the strange thing. He doesn't seem to have any obvious symptoms. He just doesn't seem to care. He's just lifeless – and getting weaker by the hour. Martha and Mary are at their wits' end, not knowing how to cope with him. Nothing they say or do seems to interest him. He almost seems to want to die.'

Jesus nodded slowly.

'I see. Please tell Martha that I will come to see him at Bethany soon.'

'Don't you think you should come straightaway?' asked the youth, full of concern. 'He's pretty bad – really he is.'

Jesus laid a hand on his shoulder and smiled briefly.

'You've done as you were asked, lad,' he said. 'Tell Martha that I understand and will come as soon as I can, but we have to fulfil our mission here first. Lazarus will not die, don't fret.'

The messenger's face betrayed his doubts, but he said nothing further. When he had departed, the disciples, knowing just how much Jesus loved Lazarus and the whole family at Bethany, tried again to persuade him to go there straightaway.

'We can cope here,' said Peter. 'We coped on our own before, didn't we? You go and see your friend.'

'You had time to prepare last time,' replied Jesus. 'I was able to give you plenty of time ahead of the event, but this time you're not ready. In addition, we are pretty near Jerusalem, with all that that means in terms of the possibility of awkward questions! No. I'd better stay here for the time being. Don't worry. I know what I am doing. Trust me. We'll stay here for a few more days, then go to Bethany.'

Nothing they could say would change his mind, so they changed the subject, but Jesus was obviously preoccupied over the next few days and very serious all the time, which was unlike him. Usually, he would wear a broad smile and have cheery things to say from time to time throughout the day, but now he seemed totally withdrawn. The disciples concluded that he must be worrying over his friend, and Peter tried again to express their concern, but Jesus shook his head enigmatically.

'There's nothing to be done for the present,' he said. 'I'm sure that Lazarus is only asleep.'

'Well, if he can sleep, that's a good thing. He'll probably wake up feeling better,' replied the big fisherman.

'This is not a normal sleep,' said Jesus slowly, shaking his head. 'We'll have to wake him, in more than one sense, when we arrive.'

The disciples couldn't make out what he was talking about, so they held their peace. In fact, it was fully five days before they were able to make their way to Bethany. They arrived mid-afternoon, and Jesus left the disciples on the outskirts of the village looking for a suitable place to camp, while he made his way to the house to be greeted by a tearful, but slightly truculent, Martha.

'If only you had been here, Jesus!' she cried. 'Why didn't you come when we sent for you? If you had come, I know you could have cured him. As it is, he's been in his grave nearly four days now.'

Jesus took her by the hand and led her into the house. There, they found Mary, weeping and being consoled by several of the neighbours. Lazarus, for all his peculiar ways and unusual lifestyle, had been well respected in the village, and the sisters were greatly loved. When the villagers saw Jesus, they took the hint and departed, leaving the two sisters to talk quietly with their friend.

'Now, just tell me what happened,' he said.

Martha began, between sobs. 'Well – about ten days ago, four of the Essenes from the community where Lazarus was staying brought him home on a litter. They said that he had fallen ill at the community but that there was nothing now that could be done for him. We should prepare the sepulchre, for he would die shortly…'

Mary intervened. 'They were so cold about it – so, well, calculating. There was no sympathy, no love – just a statement. "He will die shortly." It was awful.'

Jesus nodded slowly. 'Please go on,' he said.

Martha spoke again. 'It was just as they said. We put Lazarus to bed and tried to nurse him, but he refused all food and didn't seem to care at all. He seemed to want to die. He kept saying, in a voice like a zombie, "Take me to the sepulchre". It was terrible.'

She burst into a fresh flood of tears. Mary spoke again, in a low voice.

'I believe he wanted to die, Jesus. Whatever could have made him want to go? What did they say or do to him in that terrible community to bring him to such a pass? He's been unsettled for years, as you know, and, yes, it's true, increasingly unhappy, but not this…'

Jesus took her hands in his and spoke gently. 'And he died four days ago?'

'Yes. We laid him in the family tomb just beyond the village. You should have come when we sent for you, Jesus. We needed you.' Mary looked at him with a mixture of love and accusation.

'Take me to him now, will you?'

The trio made their way slowly and sorrowfully to the sepulchre. Seeing them depart, a number of the neighbours followed them down the road and out of the village to the burial site. The family grave, a small cavern, was cut into the side of a steep slope, with a large stone rolled across the entrance. Nearby, the olive trees provided a little shade from the autumn sun, still quite hot at that time of day. The mourners were perspiring freely after their little walk and gathered in the shade. Jesus spoke to a couple of men in the party.

'Help me to move this stone, please,' he said.

While they hesitated, Martha came over and tugged at his sleeve, saying, 'You mustn't do that, Jesus! He's been dead four days and decay will have set in. In any case, there's no point…'

Jesus turned to her and murmured gently, 'Trust me, Martha. Let me have my way.'

He signalled to the men and slowly and painfully, sweat glistening on their brows, they heaved the great stone back, revealing the tomb's dark interior. Inside could just be seen the first of recesses cut into the rock where bodies had been laid out in their eternal sleep.

'Where is Lazarus?' asked the preacher.

'He's laid out further into the hillside, Jesus,' answered Mary in a low voice.

Jesus went slowly to the mouth of the tomb and called out gently into the gloom, 'Lazarus! Lazarus, where are you?'

There was utter silence. Nobody could believe what they were hearing. There was a long pause, then Jesus, with increasing authority in his voice, called again into the gloom, 'Lazarus! It's time to awaken. Get up and come out.'

Again there was a long period of silence, but this was broken eventually by a slight noise from within the tomb. The crowd strained forward to see what was happening, half fascinated, half terrified. Then, from the gloom, they saw a white figure emerging. Stunned, they drew back. There were muffled cries of 'My God!' and 'It's him!'

It was true. The figure, dressed in grave clothes and therefore barely recognisable at first, was indeed seen to be the unfortunate Lazarus, very weak and unsteady on his feet, but nonetheless alive.

'Help me release him from these bindings,' said Jesus to Martha, starting forward to help the weak man, who swayed unsteadily in the entrance to the sepulchre. The two sisters ran to their brother, hardly able to believe that he was with them again, smiling and weeping by turns, their minds a whirlpool of incredulity, hope and delight. They loosed the grave clothes and started to lead him slowly and painfully back up the hill.

'Jesus – how can we thank you?' Mary was trying to bring together her thoughts in her bewildered mind.

'Later, Mary.' Jesus was smiling now.

They made their way slowly back to the house. Many times Lazarus had to stop to recover his breath or his balance, but eventually he was safely installed on a couch in the living area.

'Take something to drink, Lazarus,' said Martha. 'I'll make some soup directly. We're going to have to build you up again. I just can't believe that you're here at all…'

Mary insisted on sitting by her brother, holding his hand. 'You're warm again,' she said. 'You were so cold when you …'

Her voice broke down as she recalled the moment when she had first seen the ghostlike figure emerging from the cavern. Jesus sat across the room, a slight smile playing on his face. For a while, he let the sisters talk with their brother, who said very little, but eventually the preacher spoke softly, but urgently, to his friend.

'Now, Lazarus. Tell us what you can of your long struggle. You've clearly been though a great ordeal. What is it all about?'

The tone of the question surprised the two women. Martha turned to Jesus almost hysterically and cried out, 'We should be asking questions of you, Jesus! How can Lazarus tell us anything? It was you who brought him back from the dead. How can we thank you enough?'

Mary, too, joined in, neither of them finding the right words to use in their unique situation; but Jesus gently silenced them with a gesture and resumed his questioning of Lazarus.

'Won't you tell them, Lazarus, what you have done? I think I know, but now your sisters need to know too.'

The weak man settled himself on his pillow looking straight ahead and, after a long pause, spoke slowly and quietly, apparently addressing the roof.

'Obviously, Jesus, you realise what a fool I've been,' he said, 'for you know about the great ordeal. I went to that community way out in the Jordanian desert hoping to find the spiritual home I had been seeking all my life. They took me in as a novice, and for three months they taught me their doctrines and some of their practices, but they said that they would only initiate me into the next stage of the process leading to membership if and when I had passed through the great ordeal.'

The skeletal figure on the couch paused, screwed up his eyes to blink back the tears and continued in a whisper.

'The great ordeal consists of death and rebirth. Every novice seeking admittance to the community has to submit to being drugged with a special herb concoction that the brethren have perfected. This gradually decreases vitality – it makes you feel ghastly and devoid of all feeling. Eventually you become totally unconscious and apparently dead. Of course, you are then buried, because your family and friends believe that you are truly dead. This group of Essenes need all your former acquaintances to believe that you have indeed gone. Several days later, they come and secretly steal you away from the tomb and resuscitate you; I don't know quite how, but presumably they have worked out a system, or found a suitable drug to do so. Perhaps the effects of the original drug wear off about then – I don't know. But the thing is that you have to endure all this before you can be accepted as a member of their community and therefore fully acceptable to God. Only then can you take up your life in the community for the rest of your existence, completely cut off from all you ever knew before – a totally new life… That's the theory, anyway.'

'And we were never to know that you were still alive?' asked Mary, horrified.

'No. I had to promise never to attempt to contact you again. You had to believe that I had died, so that I could live a completely new life in the future, only concerned for the good of the community. I would have been practising a terrible deceit on you both.'

'I think that's disgusting.' Martha sounded distraught. 'How could you treat us like that?'

'I had been taught that this was the only way to please God,' was the reply from the bed. 'All my life I have been looking for the right way to honour God and I thought that this might be it…'

'But it's against all that we know about being a family!' Martha burst into tears again.

Jesus caught her hands in his and looked deeply into her streaming eyes.

'It's done now, Martha,' he said softly. 'You must forgive Lazarus. I think that he's trying to tell you that he regrets what has happened. I think he sees now that this is not the way of love and cannot, therefore, be the way of God. He meant well, but was led astray…'

'That's it, Jesus.' Lazarus struggled to rise a little in his bed, but had to give up. Lying back, he continued talking.

'I have always wanted to make a supreme sacrifice for God, to show him just how much I want to serve him. I thought that, this time, this was what I was doing. But you have intervened to restore me to my senses and my family. You have saved me from a great mistake. To have let everyone believe that I was dead… to have left my sisters to fend for themselves, without a man to provide for them… that would have been unforgivable. You did warn me, Jesus, but I wouldn't listen.'

The preacher smiled as he stood by the bed. He spoke again.

'It is a great mistake to believe that service to God inevitably involves some flamboyant gesture – an unusual lifestyle – the need to go to the ends of the world. Some people are indeed called to special service, but not all – not the majority. How would the world continue if everyone were constrained to move away from home and family to do strange feats of service to God? It just couldn't work. You know that I have left my own family, to their disgust; but most people are required to serve God in the context of own homes and among their own kin. God builds on the natural ties of family to forge even greater bonds of love and caring.'

Lazarus managed a slight smile.

'I don't think I shall feel like leaving my family again in future. I have now, at last, realised where my life should be lived and my service given.'

★

The weather was becoming increasingly unpredictable. The long, hot, dusty summer was at an end and already several short sharp storms had reminded the party that they must soon head for home or face an increasingly uncomfortable life in the open. Mud was becoming an unpleasant fact of life in the camp. Jesus decided to finish his mission in Judaea straight away and seek shelter for the winter. The disciples were tired after all their exertions throughout the summer and glad to be going home. Judas thought that this winter he would make for Gaza to look up his contacts there. The rest, of course, wanted to be on their way to Galilee, and this year Jesus thought he would go there also, though he knew he could have stayed at several places in the Jerusalem district.

He held a final meeting with the group after supper.

'Next season, we must take our ministry to Jerusalem itself,' he announced. 'The whole history of our religion and culture has been centred on Zion, ever since the great King David took the city and made it his capital a thousand years ago.[4] I must go there to teach and proclaim the coming of the Kingdom of heaven. There I hope to be recognised generally as the Messiah. I believe that God will bring about something really special in Jerusalem, enabling those who have the spiritual sensitivity to accept me and follow the way I recommend. We must serve there and be prepared for anything that God sets before us.'

Silence greeted this statement. The disciples were hoping that Jesus was indicating that he thought that this time, at last, God's Kingdom would be established in all its glory, but they had tackled him so often on the topic without receiving a definite answer that they held their peace on this occasion.

Eventually Peter broke the silence. 'When do you want us all to meet and where?' he asked. 'Judas is going south for the winter and needs to know...'

'We need to be in Jerusalem in good time for the Passover next spring,' replied his leader. 'We'll meet Judas in Bethany about a week before Passover – is that all right, Judas? The rest of us can meet up in Capernaum ten days before that to walk south together.'

★

They took the usual route, east to Jericho and then north up the Jordan Valley. Jesus called a halt at Jericho, as he wanted very much to spend a few hours with John barHelez and inform him of all that had happened to their friend Lazarus. He left the disciples to make camp and fend for themselves regarding supper, and made his way to his friend's house, to be greeted warmly by the old servant.

'Come in, sir,' effused that worthy. 'I'll call the master directly. He'll be so pleased to see you.'

Jesus was shown into the large opulent living room and offered a comfortable chair, for it was becoming too cold to sit comfortably outside once the sun was nearing the horizon. It was not long before the priest appeared, beaming all over his face.

'It's so good to see you, my friend,' he began. 'You look well.'

It was true. A long summer living and working continuously in the open air had left Jesus's face as brown as a berry.

'But you look tired.' On closer inspection, John could see the dark shadows under his friend's eyes and the worry lines on the brow. A few hairs were showing grey at his temple.

The two friends laughed and relaxed together for a few minutes before the priest suggested that he stop for supper and overnight, if he wished. Jesus was pleased to agree, knowing that he would be treated royally. John despatched a servant to the camp to inform the others and the two friends settled down to enjoy their evening together. Jesus was able to bathe, change into fresh clothing and enjoy the best well-cooked and well-presented meal he had eaten in a long time.

'I'm just sorry I couldn't extend the hospitality to all your people,' said John, 'but there's too many even for my kitchen at short notice. In any case, I'm selfish enough to want you to myself!'

'That's just what I need myself,' replied Jesus.

After supper, they moved back to the living room, nursing goblets of wine. Each enquired about the other's work, and Jesus was able to update John on the topic of Lazarus. He told his friend all that had happened and asked him if he was aware of the activities of the Essene group in the desert.

'Well, of course we weren't aware of all the detail you have now given me, which seems extremely bizarre, but we did know that they were rather weird in their views and practices. We leave them alone as a matter of policy. Sometimes, the more you try to stamp things out, the worse they become.'

Jesus nodded, understanding the logic. John, however, leaned forward in his chair and continued speaking in a more serious tone.

'Actually, this business with Lazarus had already come to the attention of the Temple authorities. It was reported, as you must have expected it would be, that you actually raised him from the dead!'

'The High Priest already knows about Lazarus?' Jesus sounded surprised.

'Oh, we keep our ears to the ground!' John permitted himself a slight smile. Then, reverting to his more usual serious demeanour, he went on, 'But, as I say, it was reported that you actually revived someone who had been dead for four days! You surely didn't think to keep that quiet, did you? That sort of news flies around at great speed and is quickly picked up by our agents and reported back to base. Of course, things sometimes get exaggerated in the process, or, as in this case, misrepresented – quite unwittingly. How were our agents to know about these Essenes and their ways?'

Jesus shook his head and pulled at his beard.

'I suppose the mistake was natural enough.'

John continued. 'The thing that concerns the Temple authorities is the possible reaction within the population. There will be some – perhaps many – who will believe that this "miracle" is some sort of sign from heaven. They fear that you will now be surrounded by fanatics expecting you to do other similar stunts. You know what that can lead to! You saw it in Galilee. In these times, any miracle worker is linked, automatically it seems, with the notion of Messianism – and that, in its turn, is linked by many to revolution and freedom from Rome…'

John left the sentence unfinished, his eyebrows arched into his forehead. There was a pause and then he continued.

'You see what a wasps' nest you have stirred up, unwittingly. Frankly, you have the High Priest worried, and when the boss is worried, he is greatly to be feared. I am very relieved that you are already going north out of Judaea. If you weren't, I'd be advising you to go immediately!'

Jesus sat very still, his head in his hands. 'How easy it is upset people who are frightened for their position in life,' he murmured.

'It isn't just Caiaphas's personal position,' said John gently. 'If a revolution started, the whole community – perhaps the whole nation – would be involved. In the extreme case, the nation could be destroyed. Rome could move in and annihilate all that we have and are. That's what the High Priest is fearful of. He went so far as to say in Council, "It would be better that one man should die, rather than the whole nation perish."[5] He's that worried.'

'Are you on the Council now, then?' Jesus asked.

John grinned and snorted. 'Oh, no! It'll be years before I attain that seniority, but I am needed to attend as an advisor to the High Priest, and I sometimes take the minutes. I may not speak or vote.'

Jesus sat thoughtfully for a moment, then asked, 'Do you know a councillor named Nicodemus?'

'Of course. He's quite influential and has a few friends on the Council who think along similar lines. He's friendly with the Prince of Arimathea, for one – they often vote together.'

'The Prince of Arimathea is also on the Council, is he?' Jesus shook his head wonderingly. 'No wonder he couldn't follow me!'

'What was that?' John looked perplexed. Jesus told him about the Prince's visit to the camp and the outcome. 'I'm afraid I offended him that day,' he finished.

There was a pause, and then the preacher spoke again.

'What did Nicodemus make of the stories about Lazarus?' he asked.

John grimaced and threw up his hands in uncertainty.

'He seemed to feel that it must be a sign from God, and that you must therefore be respected, rather than feared. I believe that Prince Joseph supported him, but I could be wrong; many councillors spoke that afternoon. Do you know Lord Nicodemus as well?'

Jesus told him of the councillor's visit late one night.

'That figures,' murmured John. 'He wouldn't want to be seen hobnobbing with the likes of you! Even before the Lazarus incident, you weren't exactly persona grata with the Temple authorities, as you know!'

There was a long silence. Jesus sat with bowed head, his mouth working. Eventually, he looked up at his friend.

'Thank you for telling me all this, John,' he said. 'I realise what I'm up against. Nevertheless, I must bring my mission to Jerusalem and preach the Kingdom there. I believe the people will welcome me – I shall just have to consider how to deal with the possible reaction from Caiaphas and his party…'

'I have warned you, Jesus, because I care greatly for you. Do be careful. When do you intend to preach in Jerusalem?'

'We shall be back in time for next Passover. That is when I shall come to Jerusalem. I want it to be a triumph for God – I shall cleanse the Temple and introduce the Kingdom to all who will listen…'

★

The long walk home seemed longer than ever this time. The weather didn't help – several times they were caught in quite severe storms, the rain lashing down, accompanied by brilliant lightning and rolling thunder. It was no weather to be sleeping out, but there was no money to spare for taverns. Eventually they reached Magdala late in the morning, with only a few miles to go to Capernaum, where they would disperse. There, Jesus called at Nimrah's house, where he knew he could be sure of a welcome. He took Andrew and Peter with him, for form's sake. They were not disappointed. The lady of the house let them in with ecstatic cries of welcome, insisting that they take their time to wash, cleanse the mud from their feet and then come and be fed.

Mary joined them for the meal, of course. She radiated joy at seeing Jesus, her smile as wide as the river Jordan. It was amazing the way in which she had changed since she had known him. With very few exceptions, she cooperated well with her mother nowadays, helping her around the house and joining in her activities. Gone were the displays of rebellion, the sullen silences, the urge to leave home and go out on the town. Both she and Nimrah were keen for Jesus to stay a little while and rest.

'You've had a long, hard summer in the field,' said the older woman. 'You need someone to look after you and pamper you a bit!'

'I know you mean well, and I'm grateful,' replied Jesus kindly, 'but my friends have got their homes to go to – some of them have wives who haven't seen them in months. We have to press on for their sake.'

'I'll have a big supper for them all tonight,' said Nimrah. 'I'm sure we can sleep them all somewhere.'

She saw that Jesus was going to insist on moving on.

'Please! Spend just a few hours with us,' she whispered. Nimrah, like her daughter, could be very charming when she put herself to it. Jesus smiled and said he would ask the others. After a little discussion, they all agreed that a splendid supper and the opportunity for a good bath was too good to miss. In those circumstances, one more night away from home could be endured.

Nimrah was supervising the preparation of the meal when a knock came at her door. The servant went to see who was there and returned to her mistress with a puzzled expression on her face.

'It's a woman, for you, ma'am,' she said. 'She's well dressed and has two servants with her – she looks rather important. I've never seen her before. She can't be from round here.'

'Show her in.'

Nimrah stood as her visitor entered the room.

'I'm so sorry to intrude upon you,' the latter began. 'I see that you are very busy. I wonder if you can tell me where I can contact Jesus, the preacher from Nazareth. I know he's in this area and, when I enquired locally, I was told you might have seen him.'

Nimrah was amazed. 'He only arrived in Magdala earlier today,' she said. 'Your information is remarkably up to date!'

'We have a good system,' replied her guest, smiling. 'Can you tell me where to find him?'

'Well, he's coming here for dinner in about an hour,' replied Nimrah. 'You could wait here and see him, if you wish.'

So it was arranged. Joanna (for it was she) introduced herself and told Nimrah of her meeting with Jesus earlier in the year and her interest in his work.

'We – that's Lydia, Susanna and myself – follow his progress everywhere. My husband is Herod Antipas's steward. It's easy for him to find out all the news when he's in Galilee. You know, of course, that the King keeps spies all over his realm to inform him of potential troublemakers; I'm afraid they see Jesus as just that.'

'I know. I have warned him to be careful.'

Nimrah paused before continuing, evidently puzzled. 'But Jesus has been in Judaea most of the summer,' she said. 'How do you know what happens to him there?'

'Well, we haven't heard so much, of course,' replied her guest, 'but Herod has a few agents in Judaea also, and, of course, as soon as anyone of interest crosses the border back into Peraea or Galilee then the information flows again. It must cost the King a fortune to keep so many people employed in this work, but he does it. That's another reason why the taxes are so high, I suppose.'

The two women gossiped on until Jesus and his party arrived. He seemed very pleased to see Joanna again, and immediately sat down with her to find out what brought her to Magdala.

'My husband is away from home at present, so I thought I should take this opportunity to come to find out how things have been going in Judaea,' replied Joanna.

'So you know we've been in the south?'

'Of course! We get to know most things, in the King's service!'

Jesus briefly recounted their experiences across the summer. He finished by saying that he intended taking the mission to Jerusalem in time for next year's Passover.

'You'll really go to Jerusalem this time?' asked Joanna, her eyes kindling. 'You realise the risk?'

'Yes. I know, but I must go. I must preach the Kingdom there and seek to establish it in the centre of our nation. I believe that at last I shall break through in some way.'

'Then we must come with you,' said Joanna, with great emphasis.

'Oh no,' replied Jesus, smiling. 'You can't be serious. I can't have women in our midst – it would be unthinkable. Whatever would people think? And what would your husband say?'

Joanna giggled briefly.

'Of course we won't travel or camp with you,' she said. 'That wouldn't do your reputation any good – or mine, for that matter. No. My friends and I will go to Jerusalem for the Passover, like good Jewish women – even though the Law does not require it. My husband won't mind. He can't leave his office, so I will persuade him that I am going on his behalf!'

'You've got it all worked out!' said Jesus. 'Well, under those conditions, of course I shall be glad to have you near us.'

He mentioned Justus's inn and said that he could be contacted through the landlord, if they wished to see him. Then he continued.

'If you are really coming to Jerusalem, I wonder if you'd do something for me?' he asked.

'Of course.'

Jesus spoke with great emphasis. 'Invite Nimrah and Mary to come with you. They have really supported me ever since I first met up with them and I know it would give them a thrill to see the Holy City.'

And so it was arranged.

NOTES

[1] Mark 10:35–37.
[2] Mark 9:35.
[3] John 11:3.
[4] II Samuel 5:7.
[5] John 11:50.

Judas, John and Jericho

Judas had looked forward to his visit to Gaza. It wasn't that he particularly cared about his aunt and uncle. After all, though they had brought him up and educated him, they had shown him little affection, but had merely done what they perceived to be their duty. He would go and see them, of course, but he too would do so merely as a duty. What he really hoped to do, though, was to renew his acquaintance with his friend Jacob, the lad who had befriended him but they had so often been kept apart by antagonism between the adult relations.

After making a few enquiries, Judas learnt that Jacob had recently moved away from Gaza and had been seen heading south towards Beersheba. A neighbour told him that there had been some sort of family quarrel and the younger man had left home in a huff. Judas was, of course, exceedingly short on funds and could not afford to go any further immediately, so he sought work in Gaza, hoping that with increased funding he might be able to look Jacob up later.

He was lucky. He came across a young man named Malluch, who had newly inherited a business trading in pottery from his father, who had died suddenly a couple of weeks earlier. Malluch had been almost entirely excluded from the business side of the enterprise during his father's lifetime, being used merely as slave labour. He had no brothers, only two younger sisters who were, of course, even more ignorant than he was of business matters. Now, suddenly, he had to deal with all the commercial aspects, with only the most sketchy knowledge and no experience. He was therefore pleased to engage Judas, an accountant who could give him a few weeks' guidance and assistance, leaving him better equipped to deal with everything by the spring.

Judas set to work with a will. This was just his scene, taking hold of an enterprise and helping to realise its potential. As he examined the books and the stock and interviewed the suppliers, it occasionally crossed his mind that he might be better employed returning to commercial life, rather than engaging in the life of an itinerant preacher, but the thought didn't persist. He knew, deep down, that the life he had spent with Jesus had a special quality about it, hard and uncertain though it was. He knew that he was committed to the Galilean and he had to see that life through to its conclusion.

Three months passed by quickly and happily. Malluch showed signs of understanding something of what the business was all about and began to acquire some self-confidence, so that Judas felt that he could begin to detach himself. With a little reluctance, Malluch agreed and Judas decided to follow up on his first objective: to find Jacob and renew their old acquaintance. Early one morning late in February, he set out for Beersheba. Before him stretched a journey of over twenty miles.

He arrived late in the afternoon and was amused to find an inn called the Candid Camel, where he found a bed space available. Next day, he started on the difficult task of finding a friend whom he had not seen for nearly fifteen years, in a town he had only visited once before in his life. He began to realise the enormity of what he had taken on – it was like looking for the proverbial needle in a haystack. However, Judas was not the sort to be easily discouraged. He regarded it as something of a challenge, something to occupy his mind while he took a few days off from work. Judas remembered that Jacob's father had been in the fruit trade, and he guessed that his son would probably follow his father's occupation, so he went to the marketplace to talk to the traders there to see if they knew of a young man recently arrived from Gaza.

Some of the older men in the market looked suspiciously at him as he asked his questions – even this far south, there were official spies employed by both the Roman and the Judaean authorities – so most of the traders were extremely guarded in their replies, claiming to know nothing. However, he eventually found a woman selling pots who vaguely remembered a stranger of about thirty years of age who had recently arrived from 'somewhere up north', looking for a job in the fruit trade. She recalled thinking how good-looking he was. She had only seen him once (which she regretted) but she had told him of a fruiterer just outside town, which might be the place he was looking for. Judas took details of the business and found it after another hour's search. He told his story yet again to the wizened old man who seemed to be in charge there.

'Jacob?' he queried, grimacing and pulling at a thin grey beard. Then, turning to an equally wizened old hag, presumably his wife, he asked, 'What was the name of that young feller who came here looking for work a while back?'

'I believe it was Jacob,' said she, 'but we had no work for him.'

'Where did he go from here? Did he say?'

The old couple cogitated for several minutes on the matter, but the upshot was that Judas was no further forward. He wandered out into the yard and was just about to leave for town again when a dark-skinned man of about twenty shuffled over to him and muttered, 'Are you looking for a Jacob, who was here a few weeks back?'

'I most certainly am,' replied Judas, wondering why the man hadn't come forward earlier, while he was in the office. Presumably he had overheard the conversation with the elderly couple.

'I might be able to help,' growled the man. 'Meet me here at sundown, when I leave work, and we'll see.'

Judas didn't know quite what to make of all this. He couldn't see why the fellow couldn't give him the information straight away; but, not having anything else to do, he agreed to the man's suggestion. He made his way back to town for a couple of hours, where at least he could sit in the shade and find a drink, before trudging back to the fruiterers, hoping that he wasn't wasting his time. At sunset the man emerged from the office and the two walked slowly back towards the town. The man began by asking Judas who he was, and why he wanted to see this 'Jacob'. Having nothing to hide, Judas told him the truth, wondering why the man was being so mysterious about the whereabouts of his friend, if, indeed, he knew him at all. There was something strange about his whole demeanour.

Eventually, the man, who still hadn't introduced himself, seemed satisfied with Judas's answers and said, 'I'll take a message to the young man who I think maybe is your friend. Perhaps he'll want to see you – perhaps he won't.'

'Just tell him that I'm down in this district for two or three days at the most and I'd like to renew an old acquaintance. If he's interested, I'll wait in at the Candid Camel all tomorrow, and hope to see him.'

The man nodded and slunk away without a further word. Judas watched him go, wondering what on earth made people quite so sullen and difficult. Perhaps he has a bad conscience, he thought.

Nobody came to the inn all through the next day, much to Judas's frustration. He whiled away the time reflecting on all that had happened to him over the past two years, ever since he had met with the prophet from Galilee. Was Jesus really the Messiah? If so, and Judas thought he probably was, why didn't things happen more quickly? What had they really accomplished by all their wanderings so far? Had it really been worth it? Certainly Jesus had a great message to offer, and of course his work for the poor and sick had been wonderful, but what did it really amount to – in historical terms – in the life of the nation as a whole? Judas had big ideas and dreamed of establishing God's Kingdom for all to see. It would have to be in Jerusalem – Jesus was right about that. For Judas, Jerusalem should be the centre of the whole world, and God should rule from the cleansed and purified Temple there for evermore. Was that what Jesus intended to achieve next Passover? The boss still seemed to be unsure about his plans. Why did he not trust God to strengthen his arm and help him to bring in the Kingdom? It was all so puzzling.

Judas started to think about the other followers of Jesus, the disciples he had spent the last two years with. They were splendid fellows, of course, and Judas liked them all. He'd actually become quite fond of young Thaddeus, with whom he had been partnered by Jesus, but, when you came right down to it, they weren't really up to the job – only Nathaniel and Matthew were at all educated. The others seemed not to have a brain between them. They quarrelled from time to time about who would do what in the Kingdom, when it came; he thought of the row that had occurred when James and John had asked for favoured positions, and Jesus's reaction.

Peter seemed to be the one whom Jesus favoured, but that was probably only because Peter's temperament took him naturally to the front of any discussion or argument. Jesus seemed rather fond of young John the fisherman too, but that was probably only because he was the youngest and inclined to be a bit of a dreamer. Perhaps Jesus liked that. No, the more he thought about it, it was he, Judas, that Jesus would have to rely on for any real initiative from the group. He felt certain that Jesus would increasingly look to him for guidance and support. So what should he suggest when they reached Jerusalem? In his mind's eye, he saw Jesus standing up in the Temple at Passover and proclaiming himself to everybody as the Messiah. Then the great crowd of pilgrims from all over the known world would rally to him and acclaim him – then, perhaps God would break through with an army of angels and vindicate his Messiah, his favoured son. This would signal the end of the present order and the advent of the new Kingdom. If only Jesus would act decisively…

Judas had almost given up hope of seeing anyone that day, when, just after supper, a man of about Judas's age arrived at the inn and asked for him. The two men looked at one another for just two seconds, then they knew. People don't change, and in a trice the fifteen years of separation slipped away and they were lads again. They hugged each other for a long moment and called for wine while they caught up with all their news.

'What kept you?' asked Judas. 'I've been hanging around for hours waiting to see you.'

'I'm sorry, Judas,' replied the other. 'I couldn't get away.'

Jacob didn't seem to want to be more explicit. Instead he quizzed Judas on all that had happened to him since they had been parted, expressing great surprise at his decision to leave the well-paid and secure job in the Temple for the life of a wandering preacher.

'I thought you had too much commercial sense to do that, my friend,' he chided, but with a grin. 'I thought you liked the good life.'

'I like success, yes,' replied his friend more soberly, 'but there was no satisfaction in swindling people who were poor anyway. I must admit that I don't particularly enjoy the long road and the outdoor life, but I do believe that with Jesus we are heading towards a better world.'

'But when will this new and better life dawn?' asked Jacob. He looked sceptical.

'I don't know, but it *will* come, we're sure. Jesus lays some stress on the fact that, for him, the better life has already started – it's a life of love for God and caring for one another. It's a life of integrity and trust.'

'But you don't share that view?'

Judas paused before replying, pulling at his beard.

'There's something in the idea, of course, but I put more faith in what is to come, when Jesus declares himself and is accepted as the Messiah. Then we shall see the real Kingdom dawn.'

Jacob thought for a moment.

'And when will that be? Will Jesus make a move shortly?'

'I believe that Jesus will act next Passover,' replied his friend. 'The more I think about it, the more this seems right. We covered Galilee with our preaching mission during our first season and early in the second. We toured Judaea this last summer. Jesus is planning to go to Passover next April, and then we shall see…'

'What will we see?'

Judas had to admit that he didn't know, precisely. 'He never lets us know in advance what his plans are,' he had to admit. 'I think perhaps he was waiting for this winter to finalise in his own mind what he should do – and how.'

Jacob paused again before continuing, then he said, slowly, 'Perhaps – it's just possible – our paths are crossing in a more significant way than we imagined,' he said. 'Let me tell you what I've got myself involved in.'

Jacob briefly sketched out his life since they last lived in the same street. He had completed his education and been set to work in his father's business. His father's employees would arrange for quantities of olives, mulberries, apricots, figs, grapes, pomegranates and plums to be purchased from growers all over the south of Judaea and shipped into Jerusalem and other towns for sale. They had contacts all over the southern area of Judaea. Jacob had been started at the bottom of the ladder. His first task was in the warehousing side of the business, a hard and sweaty existence moving fruit all day from wagons to the warehouse and back again, which he recalled with no pleasure. Later, he was sent round the countryside dealing with the suppliers. He had enjoyed the travel for a while, but that too palled after a time, especially in the summer months. He was then sent, as the owner's son, to be familiarised with the office systems and learn the commercial side of the business. This was more congenial, so for some time the years had passed agreeably enough, but as Jacob approached his thirtieth birthday his father still showed no sign of taking him fully into his confidence and making him a partner in the business.

'I just felt used – that I was getting nowhere,' grumbled Jacob. 'Oh, life was secure, but deadly dull and repetitive. Finally, Father and I had a hell of a row, which finished with me walking out. I had saved some money – enough to see me through for some time, if necessary – so I could be independent. I just wanted out.'

'When was this?' enquired Judas.

'About six weeks ago. I decided to come here to Beersheba. I'd been here on business a few times years ago. I thought that father wouldn't dream I'd go south. Most of anywhere is to the north of Gaza, as you know. So I came here and looked up my old contacts, but without any success. Then I happened on the old couple you met yesterday and they said they might be able to help me.'

'And did they?'

Jacob grimaced as he considered how best to reply.

'They've certainly found me an occupation,' he said, finally. 'They introduced me to the young man you met there, when you were enquiring for me. He asked me what my hopes and ambitions were, and when I said I wanted a life with a bit more point to it and I wasn't afraid of taking a few chances, he started to draw me out on my political leanings.'

'Which are?' Judas prompted him as he paused.

'Well – it seems to me that we need more freedom for action, both as individuals and as a nation. As he and I talked it all through, we concluded that there was no hope for the nation unless we could get out of the Roman occupation and regain our independence. He was very clever. He got me fired up with his talk of glorious days to come, and, before I fully realised it, I had taken the plunge and committed myself to join the local band of the Zion Nationalists.'

'And what does that entail, exactly?'

'Basically, I am employed by the old couple ostensibly as a fruiterer – I have to visit fruit growers and purchase fruit, as I used to do for my father – but, this time, hidden in the fruit loads are weapons which are being stockpiled against the day when Judaea will rise to throw the Romans back into the sea. In addition, I have to keep my eyes open for any young man likely to want to join our enterprise, and report back to Samuel.'

'He's the fellow who found you for me?'

'That's right.'

'He's a surly-looking fellow – is he a friend of yours now?'

'He's all right when you get to know him. I wouldn't call him a friend; he's our local officer for the movement. He'll be the one who notifies us when the call to arms is issued.'

'And when will that be?'

'I don't know,' replied his friend. 'That's a secret – and one doesn't ask too many questions in a movement like ours; but I have a feeling that the moment is coming soon.'

Jacob leaned forward and his eyes burned brightly as he looked Judas full in the face. 'Might it not be that your plans with Jesus and our plans as a movement will overlap? Perhaps your coming Kingdom and our promised freedom will be one and the same revolution!'

Judas nodded slowly.

'Perhaps God has ordained that we should meet tonight,' he said. 'Perhaps it'll all happen at the Passover this coming spring – only a few weeks away. Is it possible?'

The two men felt their pulses beginning to race. Jacob muttered under his breath and appeared to reach a decision.

'I'll talk to Samuel,' he said. 'I'll see if he feels there's a synergy here. When are you due to see your leader again?'

'Not until he comes to Jerusalem for the Passover,' replied Judas, 'but I could go to meet him – he'll use the usual route, I'm sure, and I can meet him part-way – say, in Jericho – and apprise him of the situation. Have you no idea of your people's plans?'

'None. I'm very new in the movement and, in any case, everything is very secretive. I may be in trouble for telling you as much as I have – but I don't know much anyway. I believe they may planning to organise a riot quite soon somewhere, presumably in Jerusalem, to stir the people up and get them thinking. Then I suppose that the leadership will call the entire nation to arms…'

Judas pulled a face.

'Fighting is not something that my leader has ever wanted to be involved with. He's all for peace and loving kindness. I've tried to tell Jesus that force is, in the end, inevitable, but he won't listen. We had an approach – in fact we've had more than one – from the Galilean Zealots and he didn't want anything to do with them…'

It was Jacob's turn to pull a face and snort.

'I'm not surprised,' he said. 'That lot are just a bunch of amateurs. They couldn't organise a party in a tavern. Oh, they're brave enough – we know that – but they're just local thugs, really. Our movement has links all over the Empire – we are part of the international assassins, the Sicarii. You know what that means – everyone does – our people are feared all over the Mediterranean. Jesus must know of us and know that we're worth cooperating with.'

Judas thought for a moment, before replying.

'Mention the possibility of a link to your leaders and see what they think,' he said finally. 'If they want me to, I'll give a message to Jesus before he reaches Jerusalem for Passover. Then we can see what transpires.'

Thus it was that, when Judas left Beersheba a day later, he carried an invitation to Jesus to meet a representative of the nationalist movement in Jericho about a week before the Passover. They were to meet at the Parrot, one of the largest inns in town, to see if there was a basis for cooperation.

★

Winter finally gave way to spring in Galilee. The almonds had blossomed and the swallows had returned. The sun gradually increased its power and the rainstorms lessened. The hillsides blossomed with wild flowers, carpeting the ground with yellow, white, red, purple, blue and many other shades. The wayside verges were green with lush growth, as the soil enjoyed the input of rain and the increasing warmth. Jesus and his followers had fully recovered from the hardships of the previous season and were preparing their minds for what was to come. The preacher had spent most of his time in Capernaum, relaxing with Peter and Ruth, but he had several times walked over to Bethsaida to spend time with Nathaniel, reading the scriptures at his Synagogue and discussing with him the significance of what he had read. More and more, he studied the prophesies to learn what the Messiah should fulfil, turning over in his mind what was best to be done in the light of the political realities of his situation.

Three weeks before Passover, all the Galilean disciples had assembled at Peter's house as arranged, ready for the journey south. The weather was still somewhat unreliable, with the occasional storm. Once or twice, the party opted to stay overnight at an inn, even though this used up precious funds, carefully saved over the winter period. The accommodation was fairly basic, but better than sleeping under a sodden hedge. Each day, they trudged along in company with the other pilgrims streaming south for the Feast. Many more would be on their way later, closer to the time of the festival, but, nevertheless, it was a goodly crowd, growing progressively more excited as they neared the holy city.

Most of the crowd remembered Jesus and the work he had done in Galilee over the past two years and they sought to engage him in conversation. He seemed pleased enough to talk to them as individuals, but made no attempt to speak more formally during the long journey by the river, which pleased the disciples. They were just glad that he was conserving his energy, pending their arrival in Jerusalem. Although they had no clear idea of what was to happen, they felt sure of the great events that were to unfold there.

As they reached the outskirts of Jericho, weary after the long slog south, and started to make their way towards the centre to find an inn for the night, they found that news of Jesus's arrival had been spread by the pilgrims who had preceded them on the road. Several locals turned out to speak to him and enquire about his intentions. Of course, the more people turned out, the greater became the interest of others, determined not to miss out on a bit of excitement, and before long quite a crowd were thronging about the Galileans. They were making their way slowly towards the centre of the town when Jesus suddenly stopped and looked up into a fig tree. There, the disciples could see a man, hanging grimly on to a branch, evidently trying to catch a glimpse of the notable stranger visiting his town.

To the disciples' amazement, Jesus called up to the man, 'Hallo, there. Did you want to see me?'

The man was initially taken aback by this greeting, but soon overcame his timidity and called back, 'Yes. I had heard about you, Jesus, and I wanted so much to meet you.'

Jesus smiled, that winning smile of his. 'Well, come on down, then, and we can get better acquainted. We can't talk properly like this!'

The man quickly shinned down the tree and the crowd parted for him to come and take Jesus's outstretched hand. The disciples saw that the newcomer was a small man, dressed in quite rich-looking clothes, though now rather torn and dirty. He had rings on his fingers and was evidently a man of some substance.

'I'm honoured that you should have gone to all that trouble just to see me,' said the preacher. 'It can't have been easy for you to get up there!'

'No, it wasn't,' replied the man, rather ruefully trying to pull his robe straight and regain some dignity. 'I'm afraid I look a bit of a sight now, but it is so good to meet you. I've heard so much about you. My name is Zacchaeus, by the way.'[1]

'It's good to meet you, Zacchaeus.'

Zacchaeus seemed delighted to make the carpenter's acquaintance. He quickly went on, 'You've come a long way – all the way from Galilee. I'm sure you must be hungry and tired. Can I invite you and your party to dine with me and stay with me tonight? I should be so honoured…'

Jesus looked round at his little party, weary after their journey. He saw their eyes light up at the prospect of a good meal, but he also noticed the faces of some of the locals. He could see some scowling, some puzzled, many disapproving. Nevertheless, he quickly turned back to Zacchaeus and accepted his kind invitation, which was greeted with a broad smile by the little man. He indicated the way to his house, which turned out to be quite a palatial affair, nearly on a par with John barHelez's house across the town. There, the travellers were shown into a marble-floored bathroom, where servants washed their dusty feet and they were offered facilities for changing their apparel. While the meal was being prepared, they were given seats on a wide veranda overlooking a beautiful garden at the back of the house, and servants brought fruit juice and wine for them to drink.

After they were settled, Zacchaeus joined them on the veranda and enquired whether everything was to their satisfaction. It transpired that he had first heard of Jesus the previous summer, when he had moved about in northern Judaea, preaching. Although Zacchaeus wasn't religious, even he had become aware that something important had been going on. There had been much speculation concerning the Galilean and his mission. Those who had great hopes that the Messiah would soon arrive were even discussing the possibility that this Galilean actually might be 'the one who should come'.

Jesus outlined the main elements of his teaching. He emphasised the fatherhood of God and his eternal love which reached out to all, and the need of all men to respond to it – in fact, to experience a complete change in both thinking and living. Zacchaeus listened carefully, saying rather little but asking the occasional question.

When Jesus finished his summary, Zacchaeus said, quietly, 'You can't know much about me, of course. I am the local senior collector of taxes for Jericho.'

When Jesus did not respond, Zacchaeus continued, 'I suppose it's just as well you didn't know that before you came to my house. Perhaps you wouldn't have come otherwise. As you must know, we tax collectors aren't very well liked – to put it mildly. In fact, we're shunned by all God-fearing men, ignored at best and spat upon by some.'

'Of course I know that, Zacchaeus,' replied Jesus quietly, 'but I've befriended quite a few tax officials in the past two years or so – and many other people who find themselves marginalised by society. In fact, one of my own followers – Matthew, sitting over there – was in the tax business. There is no need to fear; all can find a welcome in the Kingdom, no matter what they have been.'

Jesus went over to where Matthew was sitting chatting to Thomas at the far end of the table.

'I'd like you to come over here a moment and chat to Zacchaeus,' he said.

Matthew did so and Jesus left them conversing together while he moved away to engage Zacchaeus's wife in conversation, commending her beautiful house and garden. It wasn't long before Zacchaeus called Jesus back to him and told him how much he had valued his chat with the disciple.

'I've made a decision that I'd like you to know about,' he said.

'I've decided I must give half my wealth away to poorer people. I've got plenty – why do I need so much when others have so little? And I realise that some of it I was acquired illegally – it's the way things are in the tax business – so I promise to restore anything I've taken illegally. In fact, I'll do more than just restore it, I'll repay it fourfold.'

'You won't regret it,' responded Jesus warmly. 'Of course it will be a sacrifice, and there will be consequences, as there were for Matthew, but the bottom line is that you will have peace of mind and you will draw close to God's Kingdom.'

'I'm so glad that you came here today,' said Zacchaeus, smiling. 'I feel as if I have been reborn – given a new life.'

'In a way, you have been. As I have said, there will be difficulties. Matthew may have told you that his wife bitterly resents what he has done – the loss of her standard of living and her social standing with some in the town.'

Zacchaeus nodded, slowly. He said, 'But on the other hand, surely most people will now recognise and respond to her; whereas, as the wife of a tax gatherer, she has been shunned and hated like me.'

'Unfortunately, people have long memories and many cannot find it in their hearts to forgive,' replied Jesus. 'But you will come through and find a way to become accepted again, I'm sure of it.'

His kind eyes looked into Zacchaeus's face as he once again took his hand in a warm handshake.

'God bless you,' he said.

Just then, they were called to supper and were enjoying an excellent meal when a servant came in and spoke in a low voice to Zacchaeus. After the man had left the room, Zacchaeus muttered to Jesus, 'There's been some trouble near Jerusalem, I hear.'

'Oh? What's happened?'

'Apparently, there's been quite a battle west of the city – well, a sizeable skirmish, anyway. A Nationalist group ambushed a wagon train of goods bound for the capital and made off with most of the goods. Several guards were killed, I gather, and others badly wounded. The rebels got off almost scot-free, having had the advantage of surprise – they lost just two men killed and three taken prisoner.'

'The authorities won't like that!' replied Jesus. 'They're nervous enough anyway, but coming just before Passover time…'

He paused to allow the thought to sink in, before continuing.

'We all know that the Romans always bring in extra troops from Caesarea for the Feast. They'll be even more nervous now, if the nationalists are looking for a fight.'

'This won't help you, will it?' asked Zacchaeus.

'We could have done without it, that's certain,' replied Jesus. 'This must heighten the tension which always surrounds Passover – but perhaps the worst effects will have died away by next week.'

*

On the other side of Jericho, John barHelez had also heard about the battle between the Zionists and the soldiers guarding the wagon train. It was one more issue which played on his already tortured mind. Ever since his conversation with Jesus the previous autumn, he had been increasingly uncomfortable about the way he was conducting his life. The more he thought about all that Jesus stood for and, in contrast, his own position within the Temple hierarchy, the more dissatisfied he became. However much he instinctively craved the comfortable, safe life of a priest on the Temple staff, he increasingly felt that he wasn't fulfilling his life properly – he had no real contact with God and certainly no real feeling that God was his father.

Reluctantly, he had to concede that Jesus was probably right that priests shouldn't be so privileged, relative to poorer people. He had, too, to accept that Jesus was correct in his criticism of the swindling in the Temple courtyard – the exorbitant prices of animals for sacrifice, and the high rates of exchange for the coinage. He also recognised that it was scandalous that sick and handicapped people were expelled from the Temple, regarded as less than people and beyond God's love. Above all, he knew in his heart of hearts that the High Priest was far too cosy with the Roman authorities, though he understood the reasoning he gave for it. Now there was this Nationalist threat looming again and close to the capital. There was bound to be a reaction on the part of the authorities, both Jewish and Roman, which would polarise the situation further.

John knew that the time had come when he would have to make up his mind which side to support. He dearly loved and respected Jesus. He'd known him for several years now and greatly valued his deep insight into all the religious and political problems of the day. Jesus just seemed to know where to place the emphasis, no matter how complex the moral situation. John's mind increasingly turned to how best to support his friend and whether he ought, after all, to give up his rich home altogether and follow the itinerant preacher. He had almost decided to do just that when he heard that Jesus was in town again. He was, therefore, delighted when he heard from his old servant that Jesus was actually at his door. The Galilean had walked over from Zacchaeus's house in the hope of catching him at home and hadn't been disappointed. The two friends embraced warmly. It was difficult to know which was more pleased to see the other.

'Come in and sit down, my friend,' said John. He led the way to the large well-appointed living room at the back of the house and waved his guest to a chair.

'It's so good to see you,' said John. 'I've so much to tell you – and ask you.

How much time have you got?'

'I shall be here for a day or two, then I'll move on to Bethany to see the family there,' replied his visitor.

'Right. Come to dinner with me this evening. I so want to talk to you and to have a good discussion, without interruption.'

'You mean – just the two of us?' asked Jesus, smiling.

John looked awkward. ' Please. It's not that I don't want to see your friends – please understand that – but there are things I must share with you alone. Do you mind? This once…'

Jesus shook his head. 'Not at all. I have things I must share with you too – things I haven't discussed with the Galileans yet.'

'Then you'll come to supper tonight?' John was eager.

'It'll be a pleasure. I'll join you at sundown, shall I?'

'Excellent.'

But before they could continue their conversation, the servant entered again and told John that a man was at the door enquiring after Jesus. John shot an interrogative look at his friend, but Jesus indicated, by a shrug of his shoulders, that he hadn't been expecting anyone.

'Ask him in, please,' directed John, and a few moments later Judas was ushered into the room. Jesus rose and took him by the hand in greeting.

'Judas – it's good to see you, but we weren't expecting you to join us until we reached Bethany.'

Judas bowed a brief greeting to John and then responded urgently to Jesus.

'I had to come to meet you, Jesus. I have important news for you.'

John sensed immediately that Judas didn't want to share the news, whatever it was, in his presence; so, having briefly greeted his visitor, he slipped away.

'Come and sit down and tell me what's worrying you,' said the preacher.

Judas complied and responded. 'I'm not worried, Jesus, but I have, by chance, come across what may be a great opportunity. I have fallen in with a group of Nationalists, who are planning to stir the people into demanding their independence from Rome. Their leadership believes that your move to establish God's Kingdom and their movement for independence could be linked, to mutual benefit. What do you think?'

Jesus sat still for a moment, staring straight ahead, his mouth working as he considered his reply.

'Who are these people?' he asked finally.

'Evidently, they are part of a bigger movement within the Empire, called the Sicarii. They are well organised and very powerful – greatly feared, apparently, even by the Roman hierarchy.'

Judas lent forward and sought an approving look in his leader's eyes, but he immediately saw that he would be disappointed.

'I've heard of these people,' said Jesus. 'They are also known as "the assassins". They are no better than the Zealots we came across in the north – in fact, they're probably worse. They're professional killers, rather than mere amateurs! They conceal weapons under their garments and then murder their victims when they are completely off their guard. It's been known to have happened several times in recent years.'

Iscariot's face fell. 'Then… you'll have nothing to do with them?'

'You know I won't. What have you committed me to?' Jesus looked determined.

'I've done nothing more than say you were coming through Jericho about now and might be prepared to meet one of the leaders from the Sicarii.'

Jesus paused before continuing, pulling at his beard.

'Where is this fellow? When am I supposed to meet him?'

Judas perked up a little, saying, 'He'll be at the Parrot in town. I'll go and look for him and set up something more definite, if you agree…'

Jesus considered again for a few seconds, then spoke slowly.

'You know that I am not going to agree to cooperate with this kind of organisation. They are revolutionaries of the worst kind – you must have known that. There is bound to be fighting and bloodshed as soon as they launch their campaign. Rome isn't going to tolerate any dissent, much less independence; nor, for that matter, are the Jewish authorities, who value their own positions under Rome too much. For all we know, the skirmish last night was the first part of these people's attempts at destabilising the political situation.'

'But, for the sake of…' Judas began, but Jesus cut him off with a gesture.

'Nevertheless, since we are apparently somewhat committed, I will speak to this man you want me to meet. I don't want to antagonise them at this stage. Let's see what they have to say for themselves…'

*

Jesus spoke in public that afternoon for the first time in some months. He stood up in the centre of Jericho, surrounded by a crowd made up partly of pilgrims passing through on their way to Jerusalem for the Feast and partly of locals. The disciples heard the familiar message once again, the call that they had heard again and again over the past two summers, first in Galilee and later Judaea. He spoke of the Kingdom of the heart, which must precede any great outpouring of God's power.

'The Kingdom can be within you, if you will only open your lives to it,' he said, but he went on to encourage them to watch for a greater demonstration of God's power soon. 'God is your Father and loves you all, whatever your condition, whatever you have done or been. He will show you just how much, if you use your eyes. Open your hearts to him, respond to him and show your response by serving others for his sake.'

Some Pharisees on the edge of the crowd started to question Jesus and try to bait him.

'Who gave you the authority to make such statements?' they asked. 'It's all very well for you to set yourself up as somebody important. How do we know you are really from God? Give us a sign from heaven, so that we can be sure!'²

'Why do you need a sign?' retorted Jesus. 'Surely the truth must speak for itself. You have to reach out to God for yourself and not be influenced by "signs" and miracles. No. There are to be no signs, which, in the end, only mislead and confuse the issue.'

The Pharisees scoffed at this and went off wagging their heads and chuckling in their beards, but most of the crowd seemed to understand what Jesus was saying, and there were many who applauded his message.

That night, while Zacchaeus kindly agreed to continue his hospitality to his followers, Jesus slipped away to join John for their quiet dinner together. After they had eaten, John unburdened his soul to his friend, confessing his own dissatisfaction with his calling and his resolve to break with the Temple entirely and join Jesus. The preacher nodded slowly, not entirely surprised at what he heard. He rose and took his friend's hand in a warm handshake. John eagerly returned his embrace.

'I knew you to be a man of God, John,' Jesus said softly. 'Your heart was always genuinely seeking. You were always open to ideas – you always listened carefully to what I had to say – as you did to others too. I am so glad that, at last, we can stand completely together in this great enterprise to which I feel called, for I have always valued and respected you. You, above everyone else, gladden my heart and uplift my spirit.'

'But I've been so long in recognising and reacting to the truth,' replied the priest, his head cast down. 'Like Lazarus, I sought the truth, but refused to accept it all this time, even when it was staring me in the face. You represent the truth – you are the truth – you have been my greatest friend, and I still went on rejecting all you stand for.'

'That's all over now,' his friend replied. 'We're united now, in this great endeavour. I feel so encouraged.'

John released Jesus's hand and moved slowly back to his chair, sitting heavily.

'Well, now that I've thrown my lot in with you, what can I do to help?' he asked.

Jesus too seated himself, smiled and paused before replying. He stared at the reluctant priest for several seconds before saying, 'Strangely enough, I'd like you to stay exactly where you are, for the present. Let me tell you what I have in mind and then perhaps you'll realise why I say that.'

John looked disheartened. Having decided to set out on a new course of action, he felt rather let down to be told to change nothing. He threw up his arms in frustration.

'Whatever do you mean?' he protested. 'There must be something I can do, specifically, to help your cause.'

Jesus leaned forward and raised a forefinger.

'There is. I'd like you to stay within the confines and confidence of the Temple office. I intend at this Passover to teach in the Temple and, in effect, challenge the authorities directly to accept me as the Messiah. This coming week, I shall enter the east gate of Jerusalem, in procession, riding on a donkey, just as Zechariah prophesied.[3] There are sufficient of my followers and sympathetic pilgrims around to ensure that I am greeted with some enthusiasm and we will see then how the town and the Temple responds. If there is no immediate welcome from the Temple, I shall publicly disgrace them by throwing down their filthy merchandise in the outer courtyard, and then I'll preach my message in the Court of the Jews. We shall see what they do after that. They may not respond favourably, of course. I know – you have often warned me – that things may turn nasty and they may seek to silence me. So, it would be very helpful if I had someone within the Temple keeping me aware of their intentions, if at all possible. I'd like you, therefore, to stay where you are, my friend, and keep your ear to the ground on my behalf, please.'

John puffed out his cheeks in amazement. 'You're going to challenge them in their own back yard?' he said incredulously. 'They'll never respond favourably. They're too entrenched in their own ideas and self-interest. They're even worse than I have been – and how long has it taken me to see the light? You're heading for trouble – real trouble.' He shook his head ruefully.

'I have to give them the opportunity,' returned Jesus. 'Everyone must have the chance to respond to God – that's only fair. I recognise that the chances of a favourable outcome are slight, but I have to risk it.'

John did not respond, so Jesus went on to tell him of the contact that Judas had made with the Sicarii. 'Things will come to a head, one way or another, pretty soon,' he said. 'I want to be the one who is calling the tune – I need the timetable to be set by me, not by others.'

'You'll never link up with the Sicarii?' asked John, wrinkling his nose in disgust.

'Never, but I will keep in touch with them to find out what they intend,' replied the Nazarene. 'Now, will you do as I have asked?'

The priest bowed his head and spoke slowly. 'If that's what you want – that's what I will do. You are my leader now. I'll do as I'm bidden, and I just hope and pray that you've got it right.'

'That is what I believe is God's plan and purpose, so that is what I have to do,' replied his guest. 'Remember that the Messiah is called to suffer… read Isaiah!'

John again bowed his head.

'Oh, and one more thing,' said Jesus, as if having an afterthought. 'If I ever I need a hiding place in the city, can I use your office? The authorities would never think of looking there, right in the Temple itself!'

'Of course. I can certainly provide you with a refuge in time of need – and I'll be glad to do it.'

NOTES

[1] Luke 19:2.
[2] Mark 8:11.
[3] Zechariah 9:9.

Jerusalem at last

Judas reported back to Jesus when he arrived back at Zacchaeus's house.

'I met my contact, a man called Samuel, at the Parrot. He says that his leader, Abbas, will meet you there early tomorrow morning. I will go with you to introduce you to Samuel and you can take it from there. I still think it's a good opportunity.'

'You never learn, do you?' responded Jesus, with a sad shake of his head. 'These are evil people! I'm only seeing them to try to find out their intentions and make sure they don't spoil my plans. There's no way I'm getting mixed up in riotous bloodshed.'

'Just listen to what they have to say – please. You may yet feel that there's something in it for us,' pleaded Judas. 'I feel we will have to get involved with them to some degree if we are to succeed, or we shall cut each other's throats.'

'An unfortunate expression! We'll see,' was all Jesus would say after that.

They did indeed meet up with Samuel the following morning and he, in turn, took Jesus into a back room in the inn to introduce him to Abbas, who turned out to be an enormous man, well over six feet in height and broad in comparison. The giant rose as Jesus entered the room and offered his shovel-like hand, which Jesus took. Abbas glared at Samuel, who quickly took the hint and left the two leaders alone. They sat on opposite sides of the rough table, weighing each other up for several seconds. Eventually Abbas began, with a hint of a sneer, 'So you are the Galilean teacher, Jesus, from Nazareth? I've been hearing a lot about you!'

Jesus nodded. 'I am he,' he said evenly, 'and of course everyone knows of the Sicarii.'

'I understand that you are proclaiming the coming of a new kingdom?' ventured the other.

'Yes. I preach the coming of God's Kingdom among men. It is not a political kingdom. It is a movement within men's minds and hearts, in which they open themselves to God's way of doing things – and they look forward to the day when God will demonstrate his power and release his love in every heart.'

The Nationalist grunted. 'And how is this change to be accomplished?' he asked. 'Will God come with heavenly angels to achieve this breakthrough? Or will he not, rather, look to us to take up arms on his behalf and achieve his rule in this land, rather than the rule of Caesar?'

Jesus replied softly but firmly, 'God can achieve his own purposes in his own way. I don't believe in bloodshed, even in a cause like this. Killing only increases hatred and revenge in future generations.'

Abbas rose and towered over the smaller man and waved a grim forefinger.

'Listen! We are going to boot the Romans out of Judaea very shortly,' he growled. 'We could help you, if you'd cooperate with us. We have the arms. You have the words, the charisma – men will follow you. Join with us and together we can bring about both our ideals. What do you say?'

Jesus paused before replying, his hand on his chin. 'What exactly have you in mind – and when?' he asked.

'At the right moment, we shall launch our attacks on strategic targets. We shall employ hit-and-run tactics to begin with, taking valuables, dealing with local opposition and then melting away into the hills before any large-scale reaction can be mustered. As things progress, we shall hope to rally the nation more generally – that's where you will come in – and then we shall see whether a pitched battle will finally end things. When? As soon as possible. As I have indicated, your campaign might well help to galvanise public opinion. You don't have to soil your own hands; you can rely on us to do all the dirty work...'

He paused.

'Now, is it a deal?' he challenged.

Jesus held his peace for a moment and then stood, eye to eye with the larger man. Then he said, slowly and deliberately, 'You have your way of working, I have mine; but I will consider carefully what you have said and see if there is any basis for cooperation. I'll let you have my answer very shortly.'

'*When?*' demanded Abbas. 'We want to move very shortly – in fact, our campaign has already started.'

'So it was your people who clashed with the wagon train a couple of days ago?'

'Of course. We got quite a haul too – and lessened the opposition by a couple of dozen men.' The big man threw his head back and laughed.

'But you lost some men yourself?'

The giant suddenly sobered up as if hit by a shovel. 'You know about that?' he asked.

'I heard that some of your men were killed and a few taken prisoner,' returned Jesus. 'Was the prize you took worth the loss of even one man – let alone more than twenty?'

Abbas sat down, his face very serious, his mouth twitching. 'In warfare, you are bound to lose men,' he growled, 'but when it's your own, it's different. My son was one of ours taken prisoner. I would have preferred it if he had been killed in battle. The Romans, when they get hold of him – and they will – they'll...'

The giant put his hands to his face to hide his emotions. Jesus said nothing, knowing full well what the man had in mind. Finally, Abbas continued, growling under his breath.

'They will torture him to get him to give information about our intentions. He'll hold out – he's a brave lad – but you don't know what Romans will do to a man when they want information. I'd much rather he was already dead...'

Again, he bowed his head. Jesus caught him by the hand and whispered, 'Don't despair. Even in the greatest moments of trial, God can bring help.'

Abbas immediately pulled his hand roughly away, looked up and glared at Jesus belligerently.

'Don't preach at me, Jesus,' he snarled. 'Keep that for the crowd. They might believe you. I know what's what in the real world. My boy is probably already going through hell and will not survive. He'll be lucky if he dies quickly.'

Jesus shrugged slightly and made to leave.

'I will give you my answer shortly,' he said. 'I am going to Jerusalem within the next few days. If I enter the town on horseback, you will know that I have come ready to fight. In that case, I look to you to contact me again for more detailed planning. But if I come into the Holy City walking, or riding on a simple donkey, you'll know that I have chosen to continue on the path of peace and want no further business with you. You must then go your own way.'

★

After a brief lunch, Jesus took his leave of Zacchaeus, with many thanks for all his kindness and hospitality. His host, for his part, couldn't thank Jesus enough for all he had done for him.

'I am a new man,' he declared. 'You have brought me back into the human race and made me feel welcome.'

'God bless you, Zacchaeus.' Jesus held his hand for a last moment before setting out at the head of the disciples.

Leaving the valley behind, they headed west into the hills, climbing all the while, until they came to Bethany, where they made their way to the home of Lazarus and his sisters. There they received the usual warm welcome. The family provided a light lunch for everyone and arrangements were made to sleep them all that night, either in homes in the village or out in the open nearby. Jesus himself was, of course, to stay at Lazarus's home. The four friends could hardly wait to share their news.

The following day, Jesus excused himself, saying he had to attend to some business nearby. He declined all offers of company and left mid-afternoon to walk the couple of miles to Bethphage, where he called at the house of Matthias. That worthy was also delighted to see Jesus and insisted that he come in and have some refreshment. They exchanged the usual pleasantries, enquiring after each other's health and all the news since they had met the previous autumn. Matt had little of substance to report but listened intently while Jesus told him of his plan to take his ministry to Jerusalem, making an unspoken claim to Messiahship and see whether the city, and particularly the Temple authorities, would respond.

'Then the day has come at last!' breathed Matthias. 'Very soon the Kingdom will be established for all to see!'

'That depends on the response to my call,' replied Jesus. 'It may be that many ordinary pilgrims will accept me, but will the Temple authorities? They may be indifferent, or, more likely, even hostile. If they move against me, what will the people believe and do then? Will they shrug their shoulders and say that they were mistaken in me, or will they back me against the High Priest and his entourage?'

Matt looked serious.

'I remember all too well what happened to my friend, John,' he said grimly. 'Let's hope that nothing like that could ever happen to you.'

'I am fully aware of the possibilities,' replied Jesus soberly. 'You remember that the scriptures prophesy a suffering Messiah. I am prepared to suffer, if that is God's will. But perhaps God will break through with a plan to save the situation. Whatever happens, I trust him. We'll see.'

'What can I do to help?' asked Matt.

'There is one small thing you can do,' replied the Nazarene. 'Do you know anyone who could lend me a donkey? You see, I'd like to enter Jerusalem riding on a young donkey, just as was prophesied. That way, I don't have to proclaim my Messiahship by word of mouth – all Jews who follow the tradition will have been taught from childhood that this is the way the Messiah will arrive, and they will, I'm sure, know what I am about. I can count on my followers and sympathetic pilgrims to welcome me, singing the traditional Hallel Psalms.'

'I have a donkey colt you can have at any time,' smiled Matt. 'It will be a privilege to provide the Messiah with his mount! I will, of course, come with you too and join in the Hallel.'

'Thank you, Matt. You'll know that it is I who need the animal because I will tell my disciples – whoever it is who comes – when they ask for the beast, to say, "Our master needs it."[1] That'll be a kind of password. Is that all right?'

'Fine. When am I to expect them to come?'

'In two days' time – the day after the Sabbath.'

★

The same afternoon, a small party of women, accompanied by their servants, arrived at Justus's inn. Joanna, Susanna, Rebecca and Lydia had made the long journey from Tiberias, carried by litter. Though it was, of course, much easier than walking, they were still tired and dirty after their journey. It was no easy thing to be carried over rough tracks, being jolted and jostled, even when all possible care was taken. The servants who had carried them were naturally worn out, even though they had done the journey, or similar excursions, many times. On their arrival, they had found that Nimrah and Mary from Magdala had arrived a couple of days earlier. This being her first visit, the young woman was particularly thrilled to be in the Holy City. She was still in raptures over the great buildings. There was the palace of the old King, Herod the Great, on the western side of the city, its halls trimmed with alabaster and its floors flagged or decorated with wonderful mosaics, in the best Greek or Roman tradition. Nearby, were the homes of the High Priest, Caiaphas, and his father-in-law, Annas, who had been High Priest earlier in his life. These houses, too, were lavish beyond anything Mary had ever seen. Joanna had to admit that they even rivalled Antipas's palace in Tiberias, on the shores of the Sea of Galilee. Then there was the older Hasmonean Palace, a little way away – another marvellous structure.

The great fort of Antonia, with four impressive towers at the corners, which housed the thousands of extra Roman soldiers brought in from the provinces to ensure that Passover passed off peacefully, stood high and forbidding, overlooking the city's centrepiece, the marvellous Temple, which had been built by the Jews who returned from captivity in Babylon, but greatly extended and beautified much more recently by Herod the Great. It now occupied almost the entire eastern section of the city and glowered down from its immense height into the Kedron Valley. Its alabaster spires glinted white and pink in the evening light, and decorative clusters of solid gold grapes adorned the eastern facade.

Being a woman, Mary could not visit the inner part of the Temple, which was reserved only for male Jews, but she had passed through the Outer Court of the Gentiles, noting with some surprise the trading and noise going on there, and had gone for prayer into the Court of the Women. What happened in the Court of the Jews beyond she could only guess at. Still more mysterious was the holy place at the very centre of the sanctuary, called the Holy of Holies, where it was said that God himself dwelt. Only the High Priest could enter the Holy of Holies, and then only once a year, on the Day of Atonement.

Mary was perplexed. She found it difficult to reconcile the idea of God living in the centre of the Temple with scriptural teaching that God dwelt in heaven. Yet one of the psalms talked of God being everywhere! Then, even more puzzling, Jesus taught that God was with all his people all the time. In fact, she remembered him teaching that the Kingdom was actually within each person, if only he or she looked for it. She must ask Jesus about this when she saw him, she thought, but for the time being, it was sufficient to be in the Holy City, at Passover time, especially as she was expecting to see Jesus within a couple of days.

Some of Jesus's family had also come to Jerusalem for the feast. Mary, James and Joseph had decided that it was time to make the long journey southward. Even the men did not always attend Passover – they lived sufficiently far away for attendance not to be obligatory – but this year they decided that the older brothers at least should make the effort and represent the family, with their mother.

Mary was now well into her forties and couldn't expect to be able to make the trip many more times. Travelling seventy or more miles to Jerusalem, and the same distance back, within a week or so, took its toll. Even though they brought the donkey, the journey was still quite rough, but she had always been devout and followed the practices of the faith, as taught by the local rabbi at the Synagogue. She had insisted on the family attending Synagogue classes from an early age and all the children had shown real devotion in turn. Jesus, of course, had become impossibly intense, going off, living rough and becoming no better than a sort of travelling salesman in religion. Much as Mary had loved her eldest son, she hadn't been able to accept this as a normal life, fitting for her family, who had always been decent, normal folk, living ordinary well-ordered lives, keeping homes and families in the traditional way. So she had tried to put Jesus out of her mind and heart over the past two years. It was difficult, as any mother would know, but she had tried. James, her second son, was also particularly serious about his religion and rather obsessive about attempting to keep every possible tenet of the law, but at least he stayed at home and lived a normal life!

They had visited the Temple soon after they arrived, making their sacrifices and saying their prayers, but Mary was tired after the journey and decided that she needed to rest for the next day or two. They would go again to the Temple, no doubt several times, and particularly on the day of the Passover itself, but she had to rest for now. In time she would join in with all her friends and relatives who had come, along with people coming from all over the known world to keep the Passover Feast, the most important feast of the Jewish year. For more than 1,200 years, Passover had recalled the release of the nation from bondage in Egypt and slavery to the Pharaoh. It was good to be in Jerusalem again.

At sundown that day, the Sabbath commenced. All good Jews would be inside their houses celebrating the seventh day, as required by the Law. Jesus and his party met in the home of Lazarus, who kindly hosted the supper for them all. After the meal, Jesus broke the news of his intentions for the coming week to all his friends, stressing the need to make their arrival in Jerusalem as close to the prophesy as possible. He reminded them of the words of Zechariah:

Rejoice, rejoice, daughter of Zion.
Shout aloud, daughter of Jerusalem;
for see, your King is coming to you,
his cause won, his victory gained,
humble and mounted on an ass…

He looked round at his friends and continued, 'It is important that we create a real sense of rejoicing. I know that you'll sing the Hallel Psalms as usual, and make something of this entrance, so that, to any Jew with a knowledge of the scriptures, there can be no mistaking the claim that I am making. I expect that many other pilgrims around us will join in. They are all ripe for the coming of the Messiah – though, as we know, they all have rather different perceptions of what that may mean! Nevertheless, Jerusalem must be awakened to the fact that I have arrived with a definite ministry to perform.'

The reaction of the disciples was very varied. Some were elated, some apprehensive, some confused. Peter, not surprisingly, was very excited by the prospect, looking forward to a great triumph for Jesus. Andrew, his brother, was not so sure. He remembered what had happened to John the Baptist and wondered what the authorities would do. Of course, the authority in Jerusalem was the High Priest, who should – in theory, at least – be more responsive to the claims of the Messiah than King Antipas had been in Galilee. Perhaps things would turn out all right. James and John, the other fishermen, followed Peter's line and dreamed of the coming Kingdom. Though they had been scolded by Jesus when they had asked for a place of honour near him when the Kingdom dawned, they still hoped that they would be recognised for their contribution over the past two years. Thomas, naturally a pessimist, could foresee trouble. He had lived long enough to sense that no authorities liked their positions challenged. He said as much to Matthew, but his partner couldn't believe that Jesus would misread the situation. He was sure things would turn out all right. Nathaniel had a great faith in God and believed that God would protect his own, whatever happened. Perhaps, after all, they would see an army of angels coming in the clouds to rescue the Messiah, if there was any trouble with the Temple. Philip had always followed Nathaniel on religious matters and saw no reason to change on this occasion. Judas was ecstatic. At last, Jesus was doing something definite. Not knowing the detail of what had transpired between Abbas and his leader, he hoped that Jesus's entrance into Jerusalem would be the signal for the Nationalist uprising and the beginning of the end of the Roman occupation of his land. He was overjoyed.

The trio of young men from the north of Galilee were confused. They listened to their colleagues discussing matters, each with a different slant on the affair. In the end, they knew they would follow Jesus whatever happened, so they gave up worrying or attempting to predict. The two blacksmiths flexed their great biceps and felt that they could cope if it came to fighting, though they recalled too the horror of the crucifixions they had seen in their home town not so long ago. Lazarus, as usual, couldn't make up his mind. He was devoted to Jesus, of course, and that made rational thought difficult. If Jesus wanted to do something, it must be right. Mary felt much the same. For Mary, the sun would turn blue if Jesus so commanded it; but Martha – practical Martha – wondered. She had overheard the conversation between Thomas and Matthew and this gave her pause for thought. In her own way, she too loved Jesus and hated the thought that any hurt could befall him.

Altogether, it was a thoughtful and perplexed assembly that sat together talking in little groups that Sabbath evening. All the following day, in obedience to the law, the party rested, each in his or her own mind and heart preparing for the coming day.

★

The next day dawned brightly, with a clear blue sky and warm sunshine. The countryside was still green and lush, following the winter rain, and wild flowers were blooming alongside every track and on every piece of waste ground between the little plots of tilled soil. There were tiny blue irises, yellow marigolds and purple gladioli. In the crevices between the rocky outcrops, cyclamen were flowering, in delicate mauve or pink. Fennel towered five feet into the air, capped by gigantic inflorescences of yellow. White wild garlic mingled with anemones of many shades – pink, blue, white, purple. It was a lovely time to be alive. The sun, though very warm, did not yet have the ferocity that it would acquire in a month or two, and walking was still a pleasure.

Jesus did not immediately put his plans into action. He decided that his entrance into the city would not be made until well into the afternoon, following the traditional period of rest after lunch. All the morning, he sat in reflective mood in Lazarus's garden, sometimes praying, sometimes moving to talk with different disciples as they chatted in twos and threes. A little while after lunch, Jesus entrusted the two blacksmiths, Simon and little James, with the task of fetching the donkey. He told them where to find Matthias's house and the password he had chosen.

'We'll meet you at the top of the Mount of Olives in an hour,' he said. 'I know you won't let me down.'

Everything went to plan. The blacksmiths, now accompanied by Matthias, met the others at the top of the hill. Peter covered the little grey donkey's back with his robe and Jesus took his place on it. The little animal was rather small for the task, but he walked on well, with Jesus's legs nearly reaching the ground as he sat aside him. The disciples began singing the well-known psalms of rejoicing, often sung by pilgrims entering the city for festivals, and waving palm branches that they took from the trees along the way. It didn't take long for their mood to be caught by the trickle of pilgrims on the road to Jerusalem. They too joined in the singing, many of them calling to Jesus, realising the significance of his simple demonstration. Cries of 'Hosanna!' and 'Blessed be the Son of David!' started to ring out, mingled with the singing, and the whole atmosphere became more and more charged with high emotion.[2] Down the slope they went, passing the entrance to the garden of Gethsemane, where the olive presses were located among the ancient olive groves, and into the Kedron Valley. Naturally enough, the ever-enlarging procession had been noticed from the city and people had started streaming out to see what it was all about. The enthusiasm of the pilgrims was infectious. The city dwellers, too, started to join in the celebration, adding their voices to the singing, throwing their garments and yet more palm branches in the way of the sturdy little donkey, who all this time struggled onwards with its heavy load.

Among the people leaving the city to meet Jesus, however, were some Pharisees. They alone looked grim and judgemental as they approached the procession, pulling at their beards and whispering to one another. Before long, one of them called to Jesus above the din, 'You hear what the people are saying? Tell them to stop. You're not the Messiah – you know that. Call a halt!'

The preacher at first ignored his critics but, as they persisted, he turned to them and called back, 'It's no use. Let them shout. If they stopped, I think the very stones in the walls of the city would shout instead!'[3]

And so the procession made its way up the steep slope towards the east gate of the city, under the towering Temple walls. Into the city they went, the crowd ever swelling and more and more excited and enthusiastic. They wended their way slowly through the narrow streets till at last they reached the entrance to the Temple itself. There Jesus dismounted and gave the donkey back into Matt's care, then led the throng into the Temple. Everywhere, the crowd was buzzing. Those who hadn't seen the procession wanted to know what was going on. They were asking questions and being bombarded with explanations, doubts and assertions from those who had come in from Bethany and Bethphage.

'This is Jesus, the prophet from Nazareth. He's ridden into the city on a donkey, just as the prophet foretold that the Messiah will come. This must be the one we have waited for.'

'Do you really think so?'

'Can anything very important come from Galilee – and especially from Nazareth?'

'I've seen him heal lame men. That must surely be a sign from heaven.'

'Isn't he the one who raised a man from the dead in Bethany not so long ago?'

'If he's the Messiah, what will happen now?'

'Will this be the end of the world?'

'I can't see the Romans liking this – there's bound to be trouble.'

'God will see to it that the Messiah is protected and triumphant.'

'This is the dawning of the new age – the Kingdom of God.'

'Amen, amen. Let God rule in Israel again. Throw the Romans out!'

'But Jesus is a man of peace. His Kingdom is one in which all love one another.'

So the comments and questions flowed back and forth. Speculation was endless as everyone sought to deal with the unique situation. Most of the crowd seemed to welcome the prophet, but some were doubtful, some fearful. The people crushed into the Court of the Gentiles behind Jesus, bringing the trading activities virtually to a halt with the rush. Onward they streamed, following Jesus into the inner courtyard, the women falling back and making their way into their own Temple precinct.

Once in the inner courtyard, Jesus bowed his head in prayer, and the gesture soon brought the rest of the crowd into a prayerful attitude. At last, the noise was stilled. Gone, temporarily, was the excitement, the waving palm branches, the ringing shouts and the psalm chanting. Stilled, for the moment, was the speculation. Instead, the whole crowd was silent, prayerful, and expectant; but, to their amazement, Jesus, having completed his prayer, merely raised his arms briefly in blessing, then strode back the way he had come. He paused for a few minutes in the outer courtyard, observing the tables of the moneylenders and animal salesmen. He muttered to the disciples to take careful note of all that was going on and then moved out through the Temple entrance. Without any delay, he walked back the way he had come, hardly noticing the debris left by the procession, the palm leaves and robes still lying on the road.

The disciples followed, puzzled, disappointed, bemused. While they had no clear idea of what they expected, they felt that Jesus would do more than just visit the Temple for prayer. They muttered between themselves as they climbed the slope back on to the Mount of Olives. Peter tugged at Andrew's sleeve and drew him a little apart to ask, 'What was it all for, d'you think? Nothing seemed to come of it. The people responded – most seemed delighted to see him. Many of them got the message, I'm sure – they knew what he meant by it all – yet he let the occasion go.'

Andrew waited a while before replying. Eventually, he offered, 'I can only assume that Jesus knows what he's about. Have we ever known him to misjudge a situation, or misread a crowd?'

'No – that's true,' returned his brother, 'but there's always a first time for everything!'

'Jesus knows what he's doing,' said Andrew stolidly.

The brothers James and John joined them, wanting to know what they were talking about.

'It's just what we were saying,' said John. 'I expected Jesus to hold forth with a great sermon in the Temple. He had the crowd in his hand and could have moved them to anything.'

'Perhaps that was the point,' replied Andrew slowly. 'Perhaps they were too wound up. You know that Jesus likes people to be guided by their brains as well as by their hearts. Emotion is all very well, but, in a crowd, it can often do a lot of harm. He wouldn't want to cause any trouble.'

'I see what you mean.' James entered the conversation. 'But I still think he could have used the opportunity in some way. Still, what's done is done. He certainly threw down a challenge to the Temple! I wonder what they're thinking now – those priests and scribes?'

Further down the road, Thomas and Matthew had had a similar exchange of view. Nathaniel too was disappointed that Jesus had not preached a great sermon, thus losing a blazing opportunity to proclaim his Messiahship by word as well as demonstration. Judas, hanging back from the rest, was bitterly disappointed. Whatever was Jesus doing, letting such a chance go by? What would the Nationalists think now? Surely they would have expected more from Jesus – a rallying cry that they could latch on to and use as a springboard for their own campaign. It was all very dispiriting, from Judas's point of view.

That evening, back in Bethany, Jesus said nothing to anyone until after they had finished eating their supper. Then, when they were finishing their fruit and sipping their wine, he called for silence and spoke quietly to them all.

'My friends, the die is now cast. While I did not claim anything directly today, there can be few devout Jews who saw what happened today who did not understand that I am seeking their endorsement as the Messiah. There were, no doubt, many points of view, but overwhelmingly the mood seemed to me to be enthusiastic and welcoming. A few Pharisees complained, but that was only to be expected. Interestingly, the Temple authorities did nothing – perhaps they were too surprised and didn't have time to react – I didn't stay long, after all. But there was no immediate call-out of the Temple Guard, which is interesting. Tomorrow may be different, for I shall then make a much more direct challenge. I intend to overthrow a few of the trading tables and set a few sacrificial animals and birds free in the outer courtyard. It won't be more than a token, of course, but it'll cause a stir and this time, I feel sure, the guards will be called out. We shall need to make some detailed plans to deal with that situation – just in case.'

Jesus then went on to explain precisely where he wanted each of the disciples to position himself as he set about upsetting the trading posts in what had become nothing more than a marketplace. He had made a careful mental note of the layout of the courtyard, observing where the guard was set and where reinforcements would most probably emerge from. He calculated that if he made the challenge brief, and limited the disciples' roles to observation and generally getting in the way of any approaching guard, as if by accident, he could achieve his objective and escape – into John's office if necessary – before any real military presence could be summoned. Nevertheless, he hoped that the crowd would rally round and support him, providing protection from the authorities if they turned nasty. That was the plan, at any rate.

★

Back at the Temple, John barHelez had been called to see the High Priest. His Lordship was not at all pleased. His secretary had briefed him about the demonstration that had occurred late that afternoon and he didn't like it – he didn't like it all. In fact, he was in a foul mood because of it. This demonstration by the man Jesus meant trouble – trouble with the Prefect, if he wasn't careful. Of course Pilate wouldn't care a fig about someone claiming to be the Messiah from a religious point of view, but if someone mentioned to him that a Messiah was also believed, at least by some, to be a kind of King, then the fat would be in the fire. The Romans recognised no Kings in Jewry unless they had made them themselves, and then only if they were under strict discipline from Tiberius Caesar in Rome – or Capri, which now, more and more, seemed to be the location favoured by the Emperor.

John stood and listened patiently to Caiaphas as he ranted on, as he had done so often before. He watched as this man in his early forties, tall and well proportioned, who carried his office with an air of righteous authority, paced back and forth across the large, ornate office, venting his feelings on the furniture, slamming his fist on his desk, the backs of chairs and other convenient objects. He had been called in as the High Priest's personal assistant and advisor, but in reality Caiaphas preferred not to take advice at all, but for others to listen to his analysis of the situation and agree with his own personal inclinations. He talked more to himself than to John, rehearsing all his problems in the hope that some answer would eventually trickle into his tortured mind. So long as John nodded his head in agreement from time to time, the High Priest was content. John knew better than to try to interrupt with his own point of view.

At last the tirade ground to a halt. After a short pause, John ventured, 'So what action does your Lordship propose, in view of this – this—'

'This *outrage*!' interjected Caiaphas. 'It's nothing less than an outrage, that this fellow – this carpenter – should set himself up in the Temple as – as the Messiah – "God's anointed one".'

'He seemed well received by the crowd,' murmured John, diffidently.

Caiaphas snorted and rubbed his chin. 'The crowd is mindless – they'll always go after every new charlatan!' he grumbled. 'Anything for a novelty. Where is their faith in the eternal, continuing God, the One who made the covenant with Abraham, Isaac and Jacob?'

He left the question hanging in the air for a few seconds, then growled reluctantly, 'However, I recognise that their enthusiasm does make it difficult for us to move against the man immediately. The last thing we want to do is to provoke a riot, or even a small disturbance. Pilate would have me removed from office before sundown if he thought that we were incapable of handling this situation peacefully.'

John risked a point of view.

'Perhaps it would be better simply to ignore it, then, and let the thing die a natural death? Ordinary folk quickly lose interest and simply move on to their next enthusiasm. Perhaps we should treat it with...'

'... the contempt it deserves.' Caiaphas broke in again. He paused, pursing his lips, and then appeared to come to a decision.

'Perhaps you're right. Perhaps we'd better simply watch and see what else happens. We'll see what this Jesus has in mind...'

'I'm sure that's the best policy, My Lord,' said John deferentially.

He waited for a merest second, just in case his boss came up with any other sudden inspiration, then he bowed and let himself out of the room.

Back in his own office, he wondered whether he should try to get a message through to Jesus, to let him know what had transpired; but, given the difficulties of communication and the fact that nothing definite was planned, he decided, like his superior, to wait and see what the morrow brought.

★

Cleopas and Nathan had had a close-up view of the events of the afternoon, for the procession had taken a route leading right past their shopfronts. They had heard the clamour some time before anyone had come into view. Then, when they saw people hurrying up the street towards the noise, curiosity had got the better of them and they had joined the crowd to see what was happening. However, by the time they had emerged on to the street, having locked up their workshops, the procession was already coming into view and bearing down on them. Fortunately, both were substantial men, tall and broad enough to be able to hold their own in most throngs, and so they found themselves well able to see the man on the donkey. They very quickly realised that it was their friend, Jesus, the man who had carried out the repairs on their shopfronts just over a year earlier.

Cleopas decided, without thinking, to hail their friend. 'Hey, Jesus! Jesus!' he called.

The man on the donkey evidently heard him over all the racket and turned to look for the source of the greeting.

'Over here!' yelled Cleopas, now joined by Nathan.

Jesus at last identified them in the crowd and smiled a greeting of his own.

'Blessings on you, Cleopas – and you, Nathan!' he called.

'And on you, friend,' shouted Cleopas.

'We haven't forgotten you, Jesus,' yelled Nathan. 'All the best!'

The procession swept on before they could communicate further.

'Are you going to see what happens?' asked Nathan.

'What do you think? Are you?'

The two men hesitated for a moment and then Cleopas made up his mind. 'Let's go,' he said. 'There'll be no business transacted anyway while all this is happening. In any case, pilgrims don't buy locks! I'm going to see what Jesus is doing.'

They pushed their way along the road in the crowd till they came to the Temple entrance, where they surged inside, following the Nazarene. They pushed through the outer courtyard, avoiding the animal droppings as best they could, and on into the Court of the Jews. Like the others, they found themselves following the example of the Galilean, in praying in silence. Gradually, the awesome presence of the Temple precinct impinged itself on them and, possibly for the first time in ages, they heard the sound of total silence. Then, suddenly, it was over and their friend was departing.

'Whatever do you make of that?' asked Nathan, when he had gone. 'I thought he would speak to us all and explain what this is all about.'

'Me, too,' replied his neighbour. 'It was all over before it had really begun.'

'A flash in a pan, then. Pity, for I thought well of Jesus. I liked his approach to things – I thought I understood what he was about.'

There was a short pause before Cleopas spoke again.

'You realise the significance of what he did, though, don't you? The Messiah is supposed to come into Jerusalem like that – riding a donkey through the east gate, and welcomed by everyone singing the psalms. Is Jesus really our Messiah? Will he liberate us from Rome?'

'As I remember it, Jesus's ideas were rather different,' replied the cobbler. 'He talked about liberating us from our worst selves – taking us out of the darkness of selfishness into the light of God. That seemed to be his essential message, as I remember it.'

'So why the procession – the demo?'

'Dunno. We'll have to see what he does now…'

Mary and Nimrah had also been caught up in the crowds watching Jesus and they too were puzzled at the outcome – or lack of it. They had discussed the whole matter with the other women who had come from Galilee specifically to be near Jesus – Joanna and her party. They had met, more by luck than judgement, on the fringes of the crowd after Jesus left the Temple. No matter which way they considered the situation, it seemed that Jesus had lost a big opportunity to promote his cause.

Mary secretly hoped to get the chance to speak to Jesus alone sometime. There were so many questions buzzing around in her mind that she wanted to put to Jesus. Why was evil so triumphant in the world, if it was God's world? Why was Rome the real power on earth, not Jewry, God's chosen people? Why were there so many beggars in Jerusalem, which, above all places, should have the financial resources to care for those who were down on their luck? And so on…

Mary put some of her questions to Nimrah, but her mother was no better able to answer them than Mary herself. She tried confiding in Joanna, but she and her friends seemed just to want to follow Jesus without thinking about any of the difficult issues.

'I just think he's wonderful,' was all she got from Lydia, and the others seemed to be of a similar mind.

I think he's wonderful too, Mary thought to herself, but I would like to understand a bit more about it all as well.

Jesus's family heard about the events of the day, rather than participating in them in any way. Mary had been resting up and her two sons had followed suit, but they had heard soon enough about the disturbance in the city. It hadn't taken them long to realise that the man on the donkey at the centre of the affair had been their own kinsman. James was the first to voice his disapproval.

'I feel so ashamed!' he said. 'Why ever does Jesus want to go making a fool of himself in Jerusalem? You know what people will say – they'll say that he thinks he is actually the Messiah! What he did is exactly what the prophet foretold. He must know that people will put two and two together...'

'... and come up with five!' burst in his brother. 'We know who he is and how ridiculous his claim is – but others may actually believe it!'

'If they do, he's in trouble,' said Mary quietly. 'If he stirs up the authorities, they'll have to act against him.'

'He's my brother and I wish him no harm,' cried James petulantly, 'but he's bringing it all on himself. We tried to warn him, months ago – didn't we? But he wouldn't listen... He just insisted on going his own way. He's always been the same!'

The conversation went on for some time in a similar fashion. Like everyone else, they could only draw one conclusion: they'd just have to wait and see what Jesus chose to do next, hoping that he wouldn't bring down the whole weight of the authorities on himself.

NOTES

[1] Mark 11:3.
[2] Mark 11:9–10.
[3] Luke 19:40.

The last week

Jesus bade farewell to the family at Bethany the following morning, saying that, for the rest of the period of the festival, he and his followers would sleep out in the open in the Garden of Gethsemane, on the Mount of Olives. It was a place commonly used by pilgrims if they could not find or afford an inn for the period of the festival. He wanted to be closer to the Temple, which he intended to be the centre of his operations over the next few days. Also, he was anxious that, if he got into any trouble in Jerusalem, he did not implicate Lazarus and his sisters.

Jesus and his followers reached the great sanctuary mid-morning, as the sun was really starting to roast the ancient city. The outer courtyard shimmered in the heat haze as pilgrims from all over the Mediterranean area greeted their friends, busily exchanged their coins and purchased their sacrificial animals and birds. The stallholders were doing a brisk trade. There was noise and bustle everywhere, with men shouting and frightened animals and birds bleating or calling. Jesus stood surveying the scene for a few minutes, while his followers moved to take up their various pre-arranged positions. When they were prepared, Jesus suddenly launched himself at the first stallholder, overturning his stall and sending his money flying.

'Away with this merchandise!' he cried. 'This is supposed to be a place of worship for the nations, but you are turning it into a robbers' cave!'[1]

The coins were scattered far and wide, rolling in all directions into nooks and crannies, and mixing with animal droppings and the dust, while startled men – both stallholders and others – started to try to collect them up. Jesus gave the traders no time to collect their wits. Immediately, he seized the next stall and overturned that too. Then he opened a large cage of pigeons and the air was briefly full of flapping wings and scattered feathers. On he went, kicking open a pen of lambs. Again, the small scared animals scattered, getting under the feet of the owners and causing widespread mayhem.

'How dare you disgrace the great Temple with all these wretched goings-on!' thundered Jesus. 'People are entitled to fair dealings here!'

'Hear, hear!' shouted one of the pilgrims and soon the crowd began to rally to Jesus, encouraging him on by yelling comments, like, 'That's it! You tell 'em.'

'I agree – go to it! – that's the way!'

'You show 'em! It's just a racket.'

Jesus continued down the line of stalls, leaving a trail of destruction and confusion in his wake. The traders, after their initial shock, started to remonstrate with this mad intruder, but they were torn between the desire for reprisal and the need to try to regain their belongings, either money or animals. Nevertheless, a few of the younger stallholders did try to restrain Jesus, only to be foiled by four of his younger and fitter disciples, Simon, little James, Philip and Thaddeus, who had been stationed near their leader for this purpose. Then, as the danger of widespread fighting increased, some of the pilgrims took a hand and began to crowd round Jesus and his followers, supporting their efforts and protecting him from the indignant response of the traders. There was quite a frenzied scene for several minutes. Then, predictably, there was a shout from the corner – it was Peter's voice – 'The guards are coming!'

Peter, Andrew, big James and John, who had been placed near the entrance to the courtyard, were deliberately slow to move out of the way as a troop of eight guards, armed with long spears and shields, moved in toward the scene of the trouble. By the time the soldiers had cleared a path and reached the scene of the overturned tables and broken cages, Jesus had made good his escape into the inner courtyard, borne along by a phalanx of excited and supportive pilgrims, urged on by the four younger disciples. This group escorted Jesus into the Court of the Jews, where the preacher was able to set himself up on a plinth and start to address the ever-increasing crowd. By the time the guards had reached the inner sanctuary, they had no means of knowing exactly who it was who had been responsible for the earlier mayhem. Jesus was already speaking to the people, having totally discarded his earlier belligerent attitude.

'I want to tell you about something I saw earlier on, at the door of the Temple Treasury – just outside the entrance over there,' he was saying. 'I saw many rich people contributing large sums of money to the Temple funds.[2] What struck me was that they seemed to me, many of them, to be very anxious for passers-by to see them making their generous gifts. Then, however, I saw a poor widow go to the contribution box, slip in a couple of mites and move away quickly, as if not wanting to be seen at all. Perhaps she thought her gift was so small that she was ashamed to be seen making it. But actually, to my mind, she gave more than anyone else, for I feel sure that, in her poverty, she was giving virtually all she had – certainly all she could spare – while the rich people, who had given so ostentatiously and proudly, were giving only a tiny fraction of their wealth to the Temple.

'You see, my friends, it isn't so much *what* you give to God that is important – it is the *spirit* and the attitude behind the gift that counts. God can look into your heart and see if you are giving willingly and generously in proportion to what you have available. God knows whether you really want to give, and he also knows if you are giving simply to win the admiration of others.'

Since the crowd was attentive, and all was peaceful and quiet, the guards had no reason to complain, still less to try to apprehend anyone. They moved around uncertainly at the back of the crowd for several minutes and then departed, shrugging their shoulders. The Captain went off to report to the authorities that, whoever it was that had caused the disturbance, had got away – or, at any rate, that everything was back to normal now.

Jesus continued teaching for an hour, setting out his view of the Kingdom, calling for everyone to enter into a new relationship with God and await the coming of the time when God would reign in every heart. As usual, he attracted questions from many in the crowd who saw the coming of the Kingdom in political terms. His response was unwavering.

'God's Kingdom will come when he wills it,' he asserted. 'Our task is to watch and pray for the outpouring of God's grace. Everyone can immediately begin to appreciate the joy of God's forgiveness and love in his inner life and can join the company of those who are taking up a new way of life. They can also anticipate the action that God himself will take shortly. It's coming – God is going to act soon! Watch and pray, therefore, for we cannot be sure when it will be!'3

★

John barHelez had been extremely apprehensive all the morning. He knew, better than anyone, the risk that Jesus was running in making any kind of disturbance in the Temple, or, indeed, anywhere in the Jerusalem district. He tried to get on with his paperwork, but all the time he was expecting to hear signs of tumult in the outer courtyard and the clash of steel as the guards reacted to any problems facing them. As it turned out, he was surprised when, having heard only a comparatively minor disturbance, the Captain of the Guard came in to report that there had been a small upset, but, by the time the guards had been called to intervene, it had all been over. Some tables had been overturned and several people had lost a little money, or a few sacrificial animals, but otherwise nothing much had happened.

'Did you apprehend the troublemakers?' asked John, as casually as he could.

'No, sir,' replied the Captain, somewhat guiltily, expecting criticism. 'Whoever it was had disappeared before we arrived at the scene. I don't know whether they went on into the Court of the Jews – there were many pilgrims making their way there when we arrived – or whether they melted away into the crowd and fled out into the city. We thought most likely that they went on into the inner courtyard, but when we went there, everything was peaceful. The man Jesus, the prophet from Galilee, who was at the centre of the demonstration yesterday, was holding forth, among others, but not saying anything out of place – so we came away.'

John listened carefully, trying not to betray on his face his inner feelings of relief. Eventually, he nodded his head and said, 'Very well, Captain. I'll report to the High Priest when I see him shortly.'

The Captain had hardly left the office when a trickle of stallholders arrived, complaining of their recent experience.

'Do you know who it was who attacked you?' asked John, again trying not to show too great an interest.

The self-elected leader of the little delegation answered, 'We're not sure, sir, but we think it was the man from Galilee, Jesus, the so-called prophet, the one who had the procession through town yesterday. We think it was him that started it, but there were others helping him – and quite a lot of the crowd were egging him on in the finish. Why weren't we protected? We are properly licensed by the High Priest to trade in the outer courtyard...'

'I know,' replied John, seeking to placate the incensed men with a gentle tone. 'It is extremely annoying and worrying when this kind of thing happens, but how were we to expect such a thing? Nothing like this has happened before. A couple of guards on the doorway are usually quite sufficient to keep order – but no doubt they had to call out the whole troop before attempting to deal with a disturbance like that... I'm very sorry it's happened. We'll make sure that it doesn't happen again. I shall, of course, report to the High Priest and I'm sure he will look into the background and see what can be done about this – Jesus, you said?'

And with that, the traders had to be content.

John made his way to the High Priest's office and gave a brief report there. Caiaphas started off again on his lengthy tirade of the previous day.

'I'd be willing to swear that it was this man Jesus again,' he said savagely. 'It sounds just like him. He thinks he is – well, we know what he thinks he is. I'll give him "Messiah" when I catch him! We're going to have to take action. These things cannot be allowed to continue. All right, barHelez. Thank you for your report. I'll take counsel with some senior colleagues and we'll consider what must be done.'

'Whoever it was, he seems to have the crowd behind him, my Lord,' ventured John diffidently. 'Whoever it was, it might be difficult to take him into custody with this many pilgrims around.'

'I know, I know,' muttered the Caiaphas, pulling at his beard, 'but I feel sure it will have been the Galilean. He's obviously looking to stir things up. We'll have to find a way of taking him when the crowd is out of the way – assuming we can find a charge to hold him on. What have we got on him?'

'Very little, in concrete terms, My Lord, to be truthful,' replied John, trying to sound disappointed. 'He's clever. He's been critical of the Pharisees, but then, so are we. He's failed to follow all their interpretations of the Law – but we don't arrest people for that. He's had some dealings with pretty unsavoury people, but that's not a crime in itself...'

'But he's set himself up as the Messiah!' exploded Caiaphas.

'Yes, My Lord. You can argue that from yesterday's demonstration – but that's not a crime either. Many have claimed to be the Messiah in the past and we've simply watched them wither away on the vine as impostors...'

'But the political implications are immense just now,' interjected the High Priest. 'The Messiah can be seen by some as a king...'

John stretched out his arms, palms upturned, and said mockingly, 'What sort of king comes into town riding on a young donkey? Even the Romans – even Pilate – isn't paranoid enough to feel threatened by that!'

Caiaphas rammed his fist into his other hand. 'We'll see!' he retorted. 'We'll see! If we lay our hands on him somehow, we'll find something to charge him with and have him silenced. See what you can come up with. You say he is preaching in the Temple now? Send out a few people to question him as he preaches, to see if we can trap him into saying something incriminating, or unpopular – or just plain stupid.'

'Very good, My Lord.' John bowed and made his escape.

*

Jesus continued teaching in the Temple all the afternoon.

'Nobody lights a lamp, or a candle, and puts it under a bucket, or down in the cellar,' he said.[4] 'The whole point of a lamp, of course, is to give off light to those around it, to help them see clearly what they are doing. So – you put a lamp on a lamp stand, in order that its light can shine to the greatest advantage. Similarly, if your life is good and, so to speak, full of light, you should shine forth as best you can, giving light and comfort and support to all those around you. You must be a light in this dark world, helping to bring God's love to all.'

One of the Temple employees, sent to try to trap Jesus, asked if he could put a question.

'Of course,' replied Jesus. 'Go ahead.'

'Well, sir, we know that you are sincere and have many interesting and challenging things to teach us. We know, too, that you will speak God's truth without fear. What is your feeling about the Roman occupation? How long are we Jews to be enslaved?'

Jesus took a good look at the questioner and sensed what he was up to. He replied carefully, 'I have said many times that all empires come to an end at some time. That is the way of things. Three hundred years ago, Greece was the most powerful nation on earth. Now it's Rome. God will end their reign too in due course, but I cannot say when.'

'That's all very well!' shouted another of the Temple stooges. 'But what do you advise us to do now? Should we pay our taxes to Rome or not?'

Jesus paused before replying. This time he knew that he was in trouble if he gave either a straightforward 'yes' or 'no' answer. The crowd wouldn't like the former and Caesar wouldn't stand for the latter. Eventually, he asked, 'Has anyone got a coin in his pocket?'

Someone in the front row of the crowd soon produced a Roman denarius and it was passed to the preacher, who examined it carefully, as if for the first time. Then Jesus showed it to a man near him, and asked, 'Tell me, whose image is this, and whose title is this on the coin?'

The bystander, amazed, said immediately, wrinkling his nose, 'It's Caesar, of course.'

Jesus nodded as if in great satisfaction and then turned to his questioner, saying, 'Then I recommend that you pay Caesar that which is due to Caesar – but pay to God what is due to him.'[5]

There was a murmur of approval from the crowd, many of whom recognised the dilemma posed by the question and the clever way that Jesus had defused the situation. Of course, some grumbled under their breath that they wouldn't pay taxes to Rome under any circumstances, but the Temple's stooge had been turned away with nothing incriminating to report back to Caiaphas.

Jesus continued his work in the Temple, preaching and telling stories, as well as talking with individuals from time to time. Finally, at the end of the afternoon, Jesus drew his work to a close and left the Temple. He dismissed the rest of his followers, asking them to go back to the garden of Gethsemane to start preparation of the supper there, while he set out for Justus's inn.

The innkeeper was delighted to see him. Jesus was especially pleased to find Nathan and Cleopas there also, for they had called in briefly following their day's work for a mug of local beer together. Jesus greeted the three friends warmly, asking after their families and listening to all their news.

'We saw you the other day, Jesus – riding on the donkey,' said Cleopas. 'I hope that you were pleased with the reception given to you by the town.'

Jesus was silent for a moment before answering, softly, 'You realised what I was doing, I hope,' he said. 'I came fulfilling Zechariah's prophesy. It was my unspoken claim to be the Messiah. Do you think that the people round you recognised that? What did they think?'

Cleopas pursed his lips and gestured interrogatively.

'Who can tell?' he said. 'I remembered the words of the prophet myself, but whether others did so, it is impossible to say.'

'What did you do today, Jesus?' asked Nathan, not wanting to be drawn into committing himself too far.

'I began by having a real go at the traders in the outer courtyard,' said the preacher grimly. 'I have always wanted to speak out against the business being carried on there and this time I did. I threw over several tables, released a few animals and birds and made quite a scene. Something they won't forget in a hurry.'

Cleopas looked horrified. 'What happened then?' he asked. 'It's a wonder you weren't run in by the guards.'

'Oh, we had it all planned out. My friends were all given specific duties to ensure that I could cover my retreat, but in the event the crowd took my part and covered me as I went into the inner courtyard, where I simply started preaching to the people. By the time the guard came in, all was sweetness and light!'

'How was your teaching received?' asked Nathan.

'As always, with a mixture of appreciation, uncertainty and hostility.'

Cleopas spoke up. 'Well, I shall be there in the morning, Jesus, if you're coming again. I should like to hear you speak again.'

Nathan nodded. 'Me too.'

Jesus smiled, glad to have the support of the pair.

'Thank you, my friends,' he said.

After the two shopkeepers had gone, Jesus turned to the inn landlord. Justus shook his head sadly.

'I'm just sorry I can't join you tomorrow as well,' he said, 'but at this time of the year, there's just too much to do in this place.'

Jesus opened his hands and smiled at the landlord. 'Of course there is – I understand, Justus – don't worry. But I want to ask a favour – something you may be able to do for me.'

'Anything'.

'I want to host an evening meal here in two days' time. I want to invite fourteen people.'

'The upper room is still available for you, and I can lay on the food,' replied Justus. 'I may need some help in preparation, though – we're very pushed at festival time.'

'That'll be fine. I'm sure some of my followers will help out. I'll send them over mid-afternoon. The only trouble is that they don't know this place. Can you suggest something?'

'I'll get young Mark to act as guide,' he said.

He called into the house and soon the young man appeared. He smiled when he saw Jesus and shook his hand gladly.

'You wanted me, Father?'

'Yes, son. Jesus is sending a couple of his men over the day after tomorrow to give us a hand in preparing a meal for his party that evening in the upper room. They don't know the way here, so I want you to meet them down by the well near the city gate.'

'No problem,' replied the young man instantly, but then his brow furrowed. 'But how will I know them – or how will they recognise me?'

The landlord thought for a moment and then an idea dawned.

'You could carry a large water pot, as if you were going to the well for water.[6] Since water-carrying is generally a woman's task, you will be sufficiently obvious to anyone looking for you.'

Mark's face was a picture! 'I'm not keen on that,' he grumbled. 'Fetching water isn't a man's job. I'll look – and feel – most peculiar.'

'Just do it for me!' Jesus laughed, clapping the young man on the shoulder. 'I'm sorry to cause you embarrassment, but it won't be for long.'

And so it was arranged.

★

By the time Jesus arrived back at the Temple, most people had drifted away to find some supper. He was able to slip into John's office unobserved, to find his friend still at work. John hurriedly closed the door behind him and took him into the inner office, hoping that nobody of consequence would come in while he had Jesus there. The Galilean was becoming hot property!

'I won't stay long, my friend,' said the preacher. 'I just wanted to ask you how things were going here.'

John briefly explained the attitude of the High Priest and cautioned Jesus yet again.

'If he can, Caiaphas will have you taken into custody and tried on some trumped up charge,' he said. 'You must be very careful. Stay in the crowd. Avoid all controversy.'

'Thank you for the warning, John. You're as good as gold, as usual.'

Then, with a wide smile, Jesus changed topics.

'Now, something much more pleasant,' he said. 'I'm hosting a supper for my friends the evening after next – Wednesday evening. Can you come? It'll be at Justus's place.'

'I wouldn't miss it for the world,' replied the priest. 'I'll be there – that'll give us another chance to compare notes.'

★

There was intense discussion as the disciples made their way back to Gethsemane, which continued while they prepared the evening meal.

'I'm not clear what Jesus hoped to achieve by that demonstration this morning,' said big James, voicing the feelings of several of the company.

Andrew gave his opinion.

'He's been wanting to condemn that business in the Temple for a long time,' he said, 'in fact, ever since I've known him. I suppose that he might have been hoping that the crowd would make more of a rumpus—'

'I thought he was trying to *avoid* a rumpus,' said Thomas.

'In fact the crowd were pretty supportive,' added Matthew. 'We had almost nothing to do in the finish – they simply carried him along with them into the inner courtyard… and it was all over. Just as well, too – the guards weren't far behind us.'

'It's all right for you!' growled Simon, gently fingering a black eye. 'I got this protecting Jesus from an irate stallholder!'

'You know you're really proud of it, too!' retorted Matthew. 'You alone have something to show for your day's work! Jesus was totally unharmed.'

'But did the incident succeed? The Temple authorities have not made the slightest move to recognise Jesus's claim to be the Messiah,' observed John.

'Did you seriously expect them to?' broke in Thomas petulantly. 'Nobody likes giving up his power base – and Caiaphas is no exception. He's in a cushy position now and he isn't going to move over for Jesus, or anyone else.'

'So where will Jesus go from here?' Peter seemed quite lost.

'Jesus will know what to do.' This from his brother. Andrew had great faith in his leader.

And so the discussion went on and on till Jesus arrived for his supper and the questions ground to a halt. They all knew that Jesus would tell them what he had in mind after supper was over. As expected, Jesus stood up to address them all when the meal was coming to an end.

'Thank you, my friends, for your support this morning. Everything went off smoothly, I thought. We made our point – the crowd, in the main, seemed to agree with the sentiments I expressed – and we made ourselves scarce pretty quickly and avoided any trouble with the guards. I gather from my contacts in the Temple that the High Priest wasn't pleased – I'm not surprised, since he gets a good rake-off from the trading. He suspects that we were to blame but isn't quite sure. Besides, he's nervous about acting against us while the crowd are around and supportive.'

'But where do we go from here?' asked Peter.

Jesus smiled and gazed at the big fisherman.

'We continue to teach in the Temple. I will teach the truth to the people and hope that they respond. Perhaps, even now, the authorities will see the truth and acknowledge it.'

Thomas decided to speak up, voicing the opinion he had expressed before Jesus came in.

'You may well be right, Thomas,' replied the preacher, 'but I can do no more than propagate the truth and hope to see a result. So it's back to the Temple in the morning. But' – and here Jesus's face broke into another wide smile – 'there's some good news. I'm hosting a Passover meal the evening after next. I know it's a day earlier than many folk celebrate the festival, but it follows the pattern laid down by the Essenes and I'd like to follow their tradition on this occasion. I owe them a lot even though I don't agree with all that they teach. It's going to be so good to celebrate the Feast together.'

★

Judas felt let down and frustrated. Another day had gone by, another opportunity had been lost. Jesus had had every chance to get the crowd going and demand changes at the Temple, yet all he had managed was merely symbolic in nature. Even when Jesus had been challenged directly about paying tribute to Caesar, he had ducked the issue. He had the world at his feet, Judas thought, yet he failed to capitalise on the fact.

The man from Gaza wandered off away from the camp up the Mount of Olives, skirting round the many pilgrim encampments and seeking solitude in the deep gloom under the ancient olive trees. There he cudgelled his brain. What could he do to help to bring in the Kingdom of God – that wonderful situation when Jews would rule and teach the whole world the truth about the Eternal One? Why wouldn't Jesus act?

He kicked impetuously at a stone on the rough path through the olive grove. The frustration was becoming overwhelming. He had followed Jesus now for two years. He had been the first to offer to follow him full-time, but Jesus didn't seem to trust him particularly, or favour him above the others.

Scowling, he recalled with disgust that Jesus seemed instead to favour those ignorant fishermen. What did they know? What could he do to hasten the coming of the Kingdom? He'd tried interesting Jesus in forming alliances with influential groups who wanted to free Israel from the yoke of the Romans, but without any sign of success. What was Jesus waiting for? Could it be that he didn't really know how to proceed and was waiting for others? It was confusing and highly frustrating.

Judas knew he was in for another bad night.

*

James and Joseph had arrived in the Temple after lunch for a time of prayer, but had been drawn by natural curiosity to join a crowd of pilgrims listening to a preacher. They quickly realised that they were listening to none other than their own brother! They stood at the back of the gathering with a torrent of mixed feelings storming through their minds. On the one hand, Jesus seemed to be putting forward eminently sensible advice and advancing cogent arguments for his way of life. You had to admire him. The crowd certainly seemed to be enthralled by his words and sympathetic to the message he preached. And it was not just the words themselves; somehow he seemed able to hold his audience with that gentle voice and those blazing eyes. Mind you, there were times when his voice rose and the attitude became stern – when, for instance, he criticised the Pharisees, or other so-called religious leaders – but generally he wrapped his listeners in a cocoon of God's love and care, making them feel wanted and part of the great family of heaven.

On the other hand, however, they realised that the criticism directed at the religious establishment could well bring trouble on their brother's head – and if he were disgraced it would bring odium on the whole family. It wasn't right that Jesus should set himself up in this way and bring all of them into disrepute. The news would be bound to get back to Nazareth, and what would people think? These feelings were greatly enhanced when they overheard a couple of fellows discussing the events of the morning. How could Jesus engage in such disgusting goings-on? Disturbing the licensed traders in the courtyard, indeed! The High Priest himself had arranged for them to trade in the precinct for the benefit of pilgrims, so who was Jesus to question their right to be there?

Meanwhile, Mary, Jesus's mother, who was visiting the Court of the Women, met up with Nimrah and Mary from Magdala. The latter had been discussing Jesus's entry into Jerusalem two days earlier, and his mother had gradually engaged herself in their conversation. She had kept her identity to herself to begin with, as she was most interested to know what the strangers thought of her son. She was soon in no doubt that they were firm supporters of the Nazarene, eccentric though she herself believed him to be.

'But what was his purpose in entering in style like that?' she asked, timidly.

The younger Mary answered immediately. 'You must know the prophesy – Jesus was inviting all of us to recognise him as the Messiah – the one who is to come.'

'Do you believe that?'

'We hope that it's so,' replied Nimrah, more carefully. 'We have followed the progress of Jesus's mission now for nearly two years. He has taught from the heart and seems to know, instinctively, what God wants from him – and us all.'

'I don't think it's instinct, Mother,' put in the young woman. 'Jesus has to listen carefully to God – you know how he always keeps quiet times early each morning for contemplation, thought and prayer.'

'You're right, of course,' smiled Nimrah. 'Jesus is a wonderful man, blessed by God with great charm and charisma – everyone loves him. He is very gifted too and has healed all manner of diseases and conditions. Surely, he must be from God. Why should he not be our Messiah?'

'Not everyone loves him,' the older Mary had said, rather grimly. 'He's in trouble with the authorities, both at home in Galilee – and here in Jerusalem, no doubt, after his activities this week. He'll make big trouble for himself if he's not careful.'

At this point, Mary's voice had begun to break and she had had to turn away to hide her distress.

'Whatever's the matter?' Nimrah's natural sympathy came to the fore immediately, even though she had only just met the other woman. She put her arm round Mary's shoulder, now shaking from emotion. The situation became clear as Mary unburdened herself of her problem, admitting her relationship with Jesus. She tried to explain her fears, her worries, her distress.

'You see, we know he's only a carpenter,' sobbed Mary. 'Why does he set himself up to be something great?'

'He may have been a carpenter in years gone by,' returned the younger Mary, 'but now he's shown us, at any rate, that he's much more than that. He's more than any ordinary man. You should be proud of him!'

'Of course I'm proud of him – in a way!' cried his mother. 'But why did he have to go off like that, leaving his family, living like a vagabond and stirring up trouble for himself, first with King Antipas and now with the High Priest? He's a good boy – none better – but...'

Mary's voice broke again and she had to cover her face to hide her tears. Nimrah drew her aside and tried to console her.

'We'll see you back to where you're staying,' she said.

They met up with Jesus's brothers and made their way back to their respective inns. But the family from Nazareth was worried and puzzled.

NOTES

[1] Mark 11:17; Isaiah 56:7.
[2] Mark 12:41–44.
[3] Mark 13:35.
[4] Luke 11:33.
[5] Mark 12:17.
[6] Mark 14:13.

The tension mounts

Jesus was hard at work the next day, all day, teaching in the Temple precinct. When he was not addressing the crowd, he was talking to individuals – befriending, encouraging, advising and counselling. His themes were the same as they had always been – God's love and forgiveness, his willingness to include all who wished in his Kingdom and his hope that all men would respond to the invitation. The preacher stressed repeatedly the need for real care to be shown to others as a measure of this response to God. Jesus continued to contrast the showy, superficial religion of the Pharisees and scribes with the genuine devotion required if life were to be lived his way. He encouraged his hearers to give themselves genuinely to God's work, rather than simply following a set of rules and regulations.

'I'm not pretending that the life in the Kingdom is easy,' he said. 'It's not. It can be very difficult and demanding, but it is really rewarding. In the end, you will know you have made the right choice. Enter the Kingdom through its narrow gate. The road to destruction is wide – there is plenty of room on it and consequently many go that way; but the gateway to real life is small and its way is narrow, and so, unfortunately, few will choose it. However, it is the only way to lasting happiness.'[1]

The Sadducees, Jews belonging to the High Priest's party, sent a representative to test Jesus, who, of course, was well aware that Sadducees didn't believe in an afterlife. He was, therefore, not surprised at the man's question.

'Master,' he said, 'can I ask a question? The Law requires that if a man dies childless, his brother should marry the widow and have children to continue the family name.'[2]

Jesus smiled and raised an eyebrow. The man continued.

'In the case I have in mind, a fellow died childless and so his brother married her, but he also died without having a child. Another brother therefore married her, but he, too, died without children. This situation repeated itself several times, till at last she had married all seven brothers! Finally, she herself died.'

'I'm not surprised,' quipped someone at the back of the crowd. 'About time too!'

The questioner turned round, irritated by the interruption, but Jesus only smiled and asked, 'So what is your question?'

The Sadducee straightened himself and asked, innocently, 'In the afterlife, whose wife will she be? After all, she's belonged to them all. Will the first get her, or the last, or…?'

'What about sharing her round? One day a week!' came another wisecrack from the crowd.

Jesus did not respond to that, but dealt with the original point.

'When we rise from the dead, things then will be very different from life here on earth. There will be no marriage as such, but we shall live more like the angels in heaven. Exactly what heaven will be like, nobody but God knows, but be assured, there is life with him, eternal life, and this term "eternal" indicates a life of a real quality, not just a life that goes on for ever. After all, Moses, in the book of the Law, refers to God as 'The God of Abraham, Isaac and Jacob.' Now, Moses is hardly likely to refer to God as a God of the dead, is he? No. God is the God of the living. Our forefathers, therefore, live still, as we shall.'

In a break between preaching, Jesus had time to greet Nathan and Cleopas, who had been in the crowd listening to him.

'You must be worn out,' commented the latter. 'I'll bet you haven't stopped all day! When you're not preaching, you're taking on board the troubles and questions of individuals. Did you get any lunch?'

'We had a short break,' replied the Nazarene, with a rueful grin.

'I wonder. Just look after yourself,' returned Cleopas. 'We need you in good shape if you are really to do the work of our Messiah and save Israel from her sins.'

'I shall try to fulfil what God has in mind for me,' Jesus said. 'That is what we all must do.'

'But when will we see the full revelation of the Kingdom?' asked Nathan.

Jesus paused and looked him full in the face before speaking.

'The Kingdom is here now, already among you and within you, if you can find it, but the Kingdom will be revealed still more clearly shortly – well within your lifetime.[3] Wait and watch and pray! The final revelation of the Kingdom is a matter for God alone – I don't know when that will be.'

'I'm not sure I understand.' Nathan puckered up his face in perplexity. 'What is it, exactly, that is to happen soon?'

'Wait and watch and pray,' was the answer.

★

Judas was in a slough of despondency. Once again he wandered off on his own up the Mount of Olives after supper, racking his brains for ideas as to how to bring Jesus to a point of real action. He was tired from lack of proper sleep, having tossed and turned all night, not only on the previous night, but for several nights before that. The question kept going round and round in his mind: Why doesn't he act?

Then an idea gradually began to form in his mind. Why shouldn't he, Judas, take the initiative? Why not? Why should it always be Jesus that called the tune? Perhaps his leader might actually appreciate some help. What could he do to help?

Perhaps he should arrange for a kind of showdown between the Temple authorities and Jesus. The seed of the idea was sown and started to germinate... What if he went to the High Priest and offered to arrange a meeting between Jesus and their representative? Would Jesus attend? Would the High Priest attend? No. Upon reflection, Judas concluded that there was no future in that idea. The more he thought about it, the more he worried that one or the other party might back out. The opportunity would then be lost. What else could he do?

Jesus had indicated that somehow he already knew the authorities were reacting adversely to his message and his claim, but how could the Temple authorities take any real action against him, when the crowd were so supportive – and so numerous? But what if Jesus could somehow be taken into custody and put on trial? Then, surely, there would be a showdown and Jesus would have to meet the challenge head-on and see it off. If he were truly the Messiah, Judas felt that ultimately Jesus must win against all the odds. God must see his Messiah safely through... But if, after all, it turned out that Jesus wasn't the chosen one, then, of course, he shouldn't win. In that case, he, Judas, would have been responsible for disposing of a charlatan... and rightly so. On that basis, what was there to lose?

So it boiled down to this. How could Jesus be brought to trial? Judas licked his lips, for his mouth had gone dry with the thought of forcing his boss into his enemies' hands, but Jesus must win the ensuing battle of wits to prove himself – so it must be all right to think the unthinkable...

He decided he would go to the Temple authorities in the morning and offer to lead them to the camp here in Gethsemane during the evening, or even better at night, when everyone else was asleep. Could he do this – for God? The question burned into his mind. Had he the courage? Yes, by heaven, he would do it. In the end, he, Judas, would be seen to be right – a servant of God and loyal at least to the purpose behind the Messiah. If Jesus hadn't the courage to see things through to their proper conclusion, he would have to force him to find the courage. He'd give him the impetus to face up to the challenge.

It was a determined Judas that made his way back to camp that evening, but, again, he didn't sleep very well. It was a long night.

★

Thaddeus had no difficulty sleeping, for he had had a fair walk at the end of the day. Jesus had asked him to walk as far as Bethany and call at Lazarus's house, to invite him to join the disciples at supper the following evening. Lazarus had, naturally, been delighted to be included with the rest of the intimate followers of Jesus and was particularly glad to hear that John barHelez was also included in the party.

'It'll be like old times,' he said. 'Jesus, John and I have been friends for years now. It'll be good to have time with them both and hear how Jesus feels his mission is going.'

'He seems very anxious to have us all there,' returned Thaddeus. 'I think he may use the occasion to say something pretty significant. He's being very guarded about his detailed plans at the moment – perhaps he'll make everything clear then. Anyway, come at sundown please. I gather you know where Justus's inn is.'

'I'll be there.'

*

The following day, Jesus made his way to the Temple again, followed by his little band. Once more he stood up in the courtyard reserved for Jewish men and started to teach the pilgrims coming to pray, contemplate and discuss all manner of religious topics. As before, between preaching episodes, Jesus talked quietly and confidentially with those who wanted a word with him, his followers trying to ensure that everyone was given some time with the teacher in something approaching privacy.

At mid-morning, Judas came and told Jesus that he ought to go and do some shopping for the group. Supper was already organised, of course, but some items were required for breakfast the following morning. Jesus nodded, happy to leave details to such a competent lieutenant, but Judas didn't spend all his time shopping in the market. Making sure that nobody from Jesus's party was around, he slipped into the offices of the High Priest and asked to see him. The Levite on duty raised his eyebrows at this strange request. What on earth would this less than ordinary-looking person want with the High Priest?

'Wait here a moment,' he said.

He left Iscariot seated in the outer office while he went through to consult John barHelez, who, like his junior, was surprised that someone should just walk in off the street and have the nerve to ask to see as exalted a personage as the High Priest himself. John went to the door and opened it a crack, so that he could form some judgement for himself of the person making such a request. He was naturally greatly surprised when he saw who it was sitting outside, for he instantly recognised the person who had come to his house in Jericho only a couple of weeks ago, asking for Jesus. Why on earth was Judas, of all people, here? wondered John. If Jesus had sent him, surely he would have asked for John personally? The priest concluded that it was most unlikely that Judas was in the office with Jesus's knowledge, so it might be that he had something in mind against his leader's interests. At all events, John decided that he wouldn't see this visitor – it would be better to be discreet and stay in the background, waiting to see what transpired.

He told the Levite to ask Judas who he was and what he wanted. The junior returned saying the matter was private and needed to be discussed with the

High Priest personally. John sent him back again with the retort that unless he at least indicated what his business was, he'd be shown the door. Judas's response to this was that he had important information concerning the man Jesus, from Nazareth, but he was not prepared to reveal any details to anyone except the High Priest. John pondered for a few moments, then told the Levite to leave Judas waiting while he went to see if the High Priest would see this intruder.

He was lucky. Nobody was with the High Priest at that moment and he was able to access him without difficulty. He passed on Judas's request. Caiaphas sat stroking his long beard for a few moments before saying, uncertainly, 'I'd better see this fellow, I suppose. Do we know anything about him?'

John lied confidently. 'He wouldn't give us his name, My Lord, and, of course, I've never seen before, but I agree it would be useful for you to see him. Shall I ask him to come in now?'

'Yes. You had better come in too, to witness what has been said.'

John thought hurriedly.

'I wonder whether I am the best person, sir,' he prevaricated. 'With chaps like this, off the street, I think you should have greater personal protection. Please allow me to call the guard. The Levite can stay with you, if you wish, as a witness.'

Caiaphas looked surprised momentarily and hesitated, but agreed.

'Perhaps you're right. I'll leave you to arrange everything, then.'

John beat a hasty retreat before his superior could change his mind. He sent the Levite to find two burly guards and tell them to march Judas under escort in to see the High Priest. He then had to wait for what seemed like an age in a frenzy of anxiety, to see what would transpire. In fact, he didn't have to wait too long. Caiaphas rang the bell for him to join him in his office only about twenty minutes later.

'The man's name is Judas Iscariot,' reported Caiaphas. 'He is a follower of this Jesus, it appears, but he wants to sell his leader to us, if you please. What do you think of that?'

'I'm amazed, sir,' replied John, this time quite honestly. 'I should have thought that a man like Jesus might have attracted some loyalty from his followers, but – apparently not. Did he say why he wanted to sell the fellow in?'

'Not really. I suspect he's had enough and wants to get out. He's tired of following a nobody around, someone who's never going to make it. He wants to return to decent living with no stain on his character. He wants our assurance that he wouldn't be prosecuted himself. I agreed to that.'

Caiaphas paused, rose from his chair and moved closer to John, before continuing.

'I told him that we were anxious to interview Jesus and we would appreciate it if he would lead us to him at a time when he was alone – or, at least, well away from the crowds of pilgrims – say, at night. Judas promised to let me know when this can be arranged, but he thinks it might be possible as early as tonight, because Jesus is apparently planning to eat in the city, then sleep on the Mount of Olives.[4] If not tonight, then tomorrow night.'

The High Priest paused to see if John had any comment, but his assistant, his head spinning with the implications of all this, could think of nothing to say. Caiaphas turned away and walked back to his desk.

'I've made it clear that the price for this task will be thirty silver shillings – not a penny more,' he concluded.[5]

John found his tongue at last.

'We've been fortunate, My Lord,' he muttered. 'It's turned out very well for us.'

The High Priest nodded. 'Yes. With any luck, we ought to have this Jesus under arrest tonight, bring him to trial tomorrow and possibly have him put out of the way before the festival proper starts. It'll mean an interview with that dreadful man, Pilate, to get the sentence confirmed, but it can't be helped.'

John, his mind whirling, excused himself as swiftly as possible and made his way back to the privacy of his own office,. Things were moving very fast and in a terrifying direction. He must warn Jesus quickly. Fortunately, he was due to see him at supper at sundown. Yes, that should give his friend time to make his escape; there was no need to worry him during the day. He'd be protected by the crowd of pilgrims till tonight. John briefly bowed his head in thanksgiving, that he was able to help his friend and protect him from the very people who ought to be welcoming him as Messiah and Lord. His head was spinning and he found himself sitting looking blankly at the wall, dazed and numb. Whatever would Jesus do now – now it was quite clear that his life was actually in danger?

★

Meantime, Jesus continued to preach and teach just outside in the Court of the Jews till lunch time. He then indicated to the disciples that he would break for lunch and they decided to take themselves outside the city walls, down into the Kedron Valley. There they opened their lunch-bags, brought with them from their camp on the hill, and rested.

Jesus was sitting next to the fishermen, Peter, Andrew, James and John. A strange silence fell on the little group, with each man lost in his own thoughts. After a while, John, looking up at the towering walls of the Temple rising high above them, exclaimed, 'Look at the huge stones up there in those walls! It must have taken hundreds of men to shift them into place. The result is simply marvellous to look at. Isn't it a wonderful building?'

His brother murmured his agreement, but Jesus spoke very seriously.

'I'll make this prediction, John. Before long, this great Temple will be flattened. There'll hardly be one stone left on another! It'll be destroyed utterly.'[6]

'Whatever do you mean?' queried Peter, aghast.

'Just what I say,' returned Jesus. 'The Temple of Herod will not be here much longer.'

'When will all this happen?' asked Andrew. 'Will it be linked to the coming of the Kingdom?'

Jesus replied, 'There are going to be all manner of disturbances. Many men will set themselves up claiming to represent me, or claiming to be the Messiah themselves. Some people will follow them and be disappointed. There are going to be all manner of riots and wars... it's bound to happen. You've seen the mood of the people so often – they're ready for it. The nation will be in tumult. Family members will fight each other, father against son, brother against brother, children against parents, and, in this situation, many will turn on you because of your friendship for me. I'm afraid that you are going to be called upon to suffer – you'll be hauled up before judges, maybe even governors or kings – you may well be beaten in the Synagogues – all for the sake of the gospel message that I have taught.[7] But you must keep the faith and continue to proclaim the good news... You mustn't be alarmed – God will tell you what to say in every circumstance. Hold on to the end – it'll be worth it. I hope that this warning will help you to be forearmed.'

The fishermen didn't know how to reply to this catalogue of disaster. Their faces betrayed their inner confusion and feeling of foreboding and desolation.

Jesus continued, 'You remember the saying of the prophet Joel?

"I will show portents in the sky and on earth,
blood and fire and columns of smoke;
the sun shall be turned into darkness and the moon into blood,
before the great and terrible day of the Lord comes."[8]

'Joel is giving us a picture of the terror that will befall before the Kingdom finally dawns, but when that day comes, the Son of Man will come in glory and the Kingdom will be opened to everyone – yes, everyone.'

'When is all this to come about?' quavered John, his voice barely audible.

'I don't know the hour or the day – that is a matter for God, as I have often told you before – but I am sure that the Kingdom will come, essentially, in your lifetime. You will be able to testify to it.'

This flood of terrifying news was so uncharacteristic of Jesus that his friends didn't know how to respond. There was a long, difficult pause while each tried to digest and make sense of what he had said. On the one hand, he seemed to be clear that the Kingdom was really at hand, yet on the other there were dreadful implications about suffering and bloodshed and destruction... it was all very confusing.

Jesus seemed to sense their mood, for he smiled and said, in a way much more typical of him, 'Don't worry, now. I have told you these things so that when they happen, or threaten to happen, you will know that they are inevitable. Then you won't be frightened and shirk what has to be done. Be comforted. We will win through!'

With that, Jesus turned away and took himself off for a walk, leaving the fishermen to contemplate alone. Before long, however, he returned, apparently refreshed in mind and spirit. He called over to Peter and John and asked them to go to Justus's inn to help prepare for the supper that evening. He told them the arrangements he had made to find the place. They exchanged rueful smiles, knowing how much a seventeen-year-old lad would enjoy the task of carrying water! The things Jesus expected people to do for the sake of the Kingdom!

★

At sundown, the party assembled at the inn. Lazarus had walked in from Bethany that evening. Peter, John and Mark showed them to the upper room where everything had been made ready for them. A couple of large braziers had been lit at the extremes of the room, as, once the sun had gone down, the evening air would become quite chill. The men were standing around, chatting in twos and threes, when Justus arrived and made his way over to Jesus, who happened to be with Simon and little James. They were recalling the difficulties of being blacksmiths and contrasting their lives now with what had gone before.

'Would you have a few moments to greet some friends of yours?' asked Justus.

'Of course,' replied Jesus, surprised. 'Which friends are these?'

'Wait and see!' The landlord smiled, signalling to Mark to go and summon the 'friends'.

It didn't take long for Joanna and her comrades to make their way to the upper room. There they were greeted very kindly by Jesus and the rest of the Galileans. It was pleasant to be in the company of women for a change! They exchanged news, the women asking especially about Jesus's teaching mission in the Temple, and the reaction of the crowd.

'They seemed to be very interested,' said Peter. 'Jesus holds their attention better than the scribes who are lecturing there. He speaks from the heart.'

Joanna sought out Judas and pressed a gift into his hand for the funds. 'This is from us all,' she said. 'You'll put it to good use I know.' Judas acknowledged the gift with a stiff bow.

Just then, the door opened again and Mark showed Nimrah and Mary into the room. There were more greetings and more exchange of news. Nimrah was anxious to tell Jesus how she and Mary had met his mother in the Temple and how worried she had been about him.

'My mother is a real treasure,' said Jesus. 'I suppose it's natural for a mother to care about a son, but, you know, she has never really understood that I have to do my heavenly father's bidding. I'm afraid I have been a great worry to her, but I have no alternative. I have to follow the great purpose…'

'Perhaps she can't accept things with her mind, but her heart is yours, I'm sure,' replied Nimrah. 'I'm a mother too – remember?'

She looked fondly at her own daughter, about whom, not so long ago, she had had so many doubts. Thankfully, now the two were able to understand each other much better.

The door opened again to admit John barHelez. He too was introduced to everyone and the whole group enjoyed a few minutes chatting together before Justus whispered to Jesus that the supper was now almost ready for serving.

The ladies took the hint and were preparing to retire, when, just as they were leaving, Jesus caught Mary's arm and asked, 'Would you do something for me, please?'

Mary didn't hesitate. 'Of course. Anything. What is it?'

'I'd like to send a little gift to my mother. Could you get it to her for me, if I have it brought here? And give her my love…'

'That's easy. I would be very happy to see your mother again and take your gift.'

Jesus smiled his thanks. Mary was to remember that smile for years afterwards.

'I'll ask Mark to come back to Gethsemane with us tonight and bring the package back here with him. He can give it to you in the morning,' Jesus said. Then, to all the women, he added politely, 'Goodbye. Thank you all for coming.'

The women tore themselves away at last. Jesus introduced John barHelez to all the Galileans, many of whom had not had that pleasure.

'We've heard so much about you,' said Peter to him. 'My brother, Andrew, met you a couple of years ago, but I was at home earning the money – catching fish!'

'I gather you've known Jesus a long time,' asked big James, also in on the conversation.

'A very long time,' replied John. 'He's been a tremendous friend to me, through some difficult times – for both of us.'

One by one, the others shook hands with the priest. Some were a little in awe – but John soon put them at their ease. When it came to Judas, however, John had the greatest difficulty in keeping his face friendly and pretending to be pleased to see him again. As soon as he could, he drew Jesus to one side and explained all that had happened that morning at the office of the High Priest.

Jesus received the news with scarcely a flicker in his face. When John finished, the preacher pursed his lips and momentarily stroked his beard. Then he muttered to John, 'It had to happen, but it's a tragedy for the person concerned.'[9]

'I'm more concerned about you – and how you're going to get away,' urged John. 'We'd better cut this meal as short as possible, and then you can be out of here and away – perhaps back to Bethany with Lazarus… or what about your friend in Bethphage – Matthias, was it? Can you go there?'

Jesus looked at him steadily for a second, then spoke very firmly.

'I'm not running away, John. I expect I could, if I felt that that was the thing God wanted me to do, but maybe, after all, this confrontation with Caiaphas is what God wants. Let the High Priest take me and we will see what happens then.'

'What do you have in mind?' John's voice betrayed his fear for his friend.

'I must think about that and pray about it. I think I know what I'm called to do, but you've given me some warning and time to pray it through, to be sure.'

Just then, Justus called them to take their places at the table. The men reclined on low couches arranged in a horseshoe, so that everyone could easily be served from inside the half-circle. Jesus, as the host, was offered the place in the centre of the horseshoe, but before he took it, Jesus whispered something to Justus, who, with a look of great puzzlement on his face, called to Mark and sent the young man on an errand. Jesus indicated that he wished to have barHelez next to him on his right, while he asked Peter to take his place on his left, with Andrew next to him. Next to John, Jesus placed Lazarus, then Judas, then John and James, the two fishermen. He then invited the other Galileans to take their places round the room, Matthew with Thomas, Philip with Nathaniel and the two blacksmiths close to their friend Thaddeus as usual.

As the friends settled in their positions, Mark returned carrying a bowl of water and a towel. Jesus rose, removed his top garment, then fastened the towel round his waist and moved to the bottom of the table where Thaddeus was sitting.[10]

'Let me take your sandals off,' said Jesus softly.

Thaddeus could hardly believe his ears.

'What? – Why? –' he stammered.

'Let me wash your feet for you, my friend,' said Jesus, still in that low, sweet voice of his.

Staggered, Thaddeus allowed his leader to take his sandals from his feet, then he watched as Jesus stooped to bathe his feet and wipe them dry with towel. When this was done, Jesus moved on to little James, repeating his gesture, then to Simon, and so on down the table until he came to Peter.

'It's not right that you should wash my feet,' said the big fisherman. 'It's a job for a servant, that. I should rather be washing yours!'

'You may not understand what I'm doing now, Peter, but you will, one day,' replied the preacher. 'I must wash your feet, if you want to be one with me.'

'Then not just my feet, Jesus,' cried Peter. 'Wash my head and my hands too…'

Jesus smiled and held up his hands in a gesture.

'Your feet are enough, Peter. That symbolises that you are clean all over. And you will be clean – clean inside and out – all of you, all who have remained faithful to me and to all I have tried to do.'

Jesus continued around the table until all his guests had been washed. Then he removed the towel and took his place at the top of the table.

'Let me try to explain what I have done,' he said. 'Peter has rightly said that the washing of visitors' feet is usually done by a servant. It is conventionally his job to deal with dusty, smelly feet, but you must understand that, in the new Kingdom, the one who leads has to be prepared to be just such a servant to everyone. I have been your leader for nearly two years. You normally treat me with some respect because of that – and that's right and proper – but I'm saying that the leader has to be prepared to do the dirty jobs! If you want to lead, you must be prepared to do all the things that you want your followers to do. You too are going to be leaders in the Kingdom, so you had better get used to the idea of serving like that – and start by serving each other! I am showing you by example – for the Son of Man didn't come to be served, but to serve and to suffer for many.'[11]

The followers of Jesus looked from one to another. They sensed that every one around the table was feeling uncomfortable They knew well enough that Jesus had always taught that service to others was the way, yet they had been caught out; for none of them had offered to wash the feet of their friends when they arrived. It had been left to Jesus. He had seen to it that they were all comfortable after their walk up the hill to the city. It was a lesson they wouldn't forget in a hurry – it was an acted parable.

But Jesus had taken his seat again. He looked around at his friends and said sadly, 'I am so glad to have had this opportunity of eating this last Passover supper with you. I've been looking forward to this evening so much.'

The silence in the room became tangible. The question in everyone's mind was, Why a 'last supper'? But nobody could bring themselves to put the question to Jesus.

Their leader continued, 'I tell you this – I shan't eat a Passover supper with you again, until it is fulfilled in the Kingdom of God.'[12]

Jesus motioned to Justus to begin serving the Passover meal. The roasted lamb was brought and set on the table. The spices, herbs and unleavened bread were passed from person to person. Wine was passed round for every participant to fill his cup and the meal began, but it was now overshadowed with apprehension and foreboding. John bent close to Jesus and asked, hesitantly, 'What do you mean, Jesus – 'last supper'? What is going to happen? Is the confrontation with the High Priest which is coming soon going to initiate the coming of the Kingdom?'

His friend did not reply immediately. He nibbled at some herbs before indicating with a tiny nod towards Judas and saying, 'I must go the way that has been set before me, but it is so sad that one of my own people has to be the one to betray me.[13] However, my suffering will be a means of grace to all.'

John kept silent after that, not knowing what to say. Around the room, the disciples were discussing quietly between themselves what Jesus could possibly have meant.

'I think that Jesus knows he's heading for problems with the Temple authorities,' said Thomas to Matthew. 'We all knew the risks involved in coming to Jerusalem. I always thought we'd all finish up dead as a result.'[14]

Matthew snorted. 'You're always so pessimistic, Thomas! Jesus knows what he's about. I interpret his remark much more hopefully – it simply means that the Kingdom will definitely dawn before the next Passover.'

Thomas shook his head. 'No. He meant that this would be his last supper with us. We've had many, many meals with Jesus, in rich homes, poor homes, as well as many out in the countryside. Why should this be the last one? No. I've a feeling he believes that something significant is going to happen tonight, or tomorrow, which will split us away from him.'

The meal continued in the traditional way. Thanksgiving prayers were said and appropriate responses made. Ceremonial cups of wine were drunk, bread was broken and eaten, the lamb was shared. Hands were washed between the courses, as had been done through the centuries. But towards the end of the meal, Jesus rose to speak again, taking a piece of unleavened bread in his hands and breaking it into many small fragments.

'This represents my body,' he said.[15] 'Take and eat it – to remember me.'[16]

The broken bread was passed round to each person at the table and each took and ate, rather fearfully, for the words were burning into their very beings. Remember Jesus? How could they ever forget? What did all this really mean? Their faces became distorted with perplexity and fear.

Justus then served Jesus with a large mug full of wine, ruby red. The leader looked at it for a moment, then spoke in a whisper to them all.

'This represents my blood.[17] It is God's new covenant with you all – a new promise. God is telling you that his love is eternal. His love is poured out, just like this wine, to assure you of forgiveness for all your wrongdoing and inadequacy. This promise is to be sealed in my blood. Drink it now, all of you. I tell you plainly, I will not drink wine again until I drink it in the Kingdom of heaven.'

Again, the cup was passed from hand to hand, each man taking a small sip, though scarcely understanding what Jesus had said. Peter tried to engage Jesus in conversation.

'Whatever does all this mean? What is going to happen that is so final?'

Jesus replied, 'I have to go away from you all soon, Peter. I am going somewhere none of you can follow.'

This was too much for Peter. Big, brash Peter could not conceive that he was inadequate to any task or journey.

'I'll follow you anywhere,' he declared, 'even if I have to die in the process.'

Jesus looked into his eyes with sadness, sighed and replied, 'You mean well, Peter, but I have to tell you that this journey is too much even for you.'

Peter tried to interrupt, but he was silenced by a small gesture from his leader.

'Oh, yes, Peter. You will disown me, even tonight. Before the cock crows to herald tomorrow's dawn, you will have denied me three times.'[18]

Peter was hurt, deeply hurt, that Jesus should say such a thing. He decided not to say anything more, for fear that he would say something even more hurtful himself and strain their friendship. The meal continued with nobody speaking in more than a whisper to his neighbour. Philip asked Nathaniel if he knew what Jesus was talking about, but the older man shook his head in bewilderment.

'I can't be sure, Philip, but I can't escape the feeling that Jesus knows that things are coming to a head and he's going to be taken away from us. Why he's so pessimistic tonight I can't say. He's in a mood of great depression – and yet, underneath it, he seems almost – well – *exultant*. It is as if he thinks that a victory is in sight. I can't work it out.'

'What did he mean about a new covenant? What was wrong with the old one, made with Abraham and the faithful of the nation ever since?'

'The prophet Jeremiah spoke about a new covenant that would come about some day, my son,' answered Nathaniel. 'He foretold that at that time the Law would be set down, not on scrolls, but in the inner beings of men, within their hearts.'[19] Then everyone will know for themselves what God wants of them, and everyone will be close to God in a way that our present law does not permit.'

As the meal was coming to an end, Judas saw his opportunity and decided to make his escape. He waited until John was deep in conversation with Lazarus, and Peter with Andrew, and sidled up to Jesus and said, 'I thought, Jesus, that, since it is Passover, you would like me to make a gift on behalf of us all to charity. Our common purse is in reasonably good shape at present. We've had gifts from several of our rich friends lately, so, if you like, I'll go and see to that now.'

Jesus looked him straight in the eye for a long moment.

'You must go and do what is necessary,' he said.

A look of uncertainty and fear passed across the treasurer's face for a brief moment. Did Jesus somehow know what he was really intending to do? How could he? He couldn't know. It must be just my imagination, he thought. All this flashed through his mind in a second. Then he pulled himself together and said, as nonchalantly as he could, 'Right, then. I'll be off.'

And with that, he left the room.

Lazarus and John were still discussing the strange words that Jesus had used. What did Jesus mean by talking about God's forgiveness being linked to his blood? God's forgiveness had always been linked in Jewish tradition to the sacrificial blood of animals. At no time in the Jewish calendar was this more true. At Passover, thousands of lambs had always been killed as sacrifices, commemorating the deliverance of the Israelites from Egypt more than a thousand years earlier. Strict Jews would still daub their doorposts with the blood of a sacrificed animal, as the original Israelites had done in Egypt,[20] to signify to the angel of death that he should pass over them and not enter the house on his errand of doom.

'In what way can Jesus offer himself as a sacrifice?' asked Lazarus. 'Surely he cannot mean that he is to have his throat cut, as we cut the throats of the lambs at Passover time?'

'I just don't know, Lazarus,' replied John, shaking his head. 'I can't think what Jesus has in mind, but I don't like the sound of it. I've warned him tonight that I know the High Priest has a plan to capture him, and heaven knows what could result if that happens. I've urged him to go immediately after the meal with you to Bethany and escape back to Galilee, but he doesn't seem to be interested. It's almost as if he's set on following a path to disaster. I don't like it a bit.'

The two friends were still talking this over as Jesus stood at the conclusion of the meal to address his followers.

'I've talked to you many times and given you much teaching,' he began. 'I've tried to deal with a wide number of different issues that arise in life, but I cannot cover everything that will ever crop up – there will be many circumstances that occur that I haven't foreseen. However, the undergirding principle is clear and should guide you in all eventualities. That principle is love. Love for God and love for each other. If you remember nothing else, remember this; love is the fulfilment of every law. My last word to you, therefore, is to love each other, just as I have loved each of you.'[21]

Turning to Justus, Jesus extended his thanks on behalf of the entire group, coupled with a word to Peter, John and Mark who had assisted before the meal. Finally, he said, 'Come, let us sing a psalm of thanksgiving and depart.'

At Jesus's request, Mark came with them so that he could bring back the package for Mary. He was glad enough to be included in the circle of Jesus's friends, for, by now, he was very attached to the Galilean preacher. They all took their leave of Justus and Gomer, and Jesus led them out into the now quiet street. There, John bade the Galileans goodnight, but contrived to draw Jesus to one side for one last plea.

'Go out to Bethany, Jesus. It's not safe in or near town tonight – you know that.'

'I am going to Gethsemane,' replied his friend. 'There I will pray and then I shall know what I must do.'

'Please do it quickly.' John shook Jesus's hand one last time and walked rapidly away, not wanting to show Jesus the emotion in his heart. He had the horrid feeling that he would never speak confidentially to his friend again. He made his solitary way to his own apartments in the Temple complex, while the others made their way to the east gate, the one used by Jesus on his triumphal procession into the Holy City only three days earlier. From there, they stumbled down the hill into the Kedron Valley and began to climb the slope of the Mount of Olives, pausing at the entrance to the garden of the Gethsemane on its lower slopes, to bid Lazarus goodnight.

'When shall I see you again, Jesus?'

'When God allows,' came the enigmatic reply. 'Give my love to your sisters – and God bless you all.'

Lazarus departed for Bethany alone. The rest were glad to be back at their little campsite and started to get ready for sleep, but Jesus signalled to the three fishermen, James, John and Peter, that they should follow him as he made his way further up the hill into the olive groves. So preoccupied was he, that he forgot that he had asked Mark to come and collect a package. The young man was left sitting by the campfire, waiting for Jesus to return.

NOTES

[1] Matt. 7:13.
[2] Matt. 22:24.
[3] Mark 9:1.
[4] Luke 21:37.
[5] Matt. 26:15.
[6] Mark 13:2.
[7] Mark 13:9.
[8] Joel 2:30.
[9] Luke 22:22.
[10] John 13:4–5.
[11] Mark 10:45.
[12] Luke 22:16.
[13] Mark 14:21.
[14] John 11:16.
[15] Mark 14:22.
[16] I Cor. 11:24.
[17] Mark 14:24–25.
[18] John 13:38.
[19] Jeremiah 31:33.
[20] Exodus 12:7.
[21] John 13:34.

The arrest

After he had left the party at the inn, Judas had walked quickly along the narrow street towards the High Priest's office. The air was distinctly chilly after the warmth of the upper room, but, away from the charged atmosphere of the supper party, he felt, at last, quite sure of what he was doing and determined to see it through. He was glad to be acting, rather than agonising. It didn't take him many minutes to cover the distance. He knocked at the massive door and waited for what seemed like an eternity until the Levite answered. He gave his name and, this time, he was let into the office swiftly. The Levite sought confirmation of his business. Judas responded briefly.

'Yes. Good. We were hoping to hear from you this evening. You're sure you know the whereabouts of this Jesus, of Nazareth?'

'I do.'

'And you are prepared to lead us to him tonight?'

'Yes.'

'Very well.' He gestured to a rough wooden bench in the corner. 'Sit over there and wait.'

The Levite scribed a message to the High Priest informing him of the position and sent a servant to find him. The man was gone for a considerable time; it took time to locate the High Priest and get first his interest and then a note sanctioning the arrest of the Galilean trouble-maker. Eventually the messenger returned to the office, the Levite read the note and swiftly made his way to the office of the Temple Guard Captain. That official was having a quiet doze in his chair but came to his feet quickly when the High Priest's assistant entered the room. Producing the note, he said stiffly, 'The High Priest has sent instructions for you to go with a man called Judas Iscariot, who's here now. You are to arrest Jesus of Nazareth, the rabble-rouser'.

'I know all about him,' returned the Captain evenly. 'I was warned that this might happen.'

'Iscariot will identify your man for you. There are to be no mistakes. Caiaphas wants him arrested quickly. You are to take him straight to his house.'

'To his house? At this hour?' queried the soldier, amazed.

'Those are my orders, Captain.'

The Captain shrugged his shoulders. 'Right. If that's what he wants.'

The Levite led the way back to his office and introduced the officer to Judas.

'Where shall we be going to find this man?' asked the soldier roughly.

'He'll be on the slopes of the Mount of Olives, sir. The Garden of Gethsemane. He's been sleeping there the last couple of nights.'

'I'll have the guard turned out and we'll be on our way.'

It took a while for the little procession to be assembled. Judas wondered what would happen if there was a real emergency. He felt sure that the Romans would have turned out far quicker, but perhaps that was all that could be expected of mere Temple guards. Eventually, with much shuffling of feet and clanking of armour, the little procession moved off. The noise reverberated round the narrow streets as they made their way to the east gate and down the hill, following the route taken earlier by Jesus and his followers. It didn't take long for the short column to reach the entrance to Gethsemane. They entered the garden and followed Judas across the rough ground until they approached the campsite where the Galileans were sleeping. Judas spoke quietly to the Captain.

'You'll know the man you're looking for. I shall greet him personally and kiss him.'

'It seems appropriate!' said the Captain, with a laugh.

*

When John barHelez arrived back at his apartment, he was in no mood for sleep. He racked his brain to think of a way to help Jesus. He was sure that his friend was in grave danger, for Judas must by now have reached the High Priest's office and it wouldn't be long before some move would be made. How long would they take? Perhaps an hour to get the formal permission from Caiaphas, assemble the troops and get moving. It might take longer, depending on the High Priest's evening engagements, but it wouldn't take long then to march to Gethsemane, where Judas knew Jesus would be. On that reckoning, Jesus could have no more two hours of freedom left – probably less. Yet there was nothing he, John, could do. He had done his best to warn his friend and advise him to flee. Perhaps Jesus had already decided to go with Lazarus to Bethany, then, first thing in the morning, on to Jericho and north up the Jordan Valley to Galilee. Jesus would be in some danger there too, but not to the same extent as just now in Jerusalem.

Then another thought struck John. The friends of Jesus, the women staying at Justus's inn, should perhaps be warned that Jesus was in danger. In turn, they could warn his family, of whom he had heard some talk earlier in the evening. He wondered whether he should send a message right away, but on reflection he thought that it was better to await events and send a message – or, if possible, go himself – in the morning. He fervently hoped that he would have better news by then. John fretted himself around the apartment for well over an hour, unable to settle to read, or even pray. He sat dozing by the fire, lost in thought, staring at the embers and wondering what was happening across the Kedron Valley. Suddenly, the expected knock sounded at the door and a messenger arrived from his superior with a note, requiring him to present himself forthwith at the High Priest's house.

'*We expect to have Jesus of Nazareth in custody soon,*' ran the note. '*I require you here to take the minutes of a special Council Meeting that I am summoning here shortly. Come as soon as you receive this note.*'

So the troops must be on their way – or would be before long. John set out as bidden and quickly reached the High Priest's house. There he found Caiaphas in a state of high excitement. He had despatched the troops. He had also sent for what he called his 'Special Council', a group of half a dozen close friends and confidants within the Great Sanhedrin, and was now preparing to welcome them. One by one they were assembling, wondering why they had been dragged away from their gatherings with friends, or out of their beds. John was told to wait in the outer office. Evidently, the prisoner had not been brought in yet.

★

The three fishermen had followed Jesus as he walked slowly up the hill but, after only a few paces, the preacher came to a standstill.

'Are you armed?' he asked.

It was so unlike Jesus to mention such a possibility that the three fishermen could hardly believe their ears.

'I have an old sword hidden in my bag,' said Peter, hesitatingly.[1] 'I brought it with me, just in case—'

Jesus interrupted. 'That'll do. You'd better fetch it tonight.'

After a mystified glance at the other fishermen, to which they responded with blank expressions, Peter went back and collected the weapon. He slung it round his waist and started back, soon catching the rest up as they continued, slowly and painfully up the hill. They came at last to a small open space between the olive trees, in the centre of which was a large boulder. Jesus stopped by the stone and leaned heavily on it, as if he were an old man.

'I'm feeling very low,' he said wearily. 'My spirit is very troubled. I must pray.'

The three disciples didn't know how to respond, so they said nothing. Jesus continued quietly, his face more serious than the others had ever seen it, 'I'm going to pray just here. Keep watch down the hill for me, will you? Make sure nothing untoward is stirring in the camp.'

Peter and the two brothers, though puzzled, nodded their assent and turned back down the hill a little way, to watch what was happening below. They found a small area of ground clear of thistles and sat down.

'Nobody's moving down there,' said James. 'Everyone's gone to sleep by now, as usual.'

'Whatever is concerning Jesus so much tonight?' John whispered, his face showing real concern.

Peter ventured, 'He's been in a strange mood all evening – all through the meal. He scarcely spoke to me at all – and, when he did, I didn't like what he said.' He briefly recounted what had passed between the leader and himself. 'I was so hurt, I didn't dare pursue it,' he concluded.

'What are we supposed to be watching out for?' asked James. 'Every other night this week we've settled down and gone to sleep in the garden without a qualm. What is Jesus particularly afraid of tonight?'

'I've never known Jesus to be afraid of anything,' commented John. 'So why does he want us to watch tonight?'

None of them knew, so they fell silent. After a few moments, Peter murmured, 'I'll just go back to the clearing and see how he is.'

He rose and quietly made his way back up the slope, managing, with difficulty, to avoid tripping over the unaccustomed weapon at his side. When he reached the spot where they had left Jesus, he saw him kneeling at the boulder, deep in prayer, his torso pressed tightly to the flinty surface. Clearly, he was in great distress. From time to time, Jesus raised his head, the moonlight shining into his face, and Peter could see that it was contorted with perplexity and pain. He thought he could hear his friend praying out loud and strained his ears to pick up the words. When at last he was able to make them out, he wished he hadn't, for they told him all too clearly the depths of his leader's distress.

'My Father,' he heard Jesus saying, almost with a cry. 'What am I to do? What must I do?'

Then, after a long pause, as if he had been listening to a prolonged reply, he heard Jesus cry out, horrified, 'Not that, Father! Is that really your will? Is that the cup that you have prepared for me?'[2]

Another pause and then, more under control:

'You know I will do anything for you, my Father, but, if it is possible, I'd rather not face that.'

Peter watched while great drops of sweat dropped from Jesus's brow. He even thought that the sweat was becoming discoloured red, as if contaminated with blood.[3] He caught his breath and bit his lip, worried about the state that Jesus was getting himself into. He turned back to his friends, but when he arrived at the spot at which he had left them, he found them dozing, their heads on their breasts. He nudged the elder brother.

'He's in a dreadful state,' Peter whispered.

'I was afraid he might be,' replied James, jerking awake, 'but we can do nothing – nobody can, just at the moment. He'll come through – he always does.'

'I've never seen him as upset as this,' muttered Peter.

The fishermen fell quiet again and before long they were all half asleep, in spite of the cool of the night. A scops owl hooted in the distance but they were past caring. Five minutes later, Peter was snoring, but even this didn't disturb the other two. It was nearly half an hour later when they were awakened by

Jesus's return. He shook Peter gently on the shoulder, saying, 'I asked you to watch, Peter. Couldn't you do that for me? Watch, and pray, man. There is so much at stake.'

'I'm sorry, Jesus,' muttered Peter, struggling back to consciousness. The others grunted their apologies too, but Jesus, having had a careful look down the hill towards the camp, had already started back to his lonely vigil, retracing his steps to the clearing. The others watched him go and grimaced at each other, like chastened schoolboys caught cheating at their homework.

'We should have stayed awake for him,' John whispered.

'We should pray, I know, but I'm so tired,' said Peter. 'It's strange, isn't it? I can stay awake all night without any problem when I'm fishing back in Galilee. Why do I feel so fagged out tonight?'

'It's much easier when you're busy,' replied James. 'It's this waiting, and watching, without knowing what we are really supposed to be watching for.'

'It's the mental tiredness that gets to you,' said John. 'Perhaps it's a measure of our spiritual inadequacy – is that the right expression?'

The young man was clearly worn out himself. They settled down to wait again. After about five minutes, Peter struggled to his feet again and said he'd walk up to the clearing to see if Jesus needed them, but when he got there, he saw the preacher still on his knees, at prayer. This time, however, when he could make out the words, he felt that his leader had overcome the worst of his tribulation. He was speaking in a much more measured tone. Peter heard:

'If that is your will, Father, that is what I must do. Whatever you want, I will do.'

Peter slipped away, back to the others. 'He seems more in control now,' he told them.

The others nodded. It was not long before they were asleep again and they stayed that way until, once again, they were wakened by Jesus. This time, he did not complain.

'Come on, lads – wake up,' he was saying. Then, suddenly, he spoke with more urgency. 'Look, something is happening down there, near the camp.'

They all looked down the hill. It was true. A large party of men were moving towards the camp area. They could see many torches flickering in the darkness, winking as they passed between the olive trees.

The approach of the column of soldiers soon roused Mark from his doze. The young fellow had been waiting for Jesus, sitting by the camp-fire. Andrew had offered to wait for Jesus with him, but the two had become sleepy in the warmth of the fire. Mark was naturally alarmed to see the military and straightaway roused Andrew, who had told him to waken the rest of the party quickly. They were all just beginning to confront the situation, struggling to get both eyes and brains focussed, amazed to see their colleague Judas with the soldiers, when Jesus arrived, striding purposefully into the clearing, followed by Peter, James and John.

When he saw Jesus, Judas's face brightened and he moved swiftly to greet his leader, kissing him, as the custom was, on each side of the face.

'Greetings, Jesus,' he said, loudly enough for the Captain to hear.

'Are you really going to betray your leader with a kiss, Judas?' said Jesus quietly.[4] 'How ironical!'

The Captain moved rapidly towards Jesus, drawing his sword.

'Arrest this man!' he shouted, gesturing to the first two soldiers in the line. The two burly troopers moved either side of the Galilean, grabbed at his elbows and locked his arms behind his back; but when Peter saw this, he drew his own sword, moved quickly forward and made a clumsy lunge at one of the soldiers near Jesus. The man quickly brought his shield up in self-defence, but the blow was effective to a degree, drawing blood from the side of the man's head. He pulled away from Jesus with a stifled cry, clutching at the wound.

Jesus quickly intervened, saying calmly but firmly, 'Put up your weapon, Peter. That's not the way. I now know what I must do.'[5]

Using his free arm, he touched the wound, holding his fingers for a short time on the seeping blood. In a few moments, the blood congealed and the man, a puzzled expression on his face, checked his head and then grabbed Jesus's arm again.

'What do you want?' Jesus asked the Captain.

'You are Jesus of Nazareth in Galilee, aren't you? I arrest you by order of the High Priest.'

'I am Jesus. I must say I'm surprised that you found it necessary to come and arrest me like this – in the dead of night. I've been in the Temple the past three days, preaching in full view of everyone. It would have been far quicker for you to find me there! Anyway, you now have what you want, so you can leave these other men alone.'

Jesus looked around at all his followers, standing there in the flickering light from the torches and the fire, with looks of fear, horror and disbelief on their faces. Clearly, they had been caught completely unawares at this development and didn't know what to do for the best. Suddenly, fear overcame young Mark and he decided to make a run for it.

'Get him!' ordered the Captain, brusquely.

Two of the guards gave chase and nearly caught up with the fleeing youth, but, though they grabbed at his outer robe, the lad wriggled free of the garment and ran on, wearing only his loincloth.[6] The soldiers, encumbered by their armour, gave up the chase, but, as the attention of the guards was temporarily taken up with Mark, the rest of the disciples had also turned and fled in all directions. The Captain swore under his breath but called to his troops to return.

'Come back here! It doesn't matter,' he shouted. 'We've got the one we were told to get. We don't need the rest of those cowards.'

Then, as soon as the soldiers had responded, he yelled, 'Right. Let's go. Form a square round the prisoner. Quick march!'

The troop marched rapidly back to the city, with Jesus stumbling along in the centre of a square of soldiers, having to hurry to keep up with the fast march they set. Judas kept in the background. The last thing he wanted to do was to catch Jesus's eye. He felt excited at having taken action that he believed would bring about his desired end, but as he saw the soldiers' contempt for the prisoner and the way in which they shoved and jostled him if he was the least bit slow, the first seeds of doubt started to creep into his mind. Had he done the right thing, after all? He reassured himself that Jesus was bound to win through and confound his enemies, but could not quite bring himself to feel entirely confident of the matter now.

Nobody was around at that time of night. Jerusalem was fast asleep, dreaming of the great service of worship to come at the Temple on Passover day itself, when the sacrificial lambs would be slain and the nation's deliverance was celebrated once more. The soldiers marched, armour clinking, to the house of the High Priest, where the Captain reported to the gatekeeper. Sullen at that time of night, the man told him that Caiaphas wanted the prisoner taken across the courtyard to the house of his father-in-law, Annas.

The Captain was not unduly surprised – it was well known throughout the city that old Annas, himself previously a High Priest, still wielded the real power in the nation through his son-in-law. How like Caiaphas to defer to Annas in a matter like this, requiring deft handling, with the Romans bound to be involved and a great crowd of pilgrims, whose feelings could not be predicted, in the city! Since the prisoner seemed to be causing no trouble, the Captain detailed only two guardsmen to follow him with Jesus as he marched across the yard to Annas's residence.[7] There they were received by another sleepy doorkeeper and conducted into the house out of Judas's sight.

The traitor was left kicking his heels in the courtyard. After a few moments, though, he remembered that he had money to claim, so he made his way to the house of the High Priest and asked to be admitted. Having ascertained his business, the doorkeeper let him in, and, after a delay of about ten minutes or so, another official arrived with the thirty pieces of silver that he had been promised. He grudgingly muttered the thanks of the High Priest for Judas's services and promptly showed him the door. It was only then that Judas started to think about where he would stay that night. He might find a doorway somewhere, out of the draught, not too far away, but there would be little sleep for him. His heart was too full.

*

Andrew stumbled blindly through the undergrowth, away from the campsite and those threatening soldiers. He caught his legs on brambles and stinging nettles, but hardly felt them. The low hanging branches of the olive trees scratched his face, but he staggered uncaringly forward, anywhere to get away from the nightmare. His chest was heaving, his face and legs bleeding, but still he ran, till he could run no more and slumped on to the ground, utterly exhausted. His ears strained for the slightest warning of further danger but he perceived nothing. Then he heard someone else approaching clumsily through the darkness. Desperate, he tried to heave himself up for further flight – but he was utterly spent and could not move. The noise grew louder; someone else was crashing through the undergrowth and cursing quietly, as his legs were also being scratched and stung. Then Andrew realised that it was Nathaniel. The older man had made slower progress in flight and had done extraordinarily well to get as far as he had. They linked up with mutual great relief, very glad to be together in this dire emergency.

'What happened to the others?' asked Nathaniel after he had caught his breath.

'Don't know. All I did was to run and hope.'

They cautiously made their way into a little clearing between the olive trees, searching all the time for evidence of either friend or foe.

It was Nathaniel who spoke again. 'They've taken Jesus! They've arrested our leader – our friend.'

Andrew could see the worry lines on his face in the moonlight. 'Yes, and it was Judas, of all people, that brought the soldiers – who showed them where we were encamped. What a way to treat Jesus after all he has been to us all!' Andrew's contempt for the traitor was evident with every syllable he uttered.

'Did you see what happened to your brother, Peter?'

'No. He had been up the hill with Jesus, big James and John, so he was on the other side of the campsite near Jesus when the soldiers arrived... I didn't see anything. I just ran – as soon as Mark made the break.'

'Me too. Philip was near me, but he outran me, of course, and I lost him in the dark.'

'What are we going to do now?' Andrew couldn't get his brain working at all. His world had been turned upside down. It was the older man who seemed to be more in command of his senses.

'I think they must have given up looking for us by now,' he said. 'We could make our way cautiously back to the camp and see what's going on. We'll see them if they're still there, of course – we'll see their torches and hear their armour. We have to try to find out what's happening to Jesus – and the others.'

Andrew saw the sense in this and so they slowly and carefully made their way back the way they had come. Eventually, they cautiously approached the campsite again and saw, by the fireside, several of their friends, talking quietly, obviously very upset and bewildered. Philip, Simon, Thaddeus, little James – all the younger men – were there. They were overjoyed to see Andrew and Nathaniel emerge from the darkness.

'Have you found out what happened to Jesus?' asked Andrew.

'None of us stayed to find out,' admitted Simon, guiltily. 'We all scarpered.'

'There was nothing we could have done for him anyway,' offered Thaddeus, 'and he was asking them to let us go.'

'Nevertheless, I feel very bad about running and leaving him,' mumbled Andrew, and several others muttered their agreement.

'But where are Peter, big James and John – and Thomas and Matthew – and young Mark? Did none of you see them?' asked Andrew.

None of them could offer anything on that topic. There was a lengthy silence before anyone spoke again. Then it was Nathaniel who took the lead.

'We've got to decide what to do,' he said. 'It's no good standing round like lost sheep. What's done is done and can't be undone. We have to think about what is best in this new situation. We can't turn to Jesus now…'

'We've got so used to letting him lead us – now we have to think for ourselves.' This from little James.

Another pause, then Nathaniel again took the initiative.

'We can do nothing by way of rescuing Jesus, that's clear. We're not armed or equipped, and it would be stupid even to think along those lines. If we stay near Jerusalem, we may be putting ourselves at risk – and Jesus wouldn't want that. He clearly wanted us to stay at liberty, though what we can do without him is difficult to imagine. I think we'd be best getting out of here in case the soldiers come back – maybe at daybreak – to hunt us down. We know that the family – Lazarus and his sisters – will make us welcome at Bethany. I think we should head there, and perhaps Lazarus will go into Jerusalem tomorrow to try to find out what's happening. The authorities don't know he's a friend of Jesus, so he should be safe. We'll just have to hope that all the others are all safe too somewhere.'

There was a general assent to this line of thinking, and so the sorry band collected their belongings and made their way over the summit of the mountain and on to what was now their only refuge. When they arrived at their destination, they were very relieved to find that four of their colleagues had already made it there before them. Big James, John, Matthew and Thomas had all come to the same conclusion; Bethany was the place to be for the time being. They were out of immediate danger there, but near enough to find out what was happening to Jesus as soon as possible. But where on earth was Peter?

Nobody had any clue what had happened to the big fellow. Had he fallen and turned an ankle, or, worse, broken a leg in his flight from the soldiers? Was he even now somewhere out on the mountain, in pain, unable to move? Worse still, had the soldiers caught and arrested him too? Naturally, Andrew was the most worried, but all were concerned. However, they concluded reluctantly that nothing useful could be done till morning, when they could organise a search of the Mount of Olives. Similarly, they were concerned for young Mark. For the time being, they just had to hope that he too had made good his escape and got safely home. That also would have to be checked in the morning.

Not surprisingly, Lazarus and the women were beside themselves with worry for their friend, Jesus. They had known him for many years and it seemed inconceivable to them that anyone could want to hurt him, but evidently the authorities had decided to close in on what he stood for and eliminate his approach to life. None of them slept well for what remained of the night.

*

John heard the tramp of the soldiers' feet several minutes before they appeared at the gate of the courtyard. Much as he wanted to, he decided not to go out to meet them. In the first place, it might occur to someone that this was an unusual thing for him to do, but, secondly, he could not bear the sight of his friend being brought in like some kind of brigand. He peered through the window and saw that the main troop was being dismissed, while the prisoner and a small escort were moving across the yard to Annas's house.

John swallowed hard and tried to clear his mind. He'd be called before long – as soon as all the councillors had assembled. He had to get his mind working clearly. He wandered over to the window overlooking the street and peered out. Jerusalem was asleep, unaware of the tragedy taking place in the High Priest's house. The moon shone down on the empty street, a thoroughfare that would be crowded with pilgrims from all over the Mediterranean area in just a few hours' time. He stared at it glumly and then his face puckered in surprise. Something was moving out there in the shadows. What on earth was going on? Yes, now he could see that it was a man, a large fellow, moving stealthily from doorway to doorway, clearly trying to remain unobserved.

John watched carefully. The man came closer and then, for an instant, he showed his face in the moonlight. It was Peter – of all people! So the big fisherman was following Jesus as best he could, as he had sworn he would! John shook his head in wonderment. Whatever did Peter imagine he could achieve? Was he really planning to break into the High Priest's house, rescue his leader and spirit him away? Stupid, loyal Peter – he had no chance; but he was here and would want to know what was happening to Jesus.

John made his way to the side door which opened on to the street about thirty yards from where the disciple was hiding in the doorway. He opened the door and went out into the road, looking down the road in the direction of the hiding place, allowing the moonlight to fall on his face, hoping that Peter would see him. He was lucky. The fisherman, scared at being discovered, had his ear well to the ground and had flattened himself against the wall immediately he heard the door open, but a moment later he recognised the High Priest's assistant and made his way cautiously down to greet him.

'Come in, quickly,' said John.[8]

They moved inside the building and swiftly reached John's apartment. There they brought each other up to date with the situation.

'Whatever have you in mind now?' asked John, when the news ran out.

'I've really no idea,' said the big fisherman, lamely. 'I just had to come – to be near him. He needs someone. It's good to know you're here too and can…' He broke off.

'There's very little I can do – in fact,' said John, gravely. 'I'm afraid that Jesus is going to be brought to trial – any time now.'

'On what charge?' asked Peter. 'What can they possibly have against Jesus? And why take him at night, with all this cloak-and-dagger stuff? He was there in the Temple every day if they really wanted him and there was a proper charge to answer…'

John quickly had to explain that the Temple authorities were unwilling to risk a disturbance. The crowd might well have reacted adversely if the soldiers had tried to arrest Jesus during the day.

'But I must ask you to go now, Peter,' he finished. 'I'm expecting to be called into the Council Meeting at any time. You'd better not be here when I am called. What do you want to do?'

'I need to be near Jesus – and near you, so that you can keep me informed, please, as to what happens at the Council.' Peter looked deeply distressed and was almost pleading; and it was difficult for a man of Peter's temperament to plead.

'Of course,' returned John. 'I don't see what you can do, but still – I'll let you out in the courtyard. There are lots of people out there, with various tasks to be performed. Some are just waiting to be called for duty. They stand round the fire till they're called. Just go over and join them – nobody will realise that you're not on the staff in either Caiaphas's house or Annas's. You'll be all right. As soon as I can, I'll get word to you of what has happened.'

John let Peter out into the courtyard as he promised, and got back to his office just a few moments before a servant arrived to tell him he was wanted in the High Priest's office at once.

For once, the big fisherman wished he wasn't quite so big and therefore so noticeable. He just hoped that John was right, that he could remain in the courtyard, near Jesus, without anyone realising that he was a stranger. But, perhaps, someone might recognise him as a follower of Jesus. He recalled all too vividly how, for the past three days, he'd stood side by side with Jesus in the Temple precinct, in full view of everyone, listening as he preached and helping to control the crowds who wanted to talk to the leader when he had finished, or those who jostled forward during the address simply to get close to him. Jesus had that effect on almost everyone – they wanted to be close to him, to catch his eye and receive that friendly look, that glance of understanding. No matter what the problem, he seemed to be able to deal with it. No: that was an exaggeration. It wasn't the case that Jesus waved a magic wand and caused problems to disappear, but what he did was to give the recipient of his look the courage to face up to the difficulties and then, somehow, they seemed less than before. Peter recalled the storm on the Sea of Galilee – the boat had actually seemed to be sinking under them, but when Jesus woke and shared their distress, the wind suddenly seemed to be so much less terrifying. He'd seen so many people have similar experiences in the last two years, as they had journeyed round Galilee and Judaea.

Peter slunk in the shadows wondering what to do. A girl passing by, presumably on an errand for some important person in Caiaphas's house, looked at him with surprise and stopped, her eyes narrowing.

'Who are you?' she enquired. 'I haven't seen you here before.'

'No. That's right…' Peter faltered. 'I am new here – I'm hoping to be taken on to the staff permanently, but…'

'Which house?' asked the girl. 'Caiaphas's or Annas's?'

'Aah – Caiaphas's house.' Peter was late with his answer and he suspected that it didn't carry much conviction.

'What are you? What's your trade?'

Peter felt more and more uneasy. 'Um – I'm – I'm a butcher,' he said. 'I hope to get a job in the kitchens.' It was the best lie he could think up in a hurry.

'I didn't know we were looking for a full-time butcher.' The girl was evidently unimpressed. 'Are you sure you're in the right place?'

'Oh, yes.' For the first time the answer came readily.

'Your clothes smell more like a fisherman's to me,' said the girl, wrinkling her nose. Then a sudden thought struck her. 'You aren't anything to do with the preacher man who was brought in tonight, are you? He had fishermen friends, they say.'[9]

'Not I,' said Peter, shaking his head.

'Oh, well. See you.' The girl tossed her head and flounced off.

Peter breathed a sigh of relief and moved hastily away in the other direction. Then it occurred to him that he was probably actually more likely to draw attention to himself by hanging about in the shadows than if, as John had suggested, he joined the crowd by the large brazier set up in the centre of the courtyard, around which most people were gathering. He decided to take his courage in both hands and move closer to the fire and, hopefully, lose himself in the little crowd there. He edged forward and was pleased to feel the warmth. It was certainly chilly at night at Passover time; the fire felt good and his spirits rose a little. But he had only been there a few minutes when the fellow next to him started a conversation.

'Haven't seen you around before, mate,' he said.

'No. I've only come recently.' Peter felt the icy grip of falsehood enveloping him again. He was a hopeless liar. The interrogation followed the predictable route. As before, he was drawn into more and more invention. The man wasn't at all satisfied.

'I don't believe a word of it,' he said, eventually. 'You're a Galilean – I can tell that from your accent. I reckon you've got something to do with this prisoner who's been brought in – he was Galilean. Perhaps you're actually a follower of this man, Jesus.'

'N-no, you're quite wrong,' stammered Peter, by now becoming quite hot under the collar. 'I've never even seen the man, let alone spoken to him.'

'I saw someone very like you in the Temple the other day, when I was there. Yes; I feel sure that it was you that was with him – that Jesus...'

Just then, a soldier who had joined them at the fire, entered the argument.

'I was in the troop that brought him in,' he said, 'and I agree. I'm pretty certain this was one of the fellows in Gethsemane – in fact, I think he's the one who drew a sword and tried to resist arrest...'[10]

Peter swore viciously. Over the past two years, he had moderated his language quite a bit, as Jesus had encouraged him to use a more gentle vocabulary, but now all his fisherman's flow of invective rushed into his throat and poured forth in a rushing torrent.

'Look! I have never even seen the man...' he blurted out – but with considerable force and using colourful adjectival phrases.

'All right, all right, old man!' replied the soldier, taken aback by the ferocity of the reply. 'Keep your hair on!'

'Out of my way, out of my way, you –!' The big fellow pushed rudely past his two tormentors as he stumbled out of the circle near the brazier. His eyes were full, his throat was choking. He knew that he was a beaten man. He'd said that he would give his life for his friend, but when it came to it, he couldn't even own him in front of a couple of strangers, who probably couldn't really care less either way. He stumbled blindly on, not caring where he was going.

Just then, however, Jesus was hustled out of Annas's house and across the courtyard. On either side of him were the two soldiers of the Temple Guard. The Captain of the Guard led the way. Peter became aware of the little procession just in time to avoid a collision with the officer.

'Out of the way, you dog!' ordered the Captain.

Peter came abruptly to his senses and realised with a thousand emotions that he was within four yards of his friend and leader. He took a step or two backwards, out of the line of the marching soldiers and looked at Jesus, blinking back his tears. The prisoner hardly altered his step, but shot a look at the fisherman. Peter was to remember that look for years to come. There were so many emotions conveyed by that brief glance. He saw a wish not to compromise his friend in the eyes of the soldiers; but was there not also a suggestion of reproach, that he, Peter, hadn't managed to handle himself better and support his friend? Yet surely there was also, incredibly, an assurance, suggesting that things would turn out right eventually and he shouldn't blame himself too much. Peter wondered later how was it possible to convey so much in such a short time, but somehow it had happened.

The little group marched on and Peter headed for the entrance to the Courtyard, full of remorse, guilt and bitter failure. He rushed blindly into the street, not caring that the doorkeeper spoke to him, commenting on the late hour. He pulled up as soon as he realised he was in the road and stood against a wall, weeping bitterly. As he did so, he heard a cock crow and he recalled the words of his friend at supper...

'Before the cock crows, you will have disowned me three times.'

He started haltingly down the road. He hardly knew where he was going or what he was doing. Failure filled his mind and spirit. Tears filled his eyes. He'd failed to stay by his leader, his master, the one who had taught him what life was all about. He had failed – failed Jesus, of all people. The word resounded over and over in his brain. Failure. What would happen to Jesus now? He didn't know, but he feared the worst and he knew that he had let his greatest friend down. Failure. He staggered on – and on, not knowing or caring where he was going.

After what seemed like an eternity of wandering, he dimly realised that he was dog-tired and needed to find somewhere to sleep – or at least to lie down. It was well into the night by now. Where could he go? He only knew one place, and that not very well. Would Justus take him in now, he wondered? He had better try. He was cold and desperately tired. With difficulty, he worked out where he was and retraced his steps to the inn. The landlord was, of course, already in his bed, but came reasonably promptly to the door when Peter knocked uncertainly on it.

'Whatever has happened to you?'

Justus couldn't believe what he was seeing. Peter was dishevelled, his normally bronzed face pale, with dark circles under red-rimmed eyes. He couldn't find the words to tell Justus anything for a while. The landlord realised that the fisherman was all in and silently drew him inside, sat him down by what was left of the fire and poured him some wine.

Gradually, the story came out. The arrest in the garden, the piece of luck in meeting John, the events in the courtyard, the look that Jesus had given him, the triumphant cock-crow announcing his abject failure, the danger that Jesus was in – it all came out with tears and recriminations. The fisherman was not fit to follow Jesus. He wished he had never said he would follow him... The words poured out in a torrent of self-disgust.

Justus sensibly let it all come out without attempting to interrupt. At last the torrent finally subsided. Peter sat, head bowed almost between his knees, occasionally looking up and glowering at the fire. Justus let a considerable time pass before attempting to reply. Eventually, he said, softly, yet with urgency, 'Young Mark came home a couple of hours ago and told me that Jesus had been taken. He didn't know what happened to the rest of you – he just ran.'

'We all did,' mumbled Peter. 'We all ran for our lives – we never thought of him.'

'My friend, you have had a terrible experience. Jesus is undoubtedly in a tough spot – on trial before the Temple leaders – but think for a moment. What could you have done to help him? In all honesty, what can any of us do to help Jesus now? John barHelez is near him and will do all he can, but even he is virtually powerless in this situation. But, on the other hand, remember this – Jesus hasn't committed any crime. They have to prove something against him – and they won't be able to do that. Our law is weighted on the side of the defendant, and Jesus has done nothing wrong! There are no grounds for punishing him. Of course, we know the authorities are jealous of him and annoyed with him, but they can't condemn him simply on those grounds. What crime has Jesus committed? None. They may – well – rough him up a little. They may beat him, but that won't cow our friend Jesus. In a few days he'll be set free, no doubt after having endured a good talking-to, and we can then see what he thinks it is best to do. I'm sure that things could be a lot worse.'

'Do you really think so?' asked the disciple doubtfully. 'Perhaps – maybe you're right. I hope so… but what of my failure? Jesus will never trust me again…'

'Listen to me. You know Jesus much better than I do, but I know him well enough to know that he will forgive any failure on your part – or on the part of any of us. Remember this. You appear to have been the only disciple who followed the soldiers to the house of the High Priest. At least you tried to help. Not like the others, who simply ran… I suppose you've no idea what happened to them?'

'No. As soon as I came to my senses, I concentrated on following the soldiers. That was easy, with all those torches and all the noise. The others may have regrouped at the campsite, I suppose, once the danger had passed, or perhaps they fled to Bethany. Possibly, some did one thing, some another. I don't know.'

'But you tried to stay with Jesus. That was to your credit – and Jesus will appreciate that.'

'No. I failed him.' Peter's voice cracked. 'I failed him, I tell you! He knew I would. He somehow knew that I wasn't up to it. He told me at supper.'

★

Meanwhile, John had made his way into the High Priest's study, as bidden. Here he found Caiaphas, hardly able to disguise his triumph.

'We've got him – this Jesus!' he crowed. 'That fellow Judas led us straight to him and the guard brought him in with no difficulty. The so-called miracle worker couldn't work a miracle to save himself, when it came to the crunch!'

John couldn't bring himself to reply, so he held his peace.

'He's being questioned by the Lord Annas at present,' Caiaphas went on. 'The Inner Council will all be here very shortly – most are already gathered in the meeting hall. We'd better go in and join them. I shall want you to take careful notes of all that is said, for the record.'

John assented with a nod of his head. He still couldn't bring himself to speak. He followed Caiaphas into the larger room, where several councillors were already seated. They stood when they saw their leader, but he gestured to them to sit.

'The prisoner, Jesus, of Nazareth, will be here shortly,' he said. 'We've discussed his case before, so you all know the background. During the day, I have found several witnesses who will testify against him, so we ought to be able to arrive at a preliminary judgement tonight which can be ratified in full Council tomorrow. I have already sent out notices to all the members for a meeting an hour after sunrise in the morning.'

One of the councillors stood up and addressed the High Priest.

'What is your feeling, My Lord? Is this man here on a capital charge, or, if not, how serious do you judge the matter to be?'

Caiaphas scowled. 'You know perfectly well what I think of this man. We've discussed it before. He's a potential troublemaker of the worst kind. Claiming to be the Messiah is bound to stir the crowd up, and all kinds of rioting could follow. If that happens, our position with Pilate will be very difficult. We have to get him permanently out of the way.'

'What about a spell in prison – certainly over the Feast period?' asked a second councillor; but Caiaphas was uncompromising, retorting, 'I want him out of the way for good. While ever he's alive, his followers will agitate and might stir up resentment. Once he's dead, it'll be too late. As I said last time we discussed the matter, it's better that one man die, rather than the whole nation be put at risk.'

'On what charge will we proceed?' asked another.

'I agree it's difficult,' said Caiaphas, more soberly. 'He's been heard to say many things which could be construed as, well, treasonable – or at least ambiguous, as far as Rome is concerned. We'll have to see what the witnesses can remember and agree upon. In the end, though, if all else fails, we'll have to get him to admit his claim to be the Messiah and then we can tell Pilate that he has claimed to be a King, which Rome certainly won't like.'

'How do you intend to approach the matter of his so-called Messiahship?' asked the first questioner. 'Has he ever spoken of his claim? Have we any witnesses to that?'

The High Priest was getting annoyed at the continued questions.

'Hundreds of pilgrims witnessed him riding into Jerusalem this week on a donkey – just as the prophet foretold. Isn't that a claim?'

'Will that stand up in court, though, My Lord?'

'Look, if the worst comes to the worst, we can ask him the direct question.' Caiaphas was getting rattled.

'And if he remains silent? As he's entitled to do...'

'Then I will put him under the extreme oath and question him by the Holy Name.' The High Priest knew that there was no answer to that. Every Jew knew that he must answer when called upon to do so by God himself. It wasn't exactly a legal procedure, but these were difficult days and this, after all, was only a preliminary hearing. Such was the influence of the High Priest that nobody dared to pursue that matter further.

Before long, the rest of the group had arrived and eventually Annas himself entered the room. Everyone stood in deference to the old man, himself a High

Priest in years gone by. Caiaphas invited him to address the gathering.

'I have questioned the man, Jesus,' said Annas, gravely. 'He seems to know what is what, where the court procedure is concerned. He just maintained his silence – until the Captain struck him for insolence. All he said then was that he had spoken openly in the Temple and elsewhere,[11] and there were plenty who had heard him and could bear witness – which is, of course, as we all know, how our court procedure works. I couldn't get anywhere with him on an informal basis. We shall have to be careful how we proceed.'

'Let's have him in and get on with it,' said Caiaphas, annoyed.

A few minutes later, the door opened and Jesus was thrust into the centre of the arc of councillors. He stood erect, yet avoiding any display of insolence. John had to admire his friend's bearing. The High Priest called in the witnesses and, one by one, they came and told their tales, but the stories didn't agree, and the questioning councillors could get no consistent account.[12] Caiaphas was getting more and more frustrated, being unable to proceed legally without a charge that was levelled by at least two independent witnesses.

Jesus remained impassive, saying nothing and looking straight in front of him, seemingly oblivious to the danger hovering round him. John, sitting next to the High Priest, had great difficulty in keeping his admiration for the prisoner from showing in his face. Jesus has them beaten, he thought, hugging himself internally. But, at last, when the farce had continued for well over an hour and the tempers of the councillors were obviously running very high, Caiaphas decided it was time to play his trump card. He drew himself up to his full height and spoke commandingly to the prisoner standing before him.

'I'm putting you under oath before the living God,' he said.[13] 'Tell us, once and for all, are you the Messiah, the Son of the Living God?'

There was complete silence in the courtroom for several seconds. John held his breath. Would Jesus keep silence, even when confronted by the Great Oath? Finally, however, Jesus spoke, his voice never faltering, yet still without any suggestion of personal pride.

'It is as you say.'

There was a sharp intake of breath from several people in the room. The man had owned up. He had condemned himself, they all knew, for Caiaphas could tolerate no challenge to his leadership, certainly not from a mere carpenter from lowly Galilee. The High Priest used the opportunity to make the most dramatic of all gestures. He grasped the lapels of his cloak and wrenched the cloth asunder, tearing his garment to the waist.

'Why do we bother with witnesses?' he thundered. 'This man has condemned himself out of his own mouth. He has uttered blasphemy. How can a mere carpenter claim to be the Messiah?'

The councillors stood and growled their agreement.

'What is your verdict?' called Caiaphas, his voice rising almost to a scream.

His loyal allies knew their cue.

'Death! He deserves to die!' they answered.

'Very well,' replied the High Priest, obviously satisfied. 'We shall bring this determination before the full Council in the morning and seek confirmation of this decision as soon as we can see Pilate.'

Again there was a murmur of assent from around the room.

'This Court is concluded,' intoned Caiaphas.

The councillors started to file out of the room, passing the prisoner, still standing in the centre of the floor, flanked by two soldiers. Many sneered at him. One or two even went further and slapped him, inviting him to divine who it was who had struck him. Jesus maintained his dignified stance, recoiling from the blows but saying nothing. John, sickened by the events of the night, could not but admire his friend even more. How could Jesus maintain his dignified silence amidst such provocation, he asked himself?

At last, they had all left, and John saw the prisoner being taken below, to spend the night in a filthy cell, alone, cold and seemingly friendless. He so much wanted to aid his friend, but, in the circumstances, felt that he could do nothing. Even though the night was already far gone, it seemed an eternity till the dawn.

NOTES

[1] Luke 22:38.
[2] Mark 14:36.
[3] Luke 22:44.
[4] Luke 22:48.
[5] John 18:11.
[6] Mark 14:51.
[7] John 18:13.
[8] John 18:15–16.
[9] Luke 22:56.
[10] John 18:26–27.
[11] John 18:20.
[12] Mark 14:56.
[13] Matt. 26:63.

Trials and tribulation

John was up and about as soon as the sun rose. He knew he had to be present in the Great Sanhedrin in an hour, but he felt that he must get news about Jesus to his friends first, which meant a quick visit to Justus's inn – it was too risky and unsatisfactory to send a written message. When he arrived at his destination, the landlord and the staff were barely up and about, but Justus quickly put aside his chores and hastened to greet the priest, ushering him into a side room where they could talk privately.

'Whatever has been happening, John?' asked the landlord, obviously very disturbed. 'Mark came home very late last night with a story of Jesus being arrested by soldiers! He didn't know exactly what happened – he only just managed to escape arrest himself. He was pretty shaken up. Then Peter turned up much later, very upset – rather incoherent, actually. Apparently, Jesus is on trial – is that right?'

John was glad to hear that Peter had made his way to Justus's place. He'd been bothered when he had failed to find him after the council meeting. He quickly made Justus aware of the current situation. The landlord shook his head gravely when he heard about the Council's decision to press for the ultimate sanction.

'That's terrible. They're trying him essentially on an political offence, then, not a religious matter,' he observed.

'They have to, if they are to get a death sentence. Only Pilate can order that, and he won't be interested in religious niceties, but he might well react if he thinks there might be a revolt or any kind of challenge to Rome.'

Justus nodded. 'I see that,' he said.

Fortunately, Justus was one of those people who could keep a cool head in a crisis. He offered immediately to let all the friends of Jesus in the inn know the facts as soon as possible – Joanna, Susanna, Rebecca, Lydia; Nimrah and Mary, and, through them, Jesus's family. Then, of course, there was Peter. John enquired carefully after the big fisherman.

'He's in a terrible state,' said Justus, pulling at his beard. 'He was all in, last night, when he got here – well into the night it was – but it's his mental state that really worries me. He keeps blaming himself for letting Jesus down and just won't be comforted. He's almost suicidal.'

'But what could he do?' asked John. 'There was nothing that any of us could do in the circumstances. He did more than anyone else. At least he followed Jesus and tried to be there for him.'

'I've told him that but he won't listen. How he will react when I tell him that Jesus is condemned to death, heaven alone knows. Will you tell him, John? I think it will come best from you.'

John grimaced. 'Where is he now?' he asked.

'Still in his room, of course. I haven't tried to disturb him yet, even to offer him a drink. I thought it best to leave him alone to sleep – if he will.'

'I agree,' said the priest, 'but I have no time. I have to get back to the Temple where the Great Sanhedrin will meet shortly to consider Jesus's case formally. I mustn't be late. Please tell him the news later, when you think it's right – I know you will do so gently. And tell Peter I will come again as soon as I know what the Sanhedrin has decided. You had better warn him, however, that I have no real hope that they will reverse the decision of the Inner Council – I'm afraid they usually just go along tamely with any recommendation from that quarter. Nor do I think that Pilate will quibble. Unfortunately, life, especially a mere Jewish life, is very cheap to the Romans.'

'The hated Romans,' hissed Justus under his breath. 'When shall we be liberated from their barbarity? We had hoped that Jesus was to usher in the new age, which surely must have included ridding us of Roman domination. Ah, well – it was not to be.'

'No,' replied the priest, shaking his head. 'Anyway, I must be off. Thanks for all your help.'

'Just a minute – what are we to do about the rest of the Galileans? And Jesus's friends at Bethany – Lazarus and his sisters?'

'I don't know where the rest of his followers are – and I haven't time to go to Bethany,' returned John. 'I daren't send a written message – it could fall into the wrong hands and compromise my position. I will, of course, be resigning shortly from the Temple staff, but I must stay near Jesus until…' He broke off, unable to bring himself to finish the sentence.

'Yes, of course. I understand,' replied Justus softly. 'Perhaps Peter will go to Bethany when he hears your news. He will know what to do – if he is thinking straight by then. Or maybe I can send Mark. He could look in on the campsite too, while he's going past there, in case some of Jesus's men have regrouped there… We'll fix something.'

'Good man,' said John, clapping him on the shoulder. 'I'll leave all that to you, then.' And with that, he departed.

★

Lazarus, Philip, Simon and Thaddeus set off over the Mount of Olives an hour or so after sunrise. They walked together as far as Gethsemane, but there they split up, the three Galileans making their way back to what had been the campsite to start their search for Peter and Mark. Lazarus continued on into town, amazed that everything seemed to be going on normally when his own particular world was falling about his ears. How could people continue with their ordinary existence, he thought, when Jesus, that kindly friend who had sought to embrace everyone in his care and concern, had been arrested? Yet that was the way of the world, he concluded. The world would carry on somehow, even if God's Messiah himself was done away with. Lazarus couldn't bring himself to think about that. Surely Jesus would emerge triumphant. God wouldn't desert him. Perhaps Jesus would be freed after a day or two; but he was desperately worried.

Lazarus entered the city, as usual, by the east gate. His first thought was to go to the Temple to see if he could find John there. He was pretty sure that John would know what was going on, but his friend was not in his office at the Temple. A Levite told him that the priest had been called to see his boss late last night on important business, and he supposed that John was still at the High Priest's house, dealing with whatever it was that had flared up so urgently. It did not immediately occur to Lazarus that Jesus's arrest and John's sudden call to the High Priest's house might be connected. He didn't believe that the authorities saw Jesus as that much of a threat. How could he be? He preached peace and loving kindness. How could that threaten anyone?

The man from Bethany was now perplexed. He couldn't go to the High Priest's house. He'd be turned away and given a wigging for his presumption, even if he asked for John by name. Then he thought of Justus and the people at the inn who were friends of Jesus. Perhaps they would know what had happened. He had only been there on the one occasion, for the Passover supper the previous evening. Was it really as recently as last evening? It seemed like a week ago already. He retraced his steps to the place and was very relieved to find that John had already been there with news – though he was, of course, appalled at the nature of the news when he heard it. Jesus was not only in prison but already condemned by the Inner Council and appearing before the full Sanhedrin at this very moment, in all probability! It was impossible!

But the news that Peter and Mark were safe at the inn was something. Lazarus didn't know Peter very well, though he had met him several times during the course of Jesus's visits to town. He was greatly distressed to hear that the big man had virtually gone to pieces, but couldn't make up his mind up about whether or not he ought to try to help him. He got as far as the door of Peter's room, but, in the end, decided to come away without knocking

Having discussed matters fully with everyone involved at the inn, Lazarus felt that there was nothing more that could be done for the present in Jerusalem, so he decided to get straight back to Bethany and let everyone there know the latest information. He would return later in the day and find out what happened at the meeting of the Great Sanhedrin. John had promised to keep them informed, which was something. Thank God for John!

★

The seventy members of the great Sanhedrin met at the appointed hour in their council chamber next to the Court of the Jews in the Temple precinct.[1]

At Passover time, every councillor was in Jerusalem and therefore able to attend the meeting. There was a great deal of discussion and wagging of heads until the High Priest arrived, followed by John barHelez and several other court officials, and the meeting was called to order. Caiaphas briefly outlined the events of the previous evening, laying stress on the need for urgent action to get the whole matter resolved before the holiest day of the Feast, now only some thirty-six hours away.

He concluded, 'In order to expedite matters, the Inner Council examined this man last night and ascertained that he does, indeed, claim to be the Messiah. We heard it from his own mouth. We have discussed previously our attitude to such a notion from a mere carpenter from Galilee, and I think we are all agreed that it is totally preposterous. The claim is clearly false, but that is not, in itself, a capital offence, blasphemous and ridiculous though it undoubtedly is. However, the fact is that such a claim might well whip up the most unfortunate feelings among the pilgrims, especially at this time of year, which could easily lead to a riot or some other disturbance. Anything like that will certainly annoy the Romans and provoke them into taking action, not only against Jesus, but more importantly against us, for not seeing that the situation might arise. So the Inner Council's recommendation is that we report this man to Pilate, saying that he claims to be the Messiah, and the Messiah is a King – he'll understand that and certainly won't tolerate it. I feel sure that he'll have him put on a cross before we can turn round.'

He paused and looked round aggressively at the assembled Council members, as if daring anyone to challenge his logic.

'Now, are there any questions? Does the great Sanhedrin concur with the recommendation?'

There was silence for a few moments. Caiaphas thought for a moment that everything would go through on the nod. However, he saw with dismay that Nicodemus was rising to speak.

'My Lord, I understand your argument, of course, but we do seem to be proceeding with unusual haste, this being a capital charge. Surely if we keep this man in custody, he cannot create any further problem and we can, at more leisure and with greater caution, proceed against him when all the evidence has been more fully assessed?'

The High Priest ground his teeth in frustration. This was the last thing he wanted. John, standing just behind him, could sense his impatience. Before Caiaphas could speak, however, Annas rose and addressed the meeting.

'My Lords, it has been my experience over many years that it is better to proceed with some resolution. If we keep this man in prison, his followers will undoubtedly incite the crowd into demanding explanations. That could cause the very thing that we are trying to avoid: disturbance – even rioting – and so on.'

Other councillors muttered their support. The situation was moving against Jesus. But then Joseph, the Prince of Arimathea, got to his feet.

Although only a young man, he quite often carried some influence in the Council, and the chairman had little choice but to allow him to make his contribution.

'Councillors,' he began, 'I'm inclined to agree with my colleague, Lord Nicodemus. It is no small thing to take the life of a man, however lowly his station, and I for one would not like to see this matter rushed. I feel that it would be better to leave things to quieten down over the period of the festival and try the man more carefully then.'

John could sense the High Priest's blood pressure rising. The back of his neck was turning deep crimson and threatened to be a shade of purple if the pressure was not shortly relieved. He was not at all surprised when Caiaphas went on the offensive.

'Am I to understand that there are one or two councillors who doubt the wisdom or the integrity of the Inner Council?' he demanded. 'Or perhaps you think that this man Jesus really *is* the Messiah? Perhaps you are actually followers of this false Messiah in secret!'

Joseph's face fell and he could not look the chairman of the meeting in the face. Nicodemus rose again and stammered out, 'No, indeed not, My Lord. We just thought that…'

'But you did not think enough!' thundered Caiaphas, having regained the initiative. 'Now, what is the will of the Council? Do we need to see this man at all, or is the Council prepared to proceed on the basis of the earlier recommendation?'

There was general chorus agreeing to proceed.

'And is everyone in favour of seeking the death penalty?'

'Aye, aye,' echoed round the room. Few noticed that neither Nicodemus nor Joseph joined in the chorus, both of whom gazed sullenly at the floor.

'Very well,' said Caiaphas, gravely. 'I shall seek an audience with the Governor as soon as possible and we will get this matter dealt with quickly. This meeting is closed.'

John left the council chamber with a heavy heart. He had had no real hope that there would be a different result, but the closing words of the chairman struck his heart and numbed him through and through. He did as he had promised and made his way, as soon as he could, to the inn again, sought Justus and gave him the news. The landlord said that he would inform everyone there of the position but that Peter, on hearing the previous tidings, had already locked himself in his room, refusing to speak to anybody. From time to time, they had heard him sobbing like a baby.

'That's so unlike Peter,' said John. 'He's as manly a man as I've ever met – or so I thought. I knew he was devoted to Jesus, but this is too much. Watch him, Justus. I know you will. I'll let you know what transpires when Caiaphas goes to see Pilate.'

And with that, he was gone again.

★

When John returned to his office, he learned that Caiaphas had already left his house on his way to see Pilate to request an audience. He fretted while he was gone, wondering how the Governor would react to being disturbed this early in the day, for influential Romans were inclined to enjoy their evenings, drinking and gambling well into the night, and therefore disinclined to rouse themselves too early the following morning. He could foresee Caiaphas receiving a fairly frosty reception at the Antonia fortress, which was situated at the north-west corner of the Temple, where the Roman Governor had set up his court for his sojourn in Jerusalem during the Feast. It was well known, of course, that Pilate detested Jerusalem, much preferring the seaside at Caesarea, but he knew that he had to be in the capital for the festival, just in case of any trouble. He always made sure that several thousand extra Roman troops were there too, for the same reason.

There would be another reason for Pilate to be displeased, too, John realised. Caiaphas would, no doubt, refuse to cross the Roman's threshold, on the grounds that it would defile him, especially with the Holy Day of Passover nearly upon them. So Pilate would have to go out to the gate to talk to Caiaphas, which would really annoy that proud individual.

It was nearly an hour before Caiaphas returned. From his office window, John saw him stride into the courtyard looking distinctly displeased, and was not at all surprised when he was sent for almost immediately.

'That fool, Pilate, is quibbling,' snarled the High Priest, almost before he had crossed the threshold. 'First he told me to deal with this matter myself, but he knows full well that we are not permitted to condemn a man to death. It flatters his ego to have me plead with him to have the man executed. But now, if you please, he has decided that he should try the man himself! I pointed out that the matter had already been discussed in two of our councils and the proposal carried almost unanimously, but he insisted. He's just doing it to annoy me, of course. He doesn't care a fig whether a mere Jew lives or dies!'

John held his tongue. There was no pleasing Caiaphas when he was in this sort of mood. He was all too well aware of the enmity between the High Priest and the Roman Governor.

'He says he will see the prisoner later this morning,' went on the Priest. 'See that the Captain of the Guard is aware of the position, while I go to confer with the Lord Annas.'

John bowed his head briefly and made his escape. Could it be that Jesus might yet escape the extreme penalty just because Pilate disliked the High Priest? He hardly dared to hope so, but, for the present at least, all was not lost.

★

John was ordered to join the High Priest and his advisors when they made their way over to the Antonia behind the troop of soldiers escorting the prisoner. John was distressed to see the state that Jesus was in. He had obviously been ill-treated by the guards since John had last seen him. His eyes were red-rimmed and one was badly swollen and would be black within a couple of hours. He walked with a limp, suggesting that he had been kicked about, and he was holding one arm as if it pained him. There were flecks of blood on his garments. John, though naturally desperately sorry for his friend, was not too surprised. Such was frequently the fate of prisoners, especially after they had been condemned. If the soldiers believed that a prisoner would be dead shortly anyway, why should anyone care if they had a little sport with him?

They marched along at a fair pace in the bright midday sun, the prisoner, his hands bound behind his back, stumbling frequently and being goaded on by the nearest soldier. Fortunately, it was no great distance, and it was not long before Jesus was thrust into the centre of the courtyard at the Antonia, while the priests and their entourage waited at the gateway. After several minutes, a servant brought an ornate chair out on to the balcony overlooking the courtyard and, several minutes after that, the Governor, accompanied by his officials and two enormous guards, arrived and seated himself.

'Is this the man Jesus?' he asked pompously, having consulted a parchment brief.

'It is, My Lord,' answered Caiaphas, trying hard to sound deferential.

'And the charge is…?'[2] Pilate let the words hang in the hot sunshine.

Caiaphas breathed in deeply and tried hard to keep his temper.

'We would not have brought him to you if we had not already established that he is guilty, My Lord,' he said. 'We have examined him thoroughly, as I mentioned this morning, and find that he is deserving of death under our Law.'

'What is the charge?' demanded Pilate. John could see that the Roman was clearly enjoying teasing Caiaphas. The High Priest decided he would have to play his trump card.

'He claims to be a King, my Lord.'

'Does he indeed? I thought that you Jews didn't like Kings – and didn't have Kings. You have one sovereign God, don't you?'

'Indeed we do, My Lord,' agreed Caiaphas, 'but this man claims to be the Messiah – and this claim includes Kingship under God, my Lord.'

Pilate appeared to reflect for a few moments. He looked at the unkempt, battered man standing before him. He shook his head, wondering how anyone could believe that this tattered specimen could possibly be King of anything or anywhere. Then he addressed himself directly to the hapless prisoner.

'You, Jesus. Do you hear what they are saying about you? They say that you are a King. What have you to say?'

Jesus stood silent for a long time. One of the escorting guards threatened to beat him into replying and finally the answer came, Jesus speaking in a cool, quiet voice, but with emphasis.

'The Kingdom that I seek is not of this world.'

'What does that mean?' asked Pilate, confused, but Jesus gave no further answer. Pilate shrugged and turned to the High Priest.

'I can't think that this man is worthy of death,' he said. 'Look at him – he's nothing but a ragbag!'

'He stirs up the people!' cried Caiaphas, who was starting to worry that his quarry might elude him. 'He stirred up trouble first in Galilee and then, more recently, here.'

'In Galilee, you say?'

'He's originally from Nazareth, in Galilee,' replied the High Priest, but as the words left his mouth he realised that he had fallen into Pilate's trap.

'Then this matter is not really my concern at all,' said that official. 'Why have you wasted my time by bringing him to me? You should have known that he should be tried by King Herod, if he's a Galilean.[3] The King is always in Jerusalem for your Passover Feast. You can take him to Antipas and obtain judgment. I will concur with anything that the Tetrarch decides.'

That was clearly Pilate's last word on the topic, for he rose and stalked majestically from the balcony and disappeared into the forbidding castle. The priests were left to lick their wounds and have the prisoner returned to Caiaphas's house until they could arrange for him to appear before Herod. The High Priest was furious!

★

John hurried round to Justus's inn yet again to give the friends of Jesus the latest situation report. Not surprisingly, there were mixed views on whether this latest twist in the saga was good or bad news. Even Joanna and her colleagues, who all worked for Herod or were married to his employees, couldn't agree. Joanna was of the opinion that Herod would be unwilling to execute Jesus after the way he felt following the death of John the Baptist. Lydia was less optimistic. She had no time at all for Antipas, who was capricious in the extreme and therefore very difficult to predict. He was capable of the most disgusting behaviour, cheating even his own family where he felt the need and ruthlessly putting down anyone who got in his way, just as his father, Herod the Great, had done in his time. Lydia certainly felt no reassurance now that Jesus's fate was in Herod's hands.

The women conferred on the possibility of going to Herod's palace and finding out from their friends on the staff how things were going. Naturally, most of the servants in the palace were locals, but quite a few staff had also travelled down from Tiberias with the King. It might be possible to link up with the Galileans and obtain some information. At least the women would feel that they were in some small way supporting Jesus through his ordeal, even though there would be no chance of getting near him. Joanna thought it worth a try anyway, and Susanna agreed to come with her. The others wanted to go too, but thought that, on this occasion, two would have a better chance of finding out what was happening than four. How Joanna was regretting that her husband, Chuza, had not been required to come to Jerusalem with Herod on this occasion! Nevertheless, she determined to do what she could to be near Jesus in his hour of need.

Mary, on the other hand, went totally to pieces. Nimrah tried to give her hope, using every argument she could think of, but the young woman had made up her mind that Jesus was doomed, and she was already in floods of tears. She flounced out of the room and up to her own bedroom where she flung herself on the bed, sobbing. Nimrah left her alone for some time, thinking that she'd cry herself out, but when she went up to see her later, she was not much better. Nimrah let herself into the bedroom and sat by her daughter, gently caressing her long black hair, which fell in tresses around Mary's shaking shoulders. Eventually the sobbing lessened and finally ceased. Mary turned and faced her mother, her eyes red, her nose swollen.

'When will they kill him?' she asked.

'We don't know that they will,' said her mother, trying to sound confident.

'Yes, they will. He's been condemned by the Sanhedrin, and Herod won't care either way – he'll agree.'

Nimrah knew that it was more than likely. The two women sat side by side for several moments before Mary spoke again.

'If I'm feeling like this, how much worse will it be for his mother? How would you feel if it were me? We must go and tell the family what we know, before they find out in quite the wrong way – tomorrow… or whenever they…' She could not finish her sentence.

'Very well,' agreed Nimrah, 'let us go and try and find Mary, Jesus's mother, and his brothers. You're right. They have to know.'

They made their way quickly the short distance to the inn where Jesus's family was staying and found Mary in. The men had gone out into town. Gently, they told Mary what they knew and how they had come by the information. Jesus's mother listened without comment and without betraying obvious emotion, but Nimrah noticed how she constantly twisted a fold of her garment between her fingers – a sure sign of inner turmoil.

'I'm so sorry to have to bring you news like this, my dear,' she finished. 'We are all still hopeful that things will turn out well – but we thought you ought to be informed.'

Mary stared into space for several seconds, before turning to the two other women with an effort.

'I appreciate what you have done – believe me,' she said. 'It cannot have been easy for you. After all, we have only met once – you had no need to take on a burden like this for me.'

The younger Mary leaned forward to take her namesake's hand, but was gently rebuffed. 'We want to help,' she started to say.

'I know.' Jesus's mother seemed to be growing icy cold in an effort to keep herself from breaking down altogether. 'I told you how it would be – and it's just as I predicted. Jesus would persist in opposing the established order. I knew it would end in disaster… but…' Here her voice cracked and the others could see she was near to breaking point. 'I hoped that he might be spared a little longer – perhaps even long enough to come to his senses.'

There seemed to be nothing to say to that, so the other women took their leave, promising to let the family know at once if they heard anything definite about Jesus's fate.

★

When Joanna and Susanna arrived at the rear entrance of the Hasmonean Palace, they were quickly admitted. The King's steward in Jerusalem remembered Chuza well and was pleased to make the acquaintance of his wife. Joanna and Susanna feigned great interest in the great palace and were shown several of the spacious apartments, with walls lined with marble and water features making the atmosphere feel cooler. The furniture was sumptuous; Joanna and Susanna didn't have to feign their admiration for that!

Before long they got the steward talking about the local political situation and he mentioned that Pilate had, that morning, suddenly transferred judgement of a prisoner to the King. They were expecting him to hold the trial later that day. Apparently, according to the steward, Herod Antipas had been highly intrigued by this turn of events. It was very unusual for Pilate to have anything to do with him – they had been rivals for years. Antipas was certain that there was more to this than met the eye. The Sanhedrin had obviously cooked up a charge for their own purposes. This fellow might be making a claim to be the Messiah, but that was not a capital charge. They must want him out of the way for other reasons.

It looked as if Pilate either didn't want to be involved (but why should he care?), or, more likely, he was teasing the High Priest by making him wait for the decision. The excuse that, because the man was a Galilean, it really fell to Herod to make the judgement, didn't ring true. The steward knew full well that Antipas didn't really care either way about another life, even if it was a Galilean. He was taking on this business for no better reason than it would add some interest to the day, which otherwise threatened to be as boring as all the rest here in Jerusalem. He more or less had to go through the farce of attending the great festivals, but they meant nothing to him. He hated being tied up in Jerusalem when he really much preferred to be in Tiberias, by the Sea of Galilee.

The women learned that the King had sent for his secretary and demanded to know more about this prisoner. The official had obviously been almost as ignorant as his master, but was able to state that his name was Jesus and that he had come originally from Nazareth, not far from Tiberias. At this, something had stirred in Herod's memory.

'Wasn't it this fellow that caused quite a to-do in Galilee a couple of summers ago?' he had asked.

'Indeed it was, Majesty,' the secretary had replied. 'We kept a careful eye on him then. We thought at one time that we should have to bring him in, just as we did with John the Baptist. He had a similar theme to his preaching…'

At the mention of John the Baptist, the King's face had darkened. He still remembered with some regret how he had been forced to have that renegade killed – he'd been outwitted by his wife, Herodias, and her daughter, Salome. It had taken a long time for him to forget that unpleasantness, and now the sore place was being irritated again – the wound throbbed anew. He had grimaced and grumbled, 'I suppose I'd better see this fellow anyway. I can always send him back to Pilate – that'll annoy him!'

Joanna and Susanna were invited to stay for a scratch meal with the other servants and they continued chatting for some time after that. The King and his cronies were asleep at that time of day, so the servants got something of a break then too. However, later on in the afternoon, they heard that the prisoner was on his way to the Hasmonean Palace for trial, accompanied by the High Priest.

The Hasmonean Palace was a particularly beautiful building, made from snowy white marble, without a trace of grain or discoloration. The main entrance was set at the head of an incline between two vast wings, and the vestibule led directly into the great hall. However, Jesus was in no condition to marvel at the splendour of the place, even though the tall columns surrounding the entrance were truly remarkable for their beauty.

Herod was amazed to see the condition of the prisoner. He would hardly command normal attention, let alone the obeisance due to a King. He stood straight enough, but his face was a mess and his clothes were grubby and smeared with blood.

'You are Jesus from Nazareth?' he asked threateningly, as if this was a crime in itself.

Jesus did not reply, so the High Priest spoke for him.

'He is, Majesty; we bring him before you for judgement. He claims to be the Messiah, which, from a village carpenter, is nothing short of blasphemy – as you will readily recognise.'

'Yes. Yes, of course,' replied the King petulantly. He turned and addressed himself directly to the prisoner.

'I've heard about you, Jesus. Not long ago, I'm told that you were travelling about in my Kingdom of Galilee causing quite a bit of disruption. They tell me that you are a magician – that you make lame people walk and cast out evil spirits. Perhaps if you did something magical for me, I should be impressed.'

But if Herod had hoped for a positive response from the bedraggled figure in front of him, he was very disappointed. Jesus continued to stand immobile without uttering a word. His face did not betray any emotion, neither disgust, nor interest, nor fear. The King tried again, with mounting irritation in his voice.

'Come along, now. This won't do! Don't you realise where you are? I have the power of life and death over you. You might at least show me the respect due to your King and your judge, and say something.'

But Jesus still did not say anything. Time and again the King goaded him, seeking to get him to commit himself in some way, but Jesus maintained his silence.[4] Eventually, Herod, by now very annoyed, turned to the priests again.

'What charge do you bring?' he demanded.

Caiaphas replied scornfully, 'He claims to be the Messiah, that is, a King, Majesty. We know that such a claim is ridiculous and contemptible, but the ordinary people are so gullible that they may just fall for it. He might stir the people up to some kind of riotous behaviour, which would be embarrassing for all of us. He is better out of the way. We request the death penalty.'

'But all that is a matter for you, as the local authority here, and the Governor,' returned Herod. 'It has nothing to do with me; I have no jurisdiction here in Jerusalem. If this was Tiberias, or any other city in Galilee or Peraea, that would be very different; but Jerusalem is not my business. You had better take him back to Pilate. Tell him that I was very pleased to be consulted, but, on examination, I find that the matter is outside my area of authority.'

'But, Majesty...' began Caiaphas.

'Take him away!' roared the King. But as the Captain started to give the orders to the soldiers, Herod stopped them.

'Just a minute,' he said, a smile drifting across his crafty face. 'I must say, Jesus, you haven't the look of a King. If you are to impress Pilate, I think we had better dress you more suitably for the part.'

He gave orders for a crimson robe to be brought and placed on Jesus's shoulders.

'That's a bit better,' mocked Antipas. 'Now at least you look as if you might have a shred of royalty in you! Hi, you there' – he glowered at the soldiers surrounding Jesus –'bow to your King! Treat him with some respect, you dogs!'

The scene quickly degenerated into a farce, as the soldiers and other bystanders amused themselves by mocking Jesus, bowing and saluting him, trying to elicit a response from their hapless prisoner; but they were all disappointed. Jesus continued his silence and made no response at all, so that before long the soldiers resorted to physical violence in order to try to provoke him. The King smiled tolerantly at all this for a while, but he soon tired and ordered them all out.

John, who had witnessed the whole episode with an ever-increasing fear in his heart, was relieved that it was at last all over. His admiration for his friend increased as Jesus withstood all these indignities with such fortitude, but he knew that it wouldn't be long before the Galilean would be back in front of Pilate. The steward, who had been present at the so-called trial, brought the news of the outcome to Joanna and Susanna.

'So, it's back to Pilate, is it?' said Joanna, pretending that it was a matter of small importance to her. 'These politicians! They will play their little games.'

The steward nodded gravely, declining to comment further, just in case he was overheard and the matter was reported to his master. Herod had long ears!

*

When Jesus was brought back to the Antonia, Pilate was distinctly put out. He was enjoying a short break from business and greatly disliked being diverted during one of his favourite hours of the day. He had thought that he'd ducked the Jesus problem and found it very irritating that the matter should come before him again. He decided that, this time, he would interview the man indoors, without the priests being there to interrupt and complicate matters.[5] He gave the order, and very quickly the prisoner was brought before him.

John fumed with worry, waiting at the gate with the High Priest's party while the Roman interrogated Jesus. Caiaphas had taken the precaution of bringing along with him quite a party this time, all primed to put pressure on the Governor to get the right verdict. The Roman's interview didn't last very long. Pilate soon stalked out of the castle and confronted the High Priest.

'I have examined the man, Jesus, and I find him innocent,' he said, almost triumphantly.

The High Priest was astounded and dismayed. After all his endeavours, was he to be deprived of their quarry after all? But before he could formulate a reply, Pilate was speaking again.

'You told me that this man claims to be a King. I've asked him about his Kingdom and it is clear to me that his notions of kingship are quite different from yours – or mine. They present no challenge to Rome – they consist of some mystical, airy-fairy ideas that can hurt nobody. He says that he's not really a king at all – more of a witness to the truth – whatever that is!'

The Roman paused for effect, then, again before Caiaphas could think of a reply, he continued further.

'I have another suggestion to put to you. As you all know, there is a custom that I release one of the Jewish prisoners at the time of the Passover festival. I have in mind to release this Jesus.'

John couldn't believe his ears. Pilate was deliberately goading the High Priest with this offer and knew it full well. He'd clearly had his fill of Priests that day and was going to enjoy himself while he could. The last thing Caiaphas wanted was for Jesus to get off. Anything was better than that. The High Priest was turning purple with rage and John knew the signs. There would be an outburst soon. He saw him have a quick word with his father-in-law, Annas, then straighten up and call to Pilate.

'We certainly don't want Jesus released, Your Excellency. That would be most unwise. He might stir up trouble for us all. It would be better to release barAbbas than that.'

John had to admire Caiaphas's quick thinking. Everyone knew that barAbbas had been caught by the Temple Guard a week or so earlier, when a Zealot raid had been made on a caravan on its way to Jerusalem. The bandit had, of course, subsequently been handed over to the Romans, just as his father had known he would be. Caiaphas knew perfectly well that Pilate would hate to release barAbbas, but now he could hope to embarrass the Governor by forcing him both to crucify Jesus and release the bandit. Caiaphas would pretend that Jesus was a bigger threat to Rome even than the notorious Zealot. That should make the proud Gentile think!

'We want barAbbas!' The crowd at the gate knew their cue. The shout was taken up on all sides. 'We want barAbbas!'

'I shall have this man Jesus flogged, while I consider the matter further,' shouted Pilate above the din. With that, he turned and flounced back inside the castle.

John groaned inwardly. A Roman flogging could easily kill a man, especially if he was already weakened by fatigue and mistreatment. Jesus must be near the limit of human endurance by this time. He had probably not been given anything to eat or drink all day. He had been deprived of sleep. He'd been bullied and tormented. True, he was tough, after months of living rough in the Judaean countryside, but he was not trained like a soldier or gladiator, whose whole lives depended on physical prowess and fitness. The Roman scourge was a truly formidable implement, consisting of about a dozen leather thongs, each tipped with a bone or metal fragment, which bit cruelly into the back of any prisoner unfortunate enough to be under sentence. John squirmed with worry for his friend and disgust that men could mete out such treatment to anyone, let along the gentle preacher.

They waited more than an hour in the afternoon sun, growing more and more hot and impatient. At last the castle door opened again and once more Jesus was brought out behind Pilate. He was still standing, but walking with difficulty and clearly suffering dreadfully. Not only had they flogged him, but they had followed up Herod's play-acting with a charade of their own. They had decked him out again in the crimson robe, but also added a purple cloak of their own and forced a crown made from a thorn bush on to his head. The blood trickled down his face, running into his eyes and down his cheeks. He looked a forlorn, beaten figure indeed. The Governor stalked over to the Jews and addressed the High Priest.

'Here is your so-called King,' he said scornfully. 'Look at him. Does he seem regal to you? Are you seriously saying that this –' he paused, searching for the right word – 'this scarecrow – is really your King?' he concluded.

But the crowd, now well primed, started to call for Jesus's death again. The chorus rose threateningly.

'Crucify him! Crucify him!'

Pilate's face contorted with inner rage. He'd clearly had enough of this episode. His mouth twisted with annoyance. He pointed an accusing finger at the High Priest and yelled, 'You take him and crucify him! I find no fault in him to justify death.'

Caiaphas shouted back, 'You know very well that we have no authority to crucify anyone! We need your authority. We say that he's a blasphemer and he ought to die.'

Pilate turned on his heel and marched back inside the castle, signalling to the guards to bring Jesus with them. Once more the priests were kept waiting. John fell to praying silently that, even at this eleventh hour, Jesus would be saved from the cross; but, a few minutes later, Pilate returned with the prisoner stumbling behind him, goaded on by a soldier with a spear in his back. Once more he stated his judgment that Jesus had had sufficient punishment and should be released, but the crowd kept up their demand and eventually that the Governor saw that he would have a riot on his hands if he refused to budge. The words that really got under his skin were uttered by that wily old fox, Annas, who yelled, during a short lull in the shouting, 'If you let this man go, you are no friend of Caesar!'[6]

John remembered that Annas had, once before, gone over Pilate's head and petitioned Caesar directly about the Governor's conduct of affairs, making a great deal of trouble for him. Now, with a great show of reluctance, he relented. He had a bowl of water brought out into the courtyard and ostentatiously washed his hands in front of them all, saying, 'I'm innocent in this matter. I wash my hands of this affair altogether – it is your judgement, not mine. Be it on your own heads.'

'We accept the full responsibility,' replied Caiaphas, relieved to have his own way at last.

'The prisoner will be taken for crucifixion tomorrow morning,' said the Governor, dully. 'Take him away.' And with that he turned and made his escape.

*

John made his way back to the High Priest's house in a dream. His worst fears had come true. His great friend, his long-time confidant, his loyal comrade, was to be crucified. It was impossible. But, would God even now intervene to save his chosen Messiah? In any case, John knew what he must do. He sought an interview with the High Priest and, before long, a message came to say that his boss would see him. He knocked on the familiar door and entered on hearing the usual grunt.

'We got what we wanted, then!' was the High Priest's greeting. His boss's mood was totally changed to one of gloating pride. 'You see? We can still command the affairs of state round here – Pilate cannot ignore us, however much he'd like to think he can!'

John allowed Caiaphas his moment of triumph. Then, when the gushing pride died away for a moment, he made his own contribution, being fairly sure that it would prick Caiaphas's bubble more than a little.

'My Lord,' he said, 'I have decided that I must ask you to accept my resignation from my post here and terminate my office as a Priest of the Temple.'

Caiaphas was thunderstruck. He rose, eyebrows arched and eyes flashing.

'What – whatever...?' He couldn't find his question. Eventually it came to him. With slightly less volume, but with greater intensity, he asked, 'Have you any idea what you are saying, John? You have been showing the greatest promise here. You could rise to be a really important member of the hierarchy. There is really no limit to your progress here... Whatever is this all about? Why do you talk of leaving? To do what?'

John stared helplessly at him, unable to find the words to reply.

'Well?' Caiaphas spat the word in John's face.

John swallowed hard and tried to explain.

'My Lord, I have tried to serve you and the Temple well for a long time, but I have to confess that I have had reservations about many things happening within our area of responsibility.'

Caiaphas's face was a picture. He couldn't believe what he was hearing.

'Such as...?' he gasped.

'Well, I wonder sometimes about the way we raise the Temple taxes and dispose of the money. Are we doing enough for the poor and destitute, as commanded by the prophets? Is the balance of our stewardship correct?'

John kept his voice as even and calm as he could. Now he had started, his thoughts were coming faster and more vigorously.

'Is it right that I live in splendour in my house in Jericho, when I only work a few weeks of each year, but others struggle to live at all and work their fingers to the bone to do so? There are some who have no work at all and are even worse off...'

Caiaphas spluttered, 'And I suppose you think it's even worse that I live in a much bigger house than you, here in Jerusalem?'

John kept his cool and continued, 'My Lord, I don't seek to judge you. That is not my place. You asked me how I had reached my decision. I'm trying honestly to tell you.'

Receiving no answer, John went on.

'Today I have been witnessing the condemnation of a man who spoke about all these things. He put many of these ideas into my head and seemed to me to have the right on his side. Yet today the Council found against him, and he's to die in the morning. For what? For seeking justice? For wanting a better world for the downtrodden and disadvantaged? It is reported by many that he also healed folk who were ill or infirm, people whom we regard as outside the remit of God's love – because they are incomplete and therefore unworthy. Perhaps he is right about that too. Is it their fault if they are ill? Do we *know* that it is their sin that results in their illness? We also know that Jesus preached – he was talking here in the Temple until only two days ago – calling on people to open their lives up to God and let the love of God flood into their hearts.

He taught people to love one another for the sake of their common Father. What could be wrong with that? Is that not the essence of the Law?'

Caiaphas was seething impotently. Now that he was in his stride, John was in full flow.

'In any case, I cannot bring myself to believe that what he has said and done makes him worthy of death. He has spoken the truth; it is we who are in error.'

Then in a slightly more apologetic tone, he concluded, 'I'm sorry, My Lord. You have been good to me and cared about my career – my advancement – but I cannot stay in your employment any longer when such miscarriages of justice are allowed to occur.'

John came to a halt and awaited the expected onslaught. Caiaphas said nothing for several seconds, but finally he found his tongue and said sneeringly, 'Am I to understand that all this time you have been a secret follower of this – charlatan – Jesus? That you are nothing better than a snake in the grass? Is this the way you repay my trust in you, John?'

John replied wearily, 'I have tried – really tried – to be loyal to you and the traditions of the Temple, My Lord. This decision has not been easy for me. I have struggled for many months to find the right way. Meantime, I have done my duty by you at all times.'

The High Priest rose and drew himself up to his full height, seeking to cow his official. He thundered, 'Get out! Go from here and never let me see your face again. You are dismissed and forfeit your status as a Priest of the Temple. I shall see to it that you will not lead our people in worship in any Synagogue in Judaea. God is merciful, but I doubt very much whether even his mercy will cover you for what you have said and done this day.'

John inclined his head as he had done a hundred times before and withdrew from the High Priest's office. He made his way back to his own little office, his heart thumping within his chest, but with a certain elation of spirit. He knew that, at last, he had done the right thing. He had stated openly, as he had hardly dared to do previously even to himself, some of the things which bothered him in his search for the truth. He had finally cast his hand in favour of Jesus… even if it was only when it was too late. Nevertheless, his step had a new spring in it. He was free of dissimulation. He was free…

John left the High Priest's house by one of the rear exits and walked swiftly away. He was aware, however, that the porter's eyes were on him and he guessed that the man had been told to keep an eye open for him and report his egress. So that was that! As he rounded the corner, however, he accidentally bumped into a figure huddled against the wall. Standing back, he started to apologise for his mistake, but as the man turned to him, John realised that he knew him.

'Judas – Judas Iscariot,' he breathed, amazed. 'What are you doing here?'

The former disciple at first drew back, thinking that perhaps John meant to strike him; but when he saw that he was not threatened, Judas reached out for John's arm.

'What is happening to Jesus?' he asked. 'Tell me, for God's sake.'

'That's rich, coming from you,' replied the former priest. 'You were the one who betrayed him. How could you, after all he has been to you!'

The traitor looked at him, tears streaming from his eyes.

'Yes. I know. That fact has haunted me for many hours now. Over and over again, I have been asking myself, did I do the right thing? You see, I believed that Jesus, when face to face with his enemies, would overturn them in triumph. I believed that God would not let him down. I felt he must win in any significant battle… but he's still in prison, isn't he? What is to happen to him?'

John thought he saw a man in genuine trauma. He felt something of the other's anguish after experiencing his own crisis, though different in kind but with some uncomfortable similarities. Softly, he said, 'He's to die in the morning, Judas. Nothing can save him now – short of a miracle. I'm afraid the Romans are very skilled at crucifixions…'

The traitor's face became suffused with grief. His eyes closed tight, his mouth was distorted, the lines on the forehead tightly bunched. He was clearly close to fainting.

'You're sure?' he said, his voice barely audible.

John held his hand as he replied gently, 'I'm sure. I too have let him down, though in a different way, so I share your grief. His other followers feel similarly. We've all let him down, in one way or another. But they thought – I thought – that you had betrayed him just for the money – or because you had lost faith in him. Are you saying that what you did, you did in order to further his cause – as you saw it?'

'I wanted him to win through. Truly. I wanted to help in the establishment of God's Kingdom. I thought he would act, if faced with a significant challenge from the authorities …'

John looked at the man, trying to determine whether this was the truth or just the excuse of a guilty and greedy coward. He still wasn't sure.

'Where is he now?' asked Judas.

'He's in the hands of the Romans at the Antonia,' replied John, 'as you might expect. They are in charge now and will see this awful business through.'

'Is there a chance that, even at this late stage, God will come to his rescue?'

Judas was clutching at his arm as he said the words. John could feel the grip of his talons on his wrist.

'Could God even bring him down from the cross?'

John tore himself from that unnatural grasp.

'I can't tell!' he snarled. 'How do I know? How can any of us know? Frankly, I doubt it.'

The traitor looked hard at the ex-priest and then turned and stumbled away. After a few paces, he turned briefly to look again at John, then he caught up his robe and fled down the street.

★

Once more John turned his steps towards Justus's inn. There he found Lazarus, waiting for more news. John told the friends of Jesus all he knew, and of his own decision to break completely with his calling as a priest and throw in his lot with them.

'So Jesus is to die tomorrow?' Lazarus could hardly bring himself to say the words, let alone believe their meaning. 'It's all over, then?'

'Jesus is to die, certainly,' replied John dully, 'but I think his message is still relevant and worth proclaiming. That is what he would want us to do, I feel sure.'

'And you want to be part of this proclamation?' Lazarus sounded amazed.

'I realise that I am joining the mission very late in the day,' John replied sadly, 'but I suppose that late is better than never.'

Lazarus nodded and asked to be excused. He had a long walk back to Bethany for the second time that day, but the folk there would need to be told the latest position. Justus ensured that John was fed and found a space for the night, even though the inn was already teeming with pilgrims; but John was determined, before he slept, to tell Jesus's mother the sad news. Nimrah and Mary offered to accompany him.

The family received the news with little show of emotion. Like Mary, the boys seemed to regard their elder brother's behaviour as foolish in the extreme, and to consider that the outcome was highly predictable, tragic though it undoubtedly was.

'Will you go to be with your brother in the morning?' asked John.

There was a long pause while each considered this question. Eventually, James spoke, his jaw jutting. 'I shan't go,' he said. 'I can't see that it helps Jesus for us to be there, and I cannot find any joy in Roman executions.'

'Me neither,' broke in his brother.

Mary shook her head. 'Jesus is my son – my eldest,' she said. 'I agree that he has been rather foolish – ill-advised – but I must be near him in his hour of need. Yes, John, I shall be with him tomorrow.'

'Then I will call here for you early tomorrow and we shall go together.'

John held out his hand and took hers briefly. Nimrah and Mary confirmed that they, too, would accompany Mary to the cross.

NOTES

[1] Luke 22:66.
[2] John 18:29.
[3] Luke 23:7.
[4] Luke 23:9.
[5] John 18:33.
[6] John 19:12.

Crucified, dead and buried

The sky looked grey and forbidding in the morning. Instead of the bright blue sky which usually greeted Jews at Passover time, the heavens were grey and overcast. The atmosphere was heavy and sultry, and locals shook their heads, forecasting a storm sometime that day. In other parts of the world, April might be associated with gentle showers but here it could sometimes bring fierce storms.

John hadn't slept well. He still couldn't bring himself to accept that Jesus's life was about to be brought to an abrupt halt that very day and in the most degrading fashion ever devised by man – crucifixion. The thought of his friend being strung up, naked, on a cross, for all the world to see, made his stomach turn. He got up at first light, washed and tried a little breakfast, but his stomach erupted. The women had decided to make their own way over to the place of execution, a rocky outcrop outside the city walls known as Golgotha, the place of the skull. John did as he had promised and went to the inn in which Jesus's family were staying. Mary joined him with hardly a word. Her face was like marble, cold and pale. She carried herself almost proudly but John could see the inner turmoil reflected in her big brown eyes, which were red-rimmed and encased in dark circles, betraying the lack of sleep for several nights past.

Although it was still early, the pilgrims were up in force and milling about all over the city. The bazaars were open and doing brisk business. Jerusalem might be celebrating a religious feast, but that didn't stop the market from operating with all the skill for which the Jewish nation was so well known – and in places feared. John and Mary picked their way slowly over to a spot opposite the entrance to the Antonia fortress. They felt they wanted to be as near to Jesus as possible throughout his slow march to Golgotha. Mary found a low wall on which she could sit while they waited for the inevitable. Nor did they have long to wait. The gate was suddenly flung open and a sad procession appeared; a troop of Roman soldiers preceded the prisoners – three of them – while a column of soldiers marched on either side. A Centurion followed with another dozen men. It was a gruesome sight. All these prisoners were nearly naked and obviously in terrible shape, physically. Their backs were torn and covered with congealed blood from scourging. Each carried a heavy wooden beam, the crossbar to his cross. Jesus was still wearing the grotesque crown of thorns that the soldiers had made for him. He staggered along at a slow pace, goaded from time to time by the nearest soldier with his javelin. Another soldier with a whip, not marching in the ranks, was stationed near the prisoners; this he used savagely from time to time on any prisoner not making the required progress.

The sad procession wended its way through an area heavily populated by shops, along the cobbled, uneven streets, heading for the west gate. Pilgrims who had previously been busy with shopping – talking, laughing and generally enjoying their visit to the Holy City – turned to see the grisly sight, and their joy was transformed to disgust, loathing, and revulsion – and, often, hatred for the Romans. Some felt sick for the prisoners. Some felt that the condemned men were probably getting their just deserts and should be despised, but few people enjoyed the spectacle. A few women seemed genuinely sorry for the men who were to die. A little knot of them stood at one corner, weeping openly and beating their breasts. Although it was, strictly speaking, forbidden for the crowd to sympathise with any condemned man, nobody took a few charitable women seriously. The soldiers passed them by with contempt, their cold faces showing no trace of emotion.

John moved along trying to keep pace with the unfortunate men. Although their progress was very slow, he and Mary had difficulty making their way between the press of pilgrims. They could see that Jesus was in a worse state than the other two. Each prisoner carried a rough board round his neck with the charge against him written on it. The two other prisoners were condemned as bandits – thieves and cut-throats – Zealots taken into custody during the recent guerrilla raid on a wealthy caravan coming into Jerusalem from the coast. They were burly fellows, displaying magnificent physiques, the result of living rough in the semi-wilderness for months, training for their foul trade. Even the thrashing they had received at the Antonia had not cowed them completely and they managed to carry their cross-beams without too much difficulty. Jesus, on the other hand, was struggling to put one foot in front of the other. The charge on the board round his neck simply read 'The King of the Jews'.[1] John was surprised by this. Surely the High Priest would have objected to it, he thought. Presumably Pilate, having lost the main argument, had decided at least to have his way about the title. *King of the Jews*! Jesus looked anything but a King now. Indeed, at that very moment, he staggered and went down under the load of his crossbar.

The Centurion cursed and marched up to see what had happened. Jesus was struggling to his feet, trying to lift the bar again, but the officer could see that he was quite incapable of taking further punishment. If the procession was to move on at anything like a reasonable pace, the load would have to be carried by someone else. A large, dark-skinned man at the side of the road close to where Jesus had fallen was picked on by the Centurion and compelled to carry the timber beam instead of Jesus.[2]

The pace was quicker now, such that John and Mary couldn't keep up with it. Thinking back afterwards, John realised that it was possibly a good thing, for by the time they had fought their way through the crowds, through the gate and on to the rough ground outside the city walls where the executions were due to take place, the actual crucifixions had been carried out and the three men were already hanging on their crosses. John was glad that Mary had not been there to see the nails being driven through the flesh of the wrists, as the men were pinioned on to the cross-beams, and the beams, carrying the men, were lowered on to the vertical poles, already in the ground. Then there would have been the other horrific moments, when the nails had been driven through the heels into the sides of the crosses. The pain must have been excruciating, not just for the condemned men, but also for any in the crowd who loved or cared for them. Crucifixion was not just a method of killing. It was a terrifying warning to all who witnessed it: *Do not challenge the Roman system or flout its laws*!

John and Mary edged closer to the central cross, on which Jesus was hanging. He was barely conscious, but every few seconds, he was compelled to push down on the nails through his heels just to ease the pressure on his chest, so that he could take in a gulp of air. His face worked as he experienced the dreadful pain all through his body. Yet still he was thinking of other people, for he looked down at his mother, standing there with his friend, and gasped, 'Mother! I'm – glad – you have come to be with me – and with John. This man is now to be your son. My friend, take this woman to be your mother.'[3]

John did not know how to reply, but he bowed his head in acceptance. He placed a tender arm round Mary's shoulder and this time she did not attempt to draw away from him. They were able, at last, to take some comfort from each other. A few minutes later, John and Mary were joined by Mary Magdalene and her mother. After exchanging hushed greetings, they learned that the two women had been earlier at the execution site and had witnessed the crucifixion itself. Mary had nearly fainted, but just managed to retain her senses.

'Do you know what Jesus said as they actually pierced his flesh?' she said in a low whisper, her voice filled with wonder. Clearly she did not expect a reply to this question, for she continued, in a voice that betrayed her own incredulity.

'He said, "Father, forgive them. They don't realise what they are doing".[4] Can you imagine that? He was able to forgive even those who crucified him!'

John shook his head in disbelief, then glanced up at the lonely figure on the cross. He stared long and hard at the broken body, the gasping figure, trying desperately to cling on to life. Jesus looked down at him and gave the merest glimpse of a smile, which was suddenly cut short by a new stab of pain.

'Yes,' said John softly. 'I can believe it of him. I wouldn't of anyone else I know.'

The four of them stood in silence, just keeping vigil with the tortured man hanging above their heads. They were distracted occasionally by the voices of the soldiers, who were sitting on the ground a few yards away. John noticed with some disgust that they were throwing dice, gaming to see which of them should take the prisoners' clothes. Jesus had not had many things of value, but he did have a good homespun robe that he prized. There it lay on the ground, while the soldiers cast their dice to determine its new owner.[5] Was nothing sacred, thought John to himself? He shook his head at the indifference of the military to the scene before them, but his disgust was even greater when a group of men came over to the cross and started to mock Jesus.

'Is this the Messiah – the King?' one scoffed. 'He was good at helping others, they say. He's not so good at helping himself! Say, Jesus, when are you going to help yourself?'

'I'll tell you what,' shouted another, 'if you come down from the cross now and put these soldiers to flight, I'll believe in you!'[6]

The women with John drew away in horror at all this. They couldn't believe that anyone could be so callous. Here was Jesus, clearly close to breathing his last, in great pain of body, mind and spirit, and all they could do was to mock. Eventually, when they received no response of any kind, the disgusting little group grew tired of their jesting and moved on.

'How could they?' asked Mary Magdalene.

John debated with himself for a moment as to whether to enlighten them. Then he said, 'I'm afraid I have to tell you that I recognised them as fellows in the High Priest's employment. No doubt they are here to ensure that Caiaphas's wishes are being carried out.'

They waited on through the long morning, hoping that they were of some slight support to the figure on the cross simply by being there, experiencing a little of his tremendous pain and agony. Their muscles ached simply with standing – how much more must the poor wreck on the cross be suffering, stretched out, pinioned in both wrists and ankles, gasping for breath! About midday, the storm that had threatened all the morning suddenly broke. The sullen greyness of the sky darkened till it was nearly as dark as night-time. The clouds became really menacing, lowering until they seemed to be just a few feet above their heads. The ground shook with the thunder, and the lightning flashed vividly against the now darkened sky.[7] The rain suddenly lashed down in torrents, sending all the casual watchers scurrying for shelter. The soldiers cursed and huddled under their cloaks.

John and the women stood still, not caring that they got soaked within a few seconds. They stood there, eyes half closed against the lashing rain, watching the lightning play among the clouds and feeling that the end of the world was about to arrive, so great was the upheaval in the heavens. At last, after what seemed like a couple of hours, the storm decreased in intensity. The sky lightened a little, the rain eased and the world returned gradually to something like normality.

John looked up at the pathetic figure on the cross. Jesus was barely alive. The two friends exchanged looks. John would never forget that look of his friend. He felt that Jesus was expressing his gratitude for his presence, his support and his love; but, in a strange way, John also knew himself to be supported and loved by the tattered, dying man. Somehow, even in death, Jesus had this ability to reassure anyone he was with that all would be well, if only they trusted him. How absurd, in the circumstances, thought John.

The afternoon wore on. All of them, but particularly the women, and especially the older Mary, were desperately tired of standing. The ground all around them was sodden and there was nowhere they could sit, so they continued to stand there, suffering with Jesus. They all had their own thoughts. Mary thought of the baby she had borne and brought up, then the long years when Jesus had been the principal breadwinner after the death of his father, then of his marriage to Sarah and her sad demise, and finally the years of estrangement as he went off, first to learn and then to teach.

Nimrah recalled the day that Jesus had visited their house and talked to her Mary; how he had helped her to control her youthful aggression and selfish disregard of anything but her own wishes. Mary Magdalene smiled through her pain as she recalled his soft brown eyes and winning smile. She would do anything for Jesus. Of course she loved him – who wouldn't? She was quite captivated by this strange man from Nazareth, but now he was going from them. Her eyes filled with tears yet again.

At mid-afternoon, Jesus suddenly lifted his head and called out, 'My God, my God, why have you deserted me?'[8]

'I can't believe it!' exclaimed Nimrah, softly. 'Is it possible that even Jesus has lost his faith in God? I always felt that he lived the whole of his life in close contact with his father.'

Mary, too, expressed intense surprise, but John smiled slightly and reassured them.

'I suppose it's possible he's lost his faith, but I don't think so. I think Jesus is repeating one of the psalms which begins with those words – but it ends with a ringing declaration of faith, thus:

"Let all the ends of the earth remember and turn again to the Lord; let all the families of the nations bow down before him…"[9] 'No. I don't think that Jesus has lost contact with God. He is identifying with the psalmist – a moment of doubt in a midst of great trauma but, in the end, complete faith and trust.'

One of the soldiers heard Jesus cry out and came across to the foot of the cross to see what was happening. The young man seemed to be somewhat different from most of his comrades, because he showed a glimmer of compassion for the dying man.

'Want a drink?' he asked.

Jesus didn't reply, but his head slumped forward and the soldier interpreted this as an affirmative response. He went over to the pitcher that the soldiers had brought with them, soaked a sponge in the watery wine and held it up to Jesus on the tip of his spear.[10] The dying man appeared to sip for just a moment and then his head fell to his chest.

'It's finished,' he gasped,[11] but, astonishingly, his tone was not one of defeat, but of victory. 'Father, into your hands, I commend my spirit.'[12]

John gazed up at his friend for several moments. The chest had stopped heaving. The body was quite still. Gone were the restless movements as Jesus had sought to ease first one painful joint and then another. There was no movement or sign of life.

'It *is* finished,' he said. 'It's over, Mary. He's at peace now. Nobody can hurt him any more.'

Mary looked up at her son one last time and nodded slowly. She turned to John, who took his new mother in his arms and held her close to him for a moment.

'It's time to go,' he said. 'We can do no more here. You're tired, cold and wet. We must think of you now.'

The others hastened to agree with him. They looked up at the body on the cross for one last time, then made their way slowly and painfully off the hill and into the town, back to the warmth and shelter of Justus's inn.

★

Judas huddled under the city wall, looking across at the stark crosses, outlined against the fierce black sky of the storm. He still hoped for a miracle. Surely God must act now and save his Messiah… It couldn't be that Jesus would die – especially not a death like that. But as the minutes ticked by and became hours, Judas began to wonder if, after all, he had been wrong in believing that Jesus was the chosen one. If Jesus was going to die, he must have been wrong. Yet, somehow, Judas still refused to admit that he had been mistaken. Jesus was so much as he imagined that the Messiah should have been – he really knew God's purposes. He, more than anyone else he had known, had followed God's way. He cherished the people because they were God's children. He cared and befriended even the unlovely, the sick, the outcasts. That was the sort of Messiah Judas could respect and follow. Yet, in other ways, Jesus had disappointed him. He certainly hadn't triumphed in the field of politics. He hadn't driven the Romans out of the Promised Land. He hadn't even convinced the religious authorities of Jewry of his claims – they had turned on him and handed him over to the Romans…

Round and round in his brain went the argument. He still couldn't decide. Did he do right in pushing Jesus to the brink, to see whether he could triumph? Why didn't God act when the chips were down? Had he been wrong after all?

Ultimately, as the storm cleared and the figure on the central cross still hung there, seemingly lifeless, Judas made up his mind. Whether Jesus had been right or wrong about being Messiah, he couldn't decide. Whatever the truth about God's lack of care for Jesus, he, Judas, wasn't going to let it be said that he benefited from his leader's death. Right or wrong, he certainly didn't want those silver pieces, still jangling in his purse. For Judas, at last, the time for action had arrived. He got to his feet and started off into the city again, gradually gaining speed as his body, cold and wet, began to recover from hours of hanging around in doorways, huddled against walls. He ran through the west gate and through the streets, largely deserted after the terrible storm. On he went, until he came at last again to the High Priest's house. There he summoned up his courage to knock boldly at the door, trying to gain confidence from the action. A Levite answered the door and gazed at him in astonishment. He presented a grim sight, unshaven, unkempt, clothes bedraggled and wet through.

'What do you want?' said the official, disdainfully.

'I must see the High Priest,' replied the scarecrow.

'The High Priest doesn't receive vagabonds from the street. Get on your way.' The Levite made as if to close the door, but Judas was too quick for him. He jammed his foot in the doorway and continued, urgently, 'I must see the High Priest. I have money for him.'

At the mention of money, the Levite paused. 'What money have you got?' he asked sceptically.

'I have silver, belonging to the High Priest,' returned the other, jangling the coins in his purse. 'Let me in. I need to see someone in authority.'

The Levite opened the door unwillingly and Judas stepped inside, but it was a full half hour before anyone came to deal with him. He fumed and fretted, livid at the way he was being treated. Eventually, he was taken into an office, to be confronted by one of the priests who assisted the High Priest.

'What's this all about?' enquired that worthy haughtily, rising from behind a rather grandiose desk.

Judas burst out, 'You have killed an innocent man – I betrayed him to you!'

'What are you talking about, man?' asked the official angrily.

'You've killed Jesus of Nazareth – he's dying on a cross out there now.' Judas was almost hysterical.

'Listen. Take it more calmly. That man was handed over to the Romans for execution after proper judgment. He was a criminal and found guilty by the Great Sanhedrin. The Governor himself confirmed the sentence—'

Judas interrupted this official response, shrieking, 'But he was not guilty! He was gentle and kind. Why did you kill him? I was quite wrong to help you.'

He reached into the purse, gathering coins in his cold, wet hands.

'Here is the money I was given.[13] Have it back! I want no part of it.'

When the official backed away, uncertain how to respond, Judas, overcome with impatience and frustration, angrily flung the coins across the desk and all over the floor round the other's feet.

'Take your silver – I didn't do what I did for money…'

Judas turned and ran to the door, stumbling as his eyes filled with salt tears, making it difficult for him to find his way. He cursed as he hit his knee against the door jamb. He made his way uncertainly out into the street again, nearly falling headlong down a small flight of steps. There was nothing left for him now, he thought. He was nothing. He had nothing. He was nothing but a failure – a betrayer of his friend. He wanted nothing more to do with anything. He just wanted out.

Judas ran back to Golgotha, just in time to see the soldiers taking the bodies down from the crosses. Judas didn't stop to see where they were taking them. He cursed violently under his breath and turned away to run and later stumble into a small copse growing further away from the city wall, on a lonely part of the hill. There, almost without giving it any more thought, he climbed a small tree, tied one end of his girdle to a branch and the other round his scrawny neck, closed his eyes and launched himself into space.

★

Justus was a good innkeeper and knew how to anticipate the needs of his guests. As soon as he saw Mary and John, hot water was provided for them so that they could bathe themselves and get warm and dry again. A fire was lit and the crackling logs soon had the room downstairs feeling more cheerful. John didn't take long to remember to ask after Peter, only to be told that he hadn't been seen all day. Justus had tapped at his door several times, offering wine or something to eat, but had been met either with silence or a stern rebuff.

'I think it is time to break this dark mood,' said John. 'He can't go on like this for ever. Sooner or later, he has to face up to life again. The other Galileans need his support – he was one the foremost of Jesus's disciples. They'll look to him now.'

Justus shrugged. 'I agree,' he replied, 'but it's not that easy. He just won't talk to anyone at present.'

John went up and rapped on Peter's door. There was no answer, so he tried again. At last, there was a weary call from inside.

'Who is it?'

'It's John barHelez. Let me in, Peter. I must speak to you.'

There was an angry, tired retort. 'My name is not Peter – it's Simon. What do you want?'

'I just want to talk to you and share with you. You can't stay alone for ever. Of course you're grieving, my friend – so are we all. Can we not share our grief and so share the pain?'

After a short delay, the door opened and John saw Peter silhouetted in the doorway. He looked a mess. His face was unshaven, his hair matted and tousled. His eyes were red-rimmed, with black shadows encircling them. He seemed to have aged ten years since John had seen him last at the supper only two nights ago. Altogether, it was difficult to equate this figure with the big, jolly fisherman whom he had known previously.

'You'd better come in – if you must,' said the wreck.

John followed the Galilean into the room and took a seat by the bed. Peter slumped on to the bed, hands over his eyes.

'Is it all over?' he said in a low growl.

'Yes. I'm afraid our friend is no more.'

'Were you there with him?'

'Yes. I was there with his mother. Mary of Magdala and her mother were with us too. Joanna and her friends were also there, somewhere, but we didn't see them. No doubt we shall hear from them shortly.'

'Were none of the Galilean men there?'

'No, Peter. They are at Bethany with Lazarus and his sisters. They're all safe.'

'Then we all let him down.' Peter's voice broke and John realised that he was choking back tears behind his hand.

'There was nothing you – or anyone – could have done, Peter.'

The fisherman looked up suddenly and spoke with some vehemence.

'Don't call me that! That was the name he gave me, and I don't deserve it. It means "a rock", doesn't it? The one who stands fast. Well, I didn't stand fast when the moment of trial came – so I don't deserve that name.'

John turned to him and reached out to take one of Peter's enormous hands but his gesture was determinedly rebuffed.

'You did what you could. Nobody could have done more. Why do you continue to punish yourself for being a failure – if that is what it was. We all shared in that failure. I was placed much nearer to him than you were, but I could do nothing to save him. The others ran away, but came back to look for him, and then went to Bethany only because it seemed the sensible course to take. He wanted you all to be safe, not taken to prison with him. That is what you did – you made sure you were safe, so that now you will be able to carry on his work.'

Peter turned on the bed and sought John's eyes for the first time.

'Carry on?' he cried incredulously, brow wrinkling. 'We can't do anything without Jesus. He was the driving force behind all our activity. Without him, we don't know what to say or what to do.'

He paused before continuing, in a low voice. 'Besides, I'm not sure I believe in his way any more. It all seemed right when he told us about it. When he spoke, our hearts were set alight and we believed in the love of God. We resolved to love others for his sake – but look where that philosophy has landed him! Imagine! A man of love stripped and nailed to a cross! What happened to the God of love then? Where was he for Jesus?'

Another burst of grief hit the fisherman and he covered his eyes again, ashamed to be seen crying by the other man. John spoke urgently, but softly.

'Listen, Peter. I call you that because now is the time for you to be a rock. The others will need your leadership now that Jesus has gone. Together, you can somehow continue to tell the world his message and you – we – can win through.'

John paused and pursed his lips before continuing in a low voice, 'Yes, Peter. I want to join you – if you'll have me. I'd like to help. We have to carry on, so that what he has started is not wasted.'

Peter stopped choking in his grief and slowly opened his eyes again. He peered at the ex-priest in astonishment.

'You want to join us now?' he asked, confusion showing in his eyes. 'But there's nothing to join, John. There's nothing without Jesus.'

John said nothing for several moments. Then he said softly, 'I want you to come down and meet Jesus's mother, who is with me. Jesus asked me to look after her. Obviously, I shall have to contact his brothers, who are in town, or they will be worried for their mother; but for now at least she's here and I'd like you to meet her.'

'I have met her before,' said Peter, 'briefly. It was when we went through Nazareth on the mission – and again shortly afterwards. She was – well – antagonistic, to say the least, towards Jesus and his ideas then.'

'She doesn't understand him, that's true; but she still loves her son, and I believe that you, knowing Jesus so well, might be able to tell her why he went through all that he did.'

Peter turned away, growling, 'I wish I could! I don't understand myself – so how can I tell her?'

'Listen. We have to work through this together. If what Jesus said was right two days ago, it must still be right now.' John's voice was urgent, but Peter shook his head.

'Jesus was wrong! He must have been,' he said. 'How can God be loving and caring when he allowed Jesus, who loved him and served him, to go to a death like that? Why didn't he save him?'

Peter shook his head again and covered his eyes as a fresh fit of grief overtook him. John waited a moment and then rose and left the room. He had tried his best, but his best was just not good enough. Peter just couldn't be reached.

★

Joanna and her friends, Susanna, Rebecca and Lydia, were still watching the grim activities on the hill of Golgotha. They had seen John depart with the other women and guessed that the last signs of life had departed from their mutual friend. They had cried so much that day that more tears refused to come. In a way, it was almost a relief.

'At last his suffering is over,' Joanna whispered.

'Thank God for that,' murmured the others, almost in unison.

They watched as the afternoon dragged on. The sky had lightened a little, but there was no chance of the sun making an appearance that evening. In another two hours, night would be upon them and the Sabbath would begin.

'Shall we go too?' suggested Lydia.

'Let's wait a little longer,' said Joanna. 'I want to see what they do with the body of Jesus. What do they normally do?'

There was an uncomfortable silence, as it dawned on them that it was probable that the bodies would simply be dumped on the local rubbish heap. Fortunately, Jewish law did not permit the bodies to be left on the crosses on the Sabbath, as would be the case across most of the Roman Empire, but their fate on the rubbish tip wouldn't be much better. Indeed, in some ways, it could be worse.

'If we can see where they put Jesus, we might be able to give him some sort of burial,' Susanna suggested. 'At least we can cover the body…'

They waited, each minute seeming like an hour. The sky began to grow dim. Then they saw a priest, accompanied by two rather grand-looking men and two servants, coming up the hill. The newcomers strode purposefully up to the Centurion, who was still keeping watch at the site of execution, and showed him a paper. Then they watched, horrified, as one of the soldiers was summoned and sent to examine the bodies on the crosses. Horror of horrors, he was mercilessly striking the legs of one of the brigands with a heavy club.

'Whatever are they doing?' asked Rebecca. 'Hasn't that poor devil suffered enough?'

'He's breaking his legs,' replied Joanna, turning away, her eyes closed as she fought to stop her stomach rising.[14] 'I've heard about that. They do it to prevent the criminal from pushing down on them to ease the pain in his chest – so that he'll asphyxiate and die. Someone has obviously decided that it's time for the bodies to be removed, before the Sabbath dawns.'

As she spoke, the soldier with the club approached Jesus.

'Oh, no – not Jesus too.' Lydia was heartbroken.

But the soldier apparently thought better of it. He called something to a comrade, who also came to the foot of the central cross and, having studied the body, thrust his spear into Jesus's side.[15] The women turned away again in horror. When they turned back, they saw that the two grand-looking individuals were coming over to see Jesus and calling to the soldiers for a ladder. They watched while the soldiers struggled to remove the nails from the feet of Jesus, then lower the crossbar and the body to the ground.

'What's happening?' asked Susanna. 'Who are these men? They are dressed very well and seem to be important, but who are they?'

Joanna responded quietly, 'I don't know – but I'm grateful to them anyway. Let's just keep out of the way and see what happens. It looks as if someone besides us cares what happens to Jesus. The soldiers are just carting the other poor devils away – yes, there they go.'

It was true. The brigands' bodies had been thrown unceremoniously on to a cart which was departing in the direction of the common rubbish tip. The body of Jesus, on the other hand, was being covered in a fine linen cloth by the two important-looking men and then transported with some reverence by the two servants on a litter over the hill in the other direction.[16] The women followed at a distance and saw them turn into a walled garden a little way down the hill. They saw the little party make its way across the garden till it stopped at a sepulchre cut into the side of the hill. Its entrance was closed by a large stone, running in a groove. Slowly, the men pushed back the stone, revealing a small cave, into which they took the body of Jesus. They remained in the cavern for a few minutes, presumably arranging the body on the shelf cut into the rock for the purpose. Then they re-emerged, replaced the stone across the gaping hole in the cliff face, and departed. It was none too soon, for the darkness was by this time falling fast and everyone needed to be indoors before the start of the Sabbath.

'Quickly!' said Joanna. 'We've seen all we need to. Once the Sabbath is over, we can return and anoint the body properly. That's the least we can do for Jesus. Meantime, he'll be quite safe there. Someone has looked after him for us – God be thanked for that!'

*

In accordance with the Law, none of the friends of Jesus went very far on the Sabbath, but this Sabbath, in particular, they felt totally moribund. Their mental and spiritual state mirrored their lack of physical activity. All feeling was gone. They were numb. Tired. Spent. Tears no longer flowed. Words were useless.

Nathaniel decided to go to the little Synagogue at Bethany for traditional worship. At the last moment, Philip joined him, but they walked in silence to and from the service and could remember little of what was said. Thaddeus, Simon and little James sat in the garden behind Lazarus's house with Mary. Normally, they would have been delighted to spend time with this lovely girl, but this morning there was an awkward tension between them. They were all thinking of their mutual friend, now, unknown to them, cold in a stranger's grave, but nobody wanted to speak about their troubled souls.

Thomas and Matthew strolled a few yards into the vineyard below Lazarus's house, where the vines were just starting to shoot from their brown stumps. Signs of new life, thought Thomas – promise of a rich harvest in just a few months. No such hope for us, though. Our vine will never shoot again. It's been mutilated by brutal hands – Roman hands – aided and abetted by the highest Jews in the land. Cut down. Murdered. There's no hope for us now. Thomas couldn't bring himself to talk about it. Even Matthew's normally ebullient spirit was quenched; he moped around, saying little.

Andrew, James and John went with Lazarus up on to the roof of his house. There the host had rigged up a shade; they sat under it, sharing a bowl of wine, but somehow, although the sky was blue and sun beautifully warm after the darkness of the previous day, life had lost all meaning. Each tried to pray silently, but the exercise seemed pointless and nothing seemed to be real any more.

After lunch, they all discussed what they should do. If it hadn't been for Peter being separated from them, most would have opted for an immediate return to Galilee and home. The mission was over – dead. What was the point of lingering in Judaea, they argued? But Andrew, at least, needed to link up with his brother, and the others were reluctant to go until the two brothers had been reunited and Peter's state of mind assessed. In the end, it was agreed that Andrew and the other two fishermen would risk going into Jerusalem next morning to seek the big fellow and, hopefully, get him to come to Bethany, prior to going with them home to Galilee.

In Jerusalem, too, Jesus's friends were at an extremely low ebb. Joanna and her friends checked with Justus that he could supply the quantity of the perfumes and oils they would need for the burial of Jesus next day. They fretted at the delay in being able to minister to their fallen leader. The day seemed interminable. Mary Magdalene and her mother, similarly, whiled away the day as best they could, wondering why some days seemed so short, when there was much to be done, while this one seemed to last as long as an entire winter.

Peter still kept to his room and would drink only a little water, which Justus insisted he took. John called to see him midway through the morning but found the big fisherman still brooding and in the depths of depression; but at least, this time, Peter wanted to know more of the detail of Jesus's trial. John was pleased even with this hint of progress and told him all the facts.

'But why didn't Jesus defend himself? Why keep silence at the trial?' queried Peter.

'Well, under Jewish Law, silence should be the best defence,' replied John. 'It is up to witnesses to bring evidence before the court and prove their case. In Jesus's case, the witnesses just didn't agree. They brought all manner of ridiculous charges – some based on truth, but grossly distorted. Consequently, the next witness told the story very differently, with different distortions. The court clearly couldn't accept stories that were not properly corroborated. Finally, Caiaphas had to resort to the highly irregular procedure of asking the prisoner to incriminate himself. When Jesus declined – as he had every right to do – the High Priest used the extreme oath, which no practising Jew can ignore. Caiaphas asked Jesus, under oath, if he was the Messiah – and Jesus quietly agreed that he was. The court accepted this as evidence of blasphemy and likely to lead to a disturbance of the peace; then they condemned him to death. They sold the "disturbing the peace" part of the story to Pilate – with difficulty. Pilate tried to slough the matter off on to Herod, but that was never likely to work – that wily old fox wasn't going to take the responsibility. Once he'd had his fun, he handed Jesus back to Pilate.'

'Shouldn't Jesus have pleaded his case more with Pilate?' asked Peter.

'I would have thought so. Pilate was obviously reluctant to proceed, but Jesus seemed to have made up his mind to accept the Sanhedrin's verdict. I can't see why. Any more than I can see why he didn't avoid capture in the first place. I told you that I warned him that Judas had agreed with the High Priest to lead the soldiers to the campsite to apprehend him. Why didn't he simply cancel the supper at Justus's inn and go immediately to Bethany – and then home to Galilee? Or, even if he had continued with the supper, he could have gone immediately afterwards to Bethany with Lazarus, instead of waiting in the garden where Judas would know where to find him. It doesn't make sense. Why didn't he escape when he could?'

Peter shrugged his massive shoulders.

'Why would anyone seek capture?' he murmured. Then, after a few seconds, he asked, 'Could it be that he thought he'd win the argument with the Temple authorities and convince them of his claim?'

John shook his head sadly. 'There was no real chance of that. I'm sure that Jesus knew that. No. I believe now that he wanted to confront what he regarded as the evil in the nation and show that he could accept the worst that it could do – even to the bitter end. That seemed to be his reading of the scriptures; he was very taken with the last part of the prophecy of Isaiah, you know, where it is anticipated that the Messiah will suffer for the nation.'

'But what does that *achieve*?' demanded Peter. 'He's suffered, but he's lost out – as he must have known that he would. What did he gain?'

'I don't know,' agreed John. 'It's a mystery.'

John also tried to comfort the mother of Jesus, who joined him for lunch. After lunch, John was able to recite some scripture to her and pray with her, but, like the folk in Bethany, they found the usual practice of worship of little benefit. Down the road, the brothers of Jesus fumed and fretted. John had sent them a message to say that their mother was safe with him, but they couldn't understand why she was not with them. Everything that could go wrong had done so. Their brother had been executed, bringing shame on them and the entire family. Now their mother appeared to be shunning them and associating with their dead brother's friends.

Justus had to go about his business. Even on the Sabbath, a minimum effort was necessary just to keep the visitors to the inn content. Mark loafed about aimlessly, the events of the previous week still bubbling in his mind. What did he really think of this Galilean preacher who had come into his life, involving him with carrying pots in public like a woman and then near-arrest in the dead of night? At seventeen, he couldn't really make up his mind what he thought of it all, but he sensed that everyone who had known the preacher was at rock bottom, dejected, despondent and, to all intents and purposes, dead in spirit.

Over in Bethphage, Matthias had heard from a friend of the way in which Jesus had been treated. He shook his head in bewilderment. First his own leader, John the Baptist, and now the man John had said would be the Messiah. What was the world coming to? The 'high-ups' – the King, the High Priest and the Governor – were all as bad as one another. They put down all potential new leadership from whatever quarter, anything that challenged their position in the status quo. Life was pointless. There would never be a life for the ordinary man, the poor man, the man whose toil kept the whole of community on track.

Cleopas and Nathan were all too aware of Jesus's fate. They had noticed his disappearance from the scene a couple of days earlier when they had gone again to the Temple to hear him speak. They were surprised and disappointed when he was not there. Then they had heard the troops marching by their shops and had dashed out to see the three men carrying their cross-beams, realising with horror that the one stumbling at the rear was none other than the Jesus they had come to respect and wanted to follow. They had immediately shut up shop and followed the grim procession to the place of execution. There they had seen the pathetic creatures hung up to die, including the one whom they had hoped might actually be their Messiah, reduced to a mere wreck, a thing of ridicule for some and an object of pity for others.

By midday, as the great storm broke, they had returned for shelter in their shops, but knowing that they would conduct no more business that day. On the Sabbath, the high day of the festival, they had intended, of course, to go again to the Temple to worship and pray, but, by common consent, they absented themselves. Somehow they couldn't find one festive feeling after the events of the past week. How could a person as kind and friendly as Jesus be thought of as a criminal? Whatever had he done to deserve that sort of treatment?

It was a long Sabbath for everyone.

NOTES

[1] John 19:19
[2] Mark 15:21
[3] John 19:27
[4] Luke 23:34
[5] John 19:23
[6] Mark 15:30
[7] Mark 15:33
[8] Mark 15:34
[9] Psalm 22:27
[10] John 19:29
[11] John 19:30
[12] Luke 23:46
[13] Matt. 27:3
[14] John 19:32
[15] John 19:34
[16] John 19:38–40.

Victory

Mark awoke in a cold sweat early the next morning, two hours before dawn. He had been dreaming – and what a loathsome dream it had been! He had been captured and thrown into prison, just like Jesus. He too had suffered as he had been tried by false judges, mocked, scourged and led out to be crucified. Like Jesus, he had trodden the terrible *via dolorosa*, carrying the great wooden crossbar, enduring the whip of the soldier and the jeers of the crowd. He agonised as he felt his arms stretched out and aching, and then experienced the searing pain as the nails were hammered home. He felt himself lifted high into the air, attached only by those nails – the pain cut through him. He awoke in a cold sweat as the cross-member fell on to the upright with a sickening thud.

It must be awful – frightful – to be crucified. It was utterly degrading to be stripped and hung up for all to see. The pain was unimaginable. Fancy having to push down against the nails in your heels, just to breathe... It didn't bear thinking about. He couldn't get to sleep again. He tossed and turned, hoping for sleep to overtake him, but it was no use. His brain was racing and he just could not relax.

Then another thought came to him. He hadn't been able to face going out to Golgotha to see Jesus before he died. He hadn't found the courage to go and say goodbye to the man who had come to mean so much to him. But why should he not go, instead, to his tomb now, to say his farewells. Surely that would be better than lying here so restlessly? The women had told them all where the tomb was; he should be able to find it and pray there for a few minutes quietly, without disturbance, at this time of day. It would be pleasing to feel that he had perhaps been the first to visit the tomb of their fallen leader.

He got up quietly, careful not to arouse the others. He crept downstairs and out into the fresh air. It was still quite dark, but Mark was sure that the dawn would break before long. He made his way swiftly to the city gate and then over the grisly hill of Golgotha to the little garden described by the women. His heart beat faster as he approached the garden gate and for the first time he wondered whether he had been foolish to come. What if there were several tombs there? How would he know which was the right one? Perhaps, after all, he shouldn't have come. Should he try to go into the tomb? What if he couldn't shift the stone guarding the entrance? No, surely better to stay outside to pray. He wasn't at all familiar with death, and suddenly it scared him.

He made his way carefully into the garden and over to the cliff face, stumbling in the gloom. As he rounded a corner, he came upon the tomb, cut into the side of the hill. There was only the one. This must be the one they used for Jesus. Then, as he came closer, he saw, to his horror, that the stone that should have been closing the entrance had already been rolled back in its groove. The hairs bristled on the back of his neck. Whoever could have been there before him, in the dead of night? Were they still inside the tomb? What were they up to?

Mark waited for several minutes outside, half hidden behind a gnarled old olive tree. There was no sound, no light. He held his breath, straining for any evidence that anyone was in the tomb, but could detect nothing. Eventually, he took his courage into both hands and approached the entrance of the tomb. Very stealthily he looked round the opening to the cave. He had no light and could see nothing, but neither could he hear anything. By this time, dawn was just breaking, the faintest glimmer of light showing in the eastern sky. In a few minutes, he knew he would have enough light to see by. He waited, each minute seeming like an hour. At last, straining his eyes, he could see that the tomb was empty – but not only of the living – also of the dead! There was no body on the rocky shelf cut into the hillside. Had he got the wrong tomb after all? He tip-toed right into the cavern and looked more carefully. Yes, there was the shelf cut into the rock, where the body should have been. There were also some grave clothes – but there was no corpse there.

Mark breathed a long sigh, partly of relief that he had not encountered anything more sinister, and partly of perplexity. Where was Jesus's body, then? He must, after all, have gone to the wrong tomb. There must be another tomb somewhere nearby. It was the only possible explanation. But why were there grave clothes here? Mark slumped on to the slab to consider his next move. He certainly hadn't seen another tomb, but he'd better go and look again. It would be easier now the day was dawning. He must have missed it in the gloom. Yes, that was it.

But just then, he heard a sound from outside the cave entrance. Someone was coming – in fact, several people. He stiffened, wondering whether whoever it was would resent his presence. But there was no time to beat a retreat.

★

The women, too, had been up quite early. Mary Magdalene was joined by Joanna, Lydia and Rebecca. Susanna had a streaming cold, probably from staying out in all that rain a couple of days ago, so she thought she'd leave the work to the others. Nimrah asked to be excused. She felt she couldn't face a tomb at dawn – she'd exhausted herself emotionally on the day of the execution.

The women met in the kitchen of the inn to assemble all their materials, spices and ointments, wrapping cloths and linen, for the proper anointing of Jesus's body. It was least they could do. Those two rich men, whoever they were, kind though they were to give Jesus a tomb, could not have had time to do more than a rushed job of laying the body to rest. Besides, thought Mary, they were not his real friends. None of the women had ever seen them before. Of course, Jesus had known many people during his ministry, had influenced many and been loved by many, so they must be friends of a kind – but not part of the inner circle. They were the real disciples. They *were*... Mary paused as she realised that she was already thinking in the past tense. Yes, it was all over now, except for these last rites. It was important to do them properly.

The group of women approached the garden just as the dawn was breaking. They felt better for the light, slight though it was. They made their way round to the cliff face where they had seen the body of their leader laid. They suddenly realised that they might have a job, even with four of them, to move the great stone covering the entrance to the cave. But, as they reached the place, like Mark before them, they were amazed and frightened to see that it was already well back in its groove and the cave was yawning black before them.

They stopped in confusion, and, like Mark, listened to hear if there was anyone inside the sepulchre. Hearing nothing, they crept forward, Mary in the lead. Then, horror of horrors, they saw a living man sitting in the shadows of the tomb, not a body lying on a slab. The man turned as they entered the tomb and started up. The women didn't wait to hear or see more; they turned and ran.

It was Mark, of course. Although he himself was also initially scared, he recovered his presence of mind first and called out, 'Don't be frightened!'

But the women were already well on their way from the sepulchre, running as hard as they could. Mark had to shout to try to make sure they heard. 'If you're looking for Jesus, who was crucified, he's not here.'[1]

But the women had gone, terrified. It was bad enough having to go to a grave at first light, but to find, not a body, but a shadowy, living male being, was quite beyond them.

Mark shook his head in disbelief. He realised now that he recognised the group – surely that was Mary from Magdala and some of the women from Herod's palace in Tiberias. Oh, well, he'd tried to tell them. Mark scratched his chin thoughtfully, disappointed that he had not found the right tomb and paid his respects. But, then again, if he had had been at the wrong tomb, why had the women come there? They had seen the body laid to rest only two days ago – they couldn't have made the same mistake. Or did they, too, get it wrong in the dim light of dawn? It was all very puzzling. He shrugged his shoulders, able to make neither head nor tail of the situation. At all events, there seemed to be nothing left for him to do at the tomb, so he walked away slowly, still pondering.

He decided to climb the hill and go home the longer way round. It was going to be a lovely day – the sun was rising swiftly now, shining brightly out of a blue sky. The swallows were dipping and swooping all around him. High overhead, a bird of prey hung in the air, scouring the valley below for a sign of breakfast. Mark's spirits began to rise. He'd get home and have some breakfast himself – the normal appetite of a seventeen-year-old lad was beginning to reassert itself.

He climbed up the hill and entered a little copse at its brow but, as he emerged on the other side, his emotions were again assailed. He swallowed hard as he saw something strange hanging from a tree overlooking the valley. It looked like a... it couldn't be. Yes – it was a body, dangling limp on a short rope. As he approached, he saw, sickened, that the man was quite dead and had probably been dead for some time. Then he realised, with loathing, who it was. He had met Judas only four evenings ago at the supper with Jesus.

★

Mary ran with her older companions until they could run no more. They paused on the hill, near the place where those terrible vertical poles still stood, ready to receive the crossbars of some other unfortunate criminal condemned to die. At least, here in the open space, they could see if anyone tried to approach them. In fact, there was nobody about. They stopped and considered what they should do next.

Joanna shrugged her shoulders as she observed, 'There's no point in trying to go to the garden again – even if we wanted to. There is no body there. Someone must have moved Jesus to another grave.'

'Why would they do that?' Mary was puzzled. 'Who would move him? We, his friends, haven't touched him. The friends at Bethany didn't know, and they still don't know, where he was interred. Who else would move him?'

Rebecca chimed in thoughtfully, 'Would the authorities have a reason to move Jesus?'

'I can't see why. In any case, did they know where the two rich men put him?' replied Joanna. 'We were the only people around at the time they moved him from here.' She shuddered as she looked up at the central pole.

'Then where is he?' Mary was close to tears again.

Nobody knew, so nobody spoke. Eventually, frustrated beyond belief, they decided to go back to the inn and report to the men there. John listened carefully to their account of their visit to the tomb, stroking his beard in bewilderment at the news that Jesus's body had disappeared. He went to see Peter, and the story interested even that downcast individual sufficiently to rouse him to action.

'We'd better go and see for ourselves,' he said.

John concurred and they set out as quickly as they could, but Peter, after having eaten almost nothing for three days, couldn't move very quickly. John strode swiftly on, arriving at the opening in the cliff face first. He peered in at the entrance of the tomb and saw, as the women had reported, that there was no body lying on the slab; but somehow he hesitated to go inside. Although, as a priest, he had had to deal with death frequently, ministering to the dying and comforting the bereaved, somehow, now it was his own friend, he hesitated. What was there about this tomb, he wondered? How could the body have disappeared? Who could have taken it? He paused, deep in thought and grief.

A few minutes later he was joined by Peter, who, although flagging physically, was still the impetuous one. He pushed past John straight into the cavern to examine the interior.[2]

'Nothing! Nothing here!' he called, his face betraying his puzzlement. John swallowed hard and went in and joined him by the slab.

'The grave clothes are here, though,' he said slowly. 'They are lying just where the body would have been. Why remove the clothing when the body was moved? I really don't know what to make of it all.'

'Well – there's no point in staying here longer,' said Peter, disappointment showing on his face. 'I'm not sure why I came really, but I hoped, I suppose, to see Jesus again. Where is he now? Who could have moved him?'

'I can only assume that the rich men who placed him here have had second thoughts and have taken him somewhere else,' replied John.

But a further thought dawned on him.

'They wouldn't have moved a body on the Sabbath, though, and it seems highly unlikely they'd come in the middle of last night. So when was he moved?'

'That's true,' agreed Peter, with a frown. 'It's a puzzle.'

Together the two men retraced their steps to the city gate, where they met Mary Magdalene again.

'Where are you going?' asked John.

'I'm going back to the garden,' declared Mary. 'It's fully light now, so I can see better. Maybe, after all, we went to the wrong tomb.'

'We saw no other tomb,' said John. 'It's a waste of time and effort.'

But they couldn't persuade the young woman to drop her plan. Some of the obstinacy that had so bothered her mother earlier showed itself again.

'I'll be all right,' she said. 'I'll go further round the hill and into the garden at the far end. Then I can make sure that there are no more graves there. Don't worry. I won't be long. I'll be back before you can miss me. Tell Mother not to worry.'

So they parted, the younger woman returning down the hill towards the garden, the two men going back into the city. Mary made her way to the far end of the garden, seeing nobody on the way. Finding nothing of interest there, she turned back towards the tomb they visited before, but, in spite of her earlier show of resolve, she couldn't bring herself to go inside it. Instead, she waited nearby for several minutes, walking slowing up and down, keeping an eye on the gaping hole in the cliff and looking for signs of the shadowy figure who had accosted them so recently there, but the place now seemed quite deserted. Mary sat down on a boulder, wondering what she should do next. What had happened to her beloved Jesus? Her eyes filled with tears again. She had so hoped at least to have the satisfaction of helping to lay his body out decently and pay her last respects. Life was so unfair, she thought. At last she had found someone in whom she had believed, someone she could trust, but he had been taken from her, cruelly...

She looked up, thinking she heard someone coming. Through her tear-filled eyes, she saw a figure standing close by. Perhaps it was the man in charge of the garden.

'Sir,' she said, 'I am looking for Jesus, who was crucified two days ago and buried here. He's a friend of ours. If you have taken him away, please tell me where he is, so that we can help to lay him out properly and pay our last respects.'

The man looked down at her as she sat on the rock, her eyes filling with tears again, her head held low.

'Mary,' he said.[3] Just the one word.

Mary's heart stopped beating. Surely that was Jesus's voice. It was just the way he used to say her name. She jerked up, mouth agape, eyes swimming.

'Jesus! Is it really you?' She flung herself at his knees, clasping him, but the figure restrained her kindly with the words, 'Gently, now. Go to my friends and tell them that all is well. I am one with my Father and your Father. There is nothing to fear.'

Mary bowed her head and released her hold, overcome with astonishment and joy, but when she looked up again, she saw nobody.

Did I really see Jesus – alive and well? she thought, amazed. It was far too good to be true. But she knew she had seen him – and very definitely alive. He'd assured her that everything was all right – in spite of that awful Friday.

'Go and tell my friends,' he had said. She stirred herself, picked up the hem of her gown and once more ran from the tomb, but this time her heart was brimming with joy, not pounding with fear.

Mary reached the inn just as fast as her legs would carry her. What others thought when they saw her running for all she was worth through the narrow streets of the city towards the inn, it was difficult to imagine. She didn't care. She must tell the others. Jesus is alive! I've seen him. He spoke to me... She burst into the tavern and saw Justus going about the ordinary chores of his day. How crazy to be worried about such things, Mary thought, in the brief moment before she caught him by the arm and asked for Peter and John – and Mary, Jesus's mother – and Joanna and her friends. There were so many who needed to be told. She knocked urgently on Peter's door and bounded in as soon as he responded.

'Peter,' she cried, 'I've seen Jesus – alive. Believe me, it's true!'

Peter sprang up from the bed on which he had been sprawled.

'What's that you're saying?' he demanded gruffly.

'I've seen Jesus alive, Peter. I know you'll think I'm crazy.'

Peter cut in, but quite gently, taking her hands in his. 'Take it calmly, Mary. You know that Jesus was crucified two days ago. You saw him die. You saw him interred. You just can't have seen him today, and certainly not alive...'

At that moment, John entered the room, having been told by Justus that Mary had returned in great agitation. She retold her story which was met with sheer incredulity on the part of the ex-priest. They took her downstairs to see the others, who were rapidly assembling in response to the new situation. Again and again, Mary told her story, gradually filling in the details, as she found the words and in response to questions from many sides, but, of course, none of those present could bring themselves to accept the story. Dead men simply don't come back to life again. It was impossible – but Mary persevered against all the objections of her friends.

'Is it possible that he didn't really die – but was mistakenly buried when in a deep coma, from which he later recovered?' she asked.

'I saw him die – as you did,' said John slowly. 'There was no doubt in my mind. Besides, Roman soldiers are experts at killing. They certified he was dead before he was taken from the cross. '

'We saw one of them thrust a spear into his side,' said Joanna.

'How did the man you saw look, Mary?' asked Lydia. 'Did he look – ill – near to death?'

Mary considered carefully before answering, her hand to her chin.

'No. Not at all. The Jesus who spoke to me appeared to be fully fit. He stood straight. His voice was strong.' She then realised the impossibility of her earlier suggestion. 'No, that person couldn't have been near death two days ago.'

'Especially not without receiving any assistance or medical aid meantime,' chimed in John. 'It makes no sense. How did you know it was Jesus? Are you sure you really saw him, not just a – sort of – figure in your imagination?'

Mary was definite. 'I didn't see him very clearly – that's true. My eyes were full of tears, as I thought about him and his death. But he called me by name, using the inflection he always used when he said "Mary". It was him. I know it. I know him, just as you would have known him. It was Jesus, our friend and leader. We'd all know him anywhere, wouldn't we? He told me to tell you that everything was well. He was one with the Father.'

At this point, the door opened and Cleopas entered, seeking Justus. Knowing he was also sympathetic to Jesus's mission, the locksmith was drawn into the conversation and Mary told her tale yet again, but without any further light being thrown on the situation. No matter which way they looked at it, there didn't seem to be an explanation that fitted all the facts at their disposal. Mary, mother of Jesus, had remained calm and silent throughout the whole episode.

'I have the feeling,' she said quietly, 'that if anyone would know his voice, it would be you, Mary.'

Turning to the others, she continued, 'We have to take Mary's report seriously, my friends. I don't understand how or why, any more than I understood a good deal that Jesus said and did; but there's a mystery here to be solved, not just pushed aside.'

There didn't seem to be anything to add after that. The group split up. The women went off to continue with their own activities, while the men adjourned to the patio outside.

'I just don't get it,' Peter was saying. 'Mary must have been hallucinating, I should think. She was so much – in love, I suppose you'd say – with Jesus.'

'We shouldn't have let her go there alone,' observed John. 'I blame myself. I should have gone with her.'

'I've been thinking that we should link up with the disciples at Bethany,' said Justus. 'I think I'll send Mark there to ask them all to come here for supper. The large upper room is free tonight. We can share our grief. And we can, at least, do what Jesus asked us to do – break bread together, share a cup of wine, and remember him and all that he meant to us.'

'Is it safe for them to come into town?' asked John. 'What will the authorities do if they are discovered?'

'I should think they'd be all right if they come in twos and threes,' replied Justus. 'There are still thousands of pilgrims everywhere – nobody will recognise them in that crowd. I think they'll be prepared to take the risk.'

So it was agreed, but, not long afterwards, Mark returned and told them his grisly news about the fate of the traitor. John and Justus conferred and decided they should go to the place Mark had described to cut Judas's body down and cover it with stones.

'At least that will prevent the birds and wild animals from desecrating the body further,' said John. 'I guess we should do at least that much for him.'

'You're a good man,' said Justus. 'I think, left to myself, I would have been tempted to leave him there, but I expect you're right. I'm sure Jesus would have done as much.'

'It's because I'm sure he would that I'm going to do so,' responded his companion. 'Jesus is a powerful example still – he always will be, for me.'

★

Cleopas had returned to his shop and briefed Nathan on Mary's account of the strange events at the tomb that morning, but such was their deep sense of depression and loss that they, like the others, totally discounted her story. So, although festival time was usually a good opportunity for trade, they decided to shut up shop and go back to their village for a few days. Somehow, the city was poisoned, polluted. It had the smell of death about it – Jesus's death. While they hadn't been as closely associated with Jesus's work as the others, they had known him for some time now and been increasingly influenced by his words. They had come to hope that he would bring in better times. The exact nature of the 'better times' was uncertain in their minds, but they had certainly hoped – they had sat up on several occasions well into the night discussing what the future might bring – but now all their hopes had been crushed.

They set out for the walk to their little village, Emmaus, which lay about seven miles to the north west of Jerusalem. Normally, especially at that time of the year, it would have been quite a pleasant walk over the rolling hills, but today they could not feel any joy, even in the wild flowers growing in profusion along the side of the track and the pleasant April sunshine pouring down out of a steel blue sky. They laboured on, talking only occasionally, each wrapped in his own thoughts. After about an hour, they reached a little olive grove and noticed a man sitting under one of the trees, apparently resting from his journey. The stranger rose as they approached and bid them good day. The two shopkeepers were in no mood for idle gossip so they answered minimally, hoping to be left to their own thoughts. The stranger, however, was not to be put off and asked if he could walk along with them, since he was planning to go in the same direction. With some reluctance, the others agreed and they trudged on for several minutes in silence.

Eventually, the newcomer asked, quietly, 'Excuse me asking, friends, but is something wrong? You both seem very downcast.'

It was Cleopas who answered, rather impatiently, 'Where have you come from? If you had been in Jerusalem this last weekend, you must have been aware of the executions. One of the victims was someone we believed was a great prophet! They crucified Jesus, from Nazareth in Galilee. It was terrible.'[4]

'Tell me more,' said the stranger. 'You were obviously very upset by what happened.'

Slowly the pair recounted their story, recalling the occasions when they had met Jesus over the previous eighteen months. Their aspects changed as they were sometimes enthused by their memories, then crushed by the finality of the situation now. The stranger listened carefully, occasionally asking a question or seeking a clarification of their belief in Jesus.

Nathan expressed it this way, 'We thought he would be the one who would redeem Israel. He offered us hope. We believed he had the secret of...' He broke off, uncertain of how to express his belief. Cleopas came to his rescue.

'He had the secret of real life, we thought,' he said. 'He knew how to live – what life was for, and where to find real happiness.'

'And now?' queried the stranger.

'Now, it's finished,' replied Cleopas quietly, shaking his head, his face downcast. 'His message sounded fine, but how can it be continued when he himself has gone – and taken from us in such a manner?'

'Are you sure he has gone?' asked the stranger quietly.

'We saw him die,' replied Cleopas firmly. 'He's gone all right. The Romans know how to kill, damn them.'

They walked on in silence for several minutes. Then Nathan mentioned the strange happenings of the morning.

'Some of the women in Jesus's group went to anoint his body this morning,' he explained, 'but returned saying that they couldn't find it. Instead, one of them swore that she actually saw Jesus alive! Of course, it must have been her imagination, but still...'

Again, he broke off, uncertain of how to continue. This time it was the stranger who responded.

'Is it so impossible' he said, 'if you consider all that the prophets wrote and declared?'

Then their companion launched into a detailed explanation of the prophetic message, reminding them of the passages of scripture which foretold the sufferings of the Messiah, but also affirming his eventual triumph.

At this point, however, the village of Emmaus came into view. Soon, they came to a fork in the track, and the stranger indicated that he would bypass the village and walk on further. But, by this time, the two friends were not so keen to be rid of their companion.

'It's getting on now,' said Nathan. 'There's only a couple of hours of light left and you've obviously walked a good distance today. Why not stop with us tonight and then go on in the morning?'

'That's very kind of you,' replied the stranger. 'Thank you. I will do that.'

Thus it was that, after washing, the three sat down to supper, prepared by Cleopas's wife. Nathan's wife was absent, visiting her mother, since she had no expectation of seeing her husband until the end of the week. The two shopkeepers sat with their new acquaintance between them; Cleopas invited him to say the blessing on the food. They bowed their heads for prayer, but when they raised them again, they saw that the hands in which the bread was held were cruelly wounded. There were recent deep scars in both wrists...

Suddenly, the truth dawned on them both. They started up from their chairs, thunderstruck, yet joyful. Questions crowded into their minds as they looked into the stranger's face and saw that it was indeed the face of Jesus. Simultaneously they reached out to take his hands, but he pulled back a little. They glanced at one another in surprise and disappointment, but when they turned again to question him, there was nobody with them in the room.

'It was him – Jesus,' Nathan breathed. 'That's – incredible! How was it we didn't recognise him earlier?'

'I don't know,' replied Cleopas, dumbstruck. 'It doesn't make sense.'

'I suppose, in truth, I was looking at the track during most of the walk. It's rough and you have to watch your feet, and, frankly, to begin with, I wasn't very interested in what our friend wanted. We were both very low in spirits.'

'To say the least,' agreed Cleopas. 'Then, again, we all had our usual head-dresses on, which doesn't give much view of the face when you are walking side by side. And the sun was in our eyes at that time of day... Still, it's a wonder we didn't recognise the voice...'

'But we saw the marks of crucifixion in his wrists... horrible.'

'So it must be true – what Mary said this morning was right. None of us believed her. He is alive! We must go back to Jerusalem to tell the others.'

'Tonight?' asked Nathan, but the word was hardly out of his mouth when he already knew the answer. The depression of the afternoon had disappeared completely, the weariness of the journey was gone. Instead their hearts were full to bursting. Within a few minutes, to the enormous surprise and disappointment of Cleopas's wife, they were on their way again, retracing their steps to Justus's inn in Jerusalem.

Peter was still keeping to his room at the inn, face downward, flat out on the bed. The numbness of his grief was wearing off a little, replaced with a million questions. The discussions he had had with John had helped a little. John was a good sort and very knowledgeable. He'd been close to Jesus for many years, yet even he didn't understand what had happened, and certainly not why. Now Jesus was gone. The thought hammered on in Peter's head. No, he mustn't think of himself as Peter any more – he'd be Simon again, a Galilean fisherman, not Peter, the missionary, working with Israel's chosen one. How could John think that Jesus's message would stand up without him? That was madness. None of the others would have the heart to go on now, he was sure.

He realised that he would have to link up with his brother and the other Galileans soon. They'd be wanting to go back home to Galilee shortly. That was the right thing to do. It was the only thing to do. Peter roused himself and sat up. Yes, he should contact Andrew and get back to Galilee, but first, he'd need to build up his reserves a bit. He hadn't eaten properly in days. Even that short walk to the garden to see the tomb had wearied him considerably. There was no way he could walk the seventy-five miles or so to Capernaum until he'd recovered his strength a little.

It was strange about that empty tomb. Where had they taken the body of Jesus? Or had they gone to the wrong tomb after all? But the women had seen Jesus laid in that grave. Had those rich men moved him later? But when? In the dead of night? During the Sabbath? The latter was unthinkable. Peter bowed his head and closed his eyes to hold back the tears as he thought again of his dear friend, dead – and now the body was lost to all his friends, making it impossible for them to pay their last respects before they left for home. That was bitter medicine to swallow.

Suddenly, Peter became aware of a second person in the room. It wasn't that he heard the door open and close, but somehow he knew there was a presence with him. He glanced round the room through eyes still wet with tears. A figure was standing just inside the window. His silhouette was clearly visible, but the face was indistinct as the sun streamed into the room behind his head, making it look a little like the head of an angel in a picture.

'Peter, my friend,' said the figure kindly – and Peter, like Mary before him, didn't need more. He knew that it was Jesus.[5] He threw himself at his leader's feet, moaning with surprise and joy.

What transpired in the moments that followed, Peter never revealed to a living soul. All he would say when he too came downstairs, looking pale but somehow radiant at the same time, was that he had seen Jesus – that he was most definitely alive – and that he must apologise to Mary for ever doubting her word. He never again spoke of dropping the name Peter. Whatever it was that Jesus said to him left him in no doubt that the mission was not over – it was only just beginning.

Hardly had Peter finished telling his startling news, when Andrew arrived from Bethany and the story had to be retold for his benefit. At first, like the others, Andrew couldn't accept the staggering fact of the resurrection, but with both Mary and Peter affirming this, he had to concede the possibility. A similar situation transpired when the rest of the Galileans arrived, in twos and threes, that evening for supper. Only Thomas was missing. He had said that he felt too depressed to come – he wouldn't be able to manage a thing to eat. He'd stay and keep Martha and Mary company, since, of course, Lazarus was also invited to supper in the inn.

Justus asked them all to go immediately to the upper room. Then he locked the door at the top of the main stairway, so that, should the authorities come to arrest any of them, they would have some time to escape from the rear of the building, down the back stairway and through the kitchen.

Before the supper, the women joined them for a short chat. Obviously, the only topics of conversation were the two reports of Jesus's reappearance from Mary and Peter. Opinions varied from outright scepticism to hopeful acceptance. Peter was adamant: he'd seen Jesus – just now in the room upstairs. He'd stopped and talked to him for – well, it was difficult to say, but it must have been for, perhaps, two or three minutes. Mary had only heard a few words before Jesus had gone again, but she was equally sure that it had been him. The fishermen, knowing Peter as they did, felt that he wouldn't be able to concoct a story like that and were inclined to accept what he said, though it was difficult. You could never be sure with women, of course. They all knew that Mary was in love with Jesus and might well be imagining things.

The men from the north, being pretty hard-bitten, were less inclined to accept either story, much though they wished they could. Nathaniel was sympathetic. Philip simply didn't know. Matthew was completely at sea. John barHelez felt dazed and unsure. How could Jesus possibly be alive? He'd seen him die a horrible death – the death of a criminal, at the hands of hardened executioners, men whose business it was to kill efficiently. How could it be true? Lazarus, unsure of himself at the best of times, was, like Matthew, totally confused. Nimrah and the other women were becoming quite sure that the stories were true. Indeed, by the time the conversation was coming to an end as supper was called, some of them were convinced that they had known all along that this would be the way things would turn out!

Justus was just going to announce that everything was ready for the meal when there was a loud knock at the door. Everyone froze, frightened lest it was the soldiers looking for them. The Galileans started to move to the back stairs, but Justus went to the window and then called them back.

'It's all right,' he shouted. 'Come back. It's not the guards; it's our friends, Nathan and Cleopas. I thought they had decided to go to Emmaus today.'

The party reassembled and very soon they were listening, amazed, to the story the two shopkeepers had to tell.

'We just had to come and tell you, straight away,' they concluded. 'We've rushed back seven miles to tell you as quickly as possible.'

'And I, too, have news for you,' replied Peter, smiling broadly. 'My friend has also made himself known to me, in this very house.'

'Really? That's wonderful! Then he really is alive and well.' Cleopas was standing like a man bemused, grinning rather foolishly. 'I can't believe it – it's – it's …' He ground to a halt, lost for words.

Peter spoke again, this time more seriously. 'He came to me, in spite of the way I let him down.'

'We've all been guilty of that, in one way or another,' said John barHelez, 'but we know Jesus – he forgives anyone anything. He's that kind of person. And he tells us that God is like that too – even though it costs him so much to do so.'

Justus was signalling to John that he wanted to serve the meal. He, Gomer, Mark and a couple of servants had been rushing about all afternoon, preparing meat, fish, vegetables and fruit. The women excused themselves, for they were to eat separately. The men sat down to eat in much the same places as they had done only four evenings earlier, except that this time, of course, Jesus, Thomas and Judas were missing – for very different reasons – and their places were taken by Nathan and Cleopas. In the absence of Jesus, John barHelez did his best to act as host, calling for the usual drinking of the wine between courses. Towards the end of the meal, John got to his feet.

'You will remember only too well, my friends, what Jesus invited us to do when we met for a meal together,' he said. 'He gave thanks for the food and drink. Let us do the same.'

He led them in a short prayer of thanksgiving. Then he continued.

'You will also remember how Jesus told us that the bread would now represent his body – broken for us. Well, now we can see what he meant. He apparently foresaw all too clearly what was going to happen to him. His body was indeed broken – cruelly broken – on the accursed cross. So let us eat this bread now and remember him and all he means to us.'

The loaf was passed round the table from hand to hand, each person breaking off a fragment and eating, trying to understand the mystery that was being unfolded to them. Then John picked up a large mug of wine.

'You know what I'm going to say, my friends. Jesus asked us to remember him when we drink wine together. This represents his blood, he said – poured out for us. Well, it was spilled all too soon. I invite you to remember him as we drink, but now we know – at least, we are beginning to appreciate – that although he was cruelly killed, God has restored him to life – eternal life. Some of us have actually seen and heard him; but I think we all know he is alive. We are starting to realise his presence in our inmost beings. Perhaps we shall never see him ourselves, but we shall know, just the same. So this meal is more than remembrance – it is a reminder of the fact that he can be with us whenever we need him.'

The mug was shared round the table. There was silence for several minutes, then John closed the meal with a short formal prayer and the men rose to chat in twos and threes round the table. Pretty soon they were joined again by the women, who had finished dining separately. Still the conversation centred on the strange events of the day. Peter, Mary, Cleopas and Nathan grew almost weary of trying to describe their experiences and answer the questions posed by the others.

A small group of Galileans was in one corner, discussing the matter.

'I wonder why Jesus appeared to Nathan and Cleopas?' said little James. 'I mean, it's wonderful for them, but they weren't really part of our group of original disciples. I feel, well, almost...'

He couldn't find the right word, but several others of the party nodded their agreement.

'I can understand Jesus appearing first to Mary,' said Nathaniel. 'He was very fond of Mary – we all are – and she has been almost part of our group for a long time. Peter too was special to Jesus – he was one of the first to follow him, but I too wonder – why Nathan and Cleopas? They are almost – well, outsiders.'

There was a pause while the group considered this. Then Andrew volunteered, 'Perhaps that's the point that Jesus wants us to understand. His presence – his new life – isn't just for us, the inner circle – the favoured few. It is for everyone. Maybe Cleopas and Nathan represent the whole world of people who will one day come to follow our Jesus. We are the ones called to go out and tell them about him and his way of life, but hopefully there will be thousands who will respond.'

Then, for no apparent reason, the conversation died away in the room. What had they heard, that made them stop talking and listen? Nobody could remember later, but something stilled the atmosphere. Suddenly, they knew that Jesus was there in the midst. Yes. Everyone knew him now. He was there.

Living and radiant.

'Peace be with you all,' he said, softly.[6]

Even though many of them had begun to believe that Jesus could appear after death, many of his friends felt a stab of fear when they actually saw him. The hair on the backs of their necks bristled and they felt shivers of excitement and apprehension run down their spines.

'Don't be fearful,' said Jesus, smiling that winning smile of his. 'It is I. There's nothing to be alarmed about. I'm really with you. You need never be afraid again. I am always going to be with you in spirit. The Kingdom that I promised has now come into your lives and can flood your very existence.'

The disciples crowded round Jesus with increasing confidence as he spoke.

'You have been through a bad time,' he was saying. 'I had to leave you for a couple of days. It was necessary for me to demonstrate to the world that I could face evil – the worst that men could do – and conquer it. Everyone thought that I had been defeated. In a worldly sense, I had been. That's the way it often is – evil often seems to win – but, by giving me this new life which nobody can take from me, God has demonstrated that ultimately he is more powerful than the worst evil in the world. His love cannot be overcome, but must win through in the end. Now you know that his love is with you always, as long as the world exists.'

And, suddenly, he was gone again.

★

The following day, everyone went to Bethany. Gone was the despondency, the heartache, the gloom. Peter was happy to be among his friends again, indeed, seemingly happy to take the lead. The fact that they all knew that Jesus had somehow emerged victorious from the experience of death elated them all. Jesus was, after all, triumphant. The Temple authorities, the Governor, the King, had all been shown to be powerless over Jesus, when it came to the crunch. He had won through, or, more accurately, God had brought him through. Now they could look forward to going out to add to the original message the assurance of victory. Not only that, but they could insist that the love which Jesus showed on the cross, which seemed to have been overcome by the forces of darkness, was in the end seen to be more powerful than the evil that confronted it. They were exultant.

They decided, for safety's sake, to leave in small parties. The fishermen went first, followed a few minutes later by the blacksmiths and Thaddeus. Matthew, Philip and Nathaniel came later, a half-hour after that. There was no point in taking unnecessary risks and being apprehended by the guards. Maybe they were still looking for them. The others could move more freely, not being associated so clearly with Jesus

All was well. Most of them reached Lazarus's house without any delay. The last group made good progress as far as Olivet, but Nathaniel found the hill tough going and had to slow up a little. They were resting part way up when they were hailed by a figure coming down the track. At first, they wondered who it was, but then they saw that it was Matthias, on his way into town from Bethphage. It was a joyful reunion, for they had much to tell. Matthias told them that he had heard of the death of Jesus and how he had spent many hours grieving, wondering what would come of the great movement originally led by his friend, John, and subsequently taken up and expanded by Jesus and his friends from Galilee. Of course, the others were bursting to tell him of Jesus's triumph – that first Mary, then Peter, then Cleopas and Nathan, and finally all of them had seen him alive and well. Matthias, like everyone else before him, was understandably sceptical at first, but was eventually persuaded by the united testimony of all three of the Galileans.

'Would we tell you an untruth, Matt?' asked Philip. 'I'll tell you – we were as close to him then as we are to you now. He's alive. I couldn't believe Peter, when he first told me of his experience. After all, he'd been through a terrible ordeal, grieving and fasting alone – at his own insistence – and we thought that maybe he was half crazy with grief, and, frankly, ill; but I can assure you that we are most definitely not ill. I've seldom felt better in my life!'

Matthew and Nathaniel hastened to agree. 'You too may see him. He appears from time to time to all sorts of people who knew him. After all, he appeared right out of town at Emmaus.'

'I hardly know what to say,' Matt had replied doubtfully. 'It's a lot to swallow, you know. People don't come to life again after they've died – least of all, one would think, after being executed by the Romans. Think what you like about Roman soldiers (and who doesn't?), they certainly know how to kill! 'But if you are all really sure that Jesus is alive again – I have to accept it as a fact. It just goes to show that God was really with him all along and that he really was the Messiah.'

They parted a few minutes later, but not before they had promised to meet up again shortly. Matt said he would come over to Bethany that afternoon to meet the rest of the group, particularly his friend, Andrew, with whom he had the special bond of being the first in the group to meet Jesus. It seemed like a lifetime ago – was it really only two years?

The fishermen had had an even worse job persuading Thomas of their good news when they arrived in Bethany. Poor old Thomas! He was always the one inclined to see things in the worst light – the pessimist of the group. He dismissed their story rather like a kindly old grandfather dismisses the stories about fairies told by his grandchildren.

'Listen, my friends. Of course, I'd love to believe you, but it simply doesn't happen. Dead men do not rise from their tombs and walk around meeting people. Jesus was killed – brutally killed on the day before the Sabbath. He just cannot appear to you all and sit at supper with you the day after the Sabbath. It's impossible.'

'Were we all seeing things, then, Thomas?' asked Matthew. 'How do explain the fact that all of us saw him? We all saw him together – and can verify one another's story.'

'And I saw him earlier,' chipped in Peter.

'And Mary before that!' This from James.

Thomas paused and shook his head. 'I don't know what you are all describing,' he said slowly and deliberately, 'but I cannot believe that it is reality. Maybe you all saw something you wanted to see – sort of – in your mind's eye.'

'It was real enough,' said Andrew. 'Not only the ten of us saw it, but Nathan, Cleopas and Justus were all there. The first two had just come back from Emmaus – they'd seen him there too, as we told you.'

'Oh, come now,' Thomas was almost jeering, 'you don't think I can believe that Jesus was in both Emmaus and Jerusalem within a couple of hours! He must at least be very ill, even if he is not dead.'

'That's the point, Thomas,' John broke in. 'Jesus has been through death and thrown it off just like a worn out tunic – and all the hurt that was inflicted on him. He is alive, strong and well. I know it sounds nonsense but it has happened. Don't ask me to explain it – none of us can – but we know it to be true.'

'Well, I shan't believe it unless I see Jesus for myself,' exclaimed Thomas. 'When I see the marks of the nails in his wrists and heels, then I will gladly believe, but until then… I'm sorry, I can't.'[7]

Nothing they could say – nor the rest when they arrived – could shift him. That was Thomas. He was a stubborn man when he wanted to be!

★

Meanwhile James and Joseph, Jesus's brothers, were feeling pretty miffed. Not only had they lost a brother in the most tragic circumstances – and in a way that brought considerable disgrace on the family – but now their mother was absenting herself with Jesus's friends at the other inn. True, they had heard from John that Mary was safe, and as well as could be expected after the ordeal of the crucifixion, but that was scarcely the point. What was she doing with that crowd, anyway? She should be here, with her family. After all, within a few days, they would be preparing to leave for Galilee. Was she coming with them, or would she stay in Jerusalem with this fellow, John? Where might he take her? What was he up to? It was all very strange. Either way, it didn't look good.

The two brothers had been to the Temple in the morning for worship and had then had lunch with some friends from Nazareth who were also up in town for the feast. Mercifully, the friends didn't enquire too closely after Mary, assuming her to be out with other women, as was so often the custom. After lunch, they agreed to take a short siesta. They had been up early as usual and the idea of a short nap after their meal was always appealing. James lay down in his room and started to mull over Mary's strange behaviour once more, and resolve what should be done about it. His train of thought stopped him dropping off as he usually did. What had happened to his mother, usually so level-headed and family orientated? He tossed and turned, pondering over all that had happened.

Then, like Peter earlier in the day, he became aware of a presence in the room with him. He didn't hear the door open. Perhaps he had dropped off for a few moments without realising it, but there, suddenly, at the foot of the bed, was – who was it? It couldn't be – yet it was! It was Jesus, that elder brother who had so disgraced the family over the past two years. But how could that be? Was he dreaming after all? Then the figure spoke.

'James. It's me, Jesus, your brother. Don't be alarmed.'[8]

James sat up in the bed and blinked, trying to collect his racing thoughts. He rubbed his eyes vigorously, but the figure was still there when he looked up again.

'Is it really you, Jesus?' he asked, fearfully. 'How – what—?' He couldn't find the words.

Jesus spoke again – kindly, but urgently.

'It is I. God has given me new life again. Don't oppose all that I am doing, James. I'd like you now to join my friends and help them to spread the message that I brought – the message of the Kingdom – a Kingdom that is for everyone who wants to join it. Even more than we realised in the past, it's open to everyone. My life, death and new life have demonstrated, for everyone to see it, that love – God's love – is stronger than anything else in the world. Now it should be an even more powerful message for the world to accept.'

James pondered, his face working, his brow furrowed deeply.

'But – will your people accept me? I've always been antagonistic to your work. Will they welcome me?'

'They've accepted Mother, haven't they?' replied Jesus softly. 'She still doesn't quite understand what we have been about, but she is learning, slowly. Meantime, she has given her love, and that is what counts in the end. Understanding can come later.'

Suddenly, James was sure what he should do.

'I'd like to understand and accept,' he cried. 'Clearly, if God has brought you back to life, he must approve of your ministry – it must be his message after all.'

James hung his head as he continued, 'I must have been wrong all this time. Forgive me, brother. How disappointed in me you must have been—'

But Jesus cut in, his voice still gentle, but firm. 'That's enough, James. What is past is forgiven. I know that you are going to be of tremendous service to God in the future. That's what counts. The past is gone and forgotten.'

'Well, if you really think it'll be all right...'

'I know it will be. Call at the inn and talk to Mother and to John – and Justus. The others will be back from Bethany tomorrow, I'm sure, and will welcome your support and friendship. Goodbye, for the present, brother.'

They touched hands briefly, then the figure was no longer there.

★

That night, when all the Galileans were present at supper in Bethany, Peter took the lead and spoke after the meal. He talked for quite some time about the future, asking for their support in continuing the work that Jesus started. He pointed out what they had all realised, that the message would have even greater impact now, backed up by the reality of God's victory over death. All round the room there were murmurs of agreement, and one by one each of them spoke, saying they were prepared to continue with the mission. Only Thomas remained at variance. Lazarus, as ever, sat on the fence.

'I'd like to help, friends,' Thomas said, 'but I'm afraid you are deluding yourselves about Jesus's return from the grave. You must do whatever you think right. I will not oppose you, of course, but I cannot accept the idea of resurrection.'

Peter clapped him on the shoulder.

'You're a good chap, Thomas. We understand your difficulty. Perhaps Jesus, in his own time, will come to you too, then you'll know, as we do.'

Peter then mentioned a new topic. 'You will all remember that Jesus was always keen to have twelve messengers in our party. He saw us, somehow, as representing the twelve ancient tribes of Israel. It was a good idea, full of symbolic associations with our long history as Jews, sons of Abraham, Isaac and Jacob. As we all know, we are now only eleven, so I think we should replace Judas, the traitor, who has left us to go his own way. Perhaps we shall never know why he did what he did. He was a strange man, who very largely kept himself to himself and had his own ideas. He wasn't prepared to follow what Jesus said without questioning it – he sometimes thought he knew better. Perhaps he betrayed Jesus simply for the money – some of you have said so – but I doubt it. John and Justus found none on him when they buried him. I think he must have had a different motive. I feel sure that he believed himself to be worthy, even though we know that his action was terribly misplaced. Anyway, what is done is done. I think we should replace him.'

There were murmurs of assent from all round the table. Andrew was the next to speak.

'I agree with my brother. Jesus wanted twelve and he should have twelve. To me, it seems obvious that we should invite John barHelez to join us. He's known Jesus for even longer than we have. He was greatly loved by Jesus – he's steeped in knowledge and experience. We couldn't do better than ask him. We know that he wants to join with us in spreading the message.'

This idea was received enthusiastically all round and Peter was elected to meet with John and offer him the opportunity. Unfortunately, when Peter broached the topic next morning, John wouldn't hear of it.

'Look, Peter, it's very gracious of you all to invite me to join you – and I will, as a follower – but I couldn't possibly take a place among Jesus's chosen twelve. I'm totally unworthy of that. Why, I've only just come round to your way of thinking. I rejected – or at least prevaricated about – Jesus's message for years. No. It wouldn't be right for me to be so honoured.'

Nothing Peter could say could change his mind, so the disciples met again and conferred further. One or two wanted to invite Lazarus, but the rest pointed out that, good fellow though he was, he hadn't really committed to Jesus's cause as yet. Discussion then moved on to others – Nathan, Cleopas, Justus and Matthias. None of these had directly served the cause for very long, but Matthias had been associated for a long time, through his work with John the Baptist. Justus had been a tower of strength in the past week or so, and to a lesser extent earlier. In the end, the disciples couldn't chose between these two, so they prayed and then cast lots and the dice fell on Matthias.[9] When told, he was delighted and very flattered.

'You – and Jesus – have my loyalty, most willingly,' he said. 'I've been looking for a chance to serve for a long time – in fact, ever since John was killed.'

From that day on, Matthias was numbered with the other Galileans.

★

A week after Jesus's first appearances, it was arranged that all the followers of Jesus would gather at a spot just outside Bethany. The sun shone brightly out of an azure sky. The flowers bloomed in every colour of the rainbow from every spare piece of land – along the road, by the brook – everywhere was a feast of colour. The swallows swooped and dived, collecting water from the stream with which to repair their mud nests, after the damage of the winter.

As well as the twelve, there were the Galilean women, Joanna and her friends, Mary and Nimrah from Magdala, John barHelez, Lazarus and his sisters from Bethany, Cleopas and Nathan and, looking a little apprehensive, Jesus's family, Mary, James and Joseph. The family from the inn were also there, of course – Justus, Gomer and Mark. The group buzzed with joy and expectation. Perhaps Jesus would come again to reassure those who still doubted – Thomas, particularly – but also Lazarus and his sisters, who had always been a little on the fringe of things.

The group started remembering all the wonderful things that they had shared since they met Jesus. How they had started at Capernaum. Well, Andrew and Matt had been with Jesus at Jordan… They remembered the stories they had heard … the things they had seen. There were those who had been healed – the lad with the evil spirit, who had been the first they knew to be healed by Jesus. Then there were those who had been lame. Peter remembered the leper who had jumped out from the bushes and startled him, but Jesus had coped and healed him.

There were many remembered by name. John the fisherman remembered the paralytic, Alpheus, healed by the pool of Bethesda, only just down the road from the inn. Big James talked of Jairus's daughter and Zacchaeus, the tax gatherer, at Jericho. There were so many that would have loved to be here now with Jesus. Of course, there were those who hadn't accepted Jesus, or had prevaricated – Nicodemus and Joseph of Arimathea, for example; and those who had rejected him – Caiaphas, Annas and their party, Abbas, the Zealot, and his son, who had been released in Jesus's place. They wouldn't feel any loyalty to Jesus, probably, but they should have done!

Lazarus and John were deep in conversation on the edge of the group. John was still trying to enlist Lazarus as a firm supporter of the mission, but Lazarus, as always, was unsure of himself. He felt that Jesus had called him just to care for his two sisters and not seek to distinguish himself in the mission or anywhere else. Well, thought John, if that was what Jesus wanted, who was he to quibble?

The family found, as Jesus had predicted, that everyone was kind and welcomed them. There was no mention of the unfortunate incidents in Nazareth and shortly afterwards. Instead, they found themselves surrounded by people only too anxious to hear about Jesus's childhood; to know what sort of life he led as a boy and as a young man growing up. James, in particular, as the one next in age to Jesus, found himself in great demand for a chat. He was surprised and pleased.

Then, suddenly, it happened. One minute, they were all chatting together quite noisily; the next, somehow they knew that he was there, and everyone fell silent. Yes, there he was, the same loving Jesus, a smile on his face, his brown eyes flashing as he looked first to one and then another in greeting, but he singled out Thomas, going over to him and offering his hand warmly.

'Thomas, old friend. I missed you the other day, when the rest were together. How are you?'

Thomas felt his knees growing weak as he took the hand falteringly, noting the deep scars in the wrist. He couldn't answer, remembering his many doubts.

'Don't be fearful, Thomas,' continued Jesus in a low voice. 'You wanted to see my hand – well, you've taken it now[10]. That's good. Believe me, I am alive and well.'

Thomas fell at Jesus's knees, eventually finding his tongue.

'Jesus, my master and my friend. Forgive my lack of trust in you – and our father, God.'

Jesus smiled broadly and pulled him to his feet.

'Up on your feet, Thomas,' he said. 'You have much work to do for me. You can't do it from down there. You must be able to walk!'

Then Jesus sought out Lazarus and his sisters, greeting them warmly.

'You are some of my oldest friends,' he said quietly. 'It was good of you to come. Follow my way and you will find happiness and the road to God.'

Mary wept openly. Even the normally stoical Martha melted and held Jesus's hand for longer than she needed to. Lazarus seemed to be transported, absolutely delighted to see Jesus again.

Jesus didn't stay with them long. Very soon he called for quiet and blessed them all.

'I am not really leaving you, my friends, even though you will not see me again. I am always your friend. I am always with you in spirit. My Father and your Father is always within you if you only look for him. Go out into the world from here and spread the message, the promise and the power of love, and I promise to be with you all the way, wherever you go and however long it takes.'[11]

And then he was gone again, and this time, for good. But somehow it didn't matter any more. The friends of Jesus didn't need to see him; they had him always with them in their very being. He kept his promise – he was there in their hearts and lives.

NOTES

[1] Mark 16:6.
[2] John 20:6.
[3] John 20:16.
[4] Luke 24:19.
[5] I Cor. 15:5.
[6] John 20:21.
[7] John 20:25.
[8] 1Cor. 15:7.
[9] Acts 1:26.
[10] John 20:27.
[11] Matt. 28:20.

Printed in the United Kingdom
by Lightning Source UK Ltd.
117367UKS00001B/226